W9-BAD-942

PRAISE FOR
COUNTDOWN TO PEARL HARBOR

A *Smithsonian* Top History Book of 2016
A *Japan Times* Best Book about Japan of 2016

"Steve Twomey has accomplished something remarkable with *Countdown to Pearl Harbor*. With deep reporting and vivid writing, he has illumined one of the most momentous events of the twentieth century in a stunningly new and penetrating light."

—David Maraniss, Pulitzer Prize winner and bestselling author of *They Marched into Sunlight*

"Splendid . . . Even though readers already know the ending, they'll hold their collective breath, as if they're watching a rerun of an Alfred Hitchcock classic."

—*St. Louis Post-Dispatch*

"Steve Twomey is a masterful storyteller. Mining new and overlooked records, he has made the Pearl Harbor story new again—suspenseful, dramatic, intensely human, and tragic."

—Evan Thomas, bestselling author of *Sea of Thunder*

"Superb . . . The best book about Pearl Harbor I've read."

—*The Columbus Dispatch*

"A riveting narrative of the American misjudgments and mistakes that contributed to a day rivaled in US history only by September 11, 2001. It's not revisionist history so much as a poignant retelling of a familiar story."

—*Los Angeles Times*

"Outstanding."

—*The Christian Science Monitor*

"[A] crackerjack read."

—*Smithsonian*

"With thrilling speed and elegant craftsmanship, Steve Twomey recounts the catastrophe of Pearl Harbor as a classic tale of human nature, with its glories and its flaws. A wonderful, heartbreaking book."

—David Von Drehle, bestselling author of
Triangle: The Fire that Changed America

"A fine, compelling account of the immediate prelude to that infamous day in December 1941. Through dogged research and graceful writing, Steve Twomey has made the old tragedy seem new again."

—Rick Atkinson, Pulitzer Prize winner and
bestselling author of *The Guns at Last Light*

"Infusing a well-known story with suspense, *Countdown to Pearl Harbor* reconstructs the military's glaring errors of omission, the secret American effort to intercept Japan's encrypted communication, and the fruitless eleventh-hour diplomatic negotiations between Tokyo and Washington. . . . Gripping."

—*The New York Times Book Review*

"Excellent."

—*Washington Independent Review of Books*

"A pulse-quickening read that straightens out the script of an American tragedy. The surprise in Steve Twomey's superb book is that the 'surprise attack' on Pearl Harbor wasn't so much a surprise as a screwup, fed by complacency, racial condescension, and sclerotic navy tradition."

—Blaine Harden, bestselling author of *Escape from Camp 14*

"Exhaustive and unflinching . . . [Twomey] has put together the pieces of the bewildering puzzle and written a riveting account of a catastrophe that never should have happened."

—*The Washington Times*

"Steve Twomey, a careful reporter and fine writer, tells the story of Pearl Harbor in a punchy, oddly suspenseful book: you know what will happen, but you can't believe it. Twomey wipes away anyone's belief in some bring-on-the-war conspiracy. And any reader will find that he tells this saddest of stories very well."

—Don Graham, former publisher of the *Washington Post*

"Steve Twomey has written not only an elegant, suspenseful account of the attack but also a brilliant portrait of a time when the nation was not yet at war, yet sensing that everything was about to change forever."

—Jeffrey Frank, bestselling author of *Ike and Dick*

"Portrays events . . . in the style of a thriller . . . Brilliant."

—*Proceedings Magazine* (US Naval Institute)

"A well-written and engaging account that reinserts human dynamism into a history too often reduced to abstract binaries."

—*The Japan Times*

COUNTDOWN TO PEARL HARBOR

THE TWELVE DAYS TO THE ATTACK

STEVE TWOMEY

SIMON & SCHUSTER PAPERBACKS

NEW YORK LONDON TORONTO SYDNEY NEW DELHI

Simon & Schuster Paperbacks
An Imprint of Simon & Schuster, Inc.
1230 Avenue of the Americas
New York, NY 10020

Copyright © 2016 by Steve Twomey

All rights reserved, including the right to reproduce this book or portions thereof in any form whatsoever. For information, address Simon & Schuster Subsidiary Rights Department, 1230 Avenue of the Americas, New York, NY 10020.

First Simon & Schuster paperback edition November 2017

SIMON & SCHUSTER PAPERBACKS and colophon are registered trademarks of Simon & Schuster, Inc.

For information about special discounts for bulk purchases, please contact Simon & Schuster Special Sales at 1-866-506-1949 or business@simonandschuster.com.

The Simon & Schuster Speakers Bureau can bring authors to your live event. For more information or to book an event, contact the Simon & Schuster Speakers Bureau at 1-866-248-3049 or visit our website at www.simonspeakers.com.

Manufactured in the United States of America

1 3 5 7 9 10 8 6 4 2

Library of Congress Cataloging-in-Publication Data is available.

ISBN 978-1-4767-7646-0
ISBN 978-1-4767-7648-4 (pbk)
ISBN 978-1-4767-7650-7 (ebook)

For Kathleen and Nick

3019
16
1314

AUTHOR'S NOTE

S EVENTY-FIVE YEARS ON, the main actors in this drama are gone. Writing about what they did, and especially what they thought, is therefore a challenge, at least to a journalist who is used to simply asking participants to explain an event. But the attack on Pearl Harbor led to nine official inquiries, big and small, in five years. The resulting thousands of pages of testimony and exhibits form the spine of this book, along with memoirs, oral histories, and personal papers of the participants. The overwhelming majority of quotations are from those primary sources.

Even so, sometimes the civilian or military leaders involved in a conversation or a moment recollected it differently, and sometimes the same person offered varying versions of what he did, said, or thought. When conflicts arose, it seemed logical to weigh the evidence based on whose reputation had the most to gain or lose, and to rely on recollections given soon after the attack, rather than those from several years later.

Finally, this book is not offered as an exhaustive account. Numerous aspects of the attack that preoccupied investigators then, and fascinate some aficionados now, are barely explored, if at all. The focus is, instead, on the core narrative of a day with almost no equal in American history.

CONTENTS

THE BOYS AT OPANA

Sunday, 7:02 a.m.

THE DAWN WATCH had been as pacific as the ocean at their feet. Rousted by an alarm clock, they had awakened in their tent at 3:45 in the caressing warmth of an Oahu night, and had gotten the device fired up and scanning thirty minutes later, a bit tardy by the army schedule. Privates George E. Elliott Jr. and Joseph L. Lockard might have described the tall, spindly gizmo as resembling an oversize rooftop television antenna, if anybody had had a TV then. Radar in its infancy was quirky looking and far from what it would become, but the privates could still spot things farther out than anyone ever had with mere binoculars or a telescope.

Half a dozen mobile units—generator truck, monitoring truck, antenna, and trailer—had been scattered around the island in recent weeks. George and Joe's, the most reliable of the bunch, was emplaced farthest north, almost as far north as you can go on Oahu. It sat at Opana, 532 feet above a coast whose waves were enticing enough to surf, which is what many a tourist would do there in years to come. Between the privates and Alaska, two thousand miles away, was nothing but wavy liquid, a place of few shipping lanes and no islands at all. If, for some reason, a ship or a fleet of them ever wished to be alone in the Pacific, it stood a good chance of succeeding in that great void. An army general liked to call it the vacant sea.

The order of the day for the two privates was to keep vandals and the curious away from the equipment during a twenty-four-hour shift and, from 4:00 a.m. to 7:00 a.m., to sit inside the monitoring van as the antenna scanned for planes. George and Joe had no idea why that window of time was significant, if it was. Nobody had said. No fears of invasion or air raid had been conveyed. Between them, they had a couple of .45-caliber pistols and a handful of bullets. The United States had not been at war during their entire lifetimes, not since November 11, 1918, the day the Great War ended. Besides, Hawaii seemed such a peaceful place to be stationed. The local monthly, *Paradise of the Pacific*, boasted in its most recent issue that "here life is lived as it was meant to be lived, happily, close to flowers and warm surf." Hawaii was "a world of happiness in an ocean of peace," it proclaimed. No, the higher-ups had not put George and Joe out there for vigilance. There had been no briefing about tense world events and likely war scenarios. They had put them out there strictly for self-improvement.

"I mean, it was more practice than anything else," George said. Often with the coming of first light and then into the morning, army and navy planes would rise from inland bases to train or scout. The mobile crews would detect them, plot their locations, and get better at using the new devices, so they would be ready for war when it came. "There was a sergeant," George said, "that used to roll us out in the morning by saying, 'Get up and get out! The Japs are coming!' and every once in a while, why, someone [else] would say, 'The Japs are coming.' But it was all in a joking manner."

Joe, who was nineteen and from Williamsport, Pennsylvania, was in charge of the Opana station that morning, and worked the oscilloscope. George, who was twenty-three and had joined the army in Chicago, plotted any contacts on a map overlay and entered them in a log, and wore a headset connecting the duo to the other side, the populous side, of the island. Army headquarters was down there, about thirty miles to the southeast, past waves and waves of swaying sugarcane, past fields of pineapple that yielded fifteen million cases of fruit and juice a year, and between the jagged volcanic ranges of Waianae and Koolau, every inch of Oahu's six hundred square miles so exotic and alluring to anyone born on the mainland. The naval base at Pearl Harbor was down there, too.

George and Joe had detected nothing ominous during the early-morning scan; only the occasional friendly craft. It was, after all, a Sunday. Their duty done, George, who was new to the unit, took over the oscilloscope for a few minutes of time-killing practice. The truck that would shuttle them to breakfast would be along soon. As George checked the scope, Joe passed along wisdom about operating it. "He was looking over my shoulder and could see it also," George said.

On their machine, a contact did not show up as a glowing blip in the wake of a sweeping arm on a screen, but as a spike rising from a baseline on the five-inch oscilloscope, like a heartbeat on a monitor. If George had not wanted to practice, the set might have been turned off. If it had been turned off, the screen could not have spiked.

Now it did.

Their device had no ability to tell its operators precisely how many planes the antenna was sensing, or if they were American or military or civilian. But the height of a spike gave a rough indication of the number of aircraft. And this spike did not suggest two or three, but an astonishing number, fifty maybe, or even more. "It was the largest group I had ever seen on the oscilloscope," Joe said. It was, George said, "very big and it was very noticeable and it was just something out of the ordinary."

The more experienced Joe took back the seat at the screen. So unusual was the image that he ran checks to make sure the contact was real and not some electronic mirage. He could find nothing anomalous. The young privates did not know what to do in those first minutes, or even if they should do anything. They were off the clock, technically. They had not been told to expect anything threatening or large or out of the ordinary. They had not been instructed to do anything at all, other than to sit at Opana and spend the night and work the machine.

Whoever they were, the planes were 137 miles out, just east of due north. They were too far to hear. That seemed as though it could change. Two things radar could tell them were direction and speed. The unknown swarm was inbound, closing at two miles a minute, coming directly at Joe and George, directly at the flowers and warm surf, directly at the world of happiness in an ocean of peace, directly from the shimmering blue of the vacant sea.

It was just past seven in the morning on December 7, 1941.

ONE

AN END, A BEGINNING

B ENEATH OAHU'S CLOUDLESS blue canopy, men in white jackets, slacks, hats, and shoes surged over a gangway and spilled onto the polished wooden deck of a ship named for one of the forty-eight states. Every battleship in the fleet bore the name of one, as if its species embodied the very Union itself. The officers snapped salutes to the Stars and Stripes at the *Pennsylvania*'s stern, 608 feet from her bow. By now, each of the sixteen American battleships was older than most members of her crew and not exactly gazelle-like, lugging armor plating, crowded magazines, big guns, small guns, antiaircraft guns. But they remained tough and still occupied the rung of highest naval prestige, which was to sink the enemy's big ships so America could rule the waves of commerce and impose its will, should that seem desirable.

To witness a broadside from their main batteries was to see an angry Zeus hurl tons of explosives a dozen miles or more. A radioman aboard the *California* would recall the 35,000-ton ship's "convulsive lurch" as blasts from the fourteen-inch guns slammed her in the opposite direction, "sideways in the water." There would be "mighty thunderclaps of sound," and flames, and smoke that "smelled as if it had just come from the nether regions." Hanson W. Baldwin, the military-affairs reporter for the *New York Times*, found it "frightening" to be aboard a battleship and "have a sixteen-inch gun go off at full load and high elevation, because you get an awful whump in the stomach and ears, and everywhere else!" In a few months, the program of the Army-Navy football game in Philadelphia would feature a photo of the *Arizona* crashing bow-on through formidable seas, seemingly unsinkable and certainly intimidating. Battleships had panache, and people loved the sight of them.

Arriving from throughout Pearl Harbor, the guests in white uniform eddied aft and formed into a square, its center left empty, beyond the last of the *Pennsylvania*'s four main turrets, whose three barrels had been elevated slightly to make more room for the capped heads beneath. Above, on the turret's roof, stood announcers of the Columbia Broadcasting System. One microphone for the outgoing admiral had been placed in the middle of the human square, another for the admiral ascending. Two thousand ninety-one nautical miles to the northeast, on the mainland, it was Saturday afternoon.

"The ceremony is about to get under way," CBS's Victor Eckland said, "and as we take a sweeping glance from one side of this giant battleship to the other, we see an array of manhood in naval officialdom of which every American can be justly proud." The navy did seem to inflate the national pride. More than the army and the marines— there was no separate air force yet—it wore a halo of glamour, sailing the country's two flanking oceans, slicing protective wakes. As was often and simply put by press and politicians alike, America had invincible warships. Visiting Hawaii the previous September, the secretary of the navy, Frank Knox, had let himself positively roar: "The greatest, most powerful and the most effective fleet on the high seas anywhere in the world." He would utter similar claims during the coming months, including one that would be published on the front page of the *New York Times* edition that would be delivered to doorsteps on the first Sunday morning of December, the seventh. Some officers on Oahu wished Knox would be less enthusiastic. They knew the navy was not ready to fight. The public might get the wrong idea.

That day's change of command would be less celebratory than was traditional during peacetime, not because America was at war, but because it was rapidly approaching one and was rearming as fast as it could, faster than at any time in its history, racing against an emptying hourglass. Since 1939, the Nazis had overrun much of Europe and had besieged Great Britain, and since 1937, the Japanese had consumed much of China and had swarmed into Indochina. Full-dress attire would not be in order aboard the *Pennsylvania*. Guns would not boom in salute. Air fleets would not dapple the sky in review. Nor would the harbor pause in respect. "We hear the hum of work—riveters, steel workers, ship fitters, boilermakers, and all of the other men and machines that are being kept busy here at Pearl Harbor," Eckland went on.

The geologic miracle that was the harbor was a substantial reason the United States had decided it ought to own Hawaii, having egged on political unrest—minority whites versus the indigenous—that opened the door to annexation. The islands had been an independent kingdom, blessed—or maybe cursed—with a huge lagoon stamped into the southern coastline of Oahu. Its name, Pearl, may have arisen from its oyster beds. Its shape evoked an alluvial fan. Or maybe a clover: a narrow stem leading from the sea to three watery petals, west, middle, east. Echoing a Scotland that was nowhere within nine thousand sea miles, the petals had come to be called "lochs," Gaelic for "lakes."

During annexation hearings in 1898, General John McAllister Schofield, who had explored Hawaii extensively, told the US House of Representatives that Oahu's clover lagoon would be ideal for a modern navy—meaning a late-nineteenth-century one, which had no worries about being trapped in a confined harbor and riddled by airplanes, for there were none of those yet. Pearl's narrow mouth and channel could easily be guarded against an incursion by hostile warships. Any shells fired from offshore could not reach warships tethered inside. The lochs and surrounding land could support dozens of warships, as well as docks, maintenance shops, and coal stocks for ship boilers. If we don't take Pearl Harbor and Hawaii, General Schofield testified, the Spanish might. The Japanese might. Imperial lust had triumphed. On August 12, 1898, in a ceremony in Honolulu, the flag of the United States had risen above its newest acquisition, probably against the wishes of most Hawaiians.

At ten a.m., the two highest-ranking participants in the *Pennsylvania*'s formalities emerged from its innards. "With the dignity of their rank and surrounded by their fellow officers and men who share with them the tradition of 165 years of U.S. naval history," the announcer said, "Admiral James O. Richardson and Admiral Husband E. Kimmel make their appearance on deck. Admiral Richardson steps from the port hatch to the quarterdeck, and Admiral Kimmel steps from the starboard hatch to the quarterdeck. They approach Columbia's microphones together."

For Richardson, who was sixty-two, the moment overflowed with humiliation. He had risen out of the backwater of Paris, Texas, to the navy's best job, commander of the Pacific Fleet, only to have it yanked away after a dozen months, not the minimum eighteen, let alone the twenty-four that most fleet commanders actually served. "My God, they can't do that to me," he had said upon reading the message an aide delivered to him on an Oahu golf course on January 5. The public removal of a man considered smart, witty, and competent dumbfounded many serving under him who, using the initials of his first and middle names—*J* and *O*—called him Uncle Joe. The victim professed he hadn't foreseen his demise, either, but that was more fib than fact. Richardson was a font of negativity and a know-it-all. "Unfortunately," he said later, "I am definite in most of my opinions."

Attending the Naval War College in Newport, Rhode Island, in 1934, for example, he had simply declined to write his thesis on the assigned topic, the relationship in naval warfare among strategy, tactics, and command. Too broad for one paper, he had told his instructors. With sarcastic understatement, he had written that the assignment left him "confused by the multiplicity of tasks and by the realization that an industrious and gifted writer"—presumably him—"might, somewhat inadequately, cover the subject [only] in a lifetime." So he would not try. He framed his own topic and proceeded to discuss that.

Rising, nonetheless, to commander in chief of the Pacific Fleet in early January 1940, he began to question the strategy and acumen of his ultimate superior, Franklin D. Roosevelt, whom he had known a long time and had worked closely with as head of the Navy Department's personnel division. He did not care for him. The president had two hobbies, Richardson would say later, "stamp collecting and playing with the Navy," and he was accurate on both counts. Roosevelt, the assistant secretary of the navy during the Great War, did love ships. The proof dotted his second-floor study at the White House: glass cases sheltering ship models, and walls dotted with oil paintings of ships under sail, in one spot stacked four high. His fondness for things nautical was so well-known that citizens wrote with offers to sell or give him ship logs, models, and prints. His secretary, Grace Tully, once had to decline a miniature of the French liner *Normandie*, telling the owner, "He already has a model of this steamship."

The president did not merely collect knickknacks of the sea. He took the title of commander in chief to mean naval expert. Ten days from then, on February 10, for example, he would write the Navy Department that he would "hate" to see it go through with plans to sell a couple of old ships. "Let me see the bids for their sale when they come in," he would write, apparently hoping he would find them insufficiently high to warrant a sale. About the same time, he would ask if catapults to launch planes could be installed on two warships. In yet another query, he would wonder about "the use of 70- and 77-foot sea sleds with pompom and Y gun." And on April 23, he would write to Navy Secretary Knox, "Please speak to me about the possibility of a patrol on Hudson Bay this summer."

Richardson regarded Roosevelt as a meddling amateur, a dangerous one. As relations with Japan deteriorated, the admiral feared that the president did not appreciate just how undermanned and untrained his navy was, even as Roosevelt counted on it to scare the Japanese into staying in line. "If you do not tell the boss what you really know and feel about the possible cost and duration in an Orange war, NOBODY WILL," he had written the department on January 26, 1940, using the euphemism for Japan employed in American war games. It was deeply misguided to think the Pacific Fleet had the manpower, the guns, the supply system, and the training to back up the tough statements and strategies of the civilian leadership, Uncle Joe felt, and Japan knew it.

Traditionally, the fleet had lived on the West Coast, in the ports of San Diego and Long Beach, visiting Pearl only on maneuvers. The harbor's lochs had been more of a forward outpost with a small permanent flotilla, and it lacked much of the infrastructure of a major base. But on April 29, 1940, a few months after Richardson had taken command, Roosevelt ordered the entire fleet to take up station in the embracing arms of Pearl until he said differently. With France, Great Britain, and the Netherlands diverted by the brutal struggle against Germany, he had reasoned that their Far East colonies would tempt the Japanese, as indeed they did. A fleet sitting so much nearer would deter them, the president thought. But to Richardson, FDR's move smacked of bluff, given how unready the fleet was, all for the sake of a part of the world, the Far East, that the admiral thought should not mean that much to the United States anyway.

"I feel that any move west [to Pearl] means hostilities," Richardson had written to Washington on May 13, 1940. "I feel that at this time it would be a grave mistake to become involved in the [Far East] where our interests, although important, are not vital." In a September 12 memo, he told Secretary Knox that the president's policies were "aggressive." The memo had wondered whether anybody in the capital had given careful thought to anything. Not only was the navy not ready for war with Japan, neither was the public, Richardson believed, because Roosevelt had not been straight about the threat, not wishing to upset voters so near the 1940 election.

Nor did Richardson confine himself to questioning grand strategy and national policy. In the same memo, the admiral gave Knox all the practical reasons Roosevelt had erred in moving the fleet to Pearl. Morale among crews had dropped because their families remained in California; every single necessity—oil, munitions, replacement personnel, oceangoing targets for gunnery practice—had to be brought from the mainland. Oahu's recreation and training facilities could not absorb thousands upon thousands of newly arrived officers and enlisted men. The sheer volume of ships clogged even spacious Pearl.

"Americans are perfectly willing to go anywhere, stay anywhere, do anything when there is a job to be done and they can see the reason for their being there," Richardson said later, "but to keep the fleet—during what the men considered normal peacetimes—away from the coast and away from their families, away from recreation, rendered it difficult to maintain a high state of morale that is essential to successful training."

These were excellent, almost undeniable points. Putting the fleet at Pearl *was* disruptive. But by complaining so loudly, Richardson came across as uncooperative, pessimistic, defeatist. And those were unwelcome qualities in a military commander in a dangerous global environment. Summoned to the capital, the admiral sat down with the president on October 8, 1940, and promptly removed any doubt about how long he ought to serve. "Mr. President," he said, "I feel that I must tell you that the senior officers of the Navy do not have the trust and confidence in the civilian leadership of this country that is essential for the successful prosecution of a war in the Pacific." Richardson was not unburdening himself spontaneously. He had planned exactly what he would say. "I thought that the President could be shocked into either changing his policies, or providing adequate implementation of them," he said, by beefing up the fleet, especially by bringing ship companies up to full complement. In Richardson's view, a misguided civilian needed a healthy face slap of reality from a career officer. "I can state with complete accuracy that when the President heard my statement, he looked and acted completely crushed." Well, of course he did. The navy, the object of Roosevelt's lifelong affection, had just spurned his love.

After he was fired a few months later, Richardson told Knox, "I have never known a commander in chief to be detached in such a summary manner as I have been, and I feel that I owe it to myself to inquire as to the reason for my preemptory detachment." Knox must have been amused at the presumption of innocence. "Why Richardson," he replied, "when you were in Washington last October, you hurt the President's feelings by what you said to him." At least the admiral would savor a morsel of grim satisfaction. Ten months after the change of command, listening to the radio at home on a Sunday afternoon in Washington and as shocked as every American, Richardson would realize that being removed in a humiliating ceremony aboard the *Pennsylvania* in February was not as bad as commanding the fleet in December.

The other officer striding across the flagship's deck had grown up, as Richardson had, hundreds of miles from the sea, in Henderson, Kentucky. If a civilian had been told to conjure the visage, carriage, and career of an admiral in 1941, Husband Edward Kimmel would have materialized. He owned the part. During the coming summer, the most famous painter of navy officers, McClelland Barclay, would depict the new commander as regal and youthful, his face ruddy and largely unlined at fifty-nine. Above all, the oil portrait would capture confidence, its subject's clear conviction that he could do anything. This was no defeatist. Cheeky classmates, quoting the Russian novelist Ivan Tourgenieff, had written in the Naval Academy yearbook of 1904 that Kimmel "had the air of his own statue erected by national subscription." He never engaged in anything more strenuous than swinging golf clubs (which he did not do especially well), yet he stayed reasonably fit and energetic. Two inches shy of six feet, with blue eyes and sandy blond hair sliding toward gray at the temples, he spoke in the cadences of his South, sanding the edges off words. His only real physical impairment was his hearing, diminished in his left ear and made worse perhaps by having been too close to too many big guns during too many exercises, gunnery being a Kimmel field of expertise. When walking, he asked people to stay to his right, so he could hear them better.

As an ensign, a commander, a captain, and an admiral, Kimmel had sailed almost every sea the planet offered and stepped on every continent, or at least the ones that were not all ice. He had nearly four decades in uniform. He had commanded a destroyer, a cruiser, a battleship, then squadrons of destroyers, then divisions of cruisers, and even bureaus in the Navy Department, first Ordnance and then Budget. The navy was his oxygen. He had bled for it. In 1914, as he stood on the deck of a warship sent to protect American lives during Mexico's revolution, a bullet—fired from ashore by someone unknown—had struck a railing and splintered, the shards wounding him in an arm and both legs. "Lieutenant Kimmel," his commanding officer had said in a letter for his personnel file, "remained at his post." In a photo, dollops of blood stain the right sleeve of his white uniform. He looks untroubled.

He had been in the navy so long that, had he wished, he could have ridden shore duty all the way to retirement, but he had no interest. He wanted the sea beneath his feet. Being an ocean admiral was such a fine calling, he once told a friend, "I recommend it highly."

Kimmel had first seen Oahu on July 16, 1908. "I have heard for years of the beautiful country, fine climate and delightful people living here in the Islands," Ensign Husband had written his mother, Sibbella, "and am now ready to vouch for all three." He was twenty-six, four years out of Annapolis and aboard the *Wisconsin,* one of sixteen battleships that constituted the Great White Fleet, so christened because each had been painted white. The sixteen had departed Virginia in December 1907 on a feat of seamanship that President Theodore Roosevelt—the cousin of the future White House naval enthusiast—envisioned as proof of escalating American greatness. The sixteen were circumnavigating the globe. No navy had done it.

During their stop in Honolulu, Ensign Kimmel had gone to the beach, the mountains, a local aquarium, and a dance, where he "met some of the native girls." They were nicer looking than Negroes back home, he had written his mother, a sentence probably offensive to few, if any, whites back in Henderson. He was having the adventure of his days, often writing home to declare he had been to some event or dinner and enjoyed it immensely. Perhaps other ensigns in the Great White Fleet peppered their letters with insecurity and loneliness, but rarely did Kimmel. He was more likely to send mother Sibbella a drawing of fleet formations or a narrative of target practice. "As you know," he had written her on March 22, 1908, from Magdalena Bay, Mexico, "in the superimposed turrets, we have mounted two eight-inch and two twelve-inch guns." If Sibbella did know the intricacies of American battleship turrets, it was because her son's previous letters had educated her.

Considering his family history, no one in Henderson would have foreseen that he would have such enthusiasm for the naval life, especially after a young Husband and four Henderson friends had overturned in his sailboat on the Ohio River. After its recovery, a sign appeared on the little craft: "This boat for Sale Very Cheap—H.E. Kimmel." His father, Manning, was all army, a graduate of West Point and a former cavalryman. Husband had wanted an army career, too, but had to settle for the Naval Academy, finishing thirteenth in a class of sixty-two. He was "intensely earnest about everything," the 1904 yearbook said, and "the best type of greaser," academy slang for "bootlicker." He may have preferred the army, but Kimmel demonstrated an aptitude for the pinpoint requirements of naval gunnery. He liked exactitude, and putting a shell on a distant, moving target required just that. He liked procedures. He wanted order.

"He's the most honest, conscientious, dedicated man I have ever served with," said a captain, Joel W. Bunkley. Admirals wanted him assigned as an aide. When the United States entered the Great War in 1917, he was dispatched to improve the gunnery of the world's most famous navy, Britain's—an astounding endorsement. A newspaper would write that Kimmel's "invisible badges of success" were "administrative genius, insatiable curiosity about his ships, uncanny powers of observation, gunnery perfection and morale building efficiency." While he could be demanding and mercurial—ripping someone now, laughing with him later—no one doubted his integrity or zeal or patriotism. The navy, after all, was not a social club. It was a war-fighting enterprise. By 1933, a chief of naval operations was calling Kimmel "a humdinger."

Like everyone else, Kimmel had sought in vain to find a sliver of rationality behind Richardson's firing. He was working directly for him at the time, as commander of the Pacific Fleet's cruisers, and thought the admiral "absolutely top flight," though he did not know about the insult to Roosevelt. More surprising was his selection as the replacement. Fleet commanders tended to be a year or two older than Kimmel was at the time, and several admirals sat higher on the seniority ladder. "I hadn't any intimation that Richardson's relief was even being considered," Kimmel said, "and even had I known that his relief was being considered, I did not in my wildest dreams really think I would get the job."

Officially, Kimmel owed the honor to Roosevelt, who had signed off on his appointment. The two had met decades earlier, when Kimmel served as an aide to the then assistant navy secretary during festivities commemorating the opening of the Panama Canal. Since then, they had encountered each other on occasion, as presidents and ranking officers do, but friends they were not, though Kimmel found him "an engaging kind of chap." Almost certainly, the man who had pushed harder for Kimmel than anyone was the secretary of the navy, Frank Knox. Kimmel had spirit. Knox liked spirit.

Born on New Year's Day 1874, William Franklin Knox still rippled with energy at sixty-seven, a fitness fanatic. "Short, stocky, straightforward, more prepared to be friendly than hostile," in the words of Attorney General Francis Biddle, Knox "was not subtle, but he was healthy and decent to the core." Gutsy as well. Knox had experienced the mixed thrill of a bullet zinging through his hat in the charge up San Juan Hill with Teddy Roosevelt's Rough Riders, and at forty-three, had enlisted to fight in the Great War. Eventually, he wound up in a nonlethal but still combative pursuit in the form of newspapering in Chicago, where he owned the *Daily News*.

Oddly, Knox was a Republican, and quite a public one. He had been the GOP candidate for vice president in 1936. But seeking a bipartisan gloss for his policies of providing aid to embattled Great Britain and building American defenses in a world at war, Democrat Roosevelt had asked Knox to become navy secretary in 1940. Knox disliked many things about the president's New Deal, but he deeply admired his clarity regarding the Nazi threat. If anything, Knox wanted even tougher measures directed against Germany, if not all-out shooting. This had prompted Democratic senator Burton K. Wheeler of Montana to label him an "irresponsible, erratic individual." With a vehemence spelled out in capital letters, Knox loathed those who, like Wheeler, demanded that Roosevelt keep the country fully neutral in Europe's war. "Indifference to the outcome and pursuit of a policy of rigid isolationism is not only COWARDLY and DESPICABLE, but is as well a BETRAYAL of our vital interests," a *Daily News* editorial had thundered. One time while giving a speech, Knox had enthusiastically quoted a letter he had gotten from an admiral: "Always we must have no appeasement, no defeatism, no McClellanism," a reference to Union general George B. McClellan, who famously exasperated Abraham Lincoln by taking eons to engage the Confederates in a fight.

Knox had a glaring weakness. He knew almost nothing about the navy, other than that sea power mattered greatly. But employing the techniques of a good journalist, he traveled everywhere, soaking up data about navy jobs, needs, and tactics. On September 6, 1940,

Knox landed in Hawaii, where he had gone down in a submarine and up in a plane launched from an aircraft carrier, the first secretary of the navy ever to reach the air that way. Joe Richardson—still in command at that point—also put Knox aboard the *Honolulu*, the flagship of the cruiser force, led by one Husband Kimmel. During sea exercises, the secretary and the admiral chatted quite a bit. "He became very enthusiastic about what he saw in the *Honolulu* and didn't mind saying so," Kimmel said. In fact, over breakfast one day, an excited Knox vowed to return to Washington and clean out the naval deadwood, getting more of the bureaucrats out to sea "where they belong, like you are." The naval novice seemed to regard Kimmel and the *Honolulu* as models of fine seamanship. But the specter of paper-shufflers joining him on the front lines had appalled Kimmel, who, wagging a finger in the face of the secretary, bluntly told Knox to forget the idea—a bluntness that only seemed to impress Knox even more. Their time together probably led to Kimmel's new job four months later. In a subsequent letter, a Republican congressman from Minnesota, Melvin J. Maas, told Kimmel, "Frank Knox and I were at the launching of the U.S.S. *Massachusetts*, and I took the occasion to tell him that, if he had done nothing else but 'discover' you and put you in command of the Fleet, he had justified his appointment."

The news not only shocked Kimmel, it briefly worried him. He would command more than a hundred warships, hundreds of warplanes, and thousands upon thousands of men, and most likely have to lead them against the Japanese. Within days of his appointment, Kimmel had written to Admiral Chester W. Nimitz, who had been in the class behind him at Annapolis. "My satisfaction is mixed with anxiety," he had said, "as to whether or not I shall measure up." The doubt, though, soon floated away on Oahu's breezes. Kimmel had always succeeded. Always. His fitness reports glistened. All those superiors who had signed all those evaluations could not all have been wrong. "Of course," he admitted later, "I had considerable conceit. I'd done pretty well up until that time. I thought maybe I could handle it." His "wildest dreams" may not have included replacing Richardson, but he had kneaded the idea of someday succeeding *someone* as fleet commander. That day was simply now.

In a letter of congratulations sent on January 9, Joel Bunkley, by now the captain of the *California*, told Kimmel that he had forecast for years that the admiral would reach the top. "I didn't know it would be quite so soon," Bunkley had written, "only because I didn't know we were going to have a President who would scrap all hidebound traditions to reach down the list to pick the best man." "I confess it came sooner that I had anticipated," Admiral Harold R. Stark had told him, "but that it should come, I have long had in the back of my head." Stark, who had graduated in the class ahead of Kimmel's, held the service's top uniformed rank, chief of naval operations. "I am thankful that I [will] have your calm judgment, your imagination, your courage, your guts and your head at the seagoing end," he wrote to Kimmel on January 13. "Also your CAN DO—rather than *can't*." Kimmel may not have detected it, but the last words smacked of a slam at his predecessor, Richardson.

Many others felt about Kimmel as Stark did, including old friends from Henderson, classmates from the Naval Academy, and shipmates from the teens, the twenties, and the thirties. Their letters in the weeks after his appointment often reflected a foreboding that difficult days awaited. Being dragged into a second act of global violence seemed such a possibility that when the Pacific Fleet took to sea for maneuvers, it doused all visible lights at night to make itself less detectable by submarines, a highly desirable ability in time of war. And Kimmel's correspondents believed he would be the right man to have in charge if one broke out.

"You are particularly fortunate in coming to bat just now, as the Fleet is almost certain to see action during your tour of duty," one navy acquaintance wrote on January 14. "Perhaps it would be more appropriate to say that the country and the Navy are particularly fortunate in having you in command at this time." Admiral Edward C. Kalbfus, under whom Kimmel had served and who was now president of the Naval War College, had given him the most succinct endorsement of all in his letter: "I shall rest easier now."

The best missive had come from the big house at 512 North Green Street in Henderson, where Kimmel's diploma from the Naval Academy still hung in the foyer. Kimmel's mother and father had died years before, leaving only his two bachelor brothers to answer the telephone that began ringing as soon as the president's choice of a commander had come over the radio. Singleton, now seventy-one, and Lambert, sixty-eight, did not mind the loss of quietude a bit, having been "electrified and delighted" by the news about Hubbie, as they called him.

"Everybody we know called up, it seemed to me," Singleton wrote him on January 8. He was "swelling up," and "liable to blow up with pride any time." When he had gone to a picture show, he had been summoned to the stage to say a few words about the great man, who would now vie with John James Audubon, the ornithologist, as the greatest Hendersonian of all time. At work—where Singleton still went, well past retirement age—they told him he no longer had to convince them there were notable ancestors in the Kimmel tree. "Hubbie has knocked them all out," a coworker had said. "You just say you are Hubbie's brother."

Singleton, as the oldest and now the patriarch of the family, seemed to struggle to adequately convey to his younger sibling how wonderful this news was. Kimmels had fought the British in the Revolution and the Yankees in the Civil War, and had fought the Indians to subdue the West. But this—the four stars that would rest on Hubbie's shoulders—beat all. "The greatest honor that ever came to a Kimmel," Singleton had concluded, "or is ever likely to come again." In ten months, he would pen an altogether different letter, after Hubbie had acquired an altogether different kind of fame.

When Richardson and Kimmel reached their respective microphones, it was the outgoing man who spoke first. He did not take note of his premature departure, nor did CBS, nor did Kimmel. All adhered to what amounted to a fiction, that it was a good thing Richardson was heading back to Washington for the next exciting post of an illustrious career. In his remarks, he only hinted that his tenure may have had difficulties. "All of you can take pride in the work accomplished under trying conditions," he told the guests. "The path ahead is not easy. There is much to be done." While he regretted leaving, he said, his departure "is tempered by the fact that I turn over this command to Admiral Kimmel, a friend of long standing, a forthright man, an officer of marked ability and a successor of whom I am proud." It was true; he did like Kimmel. Well before his dismissal, he had put Kimmel's name on the short list of those who might succeed him.

Richardson had a final command to give. Each admiral in the navy had a pennant bearing as many stars as his rank, and it flew, day and night, from the mast of his ship for as long as he held command, giving rise to "flag officer" and "flagship." Now Richardson ordered his struck from the *Pennsylvania*. Down the blue ensign fluttered, as if Richardson had surrendered. He stepped back from his microphone.

Kimmel stepped forward. Reading through horn-rimmed glasses, he offered Richardson the thanks of the fleet and promised that whatever he and his ships were asked to do for America would be done. "I can only say this, that it shall be my personal motto, or guiding principle, to maintain the fleet at the highest possible level of efficiency and preparedness," Kimmel said. They would be busy in the coming months, he added, "in light of what we all know." He then gave his first command.

"Break my flag, sir!" and up went one of four stars, not his former two, up into the tropical sunshine, coming to rest above him, above the *Pennsylvania*, above Pearl Harbor, above the Pacific Fleet of the United States of America. "The crisp, blue-eyed Kentuckian had become now the sole, solitary, infinitely lonely figure that must henceforth bear responsibility for a million tons of fighting steel, the world's greatest aggregation of warships, the defense and security of his nation," the reporter for the *Honolulu Advertiser* wrote.

It was a day shy of the thirty-seventh anniversary of Husband Kimmel's graduation from the Naval Academy. Among the letters of congratulation he had gotten in the month since his appointment was one whose author recalled the remark Kimmel had once made about how being an admiral was so enjoyable that he recommended it highly. "I hope you still think so a year from now," the writer said.

TWO

HITOKAPPU'S SECRET

Wednesday, November 26, 1941

THE EVENING BEFORE they sailed, a young officer named Sadao Chigusa had opened a drawer aboard his warship and removed his *senninbari*, a short cloth "stitched a thousand times" by a thousand women to show solidarity with a warrior. Chigusa's mother in Hiroshima had overseen the sewing of his. He had never worn it, never had a reason to. Having learned, only two days earlier, where they were going and what they were to do, he wondered if this was the last night of his life in Japan. He would leave, but never return. "Expressing my last gratitude for my mother's affection," he had written in his diary after taking the cloth from its resting place, "I wound it tightly around my body, and I strongly made a fresh determination not to fall short of the expectation and the prayers of many people, one thousand of whom I didn't even know as faces, but they had kindly given one stich to my *senninbari*."

Lieutenant Commander Chigusa was afloat in the darkness of a place he had never seen until this visit, a bay at the northern cusp of the empire. Most of the others aboard the warships anchored near his—more than sixteen thousand men—had probably never been to Hitokappu Bay or Etorofu Island, either. It was difficult to discern a reason why anyone would go, at least at this time of year. By day, the island loomed as a domain of snow-soused volcanic peaks surrounded by scrub two or three feet high. The landscape appeared to be without towns, resorts, dockyards, farms, cars, factories, or military bases. Or trees. It seemed bereft of trees. Only scattered fishermen materialized, presumably the denizens of a clump of houses, the sole ones visible around the crescent of the bay. The weather nipped at fingers and machines alike. "It was very cold, with a driving, powdery snow all morning," Chigusa wrote after his ship arrived. Often in the ensuing days he would take note of the cold. He put on a sweater and muffler his wife had made, and stuffed scraps of fabric into his shoes to warm his toes. He considered the bay "a world of isolation" that had "no relationship with outside people."

In 1924, circumnavigating the globe to demonstrate American air power, three army seaplanes had stopped to refuel at Etorofu. Far longer than wide, it belongs to a desolate strand of islands that begins off Hokkaido, the most northern of Japan's four main isles, and stretches almost to Russia, more than six hundred miles to the northeast. The American seaplanes had not, however, touched down on the waters of Hitokappu Bay, the most obvious place, given its capaciousness. They had landed inland, on a protected lake. The bay sported too many risks. The entire chain lacked a suitable harbor, or so the Americans felt. "No anchorage in these islands can be considered safe, as there are strong currents and frequent storms," their military experts concluded in a 1940–41 report on the Chishima Islands, as the Japanese called the Kuriles.

Which is to say that for preparing a fleet whose success would depend on no one knowing of its existence, not even other Japanese, few places in the empire rivaled Hitokappu for off-putting obscurity. To render the fleet safer still, garbage would not be tossed overboard; landing parties would burn it. Etorofu's few telephone and telegraph lines had been blocked, so word of the fleet's arrival could not escape. Soon, ships' radio keys would be taped off so a bump or nudge would not send aloft a signal that might ricochet into the wrong ears. Finally, most of those aboard had not been told their mission before coming to the bay. They had not even been told the enemy. The British, some had guessed, at Singapore, far to the south. Except then they had gone in the wrong direction. Chigusa, who was about thirty-three years old and the executive officer of his ship, knew only that "something most serious was awaiting us."

Before leaving the ports of southern Japan to make the more-than-one-thousand-mile journey to Hitokappu, ships were shorn of wall hangings, musical instruments, photos, private papers, vases, excess chairs, extra tables, anything useless in a naval fight but prone to ignite or fly about, or whose weight sheered speed. "Our wardroom had been turned into a very bare room," Chigusa said. Gun crews had practiced, especially antiaircraft mounts. Ships had rehearsed—and rehearsed again—how to refuel while under way, which obviously meant they were going farther than the capacity of their tanks. A quarter of the strike fleet was gas stations: tankers with ten or twelve thousand tons of oil each. Even that was not going to be enough. Five-gallon containers of fuel had been stuffed into empty spaces on some ships.

Chigusa's was the *Akigumo*, the newest destroyer in the Imperial Navy, commissioned that very month and among the last members of the strike fleet to anchor in the bay, having arrived Saturday, November 22. "It is really encouraging to see all the ships of our Task Force steam in one after another," he told his diary, "and gather in full force by evening." Thirty would be making the voyage to wherever they were going, to do whatever they were to do. If Chigusa had any in-kling that the fleet's composition bore no semblance to any previous naval force in history—not only Japanese but anyone's, period—he did not say. He did not say that six of the ships surrounding his little destroyer were aircraft carriers, the six largest Japan possessed.

The morning after his arrival, at 8:05, with snow falling on decks and uniforms, bugles had sounded. Assembled topside, crews had come to attention and faced Tokyo, more than seven hundred miles below the bleak southwestern horizon. It was a tradition in the Im-perial Navy to mark the harvest festival by standing on deck, pivot-ing toward the capital, and saluting Emperor Hirohito and Empress Nagako, and tradition held even then and even there. Afterward, small boats bearing captains and others of rank from across the fleet had converged on the flagship, the aircraft carrier *Akagi*, and by the time they returned to their own decks, all the officers had been ad-mitted to the club of those who knew the greatest secret in the world. And with the fleet now isolated and shore leave forbidden, it was safe to tell the men of every ship.

The Inland Sea is that part of the Pacific Ocean surrounded by the Japanese main islands of Honshu, Kyushu, and Shikoku, and on the day Chigusa had taken out his *senninbari*, a diminutive admiral of fifty-seven years, with gray and close-cut hair and a deep fondness for Abraham Lincoln, had stepped aboard a ferry there. His mis-tress of many years had gone with him. The strike fleet had sailed for Hitokappu Bay several days before, heading north not as one impressive host, but by twos and threes to minimize the stares from civilians ashore, to make the departure unexciting, commonplace. With the fleet gone, the admiral who stayed behind could put on ci-vilian clothes and escape to an inn on a smaller island, if only briefly, before returning to oversee the outbreak of the war he did not want.

Isoroku Yamamoto stood only three inches more than five feet tall and weighed 130 pounds at most. Geishas who did his fingernails called him "Eighty Sen" because the regular rate was ten sen a finger and he had only eight, having given the left middle and index to vanquish the Russians in the war of 1904–5. Though his digital losses presented a challenge when, say, removing the covering from a bowl of steaming soup, they did not impede his card-carrying abilities. "Boy, he was a good bridge player, Yamamoto," an American naval officer said, having lost three straight rubbers to him one day in the late 1930s. "He played for blood."

If given another life, Yamamoto had supposedly vowed, he would choose not to spend it on his flagship, the battleship *Nagato*, but at the gaming tables of Monaco, which he had visited. The commander in chief of the Combined Fleet equated relaxation with taking chances. He did not drink much. He did bet a lot. He could beat good poker players, good bridge players, and win at Go, the East Asian board game. Roulette, pool, chess, mahjong, shogi, you'd pick and he'd play and he'd win. He would wager on bowling. "Few men could have been as fond of gambling and games of chance as he," one Japanese admiral said, adding, "Anything would do." Yamamoto bested subordinates so often he would not cash their checks. If he had, they would have run out of betting money, and he would have run out of people to beat.

The American naval officer who could not beat him at bridge, Lieutenant Commander Edwin T. Layton, believed he "possessed more brains than any other Japanese in the high command." They had first met in 1937 when Layton, who could speak Japanese, became the assistant naval attaché in Tokyo, and Yamamoto, who spoke English, was the vice minister of the Imperial Navy. He had taken Layton to his first performance of Kabuki—"Weird stuff, but it can really move you," the American said—and to geisha parties, and invited him to go "net duck hunting," in which participants used precisely that, a net. "Many Japanese are hard to get to," Layton said years later. "They are quite reserved, sometimes very aloof. One sometimes has the impression that they are like actors in a *noh* drama, wearing false faces or masks to suit their role." But Yamamoto had chatted easily with Layton, as long as they skirted the details of each other's naval operations. Isoroku loved flowers, penned poetry, enjoyed reporters, eschewed pomposity.

The man would sometimes do handstands, on eight fingers. Sometimes break into tears at the memory of lost comrades, whose names he kept in a notebook he carried. He could be surprisingly vulnerable, and quite romantic. To his mistress in 1935, he had written of his burning desire "to be embraced in your arms," and told her that he had dreamed they were driving along the Mediterranean coast of France. "How wonderful it would be if it were true," he said. Geishas from Tokyo's Shimbashi district thought he could be "rather unapproachable and taciturn at first," one of them said, "but once he let himself relax, he was something of a clown . . . with a touch of the big-baby in him as well." A clerk in the fleet's paymaster branch, Noda Mitsuharu, said that when the *Nagato* would anchor at Yokosuka, near Tokyo, the admiral would welcome aboard his mistress, Chiyoko Kawai, and some of her friends. "He was famous for his geisha lover from Shimbashi. Everybody knew about it," Mitsuharu said. "We knew her, too." She and the other visitors to the ship were hard to miss. Yamamoto would have a band ready for them, to play folk dances.

He could even seem slightly mystical, convinced, for example, that oil could be made out of water and that he could tell whether a man would be a competent pilot just by studying his face. However emotional or sentimental or even odd Yamamoto could be, though,

Layton saw "a lot of steel in his eyes." He could not have risen as far as he had otherwise. Besides serving as naval vice minister, Yamamoto had represented his country at naval arms-limitation negotiations in London in 1934; had been assigned to the United States twice, first in 1919 as a naval representative and then in 1926 as naval attaché; and had commanded the Combined Fleet since 1939. As fond and proud of Japan as anyone, as eager to see Westerners bestow some long-overdue respect for the empire's power and culture, he nonetheless had opposed its 1940 alliance with Nazi Germany and Italy, which hardly endeared him to extreme nationalists, but barely dented his renown.

"There have not been many generals or admirals, either in the history of the Western or Eastern world, who combined in a single person intelligence, humanity and courage," a writer by the name of Saburo Kuroshio had said a couple of days before Yamamoto boarded his ferry, "but I do not hesitate to accord Admiral Yamamoto first place on the list of living sea fighters of the Empire, as a model admiral belonging to that category."

During 1940 and 1941, in a small notebook, an American admiral had reportedly jotted his own personal rankings of Japanese naval officers, and put Yamamoto at the top. The Japanese commander in chief was "smart and dangerous," the American had supposedly written, and his own navy ought to "look out for Yamamoto." In a formal appraisal published in September 1941, American intelligence called Yamamoto "exceptionally able, forceful, and quick thinking." In any war with the United States, the report said, he "may be expected to adopt a bold and positive course of action." In other words, Yamamoto gravitated to the daring and aggressive play, the Hail Mary. Even before that prognostication began circulating in Washington that fall—doomed to go unappreciated—it had begun to come true.

The previous winter, in January, Yamamoto had taken up pen and set down thoughts about a bold and positive course by which to attack the United States. War with the Americans was "inevitable," he had written. Japan, as the smaller power, must settle it "on its first day" with a strike so breathtaking and brutal that American morale "goes down to such an extent that it cannot be recovered." That would not be easy, he had conceded. But if "favored by God's blessing" and if "officers and men who take part in this operation have a firm determination of devoting themselves to their task, even sacrificing themselves," a secret fleet could sail ahead of any formal declaration of war and, as the conflict's opening and most decisive moment, crush American naval power. Yamamoto wished to dispose of the Pacific Fleet in a single stroke, in or around Pearl Harbor.

He mailed the letter to the minister of the navy, and then a version of it to a subordinate admiral, seeking his opinion as well. In turn, that officer showed the three pages of fine-quality paper to a fighter pilot of wide fame and considerable passion, Minoru Genda. The first thing Genda noticed was the handwriting. Yamamoto's was impeccable, beautiful. The second was the idea. It was beautiful, too, in a can-you-believe-this sort of way.

Such an audacious raid, Genda thought, would be "like going into the enemy's chest and counting his heart beat." The admiral who had shown him the letter, Takijiro Onishi, told him to study it and return with an evaluation. "For one week," Genda said, "I forgot sleeping and eating. The work was a great strain on the nerves. The most troubling thing [would be] to keep the plan an absolute secret." Yamamoto's grand stratagem would work only if the Americans lived in ignorance through the last days of peace as the stalker sneaked to the fringe of Hawaii. That meant keeping a tight and tiny circle of those who knew; otherwise, rumors of war might slither under the door of the American embassy in Tokyo.

Genda, who was thirty-seven, had not been randomly selected for exposure to a confidential rumination of the most important naval officer in Japan. In a world that still genuflected to the battleship—the backbone of navies since cannons had made their way to wooden decks in the age of sail—Commander Genda possessed such unorthodox views on the big ships that he had become the object of a playful saying: *Genda san wa kichigai desu*, "Mr. Genda is insane." His desire, conveyed in writing while at Japan's naval war college, was that all of its battleships would morph into heaping piles of scrap metal, and that Japan would never build another. War games premised on duels between passing lines of heavy-gun ships, as if the year were still 1812 and the place were still the sea off Trafalgar, were "exercises in masturbation" involving a dead technology. Genda preached the power of the airplane. He sang the song of the aircraft carrier, ships not designed to shoot anything, and such new weapons that the Great War had been fought largely without them. Unlike battleships or cruisers, which had to sail to within sight of the enemy to sink him, aircraft carriers could lurk one hundred, even two hundred, miles away, far beyond the range of any battleship gun, and then send aloft dive and torpedo bombers to dispatch the vessels of the unsuspecting foe.

Genda's proposal to rid the Imperial Navy of its battleships had remained an amusing wish. Japan not only still had many, it was building the largest in the world. But at least it had complemented its big-gun ships with aircraft carriers, building more than any other country—ten by the end of 1941, three more than the country it expected to fight one day, the United States. And Japan had Yamamoto, who had no thought of attacking the Pacific Fleet in the classic way, with mammoth, blazing guns. He, too, had become an advocate for carrier power. They would be his instruments of lethality. "I even felt something very cold running along my spine," Genda said. After contemplating Yamamoto's scheme, he made his way back to Admiral Onishi, who asked, "Possible, right?" The pilot had detected numerous problems, and the danger would be enormous. But it could be done.

Others thought not.

In the months that followed, the naval hierarchy in Tokyo rained doubt on a Pearl Harbor raid. Many of its questions could never be answered by war games or staff research, only by actually attempting the raid. Yamamoto could not guarantee his superiors that the Pacific Fleet would be in port on the planned day of attack. It might have sailed away on an exercise, which would leave the strike fleet exposed, far from home, the enemy's naval power still intact and its whereabouts uncertain. Nor could he guarantee that his men could pull off the dozens of tanker-to-warship fuel replenishments essential to keeping the strike fleet advancing across the endless North Pacific, then get it home. Genda had chosen that obscure route because southerly ones had too much commercial shipping and American naval activity. But the North Pacific becomes tempestuous as autumn elides into winter. Destroyers, the whippets of the fleet, had the smallest fuel capacity and were most likely to pitch and yaw in turbulent seas. The strike fleet's supply tankers would face great risk each time they sidled close to string their hoses and pump their flammable contents. Nor could Yamamoto guarantee that the grand secret would hold even within Japan. Of necessity, more and more commanders, pilots, planners, and logisticians would learn it, and someone's lips could always slip.

Mostly, achieving surprise—the sine qua non of Yamamoto's vision—seemed an absurd hope, even if there were no leaks from the Imperial Navy itself. The Pacific Ocean was so vast—all the newest

world war's European and African battlefields could fit into a corner
of it—that the strike fleet would be in transit for almost two weeks,
two weeks in which it might be discovered the next minute. In a tense
international atmosphere, which it now was, American patrols would
probably be up, flying from Alaska, which the Americans owned;
from Midway Island, which they owned; from Oahu, which was the
home of the Pacific Fleet. Their submarines and surface ships would
be combing the seas. If only one enemy plane or one ship stumbled
on the empire's armada, the Americans would never conclude they
had discovered a friendly mission to Hawaii. It did not even have to
be a military patrol that found them. A commercial ship could, and
radio Oahu. Unaware they had been spotted, the Japanese might sail
magnificently, valiantly, and ignorantly to their destruction in a trap
sprung by the very Pacific Fleet they had come to sink.

"We knew that you were carrying out extensive scouting from
Hawaii, so in all probability our task force would be discovered a day
ahead of that planned for the attack," Admiral Shigeru Fukodome,
a member of the Imperial Navy staff, would tell American interrogators after the war, "and consequently would be attacked first."

Any Japanese reading the American press would have thought
so, too. "Day and night, Navy and Army planes are droning down
the warm skies in circles two hundred, five hundred, a thousand
miles wide," *Collier's* magazine said on June 14, calling Hawaii a
"billion-dollar fist" of bristling, wide-awake might, symbolized by
battleships that were "wary as lions on the prowl." The *Chicago Tribune,* never one to say anything nice about the Roosevelt administration, declared on August 17, "Destroyers, cruisers and aircraft
carriers patrol ceaselessly the seas about Oahu. Pearl Harbor, sym-
bol and keystone of defense in the West, is the concentric center of
continuous flights of warplanes on day and night patrols far out to
sea, scanning the surface for the sight of strange craft." In its May

issue, *Paradise of the Pacific* helpfully provided a "Warning to the Enemy"—unnamed, but Japan—saying that its forces "would be detected long before they were in striking distance," and if any planes got as far as Honolulu, "the Army and Navy would make quick work of them." In the media, Oahu was described as "impregnable" and the "mid-Pacific Gibraltar."

Success for Yamamoto's raiders seemed fifty-fifty, at best sixty-forty. Failure might mean more than the loss of ships and men. It might jeopardize a much higher priority that fall: a plan to invade and conquer Malaya, Singapore, and the Netherlands East Indies, as well as an American possession, the Philippines. Many officers of the Imperial Navy could not imagine siphoning aircraft carriers from that much larger scheme. Instead of adding a mission to Hawaii that might result in the demise of much of the Imperial Navy, they preferred to leave Pearl Harbor alone. If the Pacific Fleet came forth to take back the Philippines or defend the Dutch and British colonies, let it come. It might not; the United States might choose not to fight a war so far away. After all, it had yet to try to curb by force the empire's aggressive spread. The Americans had not declared war after Japan seized Manchuria in 1931, nor after it attacked China in 1937, nor after it coerced beaten France into allowing Japanese forces to occupy Indochina.

Besides, if the Pacific Fleet did come, the Japanese had long hoped that any war with the United States would unfold in the western half of the ocean, where the Americans would be far from supplies and reinforcements. It made no sense to reverse that strategy now, to sail to their half. In September, after tabletop war games in a secret room at the Japanese Naval War College suggested that the strike fleet might suffer serious losses off Hawaii, Admiral Fukodome concluded, "Japan could lose the war the very first day."

Nothing punctured Yamamoto's resolve. "I like speculative

games," he told another admiral one day. "You have told me that the operation is a speculation, so I shall carry it out." Critics had it backward. The invasions of the British, Dutch, and American possessions in the southwest Pacific would be jeopardized if the Imperial Navy did *not* attack Pearl Harbor, not if it did. Leaving the Pacific Fleet untouched would concede the initiative to the Americans. They could choose when, where, and how to contest Japan's fresh conquests, or even to attack the Japanese mainland while the Imperial Navy was engaged in the southern assaults. Roosevelt had already moved the Pacific Fleet much closer to Japan, as if he were advancing the queen on a chessboard. Yamamoto wished to take the queen now, when least expected, before Roosevelt shoved it nearer still, to the Philippines. Time was not Japan's friend. Rearmament was enlarging the American navy rapidly. If Japan had to confront it at some point, let it be before the enemy's ships were too numerous. Let us control our fate. Let us choose the time and the place for engaging the Pacific Fleet.

For Yamamoto, the place was Pearl and the time was immediately after—an hour or two after—the empire submitted a declaration of war. He believed in diplomatic norms. He believed that an honorable samurai does not plunge his sword into a sleeping enemy, but first kicks the victim's pillow, so he is awake, and then stabs him. That a nonsamurai nation might perceive that as a distinction lacking a difference did not, apparently, occur to him.

He bore no illusions that his spectacular gambit guaranteed ultimate national victory, for he had seen the power of the adversary up close. During his two tours, he had traveled the American continent and noted its energy, its abundance, and the character of its people, even attending an Iowa-Northwestern football game. The United States had more steel, more wheat, more oil, more factories, more shipyards, more of all the things the empire did not have in quantity, confined as it was to rocky islands off the Asian mainland. The year before, Japanese planners had calculated that the industrial capacity of the United States was seventy-four times that of Japan, and that it had five hundred times more oil. If pitted against the Americans over time, the Imperial Navy would never be able to make good its inevitable losses the way the United States could. In a drawn-out conflict, "Japan's resources will be depleted, battleships and weaponry will be damaged, replenishing materials will be impossible," Yamamoto wrote on September 29 to the chief of the Naval General Staff. Japan will wind up "impoverished," and any war "with so little chance of success should not be fought."

But, no doubt, it was going to be fought. Isoroku Yamamoto alone could not stop the illogical march of Japanese policy. The country's rapacious grab for China, then in its fifth year and no closer to ending, and its two bites of French Indochina, in 1940 and 1941, had been answered by Western economic sanctions, which shut off the flow of oil from the United States, Japan's principal supplier. Unwilling to give up what it wanted—greater empire—in return for the restoration of lost trade, unwilling to endure the humiliation of swift withdrawal from China, as the Americans wanted, Japan was going to seize the tin, nickel, rubber, and especially oil of the British and Dutch colonies. It would take the Philippines, too, to prevent America from using its small naval and land forces there to interfere with the destiny of the empire.

Attacking Pearl may have been the most dangerous bet of his life, but Yamamoto considered it no more ludicrous than his country's southern plan to add Britain, the Netherlands, and the United States to its roster of enemies. "My present situation is very strange," Yamamoto wrote on October 11 to a friend. He would be leading the Imperial Navy in a war that was "entirely against my private opinion," yet he was "expected to do my best." As an officer loyal to His Majesty the Emperor, he could only make the best of the foolish decisions of others to start more wars. Given that there was "little hope of success in any ordinary strategy," Yamamoto wrote to a civilian official on October 24, he would "resort to the combined strategies of *Okehazama*, *Hiyodorigoe*, and *Kawanaka-Jima*." They were battles of Japanese lore. In them, warriors triumphed by appearing suddenly, or where least expected, or at the enemy's most vulnerable point.

If he could strike the Pacific Fleet hard enough in Hawaii to knock it out of action for half a year or more—"reduce it to impotency," the operational order said—maybe Japan would have time to conquer what it wanted elsewhere, gird for the American riposte, and trust in luck and the gods and martial élan. "Military operations, in a war between Japan and the United States, would be very difficult," Admiral Fukodome would tell his American interrogators, but they "would not be altogether hopeless. There would be some chances of victory. To ward off defeat, too, would not be impossible." They had once beaten much-bigger Russia, had they not? To a sad and fatal degree, hope was Japan's strategy. Referring to a well-known hillside temple in Kyoto, Prime Minister Hideki Tojo said that as far as war with America was concerned, "occasionally, one must conjure up enough courage, close one's eyes, and jump off the platform of the Kiyomizu."

On November 17, Isoroku Yamamoto stood on the flight deck of the aircraft carrier *Akagi* hours before it sailed from the Inland Sea north to Hitokappu. Strike fleet pilots had already been made privy to the secret plan in order that they might understand why they were training on topography that resembled Oahu's, and why their practice bomb runs involved targets in a harbor, not ships under way. In its 2,600 years of history, Yamamoto told a hundred pilots that day, Japan had fought huge and powerful enemies, the Chinese and the

Russians. "But in this operation, we will meet the strongest and most resourceful opponent of all." The commander of America's Pacific Fleet is smart, and might well discover their approach, in which case "you will have to fight your way to the target."

"What came from his heart went to their hearts," his chief of staff, Matome Ugaki, had written in his diary. "I saw on their faces unshakeable loyalty, determined resolution, even a degree of ferocity. But they were all self-composed. We cannot but expect some damage to us, yet I pray that by the grace of heaven they will succeed in their objective."

A few days later, Ugaki would write:

"What a big drama it is, risking the fate of a nation and so many lives."

Late on November 23, as word of the Pearl Harbor plan spread through the enlisted men and the lower-rank officers of the warships anchored in Hitokappu Bay, a sailor named Iki Kuramoti had exulted. "An air attack on Hawaii!" he thought. "A dream come true. What will the people at home think when they hear the news? Won't they be excited? I can see them clapping their hands and shouting with joy. . . . We [will] teach the arrogant Anglo-Saxon scoundrels a lesson!" The plan offered adventure and glory, but also absurd danger. A pilot named Yoshio Shiga would tell an American interrogator just how dubious many aviators were. "Shiga stated that the consensus . . . following this startling news was that to get to Hawaii secretly was impossible," the interrogator would write, summarizing an interview conducted a month after the war's end. "Hence, it was a suicide attack." The admiral who had been given command of the attack fleet, Chuichi Nagumo, reacted as if an infected baby had been laid in his lap. He worried incessantly, especially about refueling, and expected that half his force would be sunk or damaged. An associate reassured him, saying that "if you die in this operation, then special shrines will be built in your memory."

The secret was revealed to Lieutenant Commander Sadao Chigusa when the *Akigumo*'s captain returned from the meeting aboard the *Akagi* that day. Chigusa considered himself a brave servant of the empire, and he was always resolved to do his duty well, but his ship would probably sink "off Hawaii in the greatest and most desperate battle in our history." Many men began writing wills, as men do on the edge of battle. "I wrote my own farewell message to my wife and parents," Chigusa said. He had visited his parents in Hiroshima before the strike fleet left southern waters, and now he thanked them "for their affection and care all my life." To his wife, Fumiko, he entrusted the care and upbringing of their daughter, Kimiko, who was four, and their son, Masao, two. Into the envelope went a snippet of his hair to help them remember him in the years after his death. The letters would be held ashore for delivery after the attack.

"All the crew were pleased to have warm noodles at their midnight supper," Chigusa had written on the night before departure, after slipping on his *senninbari*. In between writing wills, he and the crew had installed additional shielding against shell splinters around the *Akigumo*'s bridge and main batteries, gone over the need to keep the ship dark at night, and discussed and discussed again the entire operation. "And at 2230, I took my last sleep at Hitokappu Bay without any anxiety."

At six o'clock the following morning, Wednesday, November 26, under a sky of solid pewter, the temperature just above freezing, the anchors of thirty ships ascended from the cold, the sound of their clanking links doubtless rising above the bay's endemic stillness. Propeller shafts began spinning, and the strike fleet crept forward, taking its first hostile steps, easing out of the crescent and into the

Pacific. Two battleships. Three cruisers. Nine destroyers. Three submarines. Seven tankers. Six aircraft carriers. "The sally of our great fleet was really a majestic sight," Chigusa said.

Heading out, ships fired test rounds at the bleak landscape of Etorofu, kicking up brown clouds of smoke, a kind of farewell. Aboard the carrier *Kaga*, the pilot Shiga saw the bursts, and while he did not think his commanders meant the display to underscore the gravity of the moment, "it still remains very vivid in my mind." They were going to Hawaii, and that would be the end of them. "We all thought this," Shiga said.

A joke had filtered among the crewmembers of the *Akigumo*. For this mission, each of them would receive the Order of the Golden Kite, Japan's highest military honor, but probably not in person. Chigusa was troubled by a very personal reality. "My elder brother was living in Honolulu at that time, so I worried uncommonly," he wrote in his diary, but "I did not excuse myself from dashing to Hawaii in spite of the effect my act might have on a dear one." Tens of thousands of Japanese lived on Oahu, immigrants and their families who had come to work in the cane or pineapple fields or to open small businesses. Chigusa's brother worked in a hotel. Still, he made up his mind "to do my best in war, because I fought for my Emperor and my country."

Aboard the *Akagi* was Minoru Genda, his faith in naval air power validated all around him. In recent days, he had been patiently going over details with pilots, using large three-dimensional models that had been stored aboard the flagship—one of Oahu, the other Pearl Harbor. Wooden miniatures of American battleships, about the size of Hershey's bars, had been carved and positioned along a miniature of their regular place of berth, a large island in the middle of East Loch called Ford.

Working for many weeks on the fine points—how many carriers, what mix of planes, the types of ordnance, the sailing formations—

Genda had struggled most of all with an immutable characteristic of Pearl Harbor: its maximum depth. Forty-five feet was not enough, not for the weapon of greatest threat to a ship's hull. Dropped from a plane, a torpedo plunged deeper than forty-five feet, so instead of leveling off and racing toward the American ships, they would bury themselves in Pearl Harbor's bottom mud, unless somebody thought of a way to make the initial plunge much shallower. Only in mid-November, only at the last minute, had a method been found. "Tears came to my eyes," Genda said. There was, though, still the chance that despite how little depth there was, the Americans had strung steel nets around their anchored ships as additional security to thwart torpedoes. The pilots could not be sure until they arrived overhead.

Gradually, the snowy, volcanic peaks of Etorofu dropped below the western horizon. The strike fleet spread out, forming a box roughly twenty miles across, twenty deep, a line of destroyers out front, cruisers and tankers and more destroyers in the middle, the carriers and the battleships at the rear. The *Akigumo* fought heavy swells, rolling ten degrees, twenty.

The fleet would sail nearly blind. It did not have radar, and no reconnaissance planes would be sent aloft to see who was in front of it, because any scout who became lost would have to break radio silence to find his way back. There would be only the three submarines inspecting far ahead. The fleet would sail mute, never speaking to the homeland. Its radio operators would listen, however. One message would be Tokyo's final permission to attack, if talks in Washington failed. Others would be reports from friendly eyes on Oahu about whether it had awakened to danger, and about which ships lay in the harbor, if any.

In the long saga of combat at sea, aircraft carriers were still too novel to warrant many pages, but Japan was about to write a new chapter all by itself. It had come to understand the potency of the weapon better and faster than any nation on earth. Having a mass of them sail as one and launch simultaneously, rather than sail scattered or alone, massively enhanced the destructive power of their planes. No navy had collected as many carriers into a single fleet as were now beginning the journey across the North Pacific. No navy had even created a fleet centered on aircraft carriers, of any number. As two historians would phrase it, "For the first time in history, there existed a carrier force comprising enough aircraft to do strategically meaningful things on the battlefield." If the fleet reached Hawaii undetected and intact, the nearly four hundred torpedo bombers, dive bombers, high-altitude bombers, and fighter planes that would rise from the flight decks of the *Akagi*, *Hiryu*, *Kaga*, *Shokaku*, *Soryu*, and *Zuikaku* would deliver the largest and most powerful airborne assault from the sea ever.

If.

If the Americans did not find them first.

"I pictured to myself the situation in which we were, hearing the dashing of the waves outside," Genda said. They were, at last, advancing on the Pacific Fleet, "not in a dream, but really."

Pearl Harbor was 3,150 miles ahead.

THREE

THE ADMIRAL CHIEF OF
THE PACIFIC FLEET

Thursday, November 27
Pearl Harbor

A NY DAY THAT a passenger ship of the Matson Line blossomed into view, carving around Diamond Head on the last league from California, was Boat Day on Oahu. Pan Am's Clippers had shrunk the distance to an unimaginable sixteen hours, but the *Lurline* and the *Matsonia*—white hulls, raked funnels, six hundred feet long—remained the transcendent conveyances. People flocked to the harbor in Honolulu to greet their arrivals, draping leis over the latest cohort of mainlanders who would soon be giddy drunk on the perpetual northeast breezes, the fragrance, and the light. "The day I arrived in Hawaii was the day I vowed never to leave," Dorothy Bicknell, the wife of an army officer, remembered years later. Musicians serenaded, trunks spilled onto piers, mailbags emerged from the holds bearing letters with tales of home-state doings. "I immediately got into a taxi for a round trip around [Oahu], and feasted my eyes on the gorgeous landscape," Otto Tolischus wrote of his arrival on January 29. He was pausing on his way to Tokyo, where he would be the new correspondent for the *New York Times*. "The sun was shining, the mountain peaks looked serenely into the azure sky, the flatlands simmered in various shades of green, and the blue ocean rolled lazily against a languorous shore. Peace seemed to be written all over the scene, even over Pearl Harbor that spread itself before me on rounding a curve."

Shortly after her arrival in early November, Helen Sibbella Dauth wrote to two of her uncles in Henderson, Kentucky, to say she had never seen water of such color or flowers so breathtaking. "I marvel at the place every time I look around me," Helen said. She marveled as well that she, her son, and her daughter had not perished en route. Japan seemed so intent on conquest, so untrustworthy, that anything might have happened on their way to join her husband, an army officer. The Far East "bids fair to leap into eruptive explosion even as this is being written," *Paradise of the Pacific* had warned Hawaiians in September, which was pretty much what it had written in August, too. Happily, Helen wrote, "we didn't get bombed or torpedoed, as I had anticipated. . . . In fact, we didn't even see a submarine or a Jap on the whole trip, for which I am really very thankful, although I am sure there must be some lurking somewhere in those waters." They were crafty, those Japanese, she said.

Helen Dauth had a third uncle who lived right there on Oahu. Unable to greet the boat due to his schedule, he apologized by sending a car and driver, and when they finally met at her hotel, Helen was thrilled by the cut of Husband Kimmel. "He looks perfectly marvelous," she said in her letter to the admiral's brothers, Singleton and Lambert, "and is much more handsome than what his picture shows. He is very tanned and has a vigorously healthy appearance, and also most distinguished, and looks every inch an Admiral Chief of the United States Fleet. I am so deeply proud of Uncle Hubby." He looked so *in command.* "I still don't believe him when he says he was awfully scared when the President appointed him."

In the nearly ten months since his investiture, the Admiral Chief had shaken the Pacific Fleet with a drill instructor's gusto familiar to all who knew him, demanding more precise gunnery, crisper maneuvering, quicker responses to commands, better care of machinery, swifter damage control, sharper personal appearance—simply a keener edge than the fleet had evinced in less threatening times. In the seas south of Pearl, it had drilled by day and practiced by night, simulating and executing so much that Kimmel had become known, in the words of his intelligence officer, "for killing the fleet. Oh boy. He kept them at sea, zigzagging, blackouts at night . . . guns manned. . . . A lot of people were very unhappy with this." Kimmel characterized what he did that summer succinctly: "We put on extra steam." He pushed, he inspected, he corrected, and he cursed. "I believe that in my whole career, I had never been addressed in such colorful and foul language by a superior officer," Colonel Omar T. Pfeiffer, the fleet marine officer, said of the day during the summer when he and another officer had endured "vehement castigation" for failing to deliver a report. Laxness, lateness, and subpar performance were felonies as far as Kimmel was concerned. They would take lives and ruin ships when the shells started flying, as he felt they soon would. "Every command I ever had while I was in the Navy," he said, "I endeavored to get it ready to fight." The Pacific Fleet, when it was placed in his hands on February 1, was not ready. "I set out to make it ready."

Years earlier, then-ensign Kimmel had been reassigned from a battleship, a coveted billet, to a destroyer, where he was to fill in for its executive officer, who was ill. The prospect of even two or three months aboard a no-account little vessel had annoyed Kimmel and he had not hidden it, but he was incapable of serving out the sentence with a sulking, mediocre performance. He soon had the ship running better than ever. "He couldn't do it any other way," the destroyer's captain, Thomas C. Hart, recalled, "and he was doing his job better and better all the time." When the regular executive officer had returned to health, Hart didn't want him. He wanted to keep Kimmel. "He was a dandy in all respects. Never saw anyone better."

In the late 1920s, starting his rise into the upper ranks, Kimmel had taken command of a squadron of destroyers. "Within a matter of almost hours, things started happening," said William R. Smedberg III, then serving as a communications officer aboard the *Mullany*. "Everything was tautened, inspections were more frequent and tougher." Kimmel "put us through the damnedest paces," even when the ship was in port, supposedly relaxing. "We were not being allowed to get home to our wives and babies very often," Smedberg remembered, even though Kimmel had three sons and surely knew of the desire for family time. "That was not as important to the Navy as the necessity for each officer and man to be thoroughly trained in every aspect of his job, in his eyes."

If boiler fumes wafted too visibly from the funnels of one of his ships, signal pennants would rise on the flagship: STOP SMOKE. He did not want to make it easy for an enemy to spot them. Once, in the days when he held a lesser command, Kimmel's formation had begun drifting apart off Portland, Oregon. Two pennants had risen. Everyone knew the meaning of one: NEGATIVE. They had to look up the second: SCATTER. Only Kimmel, apparently, had memorized the entire signal book.

Every exercise, every test, reflected a battle's realities. H. Kent Hewitt, one of Kimmel's senior subordinates in the cruiser force, remembered that he "would come aboard ships unexpectedly and tell them to get up their electric submersible pumps on the fo'c'stle and see how long it would take them to pump water from one side of the ship over into the other, and little things like that. He would order all the main power switches on the terrace thrown and see how long it took them to rig emergency power leads to the turrets." One day in 1940 while commanding the cruisers, Kimmel decided to find out how long one particular ship would take to provide each of its six-inch guns with a hundred live rounds from the magazines. Sounding a drill, he told the crew to ignore the navy's rule requiring dummy ordnance in peacetime exercises, and to bring up the real thing. Chaos followed. The live ordnance hadn't been stored in the correct order, and not enough men had been assigned to retrieve it, and even those few "were falling all over each other," Hewitt said. The Bureau of Ordnance then sent Kimmel a letter for violating the live-ammunition rule. "I don't give a dang," he said. "I found out what I wanted to know." He had found out, not under fire, which could have been fatally late, but during training, when correctives could still be taken.

Kimmel's eyes could X-ray every ship, or so it seemed, and they never found a flaw not worth fixing. "I note certain material failures in the destroyers," the fleet commander wrote on August 7 to his destroyer group leader. While a certain number of problems are unavoidable, he said, "I note that this last week the *Preston* had the main bearing run hot and found it necessary to [re]enter Pearl in order to roll-in new bearings. I presume you are investigating the cause of this and other breakdowns." One of his closest acquaintances, and smartest, was the commander of the battleships, Admiral William S. Pye, but their relationship did not purchase Pye any exemptions. On September 25, Kimmel complained that Pye's ships took too long to hoist aboard their catapult-launched seaplanes after scouting missions. It should take less than twenty minutes to fish a plane out of the water, Kimmel told him. He had heard that one battleship had taken an hour.

This was, clearly, an obsession with order, a crusade against deviation, a mania for staying inside the box. Kimmel seemed unable to distinguish minute matters from the ones worthy of the time of the highest-ranking naval officer in the Pacific Ocean. One day, his chief of staff, Captain William W. "Poco" Smith, found him "personally auditing the records of the number of rounds of ammunition of all sorts" distributed to bases on American islands farther out in the Pacific. Kimmel was holding one list in his hand, and comparing it with one compiled and brought by a subordinate admiral. "The two papers disagreed," Smith recalled. "And I made the remark that the Commander-in-Chief should not be counting bullets, that he had a staff to do that. Both admirals laughed, and agreed with me." But Kimmel could not help himself. On another day in 1941, for instance, he was contemplating the best way to adjust the location of two five-inch artillery batteries on the island of Midway. It was fine to shift them to a new firing position, he told an underling, but "this movement of batteries should be so made that not more than one battery is incapable of action at any time."

Kimmel went to social gatherings, sipping one and only one Old Fashioned all evening long, and he read newspapers, magazines, and books constantly. But a fleet doctor didn't think those were enough diversions. He told the admiral's staff to get him out on the golf course more often, away from his focus on work. When he agreed to go, he raced through the holes "like a man on roller skates who wanted to get back to his job," Poco Smith said. During Smith's time as chief of staff, Kimmel "rang my bell perhaps too frequently and kept me too long in the office. He knew that because I told him so. But he was a very energetic man. He worked long hours, and when something was on his mind, he would always send for me and usually other members of his staff. I believe now that we spent entirely too much time in those discussions."

The admiral could spend too much time because he had no reason to go home. "Kimmel's staff was his family," said Captain Walter S. DeLany, his operations officer. Not long after his appointment in January, the admiral wrote a friend in Washington that he hoped his wife of nearly three decades, Dorothy, would join him "for a few months." She had yet to move from California after the fleet's shift to Pearl. In the end, Dot did not come, not for a few months, not for any, most likely because Kimmel did not want her to, for the brutally pragmatic reason that he felt she would get in his way. That meant Dot continued to live alone, too, because their sons were now out of the house, two serving as officers in the navy and one studying at Princeton University. Poco Smith, whose wife *had* moved to Oahu, asked Kimmel one day why Dorothy stayed behind. "Well, to tell you the truth, Smith, I feel that I could not do my job with my family present," he had replied. Nor had Dot accompanied him to the Philippines when he was there in the 1920s. George C. Dyer, who had been an aide to Admiral James Richardson, believed that Kimmel wanted everyone to live as he did, undistracted and totally devoted. Kimmel "did everything he could to discourage officers and men from bringing their families out to Pearl Harbor," Dyer said.

The admiral did not confine his intensity to the military. Speaking to a Chamber of Commerce luncheon at the Royal Hawaiian Hotel on September 18, Kimmel thanked residents for "keeping high the spirit of the Fleet," but then berated them at length for failing to understand how close they and the nation were to war. "Hawaii has led a soft life," he told the civic leaders. They needed to conserve resources. Roads were "hopelessly inadequate, congested and dangerous." Telephone service was so awful it might impede military operations. Soldiers and sailors, as well as civilian workers at military bases, were being gouged on rents, he said. The islands simply had to do more to help prepare and to accommodate. "The officers and men whom I command know that I am intolerant of half measures," he told the Chamber. "They know that I do not take the will for the deed. They expect me to speak bluntly."

Almost all the problems Kimmel enumerated were real, but hardly the fault of a lazy or greedy populace. Roosevelt's decision of the year before to base the fleet at Pearl had injected not only thousands of officers and enlisted men into Hawaiian life, but also hordes of mainland civilians lured by the concomitant, well-paying government jobs. In a matter of months, the workforce at the naval base had ballooned to eight thousand from less than two thousand, as the navy tackled the infrastructure deficiencies that had appalled Richardson, building recreation facilities, machine shops, ammunition dumps, fuel depots, and sheet-metal shops. The number of army officers and enlisted men in Hawaii had soared, too, as the War Department bolstered infantry units, built airfields, and set up gun emplacements to be able to drive the Japanese back into the sea, should they be so misguided as to invade. Kimmel may have left his wife back home, but civilian workers and military personnel had begun bringing theirs, and their kids. Judging by the license plates of cars delivered in ship holds, the newcomers came from everywhere. "They have with them the brisk, energetic step of the mainlander, the hurry and bustle that is so well-known in San Francisco or Chicago or New York," *Paradise of the Pacific* had said in January.

Upon returning for the summer from college on the mainland, a woman named Patricia Morgan wrote in the *Honolulu Star-Bulletin* on July 11 that the tempo of life on Oahu had shot up during her year away, and the air seemed to crackle with energy. "There were new grills, new cafes, new dance halls, new stores," Morgan's article said. Honolulu was "spreading like a great mesh out towards Pearl

Harbor," eight miles or so to the west, and spreading east toward Diamond Head and up into the hills to the north. "Where but a few months ago, there were vast sugar cane fields," Morgan wrote, "there are neat little villages [of] houses for the defense workers and service families." And more people were being recruited from the mainland, upward of nine thousand more boilermakers, machinists, carpenters, plumbers, electricians, shipfitters, pipe fitters, painters, and welders.

If Kimmel felt telephone service was lousy, the military had largely itself to blame. By September 30, 1941, the Mutual Telephone Company was billing 44,342 customers, almost 10,000 more than at the start of 1940. On the highways, where newcomers seemed to drive faster than Hawaiians, police had responded to 3,337 accidents in the first eleven months of 1941, up 42 percent over the same period in 1940. With a month to go in the year, fifty-six people had been killed in accidents, compared with thirty-eight in all of 1940. George K. Houghtailing, Honolulu's assistant planner, who had just spent ten months at Yale University pursuing studies in traffic, compared the city's mess to what he had seen in the Holland Tunnel between New York City and New Jersey.

Oahu was, in other words, an isle in boom. Other than Washington, it may have been the boomingest place under the American flag, a distinction that came with more than just mounting traffic casualties and bad phones, as the *Star-Bulletin* had catalogued on October 7: "shortage of housing; overcrowding and congestion; increased rents; transportation shortage; health and sanitation problems . . . crime and delinquency; educational problems; recreation and leisure time problems." The paper added that it was listing "only a few" of the changes wrought by the galloping expansion of the two military services. Another was the bending of society's gender boundaries, because of the labor shortage. "Women and girls are driving taxi cabs, working in service stations and barber shops, operating elevators, washing cars and performing other types of work formerly done by men," the *Star-Bulletin* said, its tone suggesting the collapse of civilization.

Kimmel's dressing-down of the islands annoyed a newspaper of the Japanese community, the *Hawaii Hochi*, which scoffed at the idea that the avalanche of problems stemmed from "a bunch of slackers derelict in our duties and lacking a sense of responsibility toward the nation of which we are a part." Not surprisingly, the paper's editors were hardly the first recipients of a blunt-force Kimmel critique to resent it. While his predecessor, Richardson, had been well liked in the fleet, even if he was not by Washington, Kimmel seemed to some subordinates to be prickly, frosty, and pedantic. His assistant communications officer, Lieutenant Walter J. East Jr., felt "Kimmel was a real perfectionist and he was not the most tender man with other people's feelings. Kimmel was very gruff." The admiral, East said, "had a habit of saying, 'Look, son,' and then plowing into you." East's wife, Joan, thought that Kimmel was a "mean, nasty old man."

Judging by his surviving letters and papers, the admiral shared few feelings or emotions with anyone, which made him still tougher to like. The captain of one battleship felt "a lot of people didn't like Kimmel, on account of standoffishness. A lot of people didn't like Kimmel." Thomas Hart, the destroyer captain who had been so impressed when Kimmel served as his executive officer, had by then risen to commander in chief of the small Asiatic Fleet in far-off and vulnerable Manila, and he found Kimmel less friendly than his predecessor. "As long as Richardson commanded there, I felt more comfortable sitting out there on a limb [in the Philippines] than I ever did again," Hart said. "With his departure, the personal touch between the two commanders-in-chief wholly ceased."

Of course, a demanding demeanor did not constitute a first in the annals of naval command. And Kimmel so clearly loved the navy and cared about getting the fleet ready that many subordinates wound up grateful to serve under him. It wasn't mere respect for him, but real fondness. If you did your job, you and he got along fine. The marine colonel who had endured profane castigation, Omar Pfeiffer, turned into a "Kimmelite," as the colonel called it. A cruiser captain still had Kimmel's photo on the wall of his home more than two decades later. "The staff learned to understand the old man, and to like him," East said. Captain John L. McCrea, who was an aide to Harold Stark, the chief of naval operations, said Kimmel "was opinionated but, by God, you have to be opinionated in a job like that. You have to call the shots as you see them."

War was coming to the Pacific, and they all knew it, and they all knew no one took that more seriously than Husband Kimmel. On April 4, he ordered ships stripped of chests, paint cans, cushions, awnings, launches, and anything else that could splinter or catch fire. He had made sure over the months that army and navy planes practiced landing, rearming, refueling, and taking off from each other's airfields on Oahu so that pilots would know where to go in emergencies, and ground crews would have a feel for the other service's aircraft and ordnance. Kimmel shuffled the moorings in Pearl Harbor so that each anchored ship's antiaircraft guns enjoyed a clear field of fire, and no Japanese plane would be able to find a safe seam of approach. The number of night-firing exercises had gone up; main and secondary batteries had practiced more often with live ammunition; live-firings from antiaircraft batteries had tripled, maybe quadrupled.

Nothing had been more challenging for Kimmel than keeping his crews trained. Enlistments kept expiring and, lured by civilian wages ashore on Oahu and the mainland, many men did not sign up again. Far more disruptive than even that was the navy's immense expansion. Washington kept tapping the Pacific Fleet to help flesh out crews of the burgeoning Atlantic Fleet, and to train recruits ashore. "At an alarming rate," Kimmel said, he lost experienced ordnance experts, flight instructors, executive officers, even ship captains. The newest battleship captain in February, out of twelve, had risen to fourth in seniority by May. In place of the departing droves, Kimmel was given raw recruits and reserve officers, all of whom had to be trained. "There were times when 70 percent of the men on board individual ships had never heard a gun fired," Kimmel said, never had been given target practice. On some of the fleet's combat ships that summer, a quarter of the crew had less than a year's service. On others, the number approached 50 percent. Some auxiliary ships were nearly 100 percent green. On April 22, Kimmel wrote Stark, saying, "We cannot produce a satisfactory state of battle efficiency unless we have some degree of permanency in [the] nucleus of personnel. We must have on board a certain number of officers and men who know the ship." He made little headway. He estimated on November 15 that he needed nine thousand men just to fill out rosters.

And yet, by the relentless force of Kimmel's will, the fleet had managed to reach the late fall an indisputably better fighting force. William Pye, commander of the battleships, thought it enjoyed "the highest state of efficiency that it ever had attained." Willard A. Kitts III, the fleet gunnery officer, would tell a congressional inquisitor that "In my opinion, sir, it was the highest state that it had ever reached in times of peace in the history of the Fleet as I have known it." Even Kimmel found a modicum of happiness. "I feel that gunnery in the Fleet is better than we have any right to expect considering the enormous changes in personnel and the lack of permanency of the officers," he had told Stark on August 12. Overall, "I feel that the morale of the officers and men of the Fleet is very satisfactory, that everyone is working to the limit of his capacity, that we are never going to be satisfied, but that we all feel that we are making progress and beginning to get some dividends for our efforts."

He had promised on the day he took command to bring the fleet to the highest possible degree of readiness. A perfectionist never announces that all is now perfect. But Kimmel had ended his August 12 letter by telling Stark, "We are ready to do our damnedest."

The *Honolulu Advertiser*, then in its eighty-sixth year, cost five cents, and a reader's nickel on the morning of Thursday, November 27, purchased this headline in the lower-right corner of the front page:

TALKS WITH JAPAN END; U.S. REJECTS APPEASEMENT

The Roosevelt administration, the accompanying article said, had taken such a firm stand with the Japanese that there was little chance negotiations would resume. But hostilities seemed unlikely. "It was believed," the article went on, without saying who believed it, "that there would be no sharp or sudden break, but that with a continuation of economic restrictions, relations would gradually deteriorate."

That morning, which was the day after Yamamoto's strike fleet had sailed out of Hitokappu Bay, a coterie of officers slipped into Kimmel's office at Pearl. With war coming, his staff was growing in number, and could not fit easily aboard his flagship, the *Pennsylvania*, so he had broken with tradition and moved, as Stark had put it, "to the beach." He and his staff had commandeered space on the top floor of the submarine force's headquarters, a two-story box of unchallenging architecture erected mere feet from the water of the harbor.

The officers, both navy and army, had gathered to discuss the defenses of two distant specks of American territory, the atolls of

Midway and Wake. Over the years, in addition to annexing Hawaii and acquiring the Philippines during the Spanish-American War, the United States had gathered unto itself a handful of microdots across the Pacific Ocean, including Christmas, Johnston, Palmyra, Guam, and Canton islands, in addition to Wake and Midway. Their combined area failed to reach even half of Oahu's. But they had uses. Midway, lying 1,134 miles to the northwest of Pearl, and Wake, which was 1,994 miles to the west, were big enough for runways. They were aircraft carriers that could not be sunk, making them ideal homes for navy search planes, their fuel, and their ground crews, all defended by small marine garrisons.

Kimmel had been dubious about using Wake, which was not only on the far side of the international date line but also merely a few hundred miles from Japanese air and naval bases in the Marshalls, a chain of islands that had once belonged to Germany but had been given to Japan as a "mandate" after the Great War, along with the Mariana and Caroline Islands. Whether to defend distant and exposed Wake, whose coral reefs greatly complicated the unloading of supply ships, was "open to very serious question" as far as Kimmel was concerned. "There was a considerable difference of opinion about whether it was advisable to put guns and Marines on Wake, and I thought a long time about it and finally decided that I would recommend that we put guns and the Marines on Wake." He did so because it occurred to him that the island might serve as honey for him to trap a bear, and Kimmel was always thinking about how he might trap the Japanese bear. Frank Knox, the secretary of the navy, had wanted spirited and aggressive leaders, not dawdling McClellans, and in Kimmel he had gotten his wish, times ten.

The admiral was unafraid to err by going after the enemy, unwilling to hunker in a trench and await the other side's charge. Captain Charles Horatio "Soc" McMorris, who was Kimmel's war plans officer, had the impression Kimmel was eager to use "the fleet of-fensively as quickly and as much as possible." That's what a fleet was for. That's why Kimmel had pushed training so hard; why he lamented the never-ending draining away of his skilled hands; why he had asked Stark, again and again and again in the summer of 1941, for more. More aircraft, more bombs for the aircraft, more armor-piercing shells for his big guns, more ships of practically every type. He asked for more so often that his staff thought his requests merely bored Washington.

Actually, in the Navy Department's latest war plan, Kimmel was not supposed to sail forth and do grand battle with Japan, at least not immediately. Main Navy, as the department was known, assumed that when war did come, the United States would be fighting not only Japan but also the Third Reich. And the Nazis, who were such a threat to Great Britain, would have priority. Early on in any conflict, therefore, the Pacific Fleet would shield the West Coast and Hawaii, and raid the Japanese in the mandate islands of the Marshalls, but it would not race to the other side of the sea to help save a beleaguered Philippines or duel with Yamamoto's main ships in their waters. Kimmel's leash would be short. Even if the plan, known as WPL46, had called for such grand expeditions, they were impossible. The fleet did not have enough support ships to sustain long-range oper-ations. As the assistant chief of naval operations, Royal E. Ingersoll, put it, "The United States at that time was too weak to engage in offensive warfare in both oceans, and a decision had to be made whether a major effort would be made in one ocean or the other." The Atlantic won out.

And thus it came to pass that only a few short months after Kim-mel had been given the command of his or any officer's life, the Pa-cific Fleet had begun to shrink beneath him. German surface raiders and submarines were swarming the Atlantic Ocean, sinking cargo ships that were hauling help to Britain. Inevitably, America was going to have to join Britain in shepherding those convoys, and the Atlantic Fleet did not have enough ships to do that. There was only one place—the Pacific—from which to get more right away. New ships were simply not being built fast enough.

Stark, a friend of Kimmel's since the Naval Academy, had a good notion of how the Pacific commander would react to surrendering even a single one of his hulls, and on April 26 he tried to temper the news with a letter that began, "Dear Mustapha." The nickname, which Stark used regularly when writing Kimmel, apparently dated from their younger days, when the most famous Turk in the world was Mustapha Kemal Ataturk. "Kemal" was close enough to "Kimmel," at least for the chief of naval operations. "This is just to get you mentally prepared that shortly a considerable detachment from your fleet will be brought to the Atlantic," he wrote. Not many days later, an aircraft carrier, four light cruisers, eighteen destroyers, and three battleships—Kimmel's best three—had vanished over the eastern horizon, a quarter of Kimmel's fighting strength gone. There was talk of losing more. Walter DeLany, Kimmel's aide, remembered, "We were continually being picked upon to get units of the Pacific Fleet moved into the Atlantic Ocean," because they were told "the war was in the Atlantic."

Husband Kimmel found himself in the wrong ocean. His theater of operations officially did not count, at least not as much. While Isoroku Yamamoto feared that the Pacific Fleet was too powerful to leave untouched during Japan's campaign to subdue the southwest Pacific, Kimmel looked out his office window each day and saw only a fleet far less magnificent than the one he had taken command of. And that was something he simply could not and would not abide. In a letter to Stark on May 26, he complained that his capabilities "for offensive operations of a decisive nature are severely crippled," the key word being "decisive," meaning operations big enough to change the course of a war. He wanted to make a difference, to matter. Further along in the same letter, Kimmel pleaded for sufficient strength "to support active operations in the Western Pacific—where the real battleground will be."

In June, he made the long journey to the capital and, in his first substantive conversation with Franklin Roosevelt since 1918, demanded that no more warships be taken from him. Such bluntness with the president had gotten Joe Richardson fired, but Kimmel's motive was so obviously pure, it hardly merited punishment. The man wanted to fight. Who could punish that?

He wrote Stark again, on September 12, saying he must be able to carry on a "bold offensive." "We cannot carry the war very far into the Pacific until we are able to meet the Japanese Fleet on at least equal terms," he said, even though he knew his job was not to meet the Imperial Navy on equal terms. "Do not misunderstand me. I do not discount the Atlantic problem—but from where I sit, I discount the Pacific problem even less. Until we can keep a force here strong enough to meet the Japanese Fleet, we are not secure in the Pacific—and the Pacific is still very much part of the world situation."

Two months later, he tried again. Washington absolutely had to give him more ships. Two new battleships, the *North Carolina* and the *Washington*, were almost ready to enter service, and he wanted them. "I must insist that more consideration be given to the needs of the Pacific Fleet," he told Stark on November 15. It had to have not only enough firepower to cruise "at will" throughout the relatively close mandate islands ruled by the Japanese, but "even on occasions to Japanese home waters." He was tired of being the minor-league team, shipping ships and sailors to the big club. The Pacific Fleet "must not be considered a training fleet for support of the Atlantic Fleet and the shore establishment."

With that, Harold Stark became peeved. He responded on November 25 by reminding Kimmel that while he may be eager to take the battle to Japanese home waters, the war plan did not call for doing that. Stark worried that Kimmel was not adapting to the reality of late 1941. There were not enough ships and planes for *anybody*. "Just stop for a minute," Stark said. Ponder the other ocean. "We are at our wit's end in the Atlantic," he went on, "with the butter spread extremely thin and the job continuously increasing in toughness." He explained what was all too evident: "You cannot take inadequate forces and divide them into two or three parts and get adequate forces anywhere."

Kimmel did not get the *North Carolina* or the *Washington*. The more than two dozen ships stripped from the Pacific Fleet never returned from the Atlantic during his watch. Yet he would not be deterred. He was going to pursue the Japanese even if he had but three-quarters of the ships he once did. The moment war broke out, he intended to race southwest to wreak what damage he could in the Marshall Islands. And, if he got lucky, maybe he could pull off something far bigger. If he put enough marines, guns, and airplanes at Wake Island, the Japanese would need a major air and landing force to subdue it—and they would want to subdue it, given how close it was to them. The Imperial Navy would have to come out in force to protect that landing. Wake "would serve as bait to catch detachments of the Japanese, the Japanese fleet coming down there, and we hoped to be able to meet them out there in sufficient force to handle them," Kimmel said.

His passion was offense, and it would be his downfall.

That morning, November 27, he and the other officers had assembled to go over an offer by the army to put some of its planes at Midway and Wake, as added muscle. The planes, which were based on Oahu at the moment, could not reach the outer islands by flying;

it was much too far. They would have to be transported by navy carrier, and flown off. The whole idea seemed so cumbersome that the navy ultimately turned down the army offer, opting to bolster Wake and Midway with marine planes instead.

At one point that morning, before that decision was made, Colonel James A. Mollison of the army wondered aloud whether it made sense to reduce the air defenses of Oahu—by far the most important American outpost in the Pacific Ocean—just to add a few planes to less meaningful places. The statement perplexed Kimmel.

"Why are you so worried about this? Do you think we are in danger of attack?" Here, he meant. On Oahu, so far from the Japanese.

"The Japanese have such a capability," Mollison said.

"Capability, yes, but possibility?"

The admiral wanted a navy opinion, and turned to Soc McMorris, his war plans officer. "Soc" was short for "Socrates"; McMorris was thought to be very smart. Is there a chance, Kimmel said, the Japanese would strike Oahu?

"None," McMorris said. "Absolutely none."

And the conversation moved on.

FOUR

BETTY

T HAT SAME THURSDAY arrived cloudless in the national capital
and would soon become quite warm, a gift of the late fall that
Harold Stark had scant chance to open and enjoy. In his two years as
the navy's highest-ranking officer, the chief of naval operations had
written innumerable messages and letters, but none as consuming
as the one before him at the Navy Department on Constitution Avenue. Stark was trying to weave facts, analysis, and instruction into
a dispatch of crisp, unambiguous English that would go to the small
American fleet in the Philippines and, of course, to Pearl. When
commanders read it, Stark expected that they would recognize how
grave the moment was, and ratchet up their vigilance. The Empire
of Japan was about to lash out somewhere in the boundless Pacific,
perhaps at the British, maybe at the Dutch, even at the Philippines.
Stark could not be certain of any target. But there was going to be
war in a matter of days, he thought.

In appearance, Harold Raynsford Stark, who had turned sixty-one earlier in the month, fell short of dashing, probably for want of trying. "He is not spectacular," the *Washington Post* had said in a 1939 profile. He had "no swank." When wearing a civilian suit, as he usually was, even at the office, Stark looked like your beloved bookkeeper uncle, the one secreting chocolates behind his back: welcoming face, smiling blue eyes, rimless spectacles, and a shock wave of hair so pure that some dubbed him Snow White, although the president of the United States called him Betty. There was, obviously, a story behind that.

Stark, of Pennsylvania money, was distant kin to a general in the Revolutionary War, John Stark, who had exhorted his troops at the Battle of Bennington with, "Tonight, the American flag floats from yonder hill or Molly Stark sleeps a widow!" A century and a quarter later, at the Naval Academy in Annapolis, upperclassmen loved to demand that Harold recite the fabled cry, except they misremembered the second half as "or *Betty* Stark sleeps a widow!" An order was an order, and so "Betty" he dutifully answered each time, and "Betty" he gradually became, even to himself. He wound up signing many personal letters that way.

A Stark letter often ended, too, with "keep cheerful," a phrase he had picked up in Great Britain during the war and felt he could never cease to employ, otherwise people would conclude he himself was not cheerful. And a morose Betty Stark would be worthy of a Mutual Radio flash. In 1919, a superior writing Stark's evaluation had, in fact, officially described him as "cheerful." So had another in 1920. And a third in 1925. Nearly everyone, of any rank, ashore or afloat, had found Stark not merely upbeat but the kindest of men as he had ascended the ranks at sea and in Washington. Approachable, encouraging, human. The admiral with the mien of an uncle actually referred to his wife, Katharine, as "Aunt Kit." According to a long-time aide, David W. Richmond, Stark sought "to be a gentleman at all costs."

Many dawns aboard the battleship *West Virginia*, then-captain Stark would appear on the bridge "dressed in blue silk pajamas, giving a cheery good morning, and stop and chat with us for a few moments, never seeming to be in a hurry," in the words of Lieutenant Walter Larned Blatchford. Remarkably, for a warship, no crewmember ever uttered "a disparaging remark about Betty Stark," Blatchford said. "There was respect and love from enlisted man and officer alike, right down the line." Likewise, Admiral Harry J. Hansen, who had gone around the world with Stark on the cruise of the Great White Fleet, wrote that he had "NEVER heard a single mention of any shortcoming or dereliction" when it came to Stark. "His reputation for honesty, Faith, Honor, Respectability and impartiality was ALWAYS on a Superb scale."

Boarding the *West Virginia* one morning, Captain Stark noticed that an overnight rain had caused an awning to sag with water. He summoned the officer of the deck and explained that the young man's job was to ensure proper conditions. The junior ensign, Magruder H. Tuttle, replied that not only had he already spotted the flawed awning, he had summoned a work crew to tighten the lines and shed the water—and at that moment the work crew appeared, validating his claim and proving that Stark's criticism was premature. Betty then apologized in the best possible way. "Within a few days," Tuttle said, "I was invited to have lunch in the captain's cabin. He had a few other guests, including a civilian couple. Without ever mentioning the specific incident, he introduced me as an alert and tactful young officer in whom he had confidence."

That quality—trust in his subordinates—stoked their affection for Stark and engendered a determination to do their jobs even better. William R. Smedberg III, another aide, believed Stark "was a wonderful man to work for, really, and the thing I liked about him was that he let me run my job and almost everything I did he agreed with. That's a wonderful feeling, that you can run the job the way you think it ought to be run and it meets with your superior's approval." Stark was intensely loyal to his people and tried to make their jobs as easy as he could, almost never getting angry, or at least never showing that he was. They could ask him anything and he would never belittle the question. "He was a very simple sort of man, you know?" Smedberg said.

His favorite person in Washington may have been his president, whom Stark did not even need an appointment to see. So thick were the two that they often digested the day's doings late in the evening, each on the phone in his home, the president often propped up in bed with a mystery novel. Their relationship had begun in amusing conflict in 1915 when the destroyer *Patterson* had received orders to take Roosevelt from Bar Harbor, Maine, to his summer home at Campobello, New Brunswick. Roosevelt knew those waters well, and proceeded to do what he had done at least once before to a captain on this annual journey.

"I'll gladly relieve you," the assistant navy secretary had told the *Patterson*'s captain, who, technically, worked for him.

"No, sir," Stark had replied. "This ship is my command, and I doubt your authority to relieve me. I shall welcome all the local knowledge you have, but I prefer to handle my own ship. Just tell me where you want to go and I will take the ship there."

They had stayed in touch through the years. "Take good care of Uncle Sam's Navy!" Stark wrote on July 28, 1933, after Roosevelt's first inauguration. "We have long been in need of a friend. And most of all, continue to take good care of Franklin D. Roosevelt, whom all these United States need and trust." When the president had named him the chief of naval operations in 1939, Stark claimed to be flabbergasted, but in reality, Smedberg said, "he had quite a bit of ego and it didn't take him very long to feel they'd made a good choice."

Stark and Roosevelt genuinely liked each other, but Stark sometimes found it exasperating to be the naval chief under a president who was a wannabe admiral. One of Smedberg's tasks was to listen to the business-hour phone calls between his boss and the president, take notes, and remind Stark later of what he had promised to do. As he recalled it, Roosevelt would begin with something like, "Betty, I want this done right away," and tick off half a dozen items in rapid fire, and Stark would say, "Yes, Mr. President. Yes, Mr. President. Yes, Mr. President."

"Have you got that, Betty?" Roosevelt would end.

"Yes, Mr. President."

This timid, even obsequious, manner suggests a man of no backbone, and some did indeed think Stark was Roosevelt's bowing butler, however bold he may have been with him aboard the *Patterson* years earlier. But Stark was bureaucratically savvy. In the words of another one of the admiral's aides, Captain Charles R. Wellborn Jr., the president was a "lunger, somebody who had a bright idea and he would go after it hammer and tongs, without really thinking it through." Stark would hear him out, nod, and let the idea marinate a few days, and by then Roosevelt would have forgotten it or Stark would have marshaled counterarguments, delivered obliquely.

In February, the president wanted to augment the small force in Manila with an aircraft carrier and several cruisers and destroyers, a notable enhancement that might appear quite threatening to Japan. Stark had replied, in essence, that the president could certainly do that if he wished, although it might well provoke a Japanese pre-

emptive strike, but if he really and truly was willing to risk the anni-
hilation of the ships, the navy would "defer to your better judgment
with a cheerful 'Aye, Aye, Sir,' and go the limit." And that killed that.

Stark would often argue vigorously with his boss for more men
and ships and, in the Atlantic Ocean, even for outright shooting at
the Germans. Like Secretary Knox, Stark thought Roosevelt should
get on with it and go to war with the Nazis, given that by 1941 America was no longer remotely neutral in the European conflict. Stark
would recall telling Roosevelt that "I considered every day of delay
in getting us into the war as dangerous, and that much more delay
might be fatal for Britain's survival."

The Atlantic Fleet had eventually begun escorting convoys to
Britain to ensure the arrival of American-made supplies, and on September 11, 1941, Roosevelt announced that he had ordered Stark to
have the navy fire at—not just to warn, but to sink—any German
submarine or surface raider found in the convoy zones. "In the Atlantic, we were doing some things which only a belligerent does,"
Royal Ingersoll, the assistant chief of naval operations, said. "There
had been no declaration of war. We had done a great many things
that under international law, as it was understood before the last
war, were un-neutral, and Germany just did not see fit to declare
war on us on many occasions when she could have assumed our acts
as unfriendly." Germany had seen fit to shoot back at the escorts,
however. The destroyer *Kearny* had been torpedoed and crippled on
October 17, killing eleven Americans; the destroyer *Reuben James*
had been torpedoed and sunk on October 31, killing all but 44 of
her 159 crewmembers.

Gradually, the bureaucratic politics, the months of escalating danger, and now death in the Atlantic had worn down Gentleman Stark.
It was hard to be cheerful in a world at war. He found he was not
acting like famously pleasant Betty Stark. "I confess to having used a

little more vehemence and a little stronger language than was becoming in fighting it out this last week for the nth time," he told Kimmel on February 10, after clashing with Cordell Hull, the secretary of state, over naval dispositions. Stark loved to make people happy, but being a naval chief on the precipice of war meant he couldn't always make them so.

Kimmel, for instance, wanted guidance about national goals and policy in the Far East, but Stark could not give it to him, because Roosevelt would not give it to *him*. The president could be maddeningly elusive about what the United States would do if Japan attacked British or Dutch colonies, or if Japan turned and attacked its old enemy Russia instead of moving south—a real possibility after the Nazis invaded the Soviet Union in June 1941. Stark had written to a friend that "to some of my very pointed questions, which all of us would like to have answered, I get a smile or a 'Betty, please don't ask me that.' Policy seems to be something never fixed, always fluid and changing."

The forces afloat, especially in the Pacific, kept demanding planes and guns and ships and people, and while the nation was rearming quickly, Stark could not fill every request. He had to disappoint people. He sometimes verged on self-pity. "Give us credit," he wrote to Kimmel on March 22, "for doing the best we can under many conflicting and strong cross-currents and rip tides." On April 19, in a letter that contained some bad news, Stark sought to head off a Kimmel explosion by saying, "First, I will put at this point, rather than at the end of this letter, 'Keep Cheerful,' and help me keep my sense of humor, which is a little taxed sometimes. . . . Just remember, 'We are doing the best we can.'" Stark had even thought of quitting. "God knows I would surrender this job quickly if somebody else wants to take it up, and I have offered to, more than once," he had written to a friend on July 31. "Some generous souls have been charitable enough to ask me to stick." He had closed by saying, "Believe it or not, I am still keeping cheerful, doing the best I can."

"He was a dear old man," Smedberg said, "and I loved him very much, but he's not the man that I would have chosen as chief of naval operations." It was not a unique assessment within the navy. Stark did a historic job of preparing the service for a two-ocean war, working tirelessly on Capitol Hill to get the funding for more ships, but he was more administrator than tough, imaginative military mind. Admiral George Dyer felt the chief of naval operations "lacked decisiveness and fire," and "did not have 'instant decision' in times of emergency." Admiral James L. Holloway Jr. thought him "probably not tough or ruthless enough." Stark carried his faith in subordinates too far, and did not carry suspicions far enough, as would become all too clear. "He was rather too optimistic a man," Admiral Thomas Hart said, "tending to see the bright side too plainly and the other side not quite plainly enough."

While Stark may have thought he was the man for the job in 1939 when Roosevelt appointed him, he may not have been thinking that by late 1941. Years later, William A. Reitzel, a former navy officer who had worked with Stark and liked him, said the admiral had mentioned to him early in 1942, after he had left the top job, "that he did not think he was suited" to be the chief of naval operations in wartime. "The conversation drifted off to other things and I got no further elaboration."

By virtue of his rank, Stark was entitled to reside on the eighty sylvan acres of the Naval Observatory not far from the White House, in a three-story brick manse constructed in 1893 and notable for its very pitched roof, wraparound porch, turret, and seclusion. In time, it would be the residence of vice presidents. On November 23, a gloomy and chilly Sunday on which more rain had fallen than on any other day that month, Stark had opened the home to a big teddy bear of a foreigner who had cloaked his journey with steps worthy of a spy, although he was decidedly not one.

Admiral Kichisaburo Nomura, retired, had walked out of the embassy of Japan a few minutes earlier and begun strolling up Massachusetts Avenue, a thoroughfare flanked by many embassies. A plain, unofficial car had come up the street. "Halfway up the hill," the driver said, "I espied the unmistakable stoutness of the Ambassador." Pulling the Plymouth to the curb and rolling down a window, the driver offered a ride, as agreed, as if he were merely showing a kindness to a man of sixty-three years on a wet day in late fall. Together, the American and the Japanese ambassador made the short drive to the observatory, where the chief of naval operations waited, also as planned.

Admiral Stark and Admiral Nomura shared the bond of the sea, and had spoken frequently since the ambassador had assumed his post in February. Perhaps their most memorable chat—certainly the most accurate—had taken place in the summer, when Stark had narrated how he believed a war between their countries would unfold. Early on, the victories would belong to the empire, given that its military and economy were already in full war mode as a result of the China conflict. But then the cylinders of American industry would begin to fire. "You will be unable to make up your losses," Stark had told Nomura, "while we, on the other hand, will not only make up our losses, but will grow stronger as time goes by. It is inevitable that we will crush you and break your empire before we are through."

In fact, that surge of production had already begun, even though the United States wasn't officially involved in any war. Germany's lightning rout of France in June 1940 had been an unfathomable and frightening event to Congress and the administration, and together they had opened the treasury and sent shipyards and factories into overdrive. If France could succumb in mere weeks, the same France that had kept Germany at bay during four years of horror in the Great War, then the world was too dangerous to believe in American immunity. The country must arm itself. It must arm the British, the only roadblock left between the Germans and the Western Hemisphere. It must arm against Japan, an equally aggressive force that had entered into a military alliance with the Germans and the Italians on September 27, 1940. And after June 1941, when Germany had turned east and swarmed into the Soviet Union, the Russians had to be armed, too.

The army and navy were now spending $39.6 million every day. American and British forces were taking delivery of seventy-two airplanes every day. In October alone, the army received 615 tanks and 985 personnel carriers, about 50 large tracked vehicles every day. Active army strength had risen sixfold, from 267,769 when France surrendered to 1,649,153 by November 1. During that period, the size of the navy and marine corps had more than doubled, to 383,769 officers and men. The number of combat ships was doubling, from 343 to 688. More than a hundred navy and civilian shipyards on the East, Gulf, and West Coasts, and even along the Great Lakes, had orders for 192 destroyers, 73 submarines, 14 cruisers, 15 battleships, and 11 aircraft carriers. In one span of just five days, the keels of two aircraft carriers, six destroyers, and two submarines were laid down. The current of isolationism in the country was strong, but its preparation for war was frenetic.

In Stark's recollection of their summer conversation, Nomura had fully understood the implications of such astounding output and manpower, and had longed to find rapprochement with his hosts. "I know how bad naval battle in Pacific will be shape," he told *Time* magazine in September, in his wobbly but determined English. With much of the planet at war, "there must be statesmen who play to be the fire extinguisher." The words seem like pabulum served for public consumption, but Stark believed Nomura really did want peace, "unless I am completely fooled," he had told Kimmel in a letter. Secretary of State Hull wrote in his memoirs that Nomura was "honestly sincere" about avoiding hostilities. The ambassador had known real violence on an intimate level. He had survived the sinking of his cruiser during the 1904–5 Russo-Japanese War when many of his shipmates had not, and had survived a terror attack in Shanghai in 1932 that cost him his right eye. (He had a rotating collection of glass substitutes.) He was, further, obviously fond of Americans and their country. Nothing pleased him more than a day-trip to, say, the battlefield at Gettysburg or to George Washington's home at Mount Vernon. An American officer would describe him as "tall, moon-faced, suave, poker-playing, bourbon-drinking, chain-smoking Nomura." "I am old man," Nomura had told *Time*. "I am most earnest. We maintained, ever since opening Japan eighty-seven year ago, good relations, you and us. Most of time we're happy hours. Now Japanese and United States policy, they are many divergencies. But human being must be able to make some formulas."

By late November, however, Nomura had despaired of making such formulas, trapped as he was between two governments pursuing goals beyond reconciliation. Japan's were, on paper, commendable: Asia should be run by Asians, not the white, Western powers that had colonized so much of it or, in the case of China, had set up their own enclaves inside it. Alas, in lieu of these masters, Tokyo merely wished to substitute itself. Its desire was a "new order," a "co-prosperity sphere," a closed economic system of Asians that it would establish and run, whether other Asians wished to belong or not. Japan had attacked China in 1937, and in 1940 bullied defeated France into allowing the Imperial Army to occupy northern Indochina, a French colony.

Acting as a sort of proxy for the world, the United States had replied to these aggressions by supplying arms to the Chinese through the Burma Road, and by creating a ballooning list of goods it would no longer sell to Japan, not until its armies pulled out of China, not until it agreed that trade in Asia must be open and unfettered. Most of all, the Roosevelt administration simply wanted the empire to renounce the use of force, to stop behaving as a Far Eastern version of the Third Reich.

In the midst of negotiations between Nomura and Hull, in July, Japanese armies seized the southern half of French Indochina to go with the northern, creating a possible staging area for military jumps into the Malay Peninsula, British Singapore, and the kingdom of Thailand; then into British Burma and India; then into Borneo, Java, and the rest of the Dutch East Indies. The complete takeover of Indochina astonished the Roosevelt administration as much as anything Japan had done, for it suggested that negotiations about pulling back its troops and reining in its aggressive urges in return for a lifting of sanctions were a sham.

It "certainly occurred at an inopportune moment," Nomura had said to his foreign ministry on July 30. "Today, I knew from the hard look on their faces that they meant business, and I could see that if we do not answer to suit them that they are going to take some drastic steps." They had. Roosevelt froze Japan's financial assets, blocking the flow of American oil. Nomura feared his superiors did not understand they could not bully their way through this impasse with the United States and were engaged in "a little too much wishful thinking." They had to offer what he called "appeasement measures." Otherwise, the Americans would use force to stop the empire's seizure of lands.

"Admiral Nomura came in to see me this morning," Stark wrote Kimmel on September 29. "We talked for about an hour. He usually comes in when he begins to feel near the end of his rope. There is not much to spare at the end now. I have helped before but whether I can this time or not, I do not know. Conversations without results cannot last forever."

By October 18, Nomura was ready to quit his job, as Stark had been. Otherwise, "I am afraid I shall be leading not only a useless existence, but even a harmful one," he wrote the Foreign Office that day. Hearing nothing, he wrote his superiors again, on October 22. "I know that for some time the Secretary of State has known how sincere your humble servant is," he told them, "yet how little influence I have in Japan. . . . I do not want to be the bones of a dead horse. I don't want to continue this hypocritical existence, deceiving other people. No, don't think I am trying to flee the field of battle, but as a man of honor, this is the only way that is open for me to tread. Please send me your permission to return to Japan."

They did not. The hour was too late, the atmosphere too tense, to send a replacement to Washington. Otherwise the Foreign Office surely would have acquiesced, because Nomura had demonstrated a propensity to go rogue, acting less like Japan's emissary than a Swiss broker of peace. He did not always relay prompt, precise, and complete summaries of his talks with Hull, leaving out items he thought might upset Tokyo. He sometimes adjusted Japan's positions on his own. Hull believed that Nomura himself, not just Japan's actions, was "a serious difficulty." The ambassador was not a professional diplomat, but a retired naval officer, and "he made blunders that embarrassed his government," Hull said.

An official of the Foreign Office wrote to Nomura on September 26 "to caution you again not to add or detract a jot or tittle on your own without first getting in contact with me." On November 4, the warning was repeated: "Follow my instructions to the letter," and "there will be no room for personal interpretation." Finally, Nomura must "compose yourself, and make up your mind to continue to do your best."

Nomura's best was surely not supposed to include a clandestine rendezvous with the American chief of naval operations, a meeting he had no intention of reporting to Tokyo. But especially in recent weeks, the tone of Tokyo's dispatches to him had grown markedly worse. On November 5, his superiors said that it was "absolutely necessary" that an agreement to restore trade and the flow of oil be signed by November 25, though they had not said why. On November 11, they told him to "redouble" his efforts, because the deadline "is absolutely unmovable." Then, on November 22, Nomura read the most disturbing dispatch of all: "There are reasons beyond your ability to guess why we wanted to settle Japanese-American relations by the 25th, but if within the next three or four days you can finish your conversations with the Americans, if the signing can be completed by the 29th (let me write it out for you—twenty-ninth) . . . we have decided to wait until that date. This time we mean it, that the deadline absolutely cannot be changed. After that, things are automatically going to happen."

Like most, if not all, of Japan's overseas diplomats, Nomura did not know of a secret fleet already assembled in Hitokappu Bay by the time Tokyo sent him the allegedly immutable deadline. But Nomura could sense the desperation between the lines of the dispatches. He knew that life at home was deteriorating with the loss of so many imported and now-sanctioned goods. "All over Tokyo are no taxicab," he had told *Time*. Oil was running out. Nomura knew the military—especially the army—had its fanatics, and knew of the plans to grab the raw materials of the southwest Pacific, and knew that any invasion there might trigger an armed American response. Someone in Tokyo had once said to him that such a war would be Armageddon.

He had never heard the word. He looked it up. Yes, that was it. It would be Armageddon.

The day after Tokyo had relayed its new deadlines, Kichisaburo Nomura went to Harold Stark's residence. It was Stark's assistant, Smedberg, who had been driving the Plymouth that picked up the ambassador and conveyed him to the Naval Observatory. As Smedberg waited, the two admirals talked for an hour. Afterward, Stark told his aide, "Nomura was extremely worried about the possibility of the war party in Japan making some drastic decisions." Nomura had explained that the Imperial Army, which controlled the government, "had no conception of America's might and potential, military, naval and particularly industrial." It would go to war if the United States did not ease its economic blockade.

It is unlikely Nomura divulged to Stark anything about dates by which things would "automatically" happen. A traitor he was not, and neither Stark nor Smedberg ever said he did such a thing. More plausibly, Nomura had hoped that if he could give the Americans, through Stark, a sense of how bad he felt things were and how worried he was, they would think of something, give a little, birth a miracle that would save everyone. Stark had been, indeed, "deeply impressed" by the visit and by Nomura's words. When the ambassador emerged from the residence, Smedberg thought he was about to cry.

Japan's coming invasions of the southwest Pacific would be so massive that Tokyo never expected it could keep them a secret, unlike its strike on Oahu. Many of the assault troops would come from the empire's armies in China and board ships in occupied Chinese ports, where they would be easily spotted by residents and Western military attachés. On November 25, two days after Nomura had met with

Stark, the War Department sent an intelligence report to Roosevelt: as many as fifty thousand Japanese troops had packed as many as thirty transports near Shanghai on the China coast.

The next morning, Henry L. Stimson, the secretary of war, went to see the president, and he mentioned the memo about an armada of Japanese troop ships. "He fairly blew up," Stimson wrote in his diary. "Jumped up into the air, so to speak, and said he hadn't seen it, and that that changed the whole situation, because it was evidence of bad faith on the part of the Japanese, that while we were negotiating for an entire truce—an entire withdrawal—they should send this expedition down there to Indochina." The scenario of July was repeating itself. In the middle of talks in which the United States was trying to get Japan to forswear the use of force, it was about to use force.

Well before this moment, however, America's chief negotiator, Cordell Hull, had lost any hope of finding commonality with the Japanese. The talks between the nations were some of the strangest imaginable, in that one side—the United States—would not have to give up anything to reach a settlement. It merely sought to have Japan stop doing what it was doing. The empire, on the other hand, would have to surrender seized land and dreams of new orders and prosperity spheres, if it wanted the United States to resume oil shipments.

By now, Tokyo saw itself not as an aggressor whose actions had provoked responses, but as a victim. Attacking China had been a mistake, Japan agreed, but America was making it difficult to get out. It was fortifying Chinese armies, and refusing to understand how Japan could not instantly withdraw all of its forces there without losing honor. It would take a great deal of time. And if, in addition, the Americans kept being difficult and refusing to resume oil shipments, well, there was oil in the southwest Pacific to be seized. In other words, having lost oil by seizing the lands of others, Japan was threatening to get oil by seizing still more places.

As far back as August 8, Stimson had written in his diary that Hull felt "there is nothing further that can be done with that country except by a firm policy and, he expected, force itself." The secretary of state had considered offering an interim arrangement by which Japan would pull back some troops in return for some trade, but the Chinese objected, and now there were these fresh reports of more Japanese troop advances. The only thing that would satisfy the empire, Hull believed, was "abject surrender to her demands as an aggressor."

At five o'clock on Wednesday afternoon, November 26, Nomura entered Hull's grand, high-ceilinged office in what is now the Old Executive Office Building, next to the White House. With him was Saburo Kurusu, a special envoy who had come to help; Kurusu's wife was an American. Hull handed over two documents that reflected a government whose patience had sailed, that saw no purpose in discussing withdrawal timetables or geopolitical boundaries or any other fine point until both sides agreed on some basic, overarching concepts.

First, Hull had listed nine principles the sides would live by, including "pacific settlement of controversies," "inviolability of territorial integrity and sovereignty," and free trade. Then he outlined ten steps—they would come to be known as the Ten Points—that the sides would take. Among them, Japan would flatly agree to pull out of China and Indochina, and never aid the Germans militarily. The United States would agree to release Japan's frozen assets and resume trade. The documents contained no threat of war if Japan did not accept the ideas, nor did the United States threaten to sever diplomatic relations or break off discussions, although it knew that might well happen. The items outlined were mostly items that Hull had been saying for months, but that Japan had never seemed to hear, as evidenced by its repeated military seizures.

Roosevelt had called the documents "magnificent," Stimson wrote in his diary, a statement of "our constant and regular position." But Nomura knew how Tokyo would respond, even as he sat before Hull and read the sheets of paper. All the pain would be Japan's, if there were to be peace. His conversation at Stark's residence had not changed a thing. In a cable marked "extremely urgent," he told the Foreign Office that afternoon how he and Kurusu had reacted in Hull's presence: "In view of our negotiations all along, we were both dumbfounded and said we could not even cooperate to the extent of reporting this to Tokyo. We argued back furiously, but Hull remained solid as a rock. Why did the United States have to propose such hard terms as these?"

It mattered not. The strike fleet had churned out of Hitokappu Bay that morning.

Hull now told the army and navy that diplomacy had run its course. The American embassy in Tokyo had already urged American citizens to leave Japan. "He [Hull] told me now that he had broken the whole matter off," Stimson wrote in his diary on Thursday, November 27. "As he put it, 'I have washed my hands of it, and it is now in the hands of you and Knox.'"

Hull did not mean that he would refuse to meet again with Nomura. On the contrary, he and Roosevelt expected a formal Japanese answer to the Ten Points. Nor did Hull intend by his remark to mean that his own military should start shooting. To keep the moral high ground, and preserve whatever chance for peace remained, the United States intended to let the Japanese fire first, if war was what they wanted. Rather, Hull's statement to Stimson signaled only that the army and navy should get ready, given the uncertainty, that they should alert their forces on the West Coast, in the Panama Canal Zone, in the Philippines, and on Hawaii.

Chatty Harold Stark had often mused to commanders at sea in the last year about a moment like this, when a war might be upon them. Another of his aides, Captain John McCrea, would type his letters and then give them back to him for a final reading, and "upon their return to me for mailing, I invariably noticed that he had included something in the way of a postscript to the effect that 'time is short,' 'war may come tomorrow or it may not come for months,' 'no one knows when the blow will come or from what direction,' etc. etc." Stark's intentions were the best, as always, and his statements were obviously true, as far as he knew. Time *might be* short. War *could* happen tomorrow. But then, time kept going, and war never came.

Stark once told Admiral Richardson, for instance, that "your flag officers and captains should be completely in the frame of mind that we will be in the fighting business most any time, and purely as a guess on my own part, I would say at any time after the next 90 days."

That was on December 23, 1940.

He told Kimmel that war "may be a matter of weeks or of days." That was on January 13, 1941. In an official dispatch on October 16, Stark told the Pacific, Atlantic, and Asiatic Fleets the situation was "grave," and Japan might attack Russia, even Britain and the United States. The very next day, he wrote a personal letter to Kimmel, retracting what he had just told him in the official communication. "Personally," he had said, "I do not believe the Japs are going to sail into us and the message I sent you [yesterday] merely stated the 'possibility.'" But then, three weeks after *that*, on November 7, Stark announced to Kimmel that the outlook was "worser and worser" and "a month may see, literally, most anything." Stark, obviously, did not grasp the yo-yo nature of his musings. He was just being himself, friendly and helpful, or so he imagined. But he was not putting himself in the mind of a commander in the field who would get such contradictory notes, or such repeated guesses that never panned out.

On that Thursday, November 27, in the wake of Hull's washing of hands, Stark and the navy composed a message that would become the most dissected in its history. Though the army was consulted, and so was Frank Knox, the dispatch was the child of three fathers: Stark; Royal Ingersoll, the assistant naval chief; and Admiral Richmond Turner, the chief of the division that planned war operations. In military-speak, it related the known facts of Japanese movements in the Far East, and ordered the Asiatic and Pacific Fleets to undertake a "defensive deployment."

By design, the most startling sentence, of nine words, was the first. It was not lifted from a book of standard message phraseology and, in fact, the expression had never been employed by the Navy Department, as far as Stark, Ingersoll, and Turner knew. That was its beauty. That was why they chose it. To stand out.

This dispatch is to be considered a war warning.

"The words 'war warning' were my own words," Turner said afterward, "and seemed to me to express the strong conviction on the part of the Department that war was surely coming."

Stark's aide, McCrea, was deeply impressed by the phrase "because I remember the thought flashing across my mind that it was a strong statement to make, that it went the whole way, and that if nothing eventuated, confidence in the Navy Department's estimate in future matters might suffer in consequence."

"We pondered almost an entire forenoon on that phrase," Stark said, "whether it was strong enough, whether it would convey what we felt, whether it was too strong." Even knowing what he knew from Nomura's visit a few days before, and even knowing Hull's belief that things seemed hopeless, Stark apparently did not want to overdo it. Maybe he was, finally, cognizant of how many times he had speculated and never been right. But with Japanese forces moving, and Hull worried, Stark eventually sanctioned the memorable expression "war warning."

"I thought it was very plain and it flew all the danger signals," Stark said.

It was "all out," he said.

It was "so outstanding."

FIVE

IT DOESN'T MEAN US

T OWARD EVENING, Stark's message raced west, back through Thursday, traversing the country and half of the Pacific Ocean, finally arriving at Pearl, where the sun still rode high in the sky.

This dispatch is to be considered a war warning X Negotiations with Japan looking toward the stabilization of conditions in the Pacific have ceased and an aggressive move by Japan is expected within the next few days X The number and equipment of Japanese troops and the organization of naval task forces indicates an amphibious expedition against either the Philippines Thai or Kra Peninsula or possibly Borneo X Execute an appropriate defensive deployment preparatory to carrying out the tasks assigned in WPL46.

If Harold Stark endorsed a single managerial tenet above all others, it was to tell people what you want done, but not how to do it. People loved him for that. The warning message reflected the Stark philosophy. It contained rich dollops of intelligence—a war is imminent, the talks have ended, Japanese landings could happen here, here, and here—but only one order: *execute an appropriate defensive deployment*. Left out, deliberately, was any hint of what qualified as that sort of response, whether it would be taking ships to sea, elevating watch levels, sending protective fighter planes aloft, or something else. That decision would be left to the recipients. Fleet commanders had gotten their jobs by demonstrating judgment and leadership. They must be given room to use their brains. Stark would never presume, "sitting at a desk in Washington," that he knew better than an admiral thousands of miles away how to dispose his forces in compliance with an order, he said, because "once I had started—if I had started—to give him directives, I would have been handling the Fleet. That was not my job."

The creed was hardly his alone. Admiral Ernest J. King, the commander of the Atlantic Fleet, insisted that senior officers give junior ones a chance to figure out how to obey an order. And that didn't happen often enough to suit King. "I have been concerned for many years," he wrote to his boss, Stark, on January 21, "over the increasing tendency—now grown almost to 'standard practice'—of flag officers and group commanders to issue orders and instructions in which their subordinates are told 'how' as well as 'what' to do to such an extent and in such detail that the 'custom of the service' has virtually become the antithesis of that essential element of command, 'initiative of the subordinate.' " If officers "are not habituated to think, to judge, to decide and to act for themselves," King warned, the navy "shall be in sorry case when the time of 'active operations' arrives." It had to "stop nursing them."

In Manila—4,767 miles from Pearl—it was already November 28 when Stark's warning reached Admiral Thomas Charles Hart, the same Admiral Hart who had once been Kimmel's temporary captain aboard a destroyer. It so happened that Hart, depicted in a white uniform with a high and rigid collar, graced the cover of that week's *Time*. He was the admiral at "the front," the magazine said, right under Japan's nose, only a few hundred miles from the island of Formosa, which was in Japanese hands. The article described the commander of the Asiatic Fleet as a "wiry little man" who was "weathered, wrinkled, tough as a winter apple" and an "indispensable oldster."

At sea, Hart had fought the Spanish in the last century and the Germans in the Great War, and then gone ashore to lead the Naval Academy for several years. Now sixty-four and in his third year as commander, Hart was six months past the age of retirement—and quite ready for it, to slip out of uniform for good and get home to Connecticut and his farm and his wife, whom he had not seen in a year. "I sort of feel finished as a public person," he had written her on June 12. But Stark had begged him to stay on. "I could think of no one else so well qualified to serve our country out there in time of stress," Stark had written him on November 1. Admiral William D. Leahy, a former chief of naval operations, told Franklin Roosevelt that Hart was one of the three best men in the navy, adding that. "Of the three, I consider Hart the most reliable and the least likely to make a mistake." An aide to Stark would say that the little oldster "was the smartest naval officer I ever ran into."

To Hart, the meaning of Stark's warning could not have been clearer: Tommy, man your guns. Tommy, watch your back. Years later, in his eighties and still sharp, Hart would slowly enunciate the opening sentence to underscore how obvious the point was: "This . . . is . . . a . . . war . . . warning." That was "the whole thing," Hart would say, the rest of the message being "yackety-yak," except for the order to *execute an appropriate defensive deployment*, which also was clear and short. "Five words."

The dispatch cited the Philippines by name as a possibly endangered locale, which Hart had long appreciated just by looking at a map. The Japanese wanted oil, as the world knew, and the place to get it was the Netherlands East Indies, as the world knew, too. They would have to cruise right past Manila to get there.

Tommy Hart had been thinking a great deal about this moment, about what the Japanese would do about the Philippines if they sailed by. "Did they dare go into the [East Indies] in force, running into British opposition perhaps, as well as Dutch—certainly Dutch— and leave the Philippines on their flank while they stuck their necks out fifteen hundred miles farther south?" Hart said. Would they assume the United States would remain on the sidelines and not use its Philippine-based forces to help its European friends? Or would Japan seek to neutralize them?

The Asiatic Fleet did not pose much of an obstacle to Japan's advance. It had no battleships or aircraft carriers, just two cruisers, a baker's dozen of destroyers, and a flotilla of submarines—and most of the vessels had been sired in the Great War. "When asked about it," Hart said, "I used to say that all of my ships were old enough to vote." His surface ships were "both weaker and slower than the Japanese," he said, "which did not give us much to work with." But he had enough submarines to be nettlesome to the Japanese. And the War Department had been reinforcing the army's Philippine airfields with B-17s flown from the mainland via Oahu, huge aircraft that had the range and bomb load to damage the Imperial Navy if the Americans chose to contest a southern grab for oil. "My own estimate was that they would not leave us on their flank and make the venture," Hart said. "Consequently, they would attack."

While his submarines would be safe, hidden beneath the waves, his overmatched surface ships would not be, and so he began to scatter them, putting distance between them and the oncoming Japanese. A wise man in his situation, Hart said, "sleeps like a criminal, never twice in the same bed.

"Really," he said, "it was quite simple." The war warning meant that "we were told that we were to await the blow, in dispositions such as to minimize the danger from it, and it was left to the commanders on the spot to decide all the details of said defensive deployment."

Unlike Hart's fleet, the Pacific Fleet at Pearl Harbor enjoyed serious distance from the adversary, days and days of it. Given the number of fleet battleships (nine), aircraft carriers (three), cruisers (twenty-two), destroyers (fifty-four), submarines (twenty-three), and planes (hundreds), it packed far more lethality, too, even after the leakage of ships to the Atlantic Fleet. It could defend itself.

So when Pearl began to parse the war warning on the afternoon of November 27, it did so in an environment altogether more secure than Manila's. Nine of Kimmel's highest-ranking officers would learn of Stark's advisory in the next few days. The fleet commander could be intimidating, but he shared. Often walking to the offices of subordinates rather than standing on rank and summoning them to his, Kimmel would let them read official correspondence, and even Stark's voluble letters, and he liked to ask what they thought. He expected them "to talk back to him if you thought you were in the right," said Lieutenant Walter East Jr., the assistant communications officer. "If you did not, he did not respect you." Poco Smith, Kimmel's chief of staff, asked him one day "why he gave so much hell to the captain of one of his cruisers. He replied, 'He won't fight back!'" The assistant operations officer, Commander Roscoe F. Good, had fought back so fiercely on one occasion that Kimmel lost his temper, and Good had then fought back even more. If the admiral wanted a yes-man, Good told him, "I'll put a phonograph over in the corner to say 'yes' all day long!" "You do," Kimmel shot back, "and I'll throw the damned thing out the [window], and you with it." However mad it might make him, Kimmel wanted your opinion.

With all the freewheeling conversations and the messages he showed them, Kimmel's subordinates were familiar with Stark's penchant for dark predictions, none of which had ever come true. Admiral William F. Halsey, who commanded the fleet's carriers and would become a figure of lore in the coming war, called them "wolf" dispatches. "There were many of these," Halsey said, "and, like everything else that's given in abundance, the senses tended to be dulled." To Admiral Pye, the commander of the battleships, the months of 1941 were replete with Stark letters that "indicated a very serious situation, and yet nothing happened." These letters were "exasperating and unsettling" to Kimmel, one staff officer wrote in a memoir, veering "wildly among cheerful reassurance, painful obfuscation and hesitant alarm."

For his part, Kimmel was "glad to have all of these warnings and forebodings." But each one reinvigorated a problem he had faced from the day in February when he took command. There was going to come a moment when war with Japan was no longer an abstraction that might be encountered in a far-off future, but a genuine likelihood. The trick would be to recognize that moment. And when he did, a smart and prudent commander would cut back the gunnery practice, the exercises involving night maneuvering or mine detection, the training flights for new pilots and navigators, and all the rest. He would elevate his wariness and begin to prepare to move on the Marshall Islands, as outlined in the war plan. And to be safe and not sorry, he would begin to search for the Japanese.

Which, thus far, Kimmel had not done.

Contrary to what the American people had been told, or at least what buyers of newspapers and magazines had been reading in 1941, the Hawaiian Islands were not being shielded round-the-clock by bevies of searchers in the skies and on the seas. It was not true, as *Collier's* said in June, that planes were flying reconnaissance circles "a thousand miles wide around Oahu." They weren't flying any circles at all. Nor was it true that warships "patrol ceaselessly the seas" nearby, or that Pearl Harbor was "the concentric center of continuous flights of warplanes on day and night patrols far out to sea," as the *Chicago Tribune* claimed in August. Authors had made assumptions, or gotten swept away by a determination to reassure their readers, or both. Then again, the Japanese had assumed similar things.

It *was* true that every day, long-range navy seaplanes were skipping and bouncing skyward from the waters of Pearl Harbor or Kaneohe Bay, on the east side of Oahu. Any resident or visiting journalist could watch them go. But the PBYs, as the floatplanes were known, were not soaring aloft to begin systematic searches of the distant perimeter. Sometimes they engaged in drills with warships, sometimes they were bound for Wake, Midway, or another island. Their more common destinations were the "operating areas," where the fleet practiced, usually south of Oahu, where the squalls were fewer and the sky's ceiling higher. As a precaution against a Japanese submarine spying on his ships during those exercises, or even taking a stealthy, peacetime shot at one of them, Kimmel always had a handful of PBYs vet the operating areas to see who was on or just below the surface. But those sweeps covered only a slim slice of the compass pie at a time. The Pacific Fleet never answered Stark's frequent musings about war by starting to look rigorously for raiders. If Kimmel had done so every time he got an alarming note, he said, his men and machines would have wound up so burned out and broken they would have been unfit to fight.

Yet, the dispatch of that day, November 27, was different. No matter how used to Stark's ominous guesses they were, "war warning" stood out. Officers at Pearl would remember the phrase long, long afterward. It was "a shock to me," one said, "to see it written down." It was unique. "I not only never saw that before in any correspondence with the Chief of Naval Operations," Kimmel said, "I never saw it in all my naval experience."

But novel did not equate to fear inducing, at least not on Oahu, not yet. The Philippine Islands, an American possession, were listed by name in the warning as one of Japan's possible destinations, but they were so much closer to the Japanese. Stark offered complete silence about Hawaii.

Further, he had not reprised what he had written only three days earlier. The day after Nomura's visit to him on November 23, Stark had written both Hart and Kimmel that continued peace with Japan was "very doubtful" and "a surprise aggressive movement in any direction, including attack on Philippines or Guam, is a possibility." The phrase "in any direction" was so broad that any piece of American territory in the Pacific, including Hawaii, including the Panama Canal, including the West Coast, could logically consider itself at risk. But those three words had vanished in the new text, which "indicated to us in the Fleet that since the earlier dispatch, the Navy Department had obtained later information, on the basis of which it could specify more probable and possible objectives," Kimmel said. Stark seemed to be narrowing Japan's initial theater of aggression to the southwest Pacific.

That seemed to comport with what else he had done. If Stark genuinely believed Oahu faced probable danger, surely he would not have suggested—as he had within the last twenty-four hours—that the navy ferry army fighter planes to the outer islands, diminishing Oahu's defenses. That suggestion "tended to, and did, reduce in my mind the chances of an attack on Pearl Harbor," Kimmel said. And surely Washington would not have commandeered so many of the fleet's combat ships recently, reducing its defensive power.

"Now, war was getting closer," Kimmel said. "We could see that. There was no question about that." But none of his officers who saw the war warning felt Stark was worried about Pearl. The dispatch seemed of a piece, its two halves to be read as a whole, the first announcing that war could erupt "in the next few days," and the second indicating where. Borneo. Thailand. Way down there. Not way up here. As one admiral remembered the conversations, "Without exception, everyone believed that the dispatch indicated an attack in Southeast Asia."

Stark's text, though, contained more than the warning. It had a command, and commands could not be ignored. Even if Main Navy had not specified Pearl as a threatened place, it nonetheless was telling Kimmel to *execute an appropriate defensive deployment.* The plain English suggests he was to spread his forces protectively in anticipation of possible enemy attack, but the plain English wasn't so plain within the Submarine Building. "There was some doubt in the minds of [some] present as to what a 'defensive deployment' was," an officer said, "because we do not use that term in the Navy." It had never cropped up "in any textbooks, tactical books, or tactical instructions and orders."

Because the command was followed immediately by *preparatory to carrying out the tasks assigned in WPL46,* Pearl blended the phrases into one belabored thought: Stark is telling us to get ready to raid the Marshall Islands, but not to do so eagerly or obviously, because the Japanese might detect our pre-positioning, claim self-defense, and shoot first. We should deploy for offense, but cautiously. "It seemed to us," Soc McMorris said, "that they [Main Navy] might have thought that in our enthusiasm to strike as promptly as possible, we might advance forces to a position that would be regarded as threatening, and thus destroy any remote chance of retaining peace."

After all, Stark had said something like this before, in October, during a flaring political crisis in Japan, when he had spoken to the fleet about "preparatory deployments" that would not disclose "strategic intent," by which he meant the plan to attack the mandate islands. The difference, of course, is that in October, Stark had not said "defensive" deployments, just deployments.

And so, for all the invested time and care, the triumvirate of admirals at Main Navy had authored a warning message that could be easily and thoroughly misconstrued, and it was, easily and thoroughly. Stark, Ingersoll, and Turner never considered that Pearl might compare and contrast the dispatches of November 24 and November 27, and note the absence of "in any direction." Stark had inserted the phrase himself in the first directive in order to get Hawaii thinking about risk, but he had forgotten to repeat it—"slipped my mind"—in the second. "Probably," he said, "it might have been better if we had put it in."

Nor had he thought that by naming certain places as potential targets he would be seen as excluding all those he did not name. He had intended the first sentence to be read alone as a simple declaration of approaching war to which all outposts should pay heed, full stop. He had then gone on to list several places that might face particular risk, not to delimit the risk to others, but only because Main Navy had more intelligence about them.

By "defensive deployment," the three authors never imagined that Kimmel would interpret that as anything but a command to assume—in Tommy Hart's words—"dispositions such as to minimize the danger." The phrase had nothing to do with cautiously preparing to attack. What they expected, above all, was that Kimmel would start combing the seas and air with surface ships and planes for his own protection against ambush. "We had assumed when we sent out that dispatch that reconnaissance would be started," Stark said, "and kept up."

He and his cocomposers were not clairvoyant. They had not an ounce of evidence that Japanese ships were bearing down on Hawaii, and thus saw no reason to name it specifically in the dispatch. Actually, the chief of naval operations considered an attack on Pearl Harbor no more likely than Kimmel did. But given how bad things seemed with the Japanese, anything could happen. It was time to be responsibly wary. Everyone in the navy knew all about Port Arthur, a widely taught example of Japanese naval treachery during the 1904–5 war with Russia. Before war had been declared, an imperial fleet had crept through the night and loosed torpedoes at Russian warships anchored off the Korean harbor of Port Arthur. The lights of the Russian ships had been burning brightly, revealing their positions, because they thought peace still prevailed.

At least Main Navy's underthought, badly worded dispatch gave the Pacific Fleet the sense that it might be executing its offensive mission very soon. For the moment, it saw itself only as an interested bystander, sitting on the periphery of coming events way to the southwest. Tommy Hart would opine years later that the warning should have left out the specific places and simply ended with the first sentence, announcing that war was going to break out, period, and not try to say where. Poco Smith thought so, too. Then everyone might have felt equally endangered and hunkered down. How that might have changed everything.

If he had wished—no regulation stopped him—Kimmel could have sought an explanation of the text. But to say that he should have is to imply that he was confused. He wasn't. If he missed Washington's true meaning, Kimmel said later, "then there must have been something the matter with the message."

The Pacific Fleet would carry on as before. Training would go forward, and so would the reinforcement of Wake and Midway with fighter planes. It was not yet time, that crucial time, for shifting to maximum protection. It was not yet time to empty Pearl of as many ships as possible. The harbor outside Kimmel's windows may have been an ideal refuge for ships in an earlier era, but the warplane had turned it into a barrel crammed with fish, tied up and stationary, without room to maneuver and with only one way out, a narrow channel that was susceptible to blockage. Going to sea, where the fleet would have room, where it would be a moving target, would be better than staying inside the barrel, when or if war was coming.

At best, Kimmel and his staff briefly considered reconnaissance flights as they mused over the war warning, if they considered them at all. None began. It was not the first time, and would not be the last, that Husband Kimmel analyzed a new dispatch or piece of intelligence in the way that least complicated or disrupted what he wanted to do—which was to execute his plan to raid the Marshall Islands, not sit around in some sort of defensive crouch.

In the days that followed, Washington had no notion of what Kimmel was doing in response to its warning. He was not required to report his actions. Not only was it Main Navy's practice to let commanders figure out the best way to comply with an order, it did not insist on knowing their choice once they had made it. "A commander-in-chief is considered by the Navy as almost a viceroy out in his own field," Royal Ingersoll said. "They tell him in broad terms what he is supposed to do, and they do not bother him with asking him how he is going to do it, or keep bothering him with whether he has done it." It's one thing, of course, to let someone figure out how to comply with an order, and altogether another thing to forgo knowing how he has, which leaves only the assumption that he has done good things.

Stark thought the war warning was a model of precision, and he had faith in Kimmel's judgment, with good reason. Although not close—Kimmel's rough style was not to Stark's gentlemanly taste—the two had known each other for four decades. Nothing got by his Pacific Fleet commander. He paid attention to everything. His spotless record testified to it. "I had every confidence in him," Stark said, "and left the matter entirely to him, after giving him a war warning, and informing him that an aggressive move by Japan was expected in the next few days."

Within twenty-four hours of receiving the warning, Kimmel lifted a restraint on his forces. Every so often during 1941, using sound-detection equipment, his destroyers came across submerged, unidentified submarines, which could only be Japanese. But Stark had barred Kimmel from attacking these unknown contacts, not wishing to provoke Japan while peace prevailed. Kimmel thought that was dangerously unfair. It left his ships at the mercy of the underwater Japanese, who could elect to fire torpedoes at his warships and slink away. Kimmel knew the fates of the *Kearny* and the *Reuben James* in the Atlantic. But using the war warning as justification, he now told his ships to fire away with depth charges whenever they detected something beneath them.

It was the one response to the war warning Kimmel did pass on to Washington. Stark did not countermand him this time, which obviously meant things were very close to war indeed.

———

The evening of November 27, the destroyer *Cummings* rode at anchor in East Loch. Its executive officer, Lieutenant William W. Outerbridge, was writing to his wife, Grace, in San Diego, as he did with punctuality. In a photo of a group of officers that would be taken two years later, Outerbridge would be the slight one in the first row, with glasses and big ears, feet jammed together, knees jammed together, hands tucked between thighs, shoulders pulled in, the absolute model of diffidence. It's as if a shy history teacher isn't sure he belongs in the navy.

Billy Outerbridge's overriding goal, at least in late November 1941, was to find any way to get transferred off the *Cummings* and be done forever with his captain, the "nasty, suspicious" George Dudley Cooper, or "Dud," as Outerbridge called him. Dud was "a small person," he had written to Grace earlier that month. Dud was "an ass." Dud was "the devil." His rules were arbitrary, his paranoia great. Outerbridge may have looked nerdy, but looks are not all; he had backbone enough to argue and argue with Dud. Outerbridge's contempt was so sizable, and apparently not hidden, that he was actually looking forward to getting his tonsils out, which had become a medical necessity. "It would tickle me if the ship got under way while I was in the Hosp.," he had written his wife.

The best solution to the Dud problem would be a shore assignment, anywhere. Outerbridge was trying. "Hope someone in the [personnel] bureau decides that we have had enough sea duty and also that we should be promoted," he wrote on November 18. A billet at a naval base would mean family reunification. Outerbridge missed his three little boys, back on Jackdaw Street in San Diego. "I wish I could be there to raise them more personally, as I feel they have the makings of good men," he wrote on November 7. He missed Grace. The two of them seemed to be entering a good phase of life, he felt, older and wiser. He was thirty-five, she forty-one. "As a matter of fact, I am very happy to have you for a wife," he wrote one day. "I only wish that we could be together more, but our time will come."

As a military family, they had a military family's financial worries. Outerbridge made $356 a month, which meant that the recent but necessary purchases of a new car and a washing machine in San Diego had drained so much from their bank account that they would have to hold back on any further large expenditures. He had made sure, however, that Grace and the boys would be all right financially without him, and had explained in a straight-ahead way why they would be. "If I am killed, you will get immediately by wire $1,500 from Navy Mutual Aid and $1,500 from the Treasury Dept. as gratuity, 6 mos., pay," he told her on April 7. "I have made provision for the amount of the policy of Mutual Life, N.Y. ($5,000.00) to be held in reserve for emergency or education of the children. It will be payable on demand." He outlined some other, smaller payments she would get, too. "This is all in case I die this year."

Death was certainly possible. Outerbridge was only a junior officer on a small ship in a fleet that had more than a hundred vessels, and he was not privy to top-level correspondence and not included in meetings with the commander in chief, and certainly did not know of any war warning on that day. But Billy Outerbridge read the newspapers. He listened to local radio. He heard the talk. A clash with Japan seemed so close now he thought it might interfere with his tonsillectomy. That evening, he wrote Grace that if nothing big happened, he would head to the hospital on Monday, December 1. "I wonder what the Japs are going to do now," he said.

He would be just about the first American to find out.

SIX

MACHINE GUN SHORT

Friday, November 28

O N MAY 18, 1775, the troops of Colonel Benedict Arnold—
not yet a traitor to the American Revolution—captured a
two-mast, seventy-ton British sloop on Lake Champlain. He christened it the *Enterprise*. One hundred sixty-six years later, the seventh
American naval vessel to bear that name, this one 827 feet long and
32,000 tons, with a main deck as flat and as big as Kansas, began
lighting boilers before dawn Friday.

After shedding the ropes binding her to Ford Island, the *Enterprise* cleared the final outbound buoy at 8:40 a.m., and soon veered
west under clear skies, a pride of destroyers and cruisers keeping her
company. Before noon, a thick pack of planes blossomed off the aircraft carrier's stern, most of them hers, coming from airfields ashore,
where they roosted when the ship was in port. Skidding onto the
flight deck with the seventy-two regulars were a dozen newcomers,
marine fighters to be ferried to the defense of Wake Island, nearly
a week of sailing away. That the *Enterprise* would not be at Pearl

nine days hence, but at sea and undamaged and her air power intact, would not only be serendipitous—it would decide the course of the coming war, as the Imperial Navy would discover in six months at a clash called Midway.

The ruler of Task Force Eight was Admiral William Halsey of Elizabeth, New Jersey, raised in the navy on destroyers but now so devoted to naval air power that he had earned his wings as a grand-father, at the age of fifty-two, far older than the typical navy pilot. Never smooth, not sage—he landed in the bottom third of his class at the Naval Academy—Halsey operated without a filter on either his emotions or his mouth. He was a character, and beloved for being one. "He grins more readily than he scowls," Lieutenant Com-mander Joseph Bryan III would write in his introduction to Halsey's autobiography.

The admiral combined the opposed passions of neatness and stuff collecting, particularly souvenir ashtrays, swords, and flags. Halsey took water with his scotch, and had doubts about anyone who did not drink at least something. As a kid, he had been known as "Billy Big Head," for the sheer size of it, and a group of pro-fessional illustrators would declare one day that his noggin was "one of the six most startling and exciting in the world," the others being those of the author Ernest Hemingway; FBI director J. Edgar Hoover; actor Tyrone Power; labor leader Walter Reuther; and Brit-ish politician Ernest Bevin. Based on the list, women did not have exciting heads.

Halsey could discuss war with a startling casualness. He believed the purpose of an aircraft carrier was "to get [to] the other fellow with everything you have as fast as you can and to dump it on him." One of his sayings would wind up emblazoned on a sign in the Sol-omon Islands in 1943 as encouragement to passing troops: KILL JAPS, KILL JAPS, KILL MORE JAPS. "When we get to Tokyo, where we're bound to get eventually," he said one day, "we'll have a little celebration where Tokyo was."

Like Kimmel, Stark, and so many other admirals of the navy in 1941, Halsey had first encountered Japan as a young officer aboard a battleship of the Great White Fleet, which dropped anchor in Yokohama Bay on October 17, 1908. Kimmel had written his mother afterward that Japan was "without doubt the most fascinating place I have ever seen, only wish I could stay here seven weeks instead of seven days." He felt that "the government did itself proud in the matter of entertaining." The young Halsey, however, had cared no more for the Japanese then than the old Halsey would three decades later. "I felt that the Japs meant none of their welcome," he said, "that they actually disliked us." He would go on during the war to dub them "stupid beasts," "rats," "yellow bastards," and "monkeys." That hardly made him a unique American.

Bill Halsey was now fifty-nine, the same age as Kimmel, both being members of the class of '04. Not only were they friends—close friends—they shared an instinct for tactical boldness, for hounding the enemy when the time came. On November 27, the day of the war warning, Halsey wondered aloud how aggressive Kimmel would allow him to be once he left in the morning on the long journey to Wake Island. "Use your common sense," his classmate had replied. The answer had hung there, unexplained, open to interpretation. Halsey had thought it clear as could be. Now he could not only sink any submarine contact, as Kimmel had just told the whole fleet it could do, but he could also fire on anything he deemed a threat, any Japanese ship on the high seas, any plane he could not identify. That was his definition of common sense. And he geared up to do it as soon as the task force left Pearl behind.

"On leaving port," Halsey said, "I directed all ships to assume a condition of readiness for instant combat." Live shells were brought from the magazines to the deck guns. Warheads were married to the principal ordnance of the *Enterprise*'s torpedo planes, and bombs were positioned for swift attachment to the undersides of the dive-bombers. Guns on every airplane were loaded. Agape at the implications of all this, Halsey's operations officer, Commander William H. Buracker, confronted his boss. "Goddammit, Admiral, you can't start a private war of your own. Who's going to take the responsibility?"

To the crew of the *Enterprise* went forth "Battle Order Number One," dated November 28; in other words, the first order of a war that had not started. "I felt that we were going to be in a fight before I got back to Pearl," Halsey said. The order ended, "It is part of the tradition of our Navy that, when put to the test, all hands keep cool, keep their heads, and FIGHT. Steady nerves and stout hearts are needed now."

Husband Kimmel shared Halsey's belief that the *Enterprise* and her escorts might encounter more than Japanese submarines as they conveyed the marine fighter planes to Wake Island. Both admirals knew the war warning had emphasized only the southwest Pacific, thousands of miles away. But Wake Island was a great deal closer to Japan than Oahu. Maybe Halsey and his forces would bump into Imperial Navy surface ships or carrier planes; maybe Japan was planning to attack his destination, Wake. Whatever the Japanese had in mind, he would be ready. That did not mean, by extension, Japanese forces could also be coming as far as Pearl. Neither Halsey nor Kimmel thought that. That would be too far. "Wake, you know, is 2,000 miles to the westward," Kimmel would say later.

Having scurried into place overnight, armed soldiers stood outside Oahu's waterworks, telephone exchanges, and commercial radio stations that Friday dawn as the *Enterprise* and her task force ploughed into the open sea. They guarded warehouses, bridges, selected roads, and other "vital places," the *Star-Bulletin* said in a front-page article, explaining that army ground and air forces in the islands were now on a "simulated emergency basis" because of "an impending failure" in talks with Japan. Around town, the newspaper noted, "machine guns were in evidence."

Which fazed few. Hawaiians were the Americans most used to military displays, and not merely because so many of them wore uniforms or worked at the bases of the army and navy. No resident could be oblivious to what Oahu now was: a highly militarized, idyllic destination. "Every day," *Paradise of the Pacific* had written a month earlier, "one sees trains of [army] motor vehicles moving swiftly along Oahu's roads." With or without a "simulated emergency basis," fighter planes darted and dodged through drills. Batteries of coastal artillery blasted test rounds seaward. Huge B-17s banked in from California and roared off for the Philippines. Anyone enjoying Waikiki Beach on a Sunday shared the sand with hundreds of soldiers and sailors who were enhancing their tans and mastering surfboards. From time to time, rumbles of thunder came out of a perfectly clear sky. Big guns out to sea. "Ever and anon, echoes of battle practice by the United States Fleet somewhere around is heard," *Paradise* had said. Blackout drills had started as far back as May 1940.

The troop deployment on Friday morning was the work of Lieutenant General Walter C. Short, or, as he was known at least to some, "Machine Gun Short." The day before, Short, the army commander in the islands, had gotten his own war warning from Washington, although his avoided a catchy alliterative phrase in favor of the pedestrian "hostile action possible at any moment." The sending of two dispatches to Oahu, one per service, reflected the peculiar reality that no one person commanded the military in Hawaii, and thus no one person or branch had the responsibility for defending it.

If things were as the military had once envisioned them, defending Hawaii would be up to the army alone. The fleet's job was *out there*, not at Pearl. Kimmel considered himself "a bird of passage," a creature not of Oahu, but one who merely alighted briefly. The island was the fleet's roadside rest area, where it filled its fuel tanks and fixed its broken parts, where crews stepped ashore to stretch legs, see a movie, visit the bars. Having been on guard and working while at sea, the fleet could hardly be expected to be on guard and working in port, too, not if it was to stay fit and fresh. "If such be the case," Kimmel had once written to Harold Stark, "the premise is so false as to hardly warrant refutation." So the army would keep the watch over Oahu while the navy rejuvenated; the army would make sure that when the navy returned from its work *out there*, the Stars and Stripes would still be flying over the rest stop.

Alas, the army couldn't do all that. It had plenty of troops in the islands—42,959 by November 30—but hardly any aircraft capable of long-range reconnaissance, hardly any capable of sinking the ships of an advancing enemy fleet, and far too few antiaircraft guns and fighter planes to keep the sky safe immediately above Pearl. Not long after his appointment as commander in chief, Kimmel had inspected the army defenses and had been "astounded." Not long after that, he decided he ought to meet Walter Short for the very first time.

As with many siblings, the army and the navy had never reflexively gotten along in Hawaii, or anywhere for that matter. They were so unsynced that no direct phone line linked Pearl Harbor to Fort Shafter, the army's lovely, palm-strewn grounds a few miles east. General George C. Marshall, the army chief of staff, had written that year that "old Army and Navy feuds, engendered from fights over appropriations, with the usual fallacious arguments on both sides, still persist in confusing issues of national defense."

Kimmel felt cooperation in the Pacific was "entirely inadequate."

He had a vivid memory of an incident in the mid-1930s when his and other battleships had arrived in darkness off Oahu to be suddenly lit up by army spotlights, which, in wartime, would quite considerably abet the aim of any enemy that happened to be in the neighborhood. The army explained that it had not known the ships were American because no one had told it when the navy would be showing up; the navy, livid, replied that it was none of the army's business what time it did anything.

During an interview with two researchers helping him write his autobiography, one of Kimmel's officers would say after the war, "As with the British, the Navy was the premier service. Yes it was. The Army was a—don't put this in the book—they were a bunch of bums." Not only that, "they were just lazy louts" who "had no pride in their uniform or service." Naval condescension seemed greatest in regard to army pilots on Oahu. The army had concluded it was unsafe to let its aviators regularly wander too far out over the ocean, there being no navigational landmarks there. In contrast, the navy's carrier pilots not only flew two or three hundred feature-less miles ahead of their ships but also then flew back to land on a stub of a runway that was both racing forward and pitching up and down. It was obvious, at least to the navy, which service had the moxie. Poco Smith, Kimmel's aide, tried to put the common naval wisdom politely: "In the operations between our planes and theirs, our aviators—possibly prejudiced—expressed the opinion that they were not very good."

Though neither Kimmel nor Short exercised any jurisdiction over the other, the admiral's uniform did bear four stars to the general's three. So perhaps to avoid the uncomfortable sense of a conversation between unequals at their first encounter in February, Kimmel had donned starless civilian attire and done the traveling, seeking out Short at his temporary residence on Oahu. The general was new to his job, too, having stepped off the *Matsonia* only a few days earlier with a résumé remarkable for how unremarkable it was. The army had sent a functionary, not a dynamo, to its premier outpost. Brooke E. Allen, an army bomber pilot on Oahu who would wind up a major general, said Short "had no imagination at all." Even Short's biographer would say that while he had a "penetrating intellect," he lacked "charisma to move masses" and his skills were not "headline-generating."

Walter Short was born in 1880 in an Illinois town so small his high school class had seven students. He had not planned on an army life, having graduated not from the United States Military Academy at West Point but from the University of Illinois. The school's president had convinced him to accept an army commission because of his "personal qualities, [his] good scholarship, and [his] interest and proficiency in military work."

One of the army's finest shots with a pistol and a whiz at math, Short had sailed to France with the American Expeditionary Forces during the Great War, and earned a Distinguished Service Medal— for the mundane feats of "inspecting and reporting upon frontline conditions" and "efficiently directing the instruction and training of machine-gun units at every available opportunity during rest periods." Short kept on training such units after the war, writing a textbook in 1922, *Employment of Machine Guns*, which explained "angles of tangent elevation," as well as "lateral wind allowances." His Capone-like nickname followed.

In a postwar and shrunken army, Machine Gun Short plodded upward through mainland assignments, a "somewhat austere" and "disciplined" officer of few words but with a talent for maneuvering troops and tanks during simulated battles. One of his aides on Oahu, Major Robert J. Fleming, would say, "I guess he was about five-nine or ten, very, very thin, very trim, kept himself in excellent condition. He had a rather sharp-featured face. He had a temper. Oh, yes, he had a temper. He didn't show it very often but when somebody goofed, Short could be very, very brutal."

He had been in charge of the First Corps in Columbia, South Carolina, when George Marshall tapped him to lead the army in Hawaii, believing Short was a "very superior officer." The nominee did not much care to move so far away—his wife's father was ill—but Marshall had insisted, and so Short wound up on an island, where the familiar notions of "the front" and "the rear" had little meaning, and where the terrain was not the tank-conducive flat farmland of, say, eastern France, but sharp mountain ranges and surf-smashed beaches.

Marshall, in a letter on February 7, schooled Short. Defending the naval base on Oahu, he had said, "is *the*, rather than *a*, major consideration for us," italics his. He had spoken to Harold Stark about Kimmel, the equally new navy commander, and learned he was "very direct, even brusque and undiplomatic in his approach to problems." The chief of naval operations "had, in the past, personally objected to Kimmel's manners in dealing with officers," Marshall wrote, but he "was, at heart, a very kindly man" who was very good at his job. The entire navy thought so, Marshall assured Short.

When the two military leaders of Oahu finally met, harmony had broken out. "I told him then," Kimmel said, "that I wanted to cooperate and do everything we could together," and Short had risen to the challenge "as a man should." The general possessed "sound judgment." Short wrote Marshall on February 19 that Kimmel was "approachable and cooperative in every way," and he would later characterize their relationship as "extremely friendly." They became golfing buddies, playing every other Sunday on a nine-hole course near Fort Shafter. On the Sundays they did not play, Kimmel often traipsed to the fort to spend the morning with Short and his wife, Isabel, who had moved to Oahu, unlike Kimmel's wife.

In the following months, army and navy forces in the islands drilled together. When the army needed to improve the skills of its radar operators, the navy invited them aboard the few ships equipped with the new technology. A commander of one of the fleet's destroyer flotillas would remember bumping into Short all the time at fleet headquarters at the Submarine Building, either as the general was leaving a meeting with Kimmel or entering one. "Really," Short said, "I felt they played the game better than I had ever seen the Navy play the game"—the game of let's get along, that is.

Their greatest act of coordination was a bifurcation of the air. With the army all but bereft of long-range bombers and modern fighter planes, the navy had no choice but to do what it did not wish to do: devote some of its aircraft to the defense of the port. By virtue of a March 1941 compact, army pilots would patrol the skies immediately above Oahu and just offshore, and navy aircraft would search the distant reaches, if and when the moment required that. In essence, the navy would find and attack the Japanese as far out as possible, and if any planes, ships, or submarines got past the navy and reached the islands, the army would respond with anti-aircraft guns, coastal artillery, fighters, and bombers. If asked, each side would lend the other any planes it could spare to carry out its mission. Stark thought the arrangement was so dandy it should be adopted any place that had dual commands.

Yet even with the goodwill, the Sunday golfing, the joint drills, and the sharing of duties in the air, neither service knew all that much about what the other was up to. There was, for example, the matter of differing alert scales. The army's lowest level on Oahu was alert one. The navy's highest was condition one. Neither was aware of the polar difference. In fact, Kimmel thought the army had but one level, namely, all-out alert. They were parallel universes that pried not into each other's business.

"When you have a responsible officer in charge of the Army," Kimmel said, "and responsible commanders in the Navy, it does not sit very well to be constantly checking up on them." Short had no idea where ships of the fleet went when they steamed away, nor what they did once they got there. He seemed awed by the navy, by the huge and powerful ships that vanished over the blue horizon, only to return in a week or two. He put his faith in the fleet's muscle and assumed its competence. Because the navy seemed maniacal about keeping secrets, he said that he "would hesitate lots of times to ask for specific information." If he had, Kimmel "would have resented it," and besides, he "felt that he could be counted on to do his job."

Kimmel, who immersed himself in the smallest aspects of fleet operations, did not immerse himself in the one army project that offered the most protection for the naval base. Short was striving to set up a network of radar units on Oahu, using mobile detectors at first, to be followed in time by permanent ones. In a simulation on September 27, a navy carrier launched planes toward Oahu, and two army mobile radar units spotted them eighty-five miles out, enabling fighter planes to intercept them at twenty-six miles. "The raiding force was theoretically destroyed before an attack on Pearl Harbor could be realized," an army report said later. In a real attack, it would be unlikely that a cadre of planes could be wiped out entirely before reaching the harbor. But radar could certainly whittle its size.

Its ability to do so depended on the quick identification of contacts. As yet, American warplanes, unlike British, did not have transponders that automatically told ground stations that a contact was friendly. On Oahu, a detected plane could, therefore, be army, navy, or hostile. The two services had to be able to confer quickly about the direction and number of planes each had aloft. Any contact left over would most likely be enemy. On Oahu, the army had constructed a makeshift "information center" atop a small concrete warehouse at Fort Shafter, to which its outlying radar units could report their contacts, and decisions could be made about friend or foe, and about where defending fighter planes ought to concentrate. Short had asked Kimmel to assign someone to the center to facilitate the essential exchange of data. "We were never able to get any liaison officer over from the Navy to take part in the exercises or carry on the work," remembered Lieutenant Colonel C. A. Powell, the army officer who commanded the information center.

"However much I should have personally checked into this thing—and God knows now I wish I had—I had a great many other things to do," Kimmel said.

Too many small ones, certainly.

That July, an unusual marine reservist reported to the fleet for a month of duty. Republican congressman Melvin J. Maas of Minnesota, the ranking minority member of the House Naval Affairs Committee, ended his tour by telling a Honolulu press conference that the navy could "wipe out virtually overnight" the capital of any country, and that no combination of enemy powers "could endanger our continental security." In other words, Maas offered the typical patriotic bluster. Actually, he was deeply troubled by what he had seen in the islands.

"While there is splendid cooperation between high army and navy command," he had written to Bill Halsey after returning home, "it depends on personal conferences, personalities, and compromises, rather than a unified plan, with the essentials of the plan known in advance to all who must carry it out." Admiral Patrick N. L. Bellinger, the leading naval aviator in the Pacific, had similar concerns, despite the aura of interservice harmony. When a Navy Department civilian complimented Bellinger on how well the services in Hawaii had divvied up defensive duties, the admiral replied, "It wouldn't work in case of war."

Maas demanded—human nature demanded—that one person be put in charge of "all military and naval and air operations" on Oahu. Otherwise, an army leader and a navy leader who share a locale but have different emphases and responsibilities can each make the same sad assumption—namely, that the other man is taking care of a problem or task, or is doing what he should. An overall leader never has to assume. All data, worries, and problems go to him, all decisions emanate from him. Maas did not care whether Oahu's leader was army or navy, but the geography suggested navy. "The only foreseeable threat that could be brought against the Hawaiian Islands is naval," he told Halsey. Concluding his letter, which was dated October 20, Maas said, "In my opinion, it is not only unwise, but may prove dangerous and tragic to leave the situation uncoordinated at the moment."

As a result of his month of active duty, Maas had many other thoughts about military issues in the Pacific, and they had reached not only Halsey but also Stark. And also Kimmel, who responded to each of Maas's observations in a seventeen-page letter to Main Navy. As far as having a single commander for Oahu was concerned, Kimmel felt the good congressman simply did not have the facts. Yes, historically, the army and the navy in the territory had not been the best of friends, but they were now. They had achieved "success," Kimmel wrote on November 13. "No change therein is recommended at the present time."

The War Department, like the Navy Department, had composed its war warning by committee. It had been chiefly worried about the exposed Philippines, but had added Oahu, the West Coast, and Panama as recipients to guard against the worst. Signed by George Marshall himself—a rare event denoting a highly serious matter—the army told Walter Short that negotiations with Japan were finished "to all practical purposes," and that the empire's future actions were "unpredictable." It might start shooting "at any moment." Do not fire first, Marshall said—unless you must in self-defense. Undertake reconnaissance and other measures "as you deem necessary," Marshall ordered, but do not "alarm civilian population." The War Department clearly had no idea how difficult it would be to frighten or panic Hawaiians with military movements.

Brigadier General Leonard T. Gerow, the dispatch's ghostwriter, would say later that the Hawaiian Department—the formal name of Short's command—should have concluded from this message that Hawaii may be endangered and that it was time to start a search and prepare "to meet any action by the armed forces of Japan." Gerow may have achieved those goals if he had written them in his message as clearly as he later verbalized them. As it was, his warning had not spoken directly of Hawaii, or of any place at all. It had mentioned reconnaissance, but in the very same sentence it gave Short the option of deeming it unnecessary. And it had told him to keep things low-key.

Earlier that day, Short had heard Kimmel's war plans officer, Soc McMorris, practically label an attack on Oahu an absurdist's fantasy. The Pacific Fleet had far more sources about Japanese naval movements and capabilities than the army did, because the army on Hawaii had none. Short believed that Kimmel's ships and aircraft were always plying and flying in the beyond, and surely had eyes on the enemy. "If that statement was made to me once, it was made a half a dozen times," said Colonel James A. Mollison, the army officer who had worried that morning that Oahu was being stripped of too many planes in order to bolster the defense of the outer islands. Major General Frederick L. Martin, commander of the army's air forces on the island, felt certain that if a Japanese attack force were coming, the navy would bump into it "in some way" because its ships were always out there, scattered, ready "to pick up information."

Under their agreement, the navy could ask for any planes the army had that might help with a search. But no request came to Short after the war warning. And he could see nothing but calm inside Pearl Harbor. There was no flight of the big ships, as there surely would have been if the navy feared a raid. Even landlubber army officers knew that staying inside the barrel carried great risk. "All you had to do was drive down here when the fleet was all in," Short said. "You can see that they just couldn't be missed if they had a serious attack. There were too many [ships]. There was too little water for the number of ships."

When Short had gotten to the portion of Marshall and Gerow's warning that involved reconnaissance, he had ignored it. Air search was not his job. "Whoever wrote it," Short said, "did not take into consideration, or overlooked, our definite agreement that the Navy was responsible for long-distance reconnaissance." Incredibly, the general had not then troubled himself to notify the War Department of what seemed to be its potentially disastrous misunderstanding about who was to search, nor had he sought to find out if his nearby brothers of the sea at Pearl were, in fact, going to start one. He had done nothing more than give Kimmel a copy of the army war warning and assume that his counterpart would read the reference to search and take care of it. "I did not pin him down," Short said, "and say, 'Are you going to send [out] a plane every hour? What is it going to search? How many degrees? How are you going to do your mission?' I did not ask him that." Exactly as Congressman Maas had feared, the two Hawaiian commanders were not meshing their efforts in the face of danger.

Short could have ordered alert three, total mobilization of his forces to repel a landing, or alert two, which was preparation for air raids or offshore shelling. But Marshall and Gerow had told him not to alarm anyone. Either of those alert levels would have been quite noticeable, even if not particularly scary to the average Hawaiian. And either would have made it difficult to continue the training of his forces, which was as much a priority for him as for Kimmel. So Short decided on the less disruptive alert one. The army would guard against subversion, which worried Short all the time anyway.

Two of every five residents of the islands were of Japanese lineage—120,552 born in Hawaii, 37,353 born in Japan. The territory was a stew of peoples, and the Japanese were its biggest ingredient, bigger than Caucasians, native Hawaiians, Filipinos, or Chinese. They worked as secretaries, craftsmen, maids, and especially as laborers in the sugarcane and pineapple fields. In an America where job ads in the *Advertiser* could casually specify racial preferences— "Haole Fountain Girls Wanted," meaning white; "Haole Girl for Clerical Work"—local Japanese were not just another "other" to the white men who commanded the military on Oahu. They were full-out suspects; they could be saboteurs waiting for Tokyo's secret go sign.

Short's intelligence officer, Lieutenant Colonel Kendall J. Fiedler, could not conceive "of that many people of a different race not engaging in some subversive activity in the event of hostilities." After all, Fiedler said, "I can't conceive of 160,000 Americans being in Japan when war is declared without them doing something against Japan." US senator Guy M. Gillette, a Democrat from Iowa, had forecast that as soon as war broke out, the local Japanese population would seek to cripple the Pacific Fleet as it rested inside Pearl. The writer of a book review in the *New York Times*, while noting how "indispensable" the Japanese were to Hawaii's economy, called them "a thorn in the side of the Navy, and of the Army, too." "For whatever their citizenship," Harold Callender wrote, reviewing Joseph Barber's *Hawaii, Restless Rampart* in the *Times* on March 2, "grave doubts are entertained as to their behavior in case this country were at war with the only naval power conceivable as an enemy in the Pacific." While conceding that most Japanese in the islands were American citizens, Callender argued they were "under the influence" of Japan's consulate in Honolulu, and "some make journeys to Japan."

Who knew what weapons these hordes of Japanese had hidden in the interior of Oahu or Maui or the Big Island? "There are great areas in the islands that are mountainous and rugged and practically inaccessible, in which the average person never goes," General Martin felt. "Those are wonderful opportunities for caches of explosives, incendiary equipment, everything of that nature."

Short told Washington during the summer that he had begun a "counter propaganda campaign" to promote loyalty and tranquility among the local Japanese. Subtle the campaign was not. At a celebration of the thirtieth anniversary of a Japanese American newspaper one night in July, Lieutenant Colonel Eugene M. Foster both praised the local Japanese as valued members of the Oahu defense team, and threatened them. If anyone in their group—he meant anyone with whom an individual associated—committed an act of sabotage, "all members of that group will be under suspicion until the guilty party is apprehended, and proof is given that his acts were not supported or condoned by others of the group." The army kept a list containing the names of more than three hundred Japanese who were more suspect than others and who were to be rounded up if hostilities began. Their homes were pinpointed, literally, on a huge army map of Oahu, "and it was a comparatively simple matter to put out our dragnet and pick them up when hostilities started," Fiedler, Short's intelligence officer, said. A second list, the B list, had still more names; those people were to be kept under surveillance if war began.

All the worry stemmed from nothing specific. "No, there was none, no indication of anything on the island that would cause unnecessary suspicion," General Martin conceded later. No discoveries of dynamite or map layouts of Pearl Harbor. No arrests of sleeper cells. No preliminary acts of mayhem, like the severing of power lines or the jamming of radio frequencies. Suspicion was rampant simply because the local Japanese looked like the potential enemy. It was a suspicion that went far beyond the Hawaiian Islands.

At least one of Short's officers—the one responsible for unmasking enemy spies—felt the fears were so much nonsense. "My feelings on that question have been expressed to practically every commanding general whom I have come in contact with," Lieutenant Colonel George W. Bicknell said, "and that was that we would never have any sabotage trouble with the local Japanese. And we did not."

Afterward, on December 15, the agent in charge of the FBI's Honolulu office would tell J. Edgar Hoover in a dispatch that there had been "no instance of sabotage." The agent, Robert L. Shivers, would write that the "Japanese populace as a whole, both alien and citizens of Japanese ancestry, have conducted themselves [in a] law-abiding manner and the latter have given every evidence of loyalty with few possible exceptions."

Within hours of dispersing troops to thwart saboteurs, Walter Short concluded he had chosen the right response to Marshall's war warning. Two more War Department dispatches—although neither signed by Marshall—arrived at Fort Shafter, reminding him to watch out for the local Japanese threat, thereby inadvertently diluting the notion of an exterior one. One of the missives said: *Desired that you initiate*

*forthwith all additional measures necessary to provide for protection
of your establishments comma property comma and equipment against
sabotage.* Well, he already had so initiated. He was on it.

The War Department, in its warning, had told him to "report
measures taken." Perhaps Marshall did not trust Short as much as
Stark did Kimmel, who was under no such obligation to explain
what he had done. Or maybe Marshall thought the moment was too
serious not to know how Oahu was responding, which would have
been a good thought to have. Whatever the reason, the Hawaiian
Department, as ordered, composed a dispatch that spilled into the
War Department code room in the wee hours of Friday, November 28. Short had written only two sentences. *Report department
alerted to prevent sabotage period. Liaison with Navy.* He ended
with this: *Reurad four seven two twenty seventh.* In army-speak, it
meant he was replying to radiogram 472 of November 27, the war
warning.

It was a careless and inattentive War Department that now
scanned that reply. Knowing that Short had been sent two follow-up
dispatches about sabotage, General Gerow assumed that Short's
first sentence—*alerted to prevent sabotage*—pertained to those two,
even though Short's reply clearly referenced, by number, only the
war warning. Gerow assumed that the second sentence—*liaison with
Navy*—meant the two services were working out reconnaissance,
even though Short meant only what he had written, that he was in
touch with Kimmel, which did not necessarily mean that they were
discussing reconnaissance. It might. It might not.

Army chief of staff Marshall read Short's reply, too. He would
have no memory of doing so, and no comprehension that Short was
telling him that he was alert *only* for sabotage. "I had an immense
number of papers going over my desk every day, informing me what
was happening anywhere in the world," Marshall said. Yes, he was in

charge of the army, he continued, "but I am not a bookkeeping machine, and it is extremely difficult, it is an extremely difficult thing, for me to take each thing in its turn and give it exactly the attention that it had merited." The word "sabotage" probably failed to register with him, Marshall said, because "sabotage was not in anybody's mind" when the War Department wrote its primary warning. Attack by Japanese forces was.

If Short's response had been analyzed more carefully—or at all—he might then have been asked why he was alert only for sabotage. He might then have been asked what "liaison with Navy" meant. It might have become clear to Washington that he was underestimating the threat, and that he had not discussed reconnaissance with the navy. It might have lead to formal discussions with Kimmel about how much risk they faced and what to do about it.

"I told them as plainly as I could. I was alerted against sabotage," Short said, adding, "They did not come back and say, 'You're doing too much' or 'You're doing too little.'" So he must have been doing it just right. "If they didn't know what we were doing, it was simply because they didn't read our messages."

By nightfall on Friday, November 28, the Hawaiian Islands were no more wary than they had been twenty-four hours before. Neither recipient of a war warning had reacted to a highly unusual message with anything approaching alarm. The senders—Harold Stark and George Marshall, the two highest-ranking officers in the United States—had sent forth messages so indirectly and clumsily phrased that they had failed to warn. The War Department, having told Short to report the measures he had taken, failed to closely read what he had in fact reported.

Washington thought reconnaissance was getting under way, but it wasn't. Short thought Kimmel was searching, but he wasn't. Kimmel saw no reason to start searching, so he hadn't.

Short did take one step that he did not tell Washington about. He ordered the six mobile radar units, which normally operated during the day and even then only for training, to fire up earlier, from 4:00 a.m. to 7:00 a.m. That was the most likely window for an air attack on Pearl, he knew. An enemy carrier would use darkness to sneak as near to the islands as possible, then launch with the rising sun.

Earlier in the year, the general had been full of urgency about getting the equipment and bureaucratic clearances for his radar network, arguing to Marshall that "defense of these islands and adequate warning for the United States Fleet is so dependent" on an early warning of approaching aircraft. "With the present international situation," he wrote in March, "it seems to me that if this equipment is to be used at all, the need for it is now."

The international situation was much worse now than it had been then. Short got the radar equipment he had demanded, and it was functioning fine. But his reason for now ordering the units to operate during the dawn hours had nothing to do with the immediate protection of the islands or the fleet he had been so concerned about. Having ordered an alert for sabotage, Short merely felt the radar units might as well go ahead and practice, "to get the battle training at the hours when it was most needed and most difficult." And because no one at the War Department realized that sabotage was Short's only concern and corrected him, the general did not know that perhaps this, finally, was the moment when radar mattered.

So as the radar crews went out to their posts around Oahu, they were not told there had been a war warning. They were not told they were searching for real.

SEVEN

AMBASSADOR JOE AND PRESIDENT FRANK

Saturday, November 29

O N THE SORT of afternoon that every afternoon in autumn ought to be, the great horseshoe of seats in deepest South Philadelphia began to fill. It filled with Admiral Harold Stark and General George Marshall. It filled with Vice President Henry A. Wallace and First Lady Eleanor Roosevelt. With senators and congressmen and governors; with 3,100 midshipmen in blue overcoats and 1,850 cadets in gray; with everyday citizens paying "as high as $25 for a single ticket," until 98,497 spectators stood or sat in the glorious sun, and there was no more room in Municipal Stadium.

Forty-one times since 1890, Army's eleven had played Navy's. The forty-second encounter was unique even before the opening kickoff on Saturday. That war warnings had been flashed to the forces in Hawaii and the Philippines, or that Kichisaburo Nomura had shed tears of despair in conversation with Stark, or that Cordell Hull had all but given up on the chances for peace, were specific acts unknown to the American people. Yet there was enough in the papers to know that war in the Pacific was as likely now as in the Atlantic, where it was practically under way already. This might be the last Army-Navy game for who knew how long.

For fifty cents, the crowd could purchase the game program, whose 212 pages included a photograph of an American battleship crashing its way through heavy seas, and a caption boasting that "despite the claims of air enthusiasts," bombs had yet to sink a big, muscular ship like this one, the *Arizona*.

Though he didn't have much of it anymore, Joe Grew still had hope on Saturday. Though he felt like a political candidate "who knows that he is going to be defeated, but he does not admit it until it is all over," he would not abandon Tokyo. "I haven't packed a thing," the ambassador of the United States told his diary that day, "and do not intend to." Even so, prudently, Grew had begun shipping documents home, including segments of the diary. Any remaining delicate papers now lived in a steel vault at his official residence, ready to be extracted and burned if—or, more likely, when—the police swarmed the embassy compound at the onset of hostilities. And, not incidentally, Grew had gotten himself a gun. He never elaborated on how he had gotten it, but he seemed aware of the incongruity of having it, given his pedigree. "I feel somewhat 'Wild West' these days," he confessed.

Ambassador Joseph Clark Grew was Boston born, Harvard educated, and career Foreign Service. And he was Groton. He was so Groton that whenever he needed a new personal secretary, he would write the headmaster of his old prep school and ask him to send over another young man for a two-year stint. Golf was so threaded through Grew's routine, even in those dark days in Japan, that when

Robert A. Fearey (Groton, '37) arrived at the embassy to succeed
Marshall Green (Groton, '35) in the summer of 1941, the new secretary already knew that "one of my principal duties would be golf."
Grew was not too good at it, oddly. Rarely broke a hundred. "His
putting style was unique," Fearey said. "Between his legs with a
croquet-type stroke. But unfortunately, no better for that fact."

Grew and his wife, Alice, the parents of three daughters who had
all gone off and married Foreign Service officers, had lived among
the Japanese for just shy of ten years. Still without fluency in the language, Grew, who was now sixty-one, had nonetheless accumulated
Japanese friends and contacts, mingled often with their officials, and
absorbed the translated contents of their newspapers day after day,
through their spasms of bellicosity. For all his upper-crust heritage,
Grew had a better feel for the Japanese psyche than did any other
American, or at least those at the State Department.

"Dear Frank," he had written one day the previous December.
Frank was the president of the United States (Groton, '00).

I find that diplomacy has been defeated by trends and forces
utterly beyond its control, and that our work has been swept
away as if by a typhoon, with little or nothing remaining to
show for it. Japan has become openly and unashamedly one of
the predatory nations.

His Japanese acquaintances were drifting away, reluctant to visit
the residence, a beautiful new, white building with elegant rooms
and perfect gardens in Tokyo's Akasaka neighborhood. They would
not join him for golf, either, afraid they would look like spies keeping in touch with their control agent. "What a sad change from the
old, friendly and congenial Japan!" Grew had written a friend in
Boston. The Japanese had allowed their ally Germany to seed the

capital with gestapo agents, who liked to vacuum up anti-Axis sen-timents and reveal the disloyal to the Japanese police. A taxi driver in Kobe had roughed up the French commercial attaché, Count Tascher de la Pagerie, breaking one of his legs in what was osten-sibly a dispute over a fare, but which Grew blamed squarely on xenophobia whipped to a hot lather by the government, through the state-supervised press. One newspaper, *Yomiuri*, had called Roosevelt a "crafty, haughty, blood-sucker." The most rabid of all, *Nichi Nichi*, would soon declare that the United States possessed "the soul of a prostitute."

Throughout the country, there was an air of righteousness that was "not the Japan that we have known and loved," Grew had writ-ten to Roosevelt. It was something that Otto Tolischus sensed, too, shortly after his arrival in 1941 as the correspondent of the *New York Times*. Tolischus had spent the two previous years reporting from Berlin, and he found that the Japanese were "more cocky and self-assured than the Germans, and they let the foreigners know it." He detected the same tension and determination that pervaded the Third Reich, "an instinctive reaction, I suppose, of the living organ-ism" steeling itself for a fight and for sacrifice. Japanese newspapers "were full of war talk," Tolischus said, "and war talk of a kind which showed me that the clock was much farther advanced in Japan, as compared with America, than a mere dateline difference."

To Grew, nothing could be as humiliating to a diplomat as the eruption of a war with the host country on his watch. If he could avoid one—"If I can help only a mite," he wrote his daughter, Anita, in July—it would cap a life of public service that had begun in Egypt in 1904 and touched down in eight other countries before Japan. "We shall feel our whole career has been worthwhile," he told her.

On the evening of September 6, Grew got into his regular car, whose regular license plates had vanished in favor of a fresh set, the better to traverse the streets of the capital with a somewhat reduced risk of being recognized by one of its 6.5 million residents. With him was Embassy Counselor Eugene H. Dooman, who had been born in Osaka. He would do the translating. The two motored to the home of a Japanese friend, a baron, and sat down for what would become a three-hour meal, although not with the baron, though his daughter served it. There were just two other people at the table: the private secretary of the prime minister of Japan, and the prime minister himself, Fumimaro Konoye.

Like Grew, the prime minister had come in a car stripped of its regular tags, so that he might remain alive. Only a few days before, a nationalist with a pistol had gravely wounded a seventy-five-year-old member of Konoye's cabinet in his home for having advocated too much restraint in dealings with the world.

"At that time in Japan, there were two camps," Grew would tell congressional inquisitors four years later. "There were the militarist war leaders who were all-out for expansion and were carrying out the plans . . . day after day, week after week, steadily. On the other hand, there were certain liberal-minded statesmen who realized the position their country had got into, realized the danger of war, and wanted to avert it, if they possibly could."

If Konoye was in the latter camp, he was a late arrival. The prime minister, who was fifty, was known for his height (almost six feet; tall in Japan), his moustache (described as "Chaplin-ish"), and his talent for having feet on both sides of any line. "Few are completely satisfied with him," Tolischus wrote in the *New York Times* on August 3, "and some accuse him of weakness, vacillation and even of lack of courage, but none knows where to get a better man to maintain the balance between various forces on which depends Japan's stability."

His actual record, though, leaned more toward the militarists than the lovers of peace. Japan had invaded China during a previous Konoye regime, and he had signed the Tripartite Pact with Germany and Italy. But of late, he had been quietly seeking to meet Franklin Roosevelt halfway. Quite literally. He had suggested Hawaii. If the president would just come, he would be pleased by what Konoye had to offer, implying that Japan would pull its troops out of China and Indochina reasonably soon, endorse free and open commerce in the Far East, and ignore its obligation to assist the Germans and Italians if America went to war with them. In return, the United States was to lift its economic embargoes and agree to a commercial treaty and financial support. Konoye claimed to have the backing of the emperor and senior military leaders.

Konoye's plea, Grew decided, reflected genuine worry. "He knew a good deal more about our country than the hot-headed militarists did," Grew said. "He had been to our country, knew something about our productive capacity, knew something about our national spirit. In my opinion, he realized that Japan, if she got into war with us and with other countries, other Western powers, would probably in the end be defeated and would emerge as a third- or a fifth-rate power."

The country's economy was already being wrecked by Western sanctions and by the war in China. Forty commodities were being rationed. No cotton was coming from India, no rubber from Malaya, no nickel from Canada. The silk industry, which normally sent 90 percent of its goods to America, no longer could, and was collapsing. The police had arrested 973,000 people for illegal barter.

Some 1.5 million workers had been stripped of their everyday jobs and ushered into armaments factories, and 2.5 million additional workers had been sucked into the army, many to fight in China. In a lecture on August 15 at the Naval War College, a Harvard professor, A. E. Hindmarsh, estimated that four years of war had cost Japan $4 billion, and had killed or wounded 1,113,000 people. Japan wasn't winning, it probably never could, and it knew it.

Seeking to meet with Roosevelt was an "act of the highest statesmanship" that reflected "a remarkable degree of courage" on Konoye's part, Grew wrote to Cordell Hull on August 19. If extremists learned of the summit beforehand or Konoye came home without a favorable agreement, he might lose not only his career "but his own life." The fanatics might kill him for having been willing to curb Japan's imperial desires and for wasting the noble sacrifices of the war in China. We should seize this opportunity, Grew told Hull.

The secretary of state, who considered Japan "one of the worst international desperadoes within the memory of man," who saw it as a nation "on the rampage, dangerous, treacherous, undependable in every way," who calculated the odds of peace with it at one in a hundred, who watched it take over all of Indochina right in the middle of negotiations, detected a whiff of Munich hovering around Konoye's proposed summit, a possible disaster of public relations and diplomacy. There would be no meeting in the Pacific unless—in advance—Konoye converted his vague promises into written details, so that a summit's success would not be left to luck, and that it would not end in squishy language that Japan could later dodge. Cordell Hull wanted to read the screenplay before going to the movie. "We asked ourselves whether the military element in Japan would permit the civilian element, even if so disposed, to stop Japan's course of expansion by force and to revert to peaceful courses," he said. "Time and again, the civilian leaders gave assurances. Time and again, the military took aggressive action in direct violation of those assurances."

At their clandestine dinner on September 6, Konoye told Grew that he understood American reluctance to trust Japan, given the Tripartite Pact and its war in China. He offered a "guarantee" to Grew that he could win approval for a settlement, and warned that if no meeting took place, his government would fall and extremists would take power. That night, Grew wrote to Hull that "Konoye repeatedly stressed the view that time is of the essence." The prime minister was so ready to go, right now, that he claimed a destroyer was waiting in Yokohama harbor, steam up, to whisk him to Roosevelt.

Evidently, Konoye hoped to inflict a fait accompli on the extremists by returning from a Pacific encounter to announce on national radio that the war in China would wind down honorably; American sanctions would be lifted soon, and the quality of Japanese lives would begin soaring. The news would "electrify the Japanese people," Konoye told Grew, "showing them that they can have what they want politically, economically and socially. They can have security without any more fighting." The radicals would not dare try to quash such mass happiness. Grew pleaded with Washington to trust him, because he trusted Konoye. A summit might fail. But a botched summit could be no worse than the war that might result if there was no summit at all.

As the summer faded, rumors reached the embassy that Washington believed "Grew had been in Japan too long, that he was more Japanese than the Japanese," Robert Fearey wrote. On September 3, the United Press cited "entirely unconfirmed reports" circulating in the American capital that Konoye had proposed a meeting with the president. Asked about it by the *New York Herald Tribune*, White

House spokesman Stephen Early had not merely denied the rumor, he had destroyed it. "The only plan the President has involving a trip on the water in the immediate future is a cruise from Annapolis on the Chesapeake Bay, and on the Potomac River," Early said. "If the *Herald Tribune* cares to follow the President to Annapolis, they will readily see the falsity of this story." If ever there was a destroyer waiting at Yokohama, it never took Konoye anywhere. Grew's hopes had been drowned by Hull's suspicions and, no doubt, his fears of being photographed with dictators who would then go on to break pledges.

In mid-October, Grew told his diary that four men had leaped onto the running board of Konoye's car as it left his residence and tried to stab him. The ambassador had found himself a gun shortly thereafter. "It would be a very simple thing for a few dagger-wielders to climb some part of our very extensive wall at night, and get into the embassy by breaking a window," Grew wrote in his diary on October 19. If they did, well, Joseph Clark Grew (Groton, '98) would exit this life with gun blazing. "I don't like heroics," he wrote, "but have no intention of letting a group of those roughnecks carve me up without a reasonable attempt at repartee."

The entry was written three days after Konoye had resigned. General Hideki Tojo of the Imperial Army had succeeded him. From then on, Grew was largely a bystander to tectonic events, ignorant of the ebb and flow in Washington between the Japanese envoys and his government. "Appeasement. Is that what the Department thinks I have been advocating?" he asked in his diary. "How completely the Department seems to misunderstand my situation."

The conservative voice of the American Midwest, the *Chicago Tribune*, took stock of the nation's industrial and military might on

Saturday, November 29, and then added, "The Administration is reported certain that Japan is aware of the odds against her and will finally elect to back down, rather than fight against such odds."

Americans, as a rule, did not credit the Japanese with having deep reservoirs of logic, as Americans defined it. Usually, they fell back on race-laden stereotypes. They reduced the entire nation to "the Jap." The Jap was a creature of the mysterious East, strange and implicitly inferior. He was inept, easily led, premodern, and uncreative. One article noted that Japan had never produced a Mozart, a Michelangelo, or a Shakespeare. Cartoonists drew the Jap as a "grinning, bowing, breath-sipping little man with horn-rimmed glasses, eager moustache and super buckteeth."

He didn't think normally, this Jap. "The Japanese mind works by intuition, apprehension, feeling, emotion, association of ideas, rather than by analysis based on logical deduction," Tolischus of the *Times* explained on September 7. "The Japanese thinks not with his head alone but with his whole being." The historian Barbara Tuchman, writing in 1936, declared the Japanese mental process was "devoid of what Westerners call logic." Colonel Kendall Fiedler, the army's intelligence officer on Oahu, considered Japanese reasoning unfathomable. "We just don't think the way they do. We can't solve their minds."

And yet there was equal conviction that in regard to one circumstance—one life-or-death circumstance—Japanese leaders, civilian and military, would reason as any American would, and that would be as they weighed national risk. They would gaze across the great Pacific and espy a gigantic, resource-rich, immensely powerful nation and recoil from armed conflict with it. They would all conclude, as Konoye apparently had, as Yamamoto had, that a war with the United States could not be won and should never be fought. Attacking it would be irrational, and Japan would see that.

"I believe that it was the consensus of the opinion of my associates and many of the high officials in Washington that it was very illogical and foolish on the part of Japan to undertake open warfare with the United States," Lieutenant Commander Alwin D. Kramer of Naval Intelligence said later. A director of Naval Intelligence, Admiral Theodore S. Wilkinson, thought the Japanese would saunter right up to the line of war with America to get what they wanted, but never step across. Senator Burton K. Wheeler, an isolationist Democrat from Montana, could not "conceive of Japan being crazy enough to want to go to war with us." Congressman Charles I. Faddis, a Democrat from Pennsylvania, had declared, "The Japanese are not going to risk a fight with a first-class nation. They are unprepared to do so, and no one knows this better than they do." The *Honolulu Star-Bulletin*'s editorial page assured nervous residents that no war was coming: "The reason is Japan is in no position to fight a war with a first-class power, and her leaders realize they will be committing suicide if they start one, or let one start." That was just common sense, and the Japanese possessed it. Only if the United States *chose* to go to war with Japan would there be war with Japan, only if America *elected* to step in to thwart Japanese aggression against other nations.

In 1939, however, a Commander J. L. Hall had offered disturbing clarity to students at the Naval War College in a lecture that suggested Japan would not rely on cold who-would-win assessments in deciding whether to begin a conflict. Hall told the students the story of a British journalist who had once heard some Westerners musing that while the Japanese were fierce and formidable when they were winning, what about when the situation was hopeless? What would they do then? The journalist, who had observed Japanese soldiers in action during the Russian war of 1904–5, enlightened the doubters. "The answer to the question is simple. They would all be dead. There would be no question how they would act in a losing game, for they would not lose and live."

It was with this mentality in mind that Ambassador Grew, now on the periphery of negotiations, wrote two messages in November. In the first, he had told his superiors, politely, not to count on Japan caving to embargoes or pressure. That would be "an uncertain and dangerous hypothesis," he said on November 3. If the empire does not get what it wants through negotiation, there could be "an all-out, do-or-die attempt—actually risking national hara-kiri—to make Japan impervious to economic embargoes abroad, rather than yield to foreign pressure." Perhaps Washington was anticipating such a self-destructive act. He did not know. "I am not in touch with the intentions and thoughts of the Administration," Grew said.

He was not advocating that Washington jettison its opposition to Japanese aggression and closed economic systems. Rather, "my purpose is only to ensure against the United States becoming involved in war with Japan because of any misconception of Japan's capacity to rush headlong into a suicidal struggle with the United States." They are not Americans. "Japanese sanity cannot be measured by American standards of logic." Do not assume their obvious war preparations or strident vows are mere theatrics. Japan might act "with dangerous and dramatic suddenness."

Two weeks later, on the evening of November 17, Grew repeated to Hull that there was "the need to guard against sudden Japanese naval or military actions," and added, "I take into account the probability of the Japanese exploiting every possible tactical advantage, such as surprise and initiative." From the American consuls in Manchuria and Formosa, he had learned that Japanese troops were massing, Grew said, suggesting possible incursions into the southwest Pacific or even Siberia, in order to stab the Russians from behind as they struggled with the Nazis on the Eastern Front. But he did not expect to ever hear of their specific military plans, he warned the State Department. All that he and his staff would be able to report was what they could see on the streets of Tokyo. Which was little. They had no expectation that Japanese friends would or could tip them off to military targets or timetables. Certainly the newspapers would not.

"Therefore, you are advised, from an abundance of caution," Grew concluded, "to discount as much as possible the likelihood of our ability to give substantial warning."

On Saturday, November 29, a spokesman for Prime Minister Hideki Tojo read a statement accusing Western countries of economically exploiting Asia, taking its resources and suppressing its peoples. "We must purge this sort of action with vengeance," he declared, so that a "chorus of victory might go up in the camp of justice as speedily as possible." In his diary, Grew called the threats, at such a time of tension, "utterly stupid." The Japanese still believe they can get what they want solely by blustering, he thought. "Once again I am impressed with the truth of a remark of a Japanese friend that when dogs are frightened, they bark, and the more they are frightened, the louder they bark."

In neither of his November dispatches to the State Department had Grew suggested that Oahu might be one of Japan's objectives if it reflexively, illogically began lashing out. The secret of Hitokappu Bay had not made its way to his ears, or anyone else's at the embassy, and it never would.

Word of Tojo's latest combustible phrases reached Franklin Roosevelt amid the pines of southwestern Georgia, where he had spent a good part of Saturday as millions of Americans had, listening to Navy beat Army, 14–6. Roosevelt and his party of forty-five—

counting reporters, but not the Secret Service detail—had arrived only that noon at the therapeutic resort of Warm Springs, after riding the Southern Railroad all night from Washington.

Though he had apparently not said so aloud, Secretary of War Stimson thought this was not a time to abandon the capital, but Roosevelt was a drained man, and had sought for days to flee. Now fifty-nine, he was in his ninth year in office, a mile marker no previous president had reached and no future one would. The last two of those years he had struggled as almost no president ever had, either, coping with the rise of swastikas over France and so many other nations; laboring without end to keep Britain alive and fighting; sending the navy so far into harm's way in the Atlantic Ocean that Americans were being killed; boosting weapons production to Himalayan levels; seeking a counter to Japan's aggression short of warring with it; fretting that Moscow would fall at any moment to German armored divisions; and, through all of that, convincing American voters in the campaign of 1940 that he deserved a third term. After seeing the president on Thursday, Ambassador Nomura had told Tokyo, "He looked very tired." Grace Tully, his secretary, would note in her memoirs that in those late November days, the White House physician, Ross T. McIntire, "was very anxious that [Roosevelt] should get away for a spell of rest and sunshine."

"The President arrived here under a cobalt blue sky," one newspaper reported with a Warm Springs dateline, "and he shelved his problems momentarily to enjoy himself and bring happiness to those at this health colony."

As Roosevelt basked in the tranquility, the Saturday papers in New York and Washington offered alarming page-one stories suggesting war with Japan was close, "closer than at any previous time," the *Times* said. This ominous outlook had been "authoritatively stated," though by whom the paper did not say. The *Washington Post* cited "a source of unquestioned authority," but nameless. In reality, the papers had spoken with the same source at the same time on Friday, not long before the source had gotten into a car at the White House for the short drive to Union Station and the train to Georgia.

"I think I could tell you for background—but only for background—that the situation seems serious," Roosevelt told the print and wire-service reporters who had crowded into his office shortly before eleven that morning. There would be peace if the empire endorsed nonaggression, its economic life would rebound, and it could have all the raw materials it needed. Instead, the president had said, it was engaged in a pattern far too Nazi-like, talking peace but taking land, as it had recently done again in Indochina. "I think a study of the map would be advisable for all of us," he had gone on, "because the Hitler method has always been aimed at a little move here and a little move there." Having seized Indochina to the west, Japan now had the Philippines bracketed, with troops also to the north of it in China and to the east in its mandate islands. But the entire Pacific seemed in jeopardy. "I don't think that any more can be said at this time," he had told the reporters. "We are . . . we are waiting."

He had one more meeting to chair before departing. Shortly after the journalists were shooed out, Roosevelt gathered with his bloc of defense strategists—Stark, Marshall, Knox, Stimson, and Hull—and for ninety minutes, the two military officers and the four civilians tried to divine where, exactly, Japanese expeditionary forces in the Far East might be bound.

In the days, months, and years ahead, a fantastical notion would find root in dark corners: that Franklin Roosevelt had hoped the Japanese would attack some place or thing American, and that he had even known where they would do so and let them, eager to rally a skeptical nation to the barricades against totalitarianism. If such word ever reached him, of course, it first would have had to pass through the hands of many others, from enlisted men in radio rooms to admirals and generals, all of whom would then have had to wink at avoidable death and destruction, and many of them would then have had to lie about it publicly and go to their graves with sealed lips. If Roosevelt did want America in the war, it already was, nakedly assisting Great Britain and Russia beyond any notion of neutrality, to the point of firing on German ships. If he did know where Japan's blows were going to fall, then the man who loved the navy would have been treasonously and fatally betraying it.

In reality, war in the Pacific, if it happened now, would be too soon for either the American army or the navy. Neither had sufficient forces to fight Japan, not yet. Both services had told the president so—twice in November alone. The Pacific Fleet is "inferior" to the Imperial Navy, Marshall and Stark wrote on November 5, and would not reach fighting strength until at least February 1942. The army chief of staff and the chief of naval operations had reiterated their plea to avoid war with Japan only two days earlier, on November 27: "The most essential thing now, from the United States viewpoint, is to gain time," they had told Roosevelt.

But far more than forcing the country to fight when it wasn't ready, a scheme to get into a war in the Pacific could hardly have been more at cross-purposes with Roosevelt's paramount goal: to help the British survive. "As you know," he had written in July to Harold Ickes, the secretary of the interior, "it is terribly important for the control of the Atlantic for us to keep the peace in the Pacific. I simply have not got enough Navy to go around, and every little episode in the Pacific means fewer ships in the Atlantic."

War in the Pacific would not only force the navy to strip ships from the Atlantic and raise the risks to crucial convoys of materials but also probably sever Britain's other essential lines of supply, those to the Far East. "Dear Joe," Roosevelt replied in January to Grew's

"Dear Frank" letter of the previous December. So far, the president wrote, the English had avoided Nazi conquest "because as the heart and the nerve center of the British Empire, they have been able to draw upon vast resources for their sustenance." Those resources would be far, far less vast if Japanese armies invaded and occupied Malaya, Singapore, Burma, and India.

But at the White House on Friday before the president's departure for Georgia, the six men had agreed that the clock was going to run out, no matter how much they wished otherwise. Japan almost certainly was going to land forces somewhere in the southwest Pacific. "It was the consensus of everybody that this must not be allowed," Stimson wrote. The country would have to go to war, a sad but unavoidable choice. Indeed, when people said war was getting closer, or felt that it was, they usually meant it in that sense, that America was approaching the point at which it would have to enter the conflict, not that the conflict would be inflicted upon America.

By late 1941, with the war in Europe now in its third year, Americans were not as isolationist as they once had been. In particular, "the press is prepared, and striving to prepare the public, for American shooting in the Far East," according to a November memo sent to Henry G. Morgenthau Jr., the secretary of the treasury. Its writer had added that "every sign that there will be no yielding on [the American] side is warmly welcomed." Sixty-nine percent of the country believed that the United States should "take steps now to keep Japan from becoming more powerful, even if this means risking a war with Japan." The number of those wishing to resist to the "last ditch" the idea of joining such a conflict had dropped by a quarter. Roosevelt's entire cabinet, polled by the president himself on November 7, unanimously declared that the country would back him "in case we struck Japan down there," in the Far East. The cabinet seemed to reflect American opinion. Nomura had told Tokyo on August 16 that the country was not yet united about going to war in Europe, but "the people are unanimous with regard to taking a strong hand in the Far East."

Roosevelt had first immersed his crippled legs in the pools of Warm Springs in 1924. There, some seventy-five miles from Atlanta, about a thousand feet above sea level, water that was heated naturally to ninety degrees welled to the surface at a steady clip of eight hundred gallons a minute. "This is really a discovery of a place, and there is no doubt I've got to do some more of it," Roosevelt had written his wife, Eleanor. Eventually, he had purchased 1,200 acres, complete with cottages and a hotel, and thus the Georgia Warm Springs Foundation took life. After he became president in 1933, one of the cottages was dubbed the Little White House, a rustic, single-story affair with a fireplace, and it was probably there that the president listened to the broadcast of the Army-Navy game from Philadelphia on that Saturday.

The game, coupled with the times and his location, evidently put the president in a wistful mood that evening. It was a Roosevelt tradition to spend Thanksgiving with friends and staff at Warm Springs, but he had not been able to get away in time for the official holiday, on the twenty-seventh. That merely meant a slight delay in the festivities. The foundation's dieticians clocked the Saturday menu at 4,300 calories, starting with popcorn, olives, and nuts; moving through turkey, oyster stuffing, whipped potatoes, and mashed turnips; and ending with apple pie, mince pie, pumpkin pie, fruitcake, macaroons, and ice cream. The president carved the bird.

He had prepared no remarks. But he spoke. In the world at that moment, he told the dinner guests, the United States was that rare large nation that was neither at war nor enduring occupation by others—"completely blotted out," as he put it. Its people remained free to pursue their work, as the foundation was, and free to play their football games, as Army and Navy had that day, and Georgia and Georgia Tech. He had listened to that game, too. He urged thankfulness for the peace that America had enjoyed since 1918, "but also think a little bit about other people, people in countries which have been overrun, people in countries that have been attacked, and, yes, people in those countries which are doing the attacking."

"It is always possible that our Thanksgiving [here] next year may remind us of a peaceful past," he went on. "It may be that next Thanksgiving these boys of the Military Academy and the Naval Academy will be actually fighting for the defense of these American institutions of ours." Great dangers "have been overhanging the future of this country."

After the president returned to the Little White House that evening, its phone rang. Hull told him of Tojo's vow to cleanse the Far East of Westerners and to do it with a vengeance. "Mr. Hull was deeply worried and felt that anything might happen," Grace Tully wrote. "He advised the President's return."

The next day, having spent a shade more than twenty-four hours resting at Warm Springs, Roosevelt and his entourage made the forty-three mile automobile trip to the nearest rail line, at Newnan, Georgia, to return to the capital. Driving through the villages of the backcountry, the president seemed to be less than his outgoing self, a reporter thought. There appeared to be no doubt, the journalist wrote, "that the showdown had come."

As he had waved good-bye to the staff and the 105 patients of the foundation, Roosevelt said, "This may be the last time I talk to you for a long time."

He would not see them again until April 1943.

Sometime that same Saturday, waiting out the wait, Admiral Matome Ugaki, Yamamoto's chief of staff, peered at a weather map of the Pacific Ocean aboard a warship in the Inland Sea. Somewhere out there was the strike fleet, dipping and rising with the swells, a muzzled ghost slipping east through thousands of miles of vacantness. In a diary entry a few days earlier, Ugaki had marveled, "The Pacific is so wide!" On Saturday, the admiral stared at the weather map and found himself "wondering how they are doing," those thirty ships going so far at such risk.

EIGHT

THEIR MAIL, OPENED
AND READ

Sunday, November 30

THE EDIFICE COLLOQUIALLY crowned Main Navy was a four-story, zeppelin-size mistake for which Franklin Roosevelt had pleaded guilty to a count of bad taste. In 1918, as assistant secretary, he had sanctioned the construction of a meant-to-be-temporary head-quarters on the National Mall, near the Lincoln Memorial and along Constitution Avenue. Temporary had now reached twenty-three years. Immediately adjacent—linked by an enclosed skyway—was the other half of Roosevelt's interim arrangement, the equally huge and graceless Munitions Building, the headquarters of the army.

The two leaky, creaky, un-air-conditioned warrens, stocked with admirals and generals, commanders and colonels, covered so much real estate that going from Harold Stark's office to George Marshall's was the equivalent of a four-block stroll. The twin military head-quarters blighted the Mall's west end thoroughly. "It was a crime,"

Roosevelt said at a press conference in August. "I don't hesitate to say so. It was a crime for which I should be kept out of heaven, for having desecrated the whole plan of, I think, the loveliest city in the world." Something better, or at least something not as poorly situated, had begun rising in September on the far side of the Potomac River, in Arlington, Virginia, a five-sided building whose shape would become its name.

On the first deck of Main Navy—the sea service did not call a floor a floor—was room 1649, and within its walls was a wooden box whose size, shape, and numerous input jacks gave it the look of a latter-day stereo receiver. Two like it resided across the way in the Munitions Building. When fed Japanese radiograms plucked from the heavens as they streaked back and forth between Tokyo and its diplomatic outposts, the boxes scrubbed away the supposedly impenetrable encryption shielding the text and spat out Japanese, ready to be translated, as great a testament to Yankee ingenuity as there ever was.

As Roosevelt's train chugged him and his party back to the capital on Sunday, which would be the last Sunday of peace the country would know for nearly four years, linguists were rendering into English a text that the navy machine had decrypted only hours before. Someone at the Foreign Office in Tokyo, it seemed, was writing to the embassy in Washington "re my #844," transmitted two days earlier. Fortunately, an army machine had already decrypted number 844.

"Well, you two ambassadors have exerted superhuman efforts," the earlier dispatch had begun, addressing Kichisaburo Nomura and Saburo Kurusu, "but in spite of this, the United States has gone ahead and presented this humiliating proposal." It was a reference to Cordell Hull's Ten Points framework for an agreement. "This was quite unexpected and extremely regrettable." The writer of number

844 had then told the embassy that a formal reply to Hull would come in a few days and when it did, the talks would end. But for now, play the Americans. String things along. Act saddened by their Ten Points. Emphasize Japan's "long-suffering and conciliatory attitude."

In the follow-up message—number 857—now being translated on Sunday, the Americans could see that Tokyo was giving specific stalling points to use with the State Department while Japan prepared its detailed, official answer. Tell them that the Hull proposal, if accepted, "would greatly injure the prestige of the Imperial Government," and therefore "we would request careful self-reflection on the part of the United States government." It added, "Please be careful that this does not lead to anything like a breaking off of negotiations."

This sudden desire to elongate the talks baffled Kurusu and Nomura. Whereas Tokyo's orders had once oozed urgency—here are the deadlines, time is dwindling, get them to agree before it's too late—"now you want them to stretch out," Kurusu complained in a reply on Sunday evening. But of course, neither he nor Nomura knew of a strike fleet, or knew that it still needed days to reach the point in the sea from which it could launch its planes and commence a war.

Such intercepts made Washington an omniscient capital, or so it would seem, incapable of being tricked by Japan, or shocked by its proposals, or surprised by its navy. They were Tokyo raw and unfiltered, the Foreign Office without the posturing. "I looked on them as I would a witness who is giving evidence against his own side of the case," Hull said. One high-ranking general called the intercepts "a priceless asset." According to lore, it was Admiral Walter S. Anderson, the director of Naval Intelligence at the time, who knighted the intercepts "Magic." The name stuck.

The art of enshrouding confidential messages in codes and ciphers had long ago—centuries ago—left behind simple schemes of substitution, like switching every *a* to *p*, or *c* to *l*. (The Japanese did, in fact, use Roman letters for their most sensitive diplomatic dispatches. Their own language, rooted in hundreds of characters, did not lend itself easily to coded radio messages.) The Japanese Foreign Office had developed a machine whose step-switches, electronic threading, and daily settings could so thoroughly muddle a text that if the original had an *m*, for example, the random substitution might be *a*—the first time. When the sender typed a second *m* from the original text, the machine might substitute *b*; a third *m*, and the result might be *r*. In a single encrypted message, *m* could have twenty-six meanings, including just being *m*. At the other end of the transmission, recipients typed the gibberish into their machine, which unscrambled the scramble, as long as its settings had been adjusted to the key, which changed every day.

Without having pilfered a machine from the Japanese, or having obtained stolen blueprints or photos, a genius band of army civilians had conjured up America's own version of one, exploiting Japanese flaws and encryption tendencies, and staring and thinking and experimenting for eighteen months. Cryptanalysts also figured out how the Japanese chose the daily key for the settings. For more than a year, it had been as if the Americans were on the Foreign Office's interoffice routing list, except, of course, the Foreign Office did not know it. The Americans dubbed their device Purple, because they had solved an earlier Japanese system by making a machine they called Red.

Usually twice a day, morning and afternoon, military couriers scurried to select government offices, and there unlocked zipped leather pouches and handed over Magic dispatches. Roosevelt and his men knew, for example, that the empire would "take measures to secure raw materials of the South Seas" (Tokyo to Washington, July 31). They knew that it was not going to compromise, because they read that it had "now reached a point where no further positive action can be taken by us except to urge the United States to reconsider her views" (Tokyo to Washington, October 21). They knew the Foreign Office was giving pep talks to itself: "Nay, when it comes to a question of our existence and our honor, when the time comes we will defend them without reckoning the cost" (Tokyo to Washington, November 4).

Washington was well aware, too, that Nomura and Kurusu had been given an "absolutely unmovable" deadline of November 25 for reaching an agreement; that the deadline had then been shoved back to November 29, after which "things are automatically going to happen"; that the embassy now had "the order and method of destroying code machines in the event of an emergency"; that Nomura had tried to quit and been told he could not.

The cryptographic coup gave the United States such a miraculous edge that not only had the news been kept out of the papers but Congress also had not been told, nor had ambassadors abroad (Grew, in Tokyo, did not know), nor had the typical admiral or general in the field, such as Husband Kimmel or Walter Short. Thousands of people worked for the government, but the intercepts went to the offices of only ten: the directors of army and navy war planning; the directors of army and navy intelligence; the secretaries of state, war, and the navy; the chief of naval operations; the army chief of staff; and the president. Anyone who knew of the existence of the machines "had to sign a paper never to disclose it, practically so long as he lived, or ever to talk about it," Harold Stark said. Keeping the material in one's office was strongly discouraged. Handing it back soon was advised. One of the couriers, Colonel Rufus S. Bratton, the chief of the Far Eastern Section of Army Intelligence, "collected all of these pouches on my next visit, or my next round, the following day, and destroyed the contents of them by burning."

Two of Stark's aides, Charles Wellborn and William Smedberg, used to watch Admiral Anderson from Naval Intelligence walk past their desks and into their boss's sanctum "with a folder under his coat," Smedberg said, "so that Wellborn and I wouldn't know that he was carrying in some 'Magic.' We weren't ever supposed—according to him—to even know there was such a thing in the Navy, because the fewer the people who knew about it the better." The two aides clearly did know, though, among others. George Marshall feared that one or two people working with the intercepts, such as one of the civilians hired to translate them after they had been decrypted, might engage in "subversive action"; namely, telling the Japanese that their system had been breached. Admiral Leigh Noyes, the director of Naval Communications, which did the actual intercepting and de- crypting along with the Army Signal Intelligence Service, stressed to his eavesdroppers "the extreme importance of allowing no inkling to reach the Japanese that we could read their messages. That would have ruined everything."

On May 3, Japan's ambassador to Berlin gave his superiors in Tokyo a tip from the Germans. The Americans were "reading Am- bassador Nomura's code messages," he told the Foreign Office, a dispatch the Americans had perused in real time, terrified the Japa- nese would now change everything, would chuck the machines and design new ones. But Nomura assured Tokyo that "the most stringent precautions are taken by all custodians of codes and ciphers, as well as of other documents." Of course, the Americans had gotten noth- ing from Nomura's custodians, nor had code or cipher pages floated out of embassy windows and onto Massachusetts Avenue, there to be picked up by a passing expert. Instead, the Americans had created Purple. But deliberately or inadvertently, a hint that they were reading Japanese diplomatic correspondence had reached the Germans. "Especially in view of the recent leak, every step possible should be taken to prevent a recurrence," Lieutenant Commander Alwin Kramer wrote in a staff memo on May 17. Kramer, who worked with the intercepts in Naval Communications, noted that "SecNav, CNO, etc., feel it would be 'calamitous' if this source folded up," right in the midst of sensitive talks with the Japanese and with the "probable" entry of the United States into the war.

The secret held, and in time couriers were delivering folders with an average of a dozen copped Magic conversations a day. Being some of the busiest people in Washington, but not allowed to hold on to the decryptions for perusal at their leisure, the recipients could not possibly read every page. To avoid inflating the folders with duplication, the army handled the messages the Japanese sent on even dates, the navy odd. The services concentrated on exchanges between Tokyo and two embassies, Washington and Berlin, culling out traffic that "dealt with administrative or personal matters at the embassy, or dealt with requests and requisitions for stationery or this, that or the other thing," the army's Bratton said. To further help the recipients get through it all, the navy's Kramer might put an asterisk in the upper-left corner of a message to denote "an item of interest." Two asterisks announced "items of the highest interest or immediate urgency." On the copies the army provided, Bratton might put red checkmarks beside the more tantalizing messages.

Even with all the steps taken to make consumption easier, Magic's recipients could not devote equal time and thought to every message. "It was entirely too voluminous for me," Marshall said. Like Stark, Marshall was overseeing an exponential expansion of his forces, and was buried in meetings, trips, and tasks. Some of the intercepts ran to four, five, fifteen pages. He could have kept up only if he had retired from the army, he said, "and read every day." And unable to retrieve previous messages from his files, spread them on a desk, and review the totality, a Stark or a Marshall had trouble catching subtle trends and shifts in tone. Each day, the recipients saw "only a single frame, so to speak, in a long motion picture film," a civilian army code breaker would complain.

Not only that, the material spewing from the Purple machines was merely the talk of Japan's diplomats, not its generals or admirals, and it was only a fraction of the diplomats' talk at that. The Foreign Office could send dispatches in any of four main encrypted systems. The Imperial Army had its own encrypted pathways. Among its many, the Imperial Navy had one code for communicating with Japanese merchant ships, one for naval administrative issues, one for flag officers, one for naval attachés, and a general fleet code, which was the most important and which in November alone carried hundreds of messages. The Americans could read some of these Japanese systems, but not the naval flag officer's code or the fleet code, known as JN-25B.

One day, Captain Arthur H. McCollum, chief of the Far Eastern Section of the Office of Naval Intelligence, tried to convince his then boss, Admiral Anderson, to stop viewing the Foreign Office decryptions as a thoroughly revealing look at what Japan was up to. "I said, 'It's not magic. This is just the blathering of some Japanese diplomats that we're getting.' He said, 'Oh, no. We're reading the mail.'" McCollum had persisted, asking Anderson, "How authentic is the mail? How much does it represent of what these little people are going to do?" The reply: "Oh, Mac. We're reading the mail."

McCollum's concern was that whatever encrypted traffic was passing between the Foreign Office and its embassies "did not necessarily reflect the opinion of the Army General Staff, which was very powerful, or the Navy General Staff, and at that time we were reading almost no Navy codes at all. I kept stressing that instead of trying to decode and translate all this mass of diplomatic stuff, we ought to be spending more time seeing if we couldn't somehow or other decode Japanese Navy traffic." But there were not enough qualified and vetted people to do all of that—and thousands of intercepted messages in multiple codes were flooding into Washington.

Even after the Americans read the Foreign Office's thoughts, they did not always understand them. When Tokyo told Nomura a deal had to be reached by November 29 or "things are automatically going to happen," neither that message nor any subsequent one de-lineated what those things were. Captain Roscoe E. Schuirmann, one of Stark's staff officers, would recall everybody wondering "what in the world this phrase meant, as to *what* things were going to happen automatically." Perhaps Japan would break off the talks. Or sever diplomatic relations. Or start attacking the British and the Dutch in the southwest Pacific, but not the Americans. Or attack the British, the Dutch, *and* the Philippines. Was November 29 the day that Jap-anese armies and naval vessels would arrive at their attack points, or the day they would start leaving Japan? "Undoubtedly, it [was] intended to mean that a course of action or policy by the Japanese— already decided upon—was intended to be carried out," the navy's Kramer said. "Just what that consisted of is a matter of interpretation or guessing."

It was now Sunday, November 30. The deadline had come and gone. Nobody had been attacked. Diplomatic ties held.

On November 26 and November 28, the navy had decrypted two messages from the Foreign Office to multiple outposts reflecting its concern that its communication links to them might be disrupted as the crisis deepened. If that happened, one of the messages had said, the embassy in Washington should tune to the regular commercial broadcasts from Tokyo and listen for certain phrases. "In case of a [*sic*] Japan-U.S. relations in danger," the phrase would be "east wind rain," it had been told. In the case of Great Britain, "west wind clear," and the Soviet Union, "north wind cloudy." "When this is heard, please destroy all code papers, etc.," the Foreign Office had said.

Here again, Magic had offered up something tantalizing but incomplete. The messages seemed to define "danger" only as an end to diplomatic relations with any country cited in a broadcast weather phrase. But on the assumption that Japan might follow such a rupture by attacking said country, the War and Navy Departments had begun a frenetic quest—still ongoing on Sunday—to hear the "winds" cues, even though Tokyo's usual communication links to its field posts obviously had not been disrupted, and there was obviously no need yet for Tokyo to switch to its backup system based on commercial broadcasts. It proved to be a pointless search for a grail that, even if it had been heard, would have told the Americans little more than what they already knew—that times were tense, relations in jeopardy, war might happen.

The diplomatic intercepts had an understandable, magnetic allure. But they created a dangerous loop of reasoning. Because the Japanese had not distributed the cipher machines to all of their embassies, only to the ones in major world capitals, and because they had been so difficult to replicate, the machines must be processing the most important traffic, the most-insider material. Reading the Foreign Office's conversations "created a sense of infallibility in Washington," an intelligence officer would say after the war, "as if we possessed a magic wand with which to divine Japanese intentions."

As a tool of counterdiplomacy, Magic was unquestionably gold. Unlike Grew in Tokyo, Hull knew the empire's bargaining ploys, heightening his wariness as he sat and listened to Nomura and Kurusu whenever they called on him at the State Department. Based on the Magic he had, for example, Hull considered Konoye's proposed summit with Roosevelt "pure blind." "They have already made up their minds to a policy of going south through Indochina and Thailand," he had told Secretary of War Stimson at the time.

Even if every privileged reader of the intercepts could not digest and compare them all, they still collectively gave the Americans a glimpse of a Japan growing more desperate and impatient. An attack in the southwest Pacific was hugely probable. But the intercepts never spelled out who might be struck, how, or when. Those scanning the diplomatic messages never saw a reference to attacks on American possessions. Not the Philippines, not Wake or Midway or the Panama Canal. Not Hawaii. Nor did they ever encounter a reference to a strike fleet coalescing in some place called Hitokappu Bay.

To get to the distant building that housed the eyes of the Pacific Fleet—its ears, rather—a visitor from Pearl first navigated the increasingly clogged streets of Honolulu, after which the Nuuanu Pali Road rose toward the spires of the Koolau Range, the air turning cooler, the plant scape lusher, the curves becoming more common. The road crested more than a thousand feet up, and then down the traveler plunged toward Kaneohe Bay on the windward side of Oahu, the northeast side, eventually to arrive at a copse of Sequoia-size radio towers planted by the sea.

The navy outpost—sheds, a barracks for the grunts, a couple of houses for the bosses, an old stone structure where they all worked—took its name from the little town nearby, Heeia. Wearing headsets and spinning the dials of radio receivers through as many as thirty frequencies, the grunts sat for hours in a high-ceilinged room, straining to overhear the tap-tap-tapping of the Imperial Navy's Morse on the far side of the Pacific Ocean, roughly nineteen messages going ship to shore or shore to ship every hour, roughly five hundred a day. The pulsing dots and dashes did not equate to the letters of the Roman alphabet, but to the syllables of spoken Japanese, rendered into a system compatible with radio. The navy had a program to teach this alien Morse to its radio operators, and it was housed atop Main Navy. Its graduates, therefore, had become known as "roofers."

With no teletype link back to Pearl—there was supposed to have been one by then—the typewritten pages containing the Heeia intercepts were gathered up and driven the twenty-one miles over the mountains not to fleet headquarters but to the Fourteenth Naval District, which was housed at the naval base in a building shaped like a fallen croquet wicket. Naval districts mostly took care of shore-based issues, such as operating dry docks, but the Fourteenth's headquarters also had a very off-limits basement. A deliveryman arriving from Heeia would walk to a door on the east patio and descend a staircase to a room a hundred feet long and fifty wide, where most of the forty or so inhabitants used tobacco-based products, and where there were no windows and dubious ventilation. Naturally, this sunless cell came to be called the Dungeon. Officially, it was the Combat Intelligence Unit, Commander Joseph John Rochefort presiding.

Rochefort, who added to the pollution by smoking a pipe, was forty-one and a "mustang," an enlistee during the Great War who had hauled himself into the ranks of officers without the benefit of a diploma from the Naval Academy. He claimed that his only regret about not having one was that he had not been "brainwashed" about the "things that you just don't do, that you don't get away with," which, of course, meant he had no regrets at all. "I didn't have that [background], so I [was] more inclined to speak up when I should have kept my mouth shut." A fellow denizen of the Dungeon, Lieutenant Wilfred J. Holmes, would remember Rochefort's "habit of caustic speech," although he did take the edge off his words with "a conciliatory smile." Another colleague said that if the commander's patience "was worn thin by a fool or an ignorant ass, then he wouldn't have any more to do with him, see? 'Can't deal with you. Can't treat with you.' He didn't suffer fools lightly, let us say that."

Fact was, Rochefort had compensating gifts. Relentlessly curious, he combined two very rare skills: he was a cryptanalyst who spoke Japanese. His parents had hoped for the priesthood after his birth in Dayton, Ohio, and he had once envisioned himself strapped in a navy cockpit, patrolling the blue yonder. But a navy superior had steered him toward the work of sleuths—toward codes and ciphers—which turned out to suit him. "It makes you feel pretty good, as a matter of fact," he said, "because you have defied these people who have attempted to use a system they thought was secure. That is, it was unreadable. It was always somewhat of a pleasure to defeat them or challenge them." He also liked the fraternity of people who broke codes. "Being a little bit nuts helps," he said. "A cryptanalyst, from those that I have observed, is usually an odd character." He did not think of himself as all that strange, though. "I like to consider myself as the exception. Maybe I'm not."

A second navy cryptanalyst who worked with him, Thomas H. Dyer, thought there were probably better pure code breakers than Rochefort, but he excelled at taking fragmentary clues and deducing the gist of the whole. "He was inspired," Dyer said. "There's no other word for it." Another Dungeon occupant, Forrest R. Biard, thought Rochefort "was intuitive, quick, sharp-thinking, [and] blessed with almost total recall."

Rochefort had learned Japanese at the source, during a three-year tour, and hadn't found it difficult to memorize hundreds of symbols. "He can translate with freedom and precision articles of the most difficult character on technical, military, political and social subjects," according to his 1932 evaluation, written by the American naval attaché in Tokyo. While in Japan, he had been expected "to pick up the mores of the people themselves," Rochefort said. "How the Japanese lived. How would they react. What did they do. And so on and so forth." By the time he took over the Dungeon, he thought of himself as "perhaps fairly well fitted to render judgment on what the Japanese intended," due to his language expertise, his experiences in Japan, and his numerous postings aboard American surface ships, which gave him a feel for how navies thought and operated.

His boys at the Combat Intelligence Unit could actually read the text of only 10 percent of the material captured and sent by Heeia. The rest was wrapped in naval codes not yet broken. But even a sealed envelope offers clues to what lies inside, written on its exterior: the addresses to and from. Similarly, warships and shore stations required call signs to identify the sender and the intended recipient of an encrypted message. The Japanese routinely changed their radio addresses every six months, but the Americans could usually figure out many of the new ones. By studying these "externals"—along with the volume of traffic—it was possible to discern command relationships, coming movements, even the identity of individual ships, all without actually reading the text of the messages themselves.

If this guy repeatedly sends to those guys, he could be their leader, the "mother" of those "chicks." If this ship is always radioed at the same time as those five ships, they could be members of the same unit. If those units are always spoken to at the same time as this unit is, perhaps they all belong to the same larger force. For example, a spike in messages between a commander and a group of fifteen ships, all of which are known to be submarines, might suggest that the submarines are about to execute a collective order. A commander who suddenly goes silent, but who is still being sent messages from shore, is quite often a commander who has gone to sea, and if he's at sea, so are his ships.

When paired with the fruits of direction finders, which pinpointed the geographic origin of a signal, the analysis of radio traffic provided some wisdom about where the Imperial Navy was and what it might have been doing. It was sophisticated guessing. It was like being allowed to see a handful of Monet's brush dabs on an otherwise blank canvas, and trying to imagine what he would wind up painting. Moreover, listeners could intercept only what the atmospheric conditions allowed them to intercept, so many messages were never heard. The assistant chief of naval operations, Ingersoll, would recall that "there were very long periods of time, and at various times, when we never knew where the Japanese Fleet was. They might go to their mandated islands, and they might just as well have been on the moon, as far as we knew where they were." One intelligence officer felt that while the accuracy of radio-traffic analysis was good, "it certainly is an inexact science." It could not be trusted blindly.

The Imperial Navy fully understood that the Americans were engaged in traffic analysis. It was, too, which made it savvy about the counterploys, above all simple silence. A ship or fleet that does not use its radios has no traffic to analyze. It could be sitting in port. It could be at sea. Moreover, a Japanese radio operator might use a certain call sign, but he could be lying. He could be pretending to be the ship or the fleet, when the real ship or fleet was elsewhere, sailing mute. The Japanese could also broadcast messages that had no addresses, neither for the senders nor the receivers. Those details would exist only in the encrypted text, which the Americans could not read.

But unlike the Magic intercepts—which the Dungeon did not know about, much less get—traffic analysis yielded actual military information. Rochefort endorsed it heartily. "With all modesty," he said, his boys were "the best communications intelligence organization that the world has ever seen," capable of making "a very, very good estimate of what the intentions will be of the enemy."

By early November, he was sure that "there was something afoot."

The Japanese navy, which was organized into fleets—First, Second, and so on, with Isoroku Yamamoto as commander of the whole, the Combined Fleet—was rearranging itself in a way that bore a strong resemblance to the volume and types of radio traffic that had preceded Japan's move into Indochina in July.

Having begun twenty-four hour staffing in August, the Dungeon was sending a report to fleet headquarters each day, recapping the previous day's radio revelations. On September 10, Rochefort's report noted that the Imperial Navy was practicing "secret communication methods and increased security." By September 28, he had the impression that "preparations are increasing for either maneuvers on a large scale or possibly a hostile operation of some kind." Radio traffic clearly indicated "deviation from the normal routine."

On October 31, the Japanese changed all their call signs, on schedule. As it began to identify the new ones, the Combat Intelligence Unit reported on November 3 that the number of messages emanating from Tokyo "is unprecedented and the import is not understood." Further, it had come across a reference to something called *itikoukuu kantai*. "The literal reading of this as 'First Air Fleet' is correct: it indicates an entirely new organization of the Naval Air Forces," the Dungeon had written. A First Air Fleet would probably involve the Imperial Navy's aircraft carriers, but Rochefort's roofers never heard mention of it again, and never did figure out why the Japanese would create such a thing, or which planes or ships were part of it. The US Navy, after all, had no such animal. The most lethal components of Japan's new air fleet were, of course, now sailing east.

By November 26, Rochefort had concluded that "a strong force may be preparing to operate in Southeastern Asia," and another one, composed of submarines and at least one aircraft carrier, was "in the vicinity of the Marshall Islands." The navy listeners also had heard the call signs of the carrier *Akagi* and the battleship *Hiei*. These were lies, or at least mistakes. Both ships were with the strike fleet, saying nothing.

Then, at 4:30 a.m. Hawaiian time, on Sunday, November 30, the Imperial Navy did something it had never done, something "rather extraordinary," one American officer felt. US Navy listeners in the Philippines realized they could not identify any Japanese ships and units. Five months too soon, they had again changed the call signs of ships afloat, wiping clean the American roster of identifications that had been compiled with patience since the last change, on October 31. They would have to start at zero.

Whatever the Japanese were planning to do, they were going to do it soon. And they were doing everything possible to befog the Americans as they did it.

NINE

THE TALENTS OF NIPPON

Monday, December 1

THE SCENE WAS "highly dramatic," Kichisaburo Nomura told Tokyo. Yammering reporters and curious staffers of the State Department lined the halls as he walked to his ten o'clock with Cordell Hull on a sunless but warm-for-December morn. The spectators seemed convinced that a moment of great significance had come, that the ambassador would deliver Japan's answer to Hull's Ten Points of November 26 and the world would know, at last, whether it was to be peace or war between Japan and the United States. The *Chicago Tribune* resorted to one of its quirky implied-subject headlines on the front page:

EXPECT JAP ANSWER TODAY

Nomura had come only to procrastinate, of course, as instructed, and as Hull already knew from Magic. The secretary of state wore a "deeply pained expression," Nomura thought, and swiftly brought

up Prime Minister Tojo's newest bombast, the promise to rid the Far
East of white overlords. Even Nomura worried that the speech had
verged on a declaration of war. He wished, although he did not say so
to Hull, that Tokyo would think a little deeper before it spoke with
such belligerence, if for no other reason than to "be in a position to
show all neutrals and outsiders the complete innocence on our part."

Saburo Kurusu, who had come with him, urged Hull to give Tojo's
speech no credence. After all, it was only "a ten-minute broadcast."
No doubt Japan's news agency had badly rendered it into English,
Kurusu said. An official translation would be delivered as soon as
the embassy had one. With that, the conversation descended into the
polite regurgitation of experienced actors. American sanctions, the
Japanese diplomats said, left their homeland no choice but to "expand to obtain raw materials." Hull lamented Japan's "bluster and
blood-curdling threats," and its "aiding [of] Hitler" by threatening
British lifelines to its Pacific possessions. "One of these days, we
may reach a point where we cannot keep on as we are," he said. The
United States could "not sit still" if the empire marched on. Without saying there would be war, Hull was saying there would be. His
country would use force to stop Japan.

The two Japanese had arrived at the State Department "seemingly
happier than for some days," a newspaper noted, though there was no
obvious reason they would be happy at all. They "departed grimly,"
with Nomura telling reporters "there must be wise statesmanship
to save the situation." Returning to their embassy, he pleaded with
Tokyo by dispatch to repropose a leaders' gathering, maybe in Honolulu, and if not between Tojo and Roosevelt, then between big-
name seconds. True, the Americans had never warmed to that idea.
"We feel, however, that to surmount the crisis with which we are face
to face, it is not wasting our efforts to pursue every path open to us,"
his message read. If Tokyo itself could not request such a high-level

conference because of "some internal condition"—presumably, op-position from extremists—"then how would it be if I were to bring up the subject as purely of my own origin, and in that manner feel out their attitude?"

Anything.

Nomura would try anything to avert what was coming, even if he did not know exactly what that was.

Perhaps on Monday, somewhere over the Pacific, his radiogram flew past two coming from Tokyo. In the first, the Foreign Office advised Nomura to check with the embassy's naval attaché when the time came to get rid of codebooks. The officer already had the chemicals to help with that. The second informed Nomura that cryptographic destruction was beginning elsewhere: "The four offices in London, Hong Kong, Singapore and Manila have been instructed to abandon the use of the code machines and dispose of them." The code machine at Batavia—today's Jakarta, Indonesia—"has been returned to Japan." Three of the cited places were British. One was Dutch. One was American.

But for now, Nomura was not to destroy anything in Washington. The Foreign Office told him to keep his machines and codes intact.

The finest Japan hand in the US Navy was overly brusque and pushy. Arthur McCollum had a quick mind, a rapid manner of speech, and "the keenness, as well as nervousness, of a terrier." He wore rimless spectacles. He wrote with unusual clarity. In the year of his graduation, 1921, his photo in the Naval Academy yearbook captured a triangular face with a sharp chin and narrow eyes. "He has the manners, politics and smooth line of the world-famous Southern Gen-

tleman," his classmates had written, adding as a dig, "If he doesn't
know what he is talking about, he throws out such a smoke screen
that no one else is aware of the fact."

The second most important thing McCollum did on Monday was
to sign, in blue ink, a memo for the chieftains of Main Navy, passing
along an overnight revelation from the Pacific that did not require
his elaboration. The note used the common in-house term for the adversary: "All Orange service radio calls for units afloat were changed
at 0000, 1 December 1941." That tied perfectly, if unexpectedly, with
the first most important thing that the navy's finest Japan hand did
on Monday.

Captain Arthur H. McCollum, who was probably the only cit-
izen of the United States who had taught American dance moves
to the emperor of Japan, had a kind of dual citizenship. A mission-
ary's kid, he had entered the world on August 4, 1898, in a city that
would one day be obliterated by a single bomb—Nagasaki, Japan.
His life and the land of his birth had been commingled ever since.
Not counting childhood, McCollum had lived among the Japanese
twice, once to master their language after graduating from Annapolis (it was during that visit that he had furthered the floor skills of
Hirohito, who had not yet ascended to the throne), and once in the
late 1920s, when he returned as assistant naval attaché. And twice he
had observed Japan from a distant perch as chief of the Far Eastern
Section of the Office of Naval Intelligence, from 1933 to 1935, and
from 1939 until now.

Since mid-autumn, McCollum and the two officers who assisted
him had kept the Far Eastern office open every minute of every day
out of a burgeoning sense of worry. One or the other of them bedded
there each night. "Heel-and-toe watch," the navy called it. As far
back as July, the section had told Harold Stark that the Imperial Navy
"has marshaled its full naval strength and is on a full wartime foot-

ing," and had "more vessels in active service than ever before." In the summer as well, McCollum had begun lobbying American universities to churn out more Japanese speakers for the government. The navy had too few, far too few. "It was as plain as the nose on your face that you had to have people who could talk the Japanese language if you were going to fight them," he said.

Daily he filled out a short form bearing the latest scraps of intelligence gleaned from Magic intercepts, radio-traffic analysis, American consulates and embassies, merchant ships on the high seas—whatever he could find that touched on the imperial fleet, where it was, and what it was doing. Had these been future times, McCollum would also have had crisp overhead photos of Japanese warships and naval ports, snapped by satellites parked high above the Inland Sea. As it was, he did not have so much as an occasional photo taken by reconnaissance planes; such flights above Japan would have been highly provocative. McCollum had no spies on Japanese land, either. As far as regular, reliable sources of firsthand information went, "my recollection is we had none," Stark said, at least none reporting from inside the three-mile limit of Japan's territorial waters, unless an American military attaché or civilian got lucky, which they sometimes did.

Unlike other navies, the Japanese navy did not issue courtesy invitations to foreign officers to come aboard its warships or stop by its ports. The American naval attaché at that moment, Lieutenant Commander Henri H. Smith-Hutton, had "very great difficulty" gathering information about the Imperial Navy, because his every trip out of the capital had to be approved, and he was never allowed to go anywhere that would have mattered. He had resorted to enlisting an apparently naive Japanese medical student to pass along what he had seen during several social calls aboard Imperial Navy warships.

Ambassador Grew had noticed that "on the railway trip from Tokyo down to Shimonoseki at the foot of Honshu Island, very close to one of the Japanese navy yards, where they were building ships, they had a big stockade erected around the yard, and as the trains passed, they always pulled down the curtains." On the shore of Tokyo Bay stood a statue of Matthew C. Perry, the nineteenth-century American naval officer who had opened reclusive Japan to the benefits of trading with the outside world. Near his likeness stood a sign, in clumsy English, clearly intended for Americans who might stop by to see the good commodore: PHOTOGRAPHY NO BECAUSE HERE. Apparently, a snapshot would have captured the beaches behind Perry, thereby aiding enemy planning for amphibious landings. "The Japanese were past masters at secrecy," Grew said, "and their secret police were constantly watching all foreigners and all Japanese who were regarded as possibly pro-American or in any way pro-foreign." Passing information to Americans could result in execution.

Despite the towering obstacles to marshaling facts about Japan's formidability, many Americans both in and out of the government had concluded with complete certainty that they knew how formidable it was. Their convictions rested on a race-flavored foundation. It was a "fact," written everywhere, heard constantly, that the Japanese, due to unfortunate physiology, were terrible at the controls of airplanes, the weapon that was coming of age in the new world war. Their airplanes were terrible, too, poor knockoffs of Western designs produced by a people incapable of innovation.

The author Fletcher Pratt, whose subjects included naval history, had informed the American people in 1939 that "the Japanese, as a race, have defects of the tube of the inner ear, just as they generally are myopic," and this gives them "a defective sense of balance" as pilots. Pratt added that as children, the Japanese had "fewer mechanical toys" than Americans, which left them "less mechanical" as adults than "any other race." An incredulous Arthur McCollum would hear people argue that Japanese pilots were no good because—as he paraphrased the argument—as babies "they're carried on the backs of their mothers or their older sisters, and their older sisters play hop-scotch, and when they play hop-scotch, the child's head bounces around and it destroys the balance in the inner ear."

Admiral Bill Halsey, the aviator leading the *Enterprise* to Wake Island, rated the Imperial Navy's carrier pilots as mediocre. Admiral Wilson Brown, the commander of the Pacific Fleet's cruisers, thought the Japanese posed a greater risk to themselves aloft than to American targets. "I based that opinion on a conversation I had with an American who had spent twenty years in Japan as head of the Singer Sewing Machine Company." The businessman had visited Brown's cabin aboard the cruiser *Indianapolis* just within the past month to aver that while he had not observed Japanese military pilots, "the civilian aviation in Japan was so badly kept up that the Singer Sewing Machine Company had issued instructions to all their employees forbidding them to ever ride in Japanese commercial aviation, and that the general belief was that the Army and the Navy were not very much better." In the same vein, reporters had once ridiculed McCollum for having taken a flight to Osaka, foolishly placing his life in the hands of a Japanese pilot.

The *Nation* told its readers on August 30 that while pilots in the Imperial Navy were better than those in the Imperial Army, "in technical achievements, especially in aviation, the Japanese bluejackets are not up to American standards," and, by the way, "witnesses report that Japanese gunnery leaves much to be desired." The *Chicago Tribune*, in an article on November 29, called the empire's aviators "only fair." They were "excellent in the mechanics of flying"—the opposite of what Admiral Brown had heard—but lacked "the initiative which makes for good air fighters," the paper said. No future aces among them, apparently.

Among Oahu's ranking naval officers, there was little trembling about the aviation skills of the likely enemy. Admiral Bellinger, the commander of Oahu's patrol planes, assumed that Japan's long war in China had created "good" Japanese pilots, but not all that good. Neither did Kimmel's aviation adviser, Arthur C. Davis, consider them a force to fear, nor did Kimmel himself.

In its March 7 issue, the *Aeroplane* magazine had attributed Japan's excessive secrecy about its military to sheer national embarrassment about its abilities. It did not want the world to see the sad quality of its weapons. "The Japanese are, by nature, imitators and lack originality," the magazine said. "This blend of characteristics makes them conscious of their failings, and they seek to hide them from the world by every means in their power." As far as the *Aeroplane* had been able to determine, Japan's warplanes tended to break down during hard use; its manufacturing plants lacked precision machinery, and its aviation development was hampered by "a native lack of self-assurance." Its aircraft carriers were "not highly rated by one German authority," even though the Germans were their ally. Three more carriers were under construction, but "they [would] not be finished before 1943." Actually, two of those three had not only been completed, they were crossing the North Pacific. "There is no doubt that Japan stands lowest in air power on the list of the Great Powers," the magazine said. The US Naval Institute thought so much of the *Aeroplane*'s conclusions that it reprinted the article in the June issue of its own magazine, *Proceedings*.

Such denigration made its way to the denigrated. "The Japanese have known what we thought of them," Grew said, "that they were little fellows physically, that they were imitative, that they were not really very important in the world of men and nations. Believe me, I have been ashamed more than once by the braggadocio, self-confidence, and condescension manifested by our English-speaking peoples."

Arthur McCollum, on the other hand, knew enough to be worried. "There were a great many people who didn't realize that the Japanese were a competent fighting machine, or refused to believe it," he said. A man named Charles Healey Day was back in the United States after having managed a Chinese aircraft factory for six years, and he was telling newspapers he had seen Japanese forces in action during the China war. They had bombed and strafed him. They had good planes and good skills, and learned from their mistakes. "For a long time, I have tried to keep my homeland from underestimating Japanese military power," Day said. "Our complacency about what we are facing is one of our greatest enemies."

Otto Tolischus, the new reporter in Tokyo for the *New York Times*, had discovered a nation squarely in the twentieth century, and decided his readers ought to know that. On September 7, he wrote, "In all the modern achievements that are the pride of the enlightened West, especially in science, industry and trade, Japan, if it has not quite caught up with the leading Western nations, is nevertheless crowding them in many fields, and has become one of the big powers of the world."

When the assistant American naval attaché for air in Tokyo had visited Main Navy, McCollum made sure he met with a group of officers to discuss what he had been able to learn about Japanese naval aviation. In his remarks in Washington, that officer, Lieutenant Stephen Jurika, praised both Japanese pilots and aircraft carriers. But the audience "would only half believe," McCollum said. They peppered Jurika with questions. Didn't the Japanese have astigmatism? Wear bifocals? Weren't they really short? It seemed to Jurika that Main Navy "just would not take seriously the fact that the Japanese carriers were a major threat, at least as good as ours." The Office of Naval Intelligence struggled and failed to offset the impact on Main Navy thinking caused by "the constant daily drumfire from our press," McCollum said, about how militarily amusing Japan was, about how "they're funny little people."

If hard data suggested a Japanese plane or weapon had excellent capability, the data were suspect. By inspecting the wreckage of a new type of Japanese fighter shot down in China, Naval Intelligence realized that the plane—the Zero—had a range of at least 1,500 miles if equipped with an auxiliary fuel tank. "We pushed this out, and the Bureau of Aeronautics just hit the ceiling," McCollum said. The Zero could not fly that far, the bureau countered, based on nothing. Likewise, using an "impeccable" source, McCollum told the Bureau of Ordnance that the Japanese had a torpedo that was faster and more potent than American ones. The bureau replied that this could not be true.

"Usually and unfortunately, the tendency was to judge technical developments on the basis of our own technology, and on the assumption that our technology was superior to any other," McCollum said. That sin has a name: mirror imaging. If our boys cannot do it, their boys cannot do it. In fact, McCollum thought, "The Japanese were probably the premier torpedo men in the world."

So common was race-based dismissal of the empire's abilities that in a few days, after Japan's warplanes had materialized in Hawaiian skies, the *New York Herald Tribune*, quoting a British general, would report that German tutors had definitely helped with the planning of the attack, and possibly had trained the pilots. There had to have been white help, in other words. Within the halls of Congress, the rumor was that Germans had actually done the flying.

The first most important thing the navy's finest Japan hand did on Monday was to stride into room 2709 on the second deck and hand three single-spaced typewritten pages to the director of Naval Intelligence, composed on his own initiative, written over the weekend, polished that morning. They were not his daily summary, or one of his twice-monthly bulletins, but something extra. Arthur McCollum's anxiety about the Japanese had driven him to offer a grand overview of their moves to the director, who had been on the job all of two months.

Within the past year—since December 1940—Naval Intelligence had had four directors, because nobody wanted to be saddled with the job for long. As a rule, careers did not get made there, but on the bridges of battleships and cruisers, girding for combat with exercises featuring roaring batteries and deft maneuvers, not the exchange of internal memos. To rise in rank, the ambitious officer had to go to sea again and again; shore assignments were mere interludes. One especially did not aspire to be director of Naval Intelligence, or to any job in it. Many thought a posting there was "the kiss of death" or a "dead end," to cite two characterizations. Scrounging for scraps of information was not serious work for manly military men.

"There was no training for intelligence officers in those days," an intelligence officer in those days said. "There was no intelligence manual, no intelligence books, no intelligence course, no intelligence school." No CIA. No NSA. No NIEs—the national intelligence estimates of today. There was no crack team of respected analysts who devoted their days to thinking as the Japanese might, or even a single person focused solely on the Magic intercepts, to catch their trends and nuances. Traffic analysis of the kind being done in the Dungeon had an aura of voodoo to those unfamiliar with it. Joe Rochefort thought most senior officers did not understand what he did and, worse, did not care to learn. Unlike gunnery, the results of intelligence work were difficult to see and impossible to hear, and therefore seemed less consequential.

By his own admission, Admiral Theodore Wilkinson, the Naval

Intelligence director du jour, had no prior exposure to collecting and vetting data on the sizes, capabilities, and movements of navies, other than "attendance at two international conferences for limitation of armaments in 1933 and 1934." But since arriving in October, Wilkinson at least had made a point of understanding what McCollum's Far Eastern Section did, even with all the work he had related to the war in the Atlantic Ocean. "He is by reputation one of our most brilliant officers," McCollum said. "It is my opinion he has a magnificent mind." Wilkinson had, in fact, finished first in his class at the Naval Academy. The respect was reciprocated. So when McCollum presented his three pages of observations about the Japanese on Monday, Wilkinson had the sense not to brush him aside.

"He read this document over, directed me to wait in his office, and disappeared," McCollum said. "He came back in about ten minutes and said, 'You be ready to go to the office of Admiral Stark with me between 11 and 11:30 this morning, and make a number of copies of this thing.'"

Arriving at Stark's suite, room 2064, the two found not only the chief of naval operations but also the two admirals who had written the war warning with him four days earlier, Royal Ingersoll, the assistant chief, and Richmond Turner, the chief of war planning. One or the other of them told McCollum to read aloud his document, which was a distillation of Magic revelations, radio tracking, and his own wisdom.

All across the Pacific, McCollum told the war warning's triumvirate of authors, Japanese citizens living abroad were returning home for good, from Hong Kong, Singapore, the Philippines, the Dutch East Indies, Australia, and India. "Many Japanese residents have recently been withdrawn from the United States, Canada and South America," he added. The Japanese had shifted the supervision of their espionage network in the Americas from Washington to Rio de Janeiro, which was solid evidence they could soon be shutting down their Washington embassy. Japan's consul general in occupied Shanghai had told Tokyo "that all preparations are complete for taking over all physical property in China belonging to British, American and other enemy nationals."

The Imperial Navy, McCollum went on, had confiscated "many" Japanese merchant ships, refitting some of them as antiaircraft platforms, and all of its warships had now completed a "repair check up." One newly organized task force was operating in the South China Sea, a second new one "in the Mandate Island area." A picket line of surface ships and air patrols ran between the Marshall Islands and the Gilberts. Some twenty-four thousand "fully-equipped veteran" troops—his total differed from the War Department's report to Roosevelt—had boarded transports, taking "a considerable number of tanks and trucks, quite a few of which were camouflaged green," to blend with jungle terrain, which meant they were going south. The first elements of these forces had reached French Indochina, Japan's new operational springboard. "All wharves and docks at Haiphong and Saigon are reported crowded with Japanese transports unloading supplies and men."

None of this surprised Stark, who had access to Magic, just as McCollum did. Nothing McCollum told the three admirals unambiguously indicated that Japan's goals included invading or bombing American places. Bringing citizens home from the United States, relocating the supervision of the North American espionage operation, preparing to seize American property in China: these might be only precautions against an American declaration of war that could follow Japan's coming southern military operations. But the chief of the Far Eastern Section did not think that was what they were. "Japan had taken every possible step in preparation for war with the United States. Her fleet was mobilized, freshly docked and was in all

respects ready for action" against the only navy that could challenge
it. McCollum asked Stark, Ingersoll, and Turner "whether or not the
fleets in the Pacific had been adequately alerted."

Neither he nor Wilkinson, incredibly, had been told about the
war warning. Betty Stark had not consulted with Naval Intelligence,
the one place that knew a few things about Japan. Nor had he given
it a copy of the warning after it had been sent. McCollum had had
no chance to offer an opinion about the message's clarity (poor) or
details (misleading), because he had never seen it. He learned of
its existence only at this very moment, in room 2064, when Stark
and Turner gave him a "categorical assurance" that "dispatches fully
alerting the fleets and placing them on a war basis had been sent,"
McCollum said.

The assurance vastly exceeded what its givers actually knew.

Stark and Turner had, it was true, sent a sharp warning to the
Pacific and Asiatic Fleets. But not having requested an explanation
of what they were doing in response, Main Navy had no way of
knowing whether they were, in fact, alert. Asking "was not Navy
custom," Stark said. And custom held even when it came to asking for a reply to a dispatch that differed in subject and tone from
all others ever sent by Main Navy; even when the subject of that
dispatch was a possible ocean-wide cataclysm; even when a failure
to understand the warning could have lethal repercussions. Stark
strove to be a gentleman. So Kimmel was to be trusted. He had
been warned. His record was superb. He would know the proper
response. Leave him be. Later, Ingersoll said it was so obvious what
the Pacific Fleet should be doing that there was no reason to ask
Kimmel to report back.

McCollum's urgency did not now prompt Stark to reconsider
whether, given the seriousness of the moment, perhaps Main Navy
should have a better idea of what steps the fleets were taking. Nor

did Stark now see fit to give McCollum and Wilkinson an actual copy of the war warning. He had merely characterized its content for them. That night, Henry Stimson happened to write in his diary that among the military and civilian advisers to the president, Stark was "the weakest of all."

And just like that, without the slightest hint or hope that he would be free of the detestable Captain George Dudley Cooper so beautifully soon, Billy Outerbridge's crusade to get off the *Cummings* ended in victory. Someone, somewhere, in the navy bureaucracy had read his request for a transfer and decided Outerbridge was ready to immediately command a ship, specifically the destroyer *Ward*. His tonsils had a stay of execution. They would not come out today, Monday, as he had planned. There was too much to do. "You may tell the boys that daddy is a captain of a destroyer," Billy wrote to Grace on Saturday, November 29, the day his plea to get off the *Cummings* had been answered.

The *Ward* was hardly a prized stallion. Her hull had first touched the water on June 1, 1918, at the Mare Island Naval Shipyard near San Francisco. Her silhouette, her size, and her passageways were as familiar to Lieutenant Outerbridge as old shoes, because he had served aboard two of her identical, four-smokestack sisters. "Being on one of these old cans seems like old times," he felt.

His new home was not assigned to the Pacific Fleet, but to Oahu's Fourteenth Naval District for close-in submarine patrol around the island. Outerbridge's days of long, long cruises on the rollicking open seas were over for now, which was fine with Billy, whose stomach had never gotten used to the rollicking-seas part of being a career naval officer. The new job entitled him to quarters ashore, maybe even in a brand-new dwelling, given how much building was under way in and around Pearl. Grace and the three boys could come out. They would be a family again. Outerbridge assured her that any house would be near a school, as well as "near the commissary, near the gas station, near the ships service store, near the hospital and not far from town," as if trying to prove that Oahu was modern and American, and not some misty, primitive isle of the sort found in *National Geographic*.

"The mess of moving and getting settled is something, but I am sure that you will enjoy living out here," he wrote. "It is expensive but everyone enjoys the climate, and I feel that we will be happy." She would have to abandon friends and familiarity, so her husband mentioned that two other officers aboard the *Ward* had wives, and "I am sure that you will like it and will be one of the girls again." If she got lucky with a booking, she and the boys could arrive aboard a Matson liner after Christmas. He had already shipped holiday packages with gifts, he said. "If Japan just stays quiet, we shall have a very happy sojourn on the island."

The *Ward* would not be his to command until a replacement executive officer of the *Cummings* was named. Outerbridge had not told Captain Cooper that their frosty service together was about to come to a close. That would be an uncomfortable conversation, though probably satisfying as well. He told Grace that he hoped he would measure up as a destroyer captain.

He would, very shortly.

TEN

THE SHIPS THAT WERE
NOT THERE

HUSBAND KIMMEL'S OFFICE was commendably utilitarian, without carpet, plush chairs, wood paneling, or other signs of leader self-regard, just a desk, a telephone, a few places to sit, and two wall maps, one of the world, one of the Pacific. Oh, but the view. From the two sizable rectangular windows of his corner space on the second deck of the Submarine Building, he could see the radio masts of the battleships along Ford Island; the submarine piers directly below in Southeast Loch; launches ferrying crews to and from shore leave; multiple destroyers and cruisers berthed across the way; the occasional floatplane rising off the water at the outset of a patrol. He could see Ten Ten Dock—named for its length, 1,010 feet—where he had taken command ten months earlier in the ceremony aboard the *Pennsylvania*, now out of the water and undergoing repair in Dry Dock Number One. Here, outside his windows, was one of the great gatherings of American power, set against the backdrop of the Waianae Range to the northwest.

Edwin Thomas Layton visited that office, and probably noted the view, every morning between eight and nine, coming from his own on the same floor. Since December 7, 1940, a day that would live in his memory, Lieutenant Commander Layton of Nauvoo, Illinois, age thirty-eight, had been the fleet intelligence officer. His daily report on Japanese naval activity drew from a slew of sources—Washington, the British, friendly diplomats in the Far East, navy radio listeners near Manila—but the best of his information came by car from the windowless nearby world of the Dungeon, whose proprietor was one of Layton's best friends.

He and Joe Rochefort had met aboard the liner *President Adams* in September 1929, outbound from San Francisco. Layton, younger by three years, was single. "His two great failings are a thorough belief in the constancy and infallibility of women," the academy class of 1924 yearbook had noted, "and an inveterate susceptibility to blind drags," a reference to blind dates, not cross-dressing, although Layton did once play a woman in an academy play, on account of a high-pitched voice. The authors of this yearbook synopsis believed the accompanying photograph required no elaboration. "Merely glance at the above masterpiece." Layton had the sexy visage of a drugstore pharmacist.

He had a sense of humor, and a better than average brain, which made him good at codes and ciphers, and once he had formed an opinion or focused on a goal, he was a "one-channel man, nicely stubborn," an acquaintance said. In those days right before the stock market vaporized, the *President Adams* was conveying him to Japan. A few years earlier, three Japanese warships had visited San Francisco on a goodwill cruise, and the navy had assigned Layton to be one of the hosts. "I found the Japanese very eager to be friendly and, surprisingly, very fine men." Half the visiting officers spoke flawless English, half admirable French. "But here was the real kicker: There wasn't one single U.S. official—no naval officer or anyone on our side—who could speak one word of Japanese. For the first time, I learned what 'losing face' was. I felt ashamed for the United States." Precociously, the young officer had promptly written to Main Navy that it was unseemly no one had been able to converse with the guests in Japanese, and he urged the department to begin enlarging the universe of those who could. If it needed volunteers, count him in.

Rochefort, whose wife and infant son were also aboard the *Adams*, was under the same orders as Layton, to report to Japan for immersion in its language under the auspices of the assistant naval attaché at the embassy in Tokyo, one Arthur H. McCollum. Layton thought Rochefort was "an easy-to-meet, an easy-to-get-on-with person," and McCollum was "the kind who would give a newcomer a cold, dry martini." (It would be McCollum who, in the summer of 1941, as the Far Eastern section chief, ordered the Tokyo language program shuttered, and told its current crop of a dozen officers to get out of Japan. He did not want assets trapped inside the enemy realm when war erupted.)

Once settled in Tokyo, the two students hired the same tutor, who came to the Rocheforts' apartment each day to spend an hour with each of them. Sometimes the instructor would order the two Americans to a movie house, where interpreters standing next to the screen would translate the captions of American silent films. Seeing the same captions and hearing their Japanese equivalents over and over, the Americans' familiarity with street Japanese rose.

Within months of returning home, they wound up on the same battleship, the *Pennsylvania*, Layton commanding the crew of turret number four, Rochefort doing double duty as assistant fleet operations officer and fleet intelligence officer. Layton liked intelligence work, too. He had no idea, he said later, that officers were supposed to avoid such a ridiculous field.

One day in 1934, when the fleet still called the West Coast its home, Rochefort heard a rumor that the Japanese Citizens Patriotic Society of Long Beach had rented an auditorium and was to show a "subversive" film to its members. He sent Layton as his spy, posing as a fire inspector. When it began to look as if he would not be allowed entry, the fire-inspecting fake said in pidgin English, "Me no here, no movies." He stayed; they got their movie. "I went around telling the crowd to put out cigarettes," Layton said, while he listened to the film, carrying a fire extinguisher as a prop. The subversion turned out to be nothing more than declarations that the emperor was good, democracy was no good, Japanese soldiers were brave and shouted "banzai," and Franklin Roosevelt had funny mannerisms. Layton had adjourned to a bar "to celebrate the successful conclusion of my first undercover operation."

In time, he returned to Japan as the naval attaché, the one who would be invited to attend a performance of Kabuki with Isoroku Yamamoto, lose badly to him at bridge, and come to believe that the commander in chief of the Combined Fleet "possessed more brains than any other Japanese in the high command."

The material Rochefort sent Layton from the Dungeon each morning was a page or two summary of the radio-intercept bounty of the previous day. A direct telephone line coursed between their buildings on the east side of the harbor, should Rochefort's roofers have late-breaking updates or Layton have a question about what he was reading. Until his anointment as intelligence officer, Layton had known nothing about this business of deducing the enemy's where-abouts by extracting tiny clues from his radio communications. "So I had to go over with them [the Dungeon] what they meant by this. They have their own jargon, they have their own language." He had to be able to explain the summaries to Kimmel, who seemed as much a novice about radio traffic analysis as he was. Sometimes, to be on the safe side, or because he had other sources, Layton would tweak Rochefort's findings before taking them to Kimmel, putting one or two more Japanese warships in a particular location than the Dungeon had. "And this infuriated me," Rochefort said. But by now the two had the bond many brothers do, affectionate but needling. "You undoubtedly have known people in your lifetime that superficially would seem to be at each other's throats all the time, and it was all good clean fun," said Lieutenant Commander Thomas Dyer, a classmate of Layton's who worked in the Dungeon with Rochefort. "If Layton was a little dense about something, Rochefort was per-fectly capable of calling him a 'dunderhead' and so forth, and Layton would come back equally strongly, probably." It was simply "a relief of tension, and meaningless."

On Tuesday morning, December 2, the Dungeon summary Lay-ton set before Kimmel began with what the admiral probably had been told hours before: at 0000, December 1, Tokyo time—very early Sunday, Hawaii time—the Imperial Navy had changed the radio address of every ship for the second time in four weeks, far sooner than its custom. "The fact that service calls lasted only one month," the summary said, "indicate[s] an additional progressive step in preparing for active operations on a large scale." With a pen-cil, Kimmel underlined the bulk of that sentence. The report contin-ued: "It appears that the Japanese Navy is adopting more and more security provisions."

To Layton, it was obvious that "they were doing everything they could to defeat our radio intelligence, that they were apprehensive that we would know of the move that was under way."

Unusually, he had one more document to present Tuesday.

Harold Stark's war warning of November 27 told Kimmel that talks with the Japanese "have ceased," and they would strike someone, somewhere, "within the next few days." It had now been five, and nothing. The newspapers Kimmel read—he would be a hungry media consumer all his life—were suggesting peace still had a pulse. The *Advertiser* and the *Star-Bulletin* reported, on November 28 and 29, that Secretary Hull was awaiting Japan's reply to his Ten Points. Then Monday morning's *Advertiser* heralded a "crucial meeting today" with the Japanese diplomats, and then Monday afternoon's *Star-Bulletin* confirmed that talks had resumed. "In the newspapers in Honolulu, and on the radio," Kimmel said, "I heard that Mr. Hull was talking to, I forget exactly, but that he was having conversations still with the Japanese ambassador. He called him down to talk to him. Mr. Welles talked to him all that week." That would be Sumner Welles, one of Hull's closest aides.

The admiral's chief of staff, Poco Smith, recalled "a great deal of confusion" at Pearl about whether diplomacy had collapsed, as the war warning had led them to believe. They had no Purple machine to guide them, and did not even know there was such a thing. Nothing from Main Navy showed up to enlighten Kimmel about what he saw in the newspapers. "He might have asked me for a clarification," said Stark, who might have provided one on his own.

Kimmel remained determined to have his ships sprint toward the Japanese in the Marshall Islands as soon as the war began, if the United States was in it, which was hardly certain. Since Stark's radiogram of November 27, he had gotten himself a to-do list, "Steps To Be Taken in Case of American-Japanese War Within the Next Twenty-Four Hours." There were eleven, the first being to tell the fleet, wherever its myriad components might be, "that hostilities have commenced." Most of the other steps reminded him of what to do with certain ships that were already at sea, so he could position them for the raid on the Marshalls, some two thousand miles away. The war, if there was to be one, was still something he would be sailing toward. It would not be coming *to* him on Oahu. None of the eleven steps pertained to defending Pearl or responding to an attack on it.

He also assigned Layton a new task. With Halsey sailing so much closer to Japan on his mission to Wake, and with the Imperial Navy's unprecedented tricks to render its radio communications as opaque as possible, Kimmel told Layton to step back from his daily, incremental intelligence reports, assume an ocean-wide perspective, and estimate the whereabouts of every Japanese warship. Their whole navy. Hampered by the change of call signs, Layton struggled to meet Kimmel's deadline, which was that day, Tuesday.

The result—five typewritten pages—was, to a civilian, a gumbo of crazy words (BatDiv, CruDiv, Desron, Subron); odd two-letter pairings (BB, CA, CV, for example); exotic Pacific places (Bako-Takao, Hainan-Canton, Kure-Sasebo, among others); and lots of numbers. Actual English comprised three sentences, two barely worthy of the name. The most important and longest was the first. In it, Layton underscored the word "thought." "From best available information, units of the ORANGE fleet are *thought* to be located as listed below." He was reminding Kimmel that divination based on radio reading was an iffy proposition.

To an admiral, the lingo of the analysis was not bizarre in the least. "BBs" were battleships, "CAs" cruisers, and "CVs" carriers. The Imperial Navy, like the US Navy, grouped ships of a kind into divisions or squadrons. A "CruDiv" was a cruiser division and a "Subron" was a submarine squadron. Under the geographic headings of "Baku-Takao" and "Hainan-Canton"—all places in, or on the shores of, the South China Sea—Layton placed more than eighty major Japanese warships. This reflected the grand advance south, in the direction of Malaya, the Dutch Indies, and the Philippines, that Stark's warning had emphasized. Layton's list declared that still more warships were in the waters of the Marshall Islands, still others already off French Indochina, still more near Japan, including most of the Imperial Navy's battleships, which suggested they, at least, would play no part in the imminent scheme, whatever it was.

Layton placed five of Japan's ten aircraft carriers with the southern invasion forces, and a sixth in the Marshall Islands. It took Kimmel but a moment to realize that the remaining four Japanese carriers, four of Yamamoto's biggest, the heart of his naval aviation, were not listed anywhere at all.

Writing in July 1940, Rear Admiral Joseph K. Taussig belittled "aviation enthusiasts who claim that aircraft have sealed the doom not only of the capital ships, but of all surface vessels as the predominating factor in sea warfare." Less-knowledgeable people were always proclaiming some new technology—submarines, torpedo boats—as the lethal answer to battleships, and they were always wrong, and they were now about airplanes, Taussig had written. "The gun for many years—in fact, since the introduction of gunpowder—has proved to be the most effective naval weapon." The secretary of the navy himself, Frank Knox, had written as recently as February that whatever the buzz about aviation, battleships remained the champions of the waves, and would continue to be "for a long time to come."

At first, aircraft carriers had seemed such quirky and vulnerable inventions. Their primary weapons, planes, were easily neutralized by weather or night; the planes had limited range and anemic bomb loads; the ship's whole purpose could be negated by a single shell punching a single hole in the unarmored runway, perhaps penetrating far enough to ignite stores of aviation fuel and consign the vessel and its aircraft to the deep. The best use of aircraft carriers seemed as scouts whose planes would find the enemy fleet, maybe even harass it, but the core combat would still resemble the days of old, with battleships showering behemoth shells on the other side's battleships until one side could go on no longer.

Carrier planes had gotten faster, though, their bombs bigger, their range greater. A carrier lacked the armor of a battleship, but it had greater speed, and could strike from much farther away through its planes. A battleship could hit only what it could see steaming a few thousand yards away. Frank Knox's love for battleships aside, even the Naval War College had heard and seen enough about naval airpower that by 1937, a standard lecture was declaring, "A fleet which lacks aviation has, in comparison with an opponent in possession of aircraft, a serious weakness which even greatly superior strength in other types [of weapons] may not counterbalance." The battleship had a rival.

On February 14, 1929, a correspondent of the *New York Times* described in overcooked prose an exercise off Panama in which aircraft from the carriers *Saratoga* and *Lexington*, sailing far below the horizon, had suddenly appeared above a knot of battleships. Plunging "so fast one could barely hold them in the eyes," the planes had swept down to the mast tops of the big ships, "simulated an attack, flattened out and, almost as though bouncing from the surface of the sea, were climbing back to safety." The little "darting bolts of wrath" returned to their distant carriers with a "technically perfect victory." The *Times* reporter had watched this seminal triumph of the gnats over the elephants from the deck of the destroyer *Litchfield*, whose captain was Husband E. Kimmel.

Judged by résumé alone, Kimmel was navy classic, raised on big-gun platforms. Battleships had always been the pathways to career greatness, and in his nearly forty years in uniform, Kimmel had served aboard eight on nine occasions, including as executive officer of the *Arkansas* and captain of the *New York*. He had never been posted to an aircraft carrier, nor did he know how to fly. (Even if he had wanted to, he could not have; he flunked the eye test required of all officers.) With Orville Wright at the controls, the first sustained heavier-than-air flight had lifted off the sands of Kitty Hawk, North Carolina, a mere six weeks before Kimmel graduated from Annapolis. Aviation was not in his upbringing.

Yet Kimmel had no Luddite's blind allegiance to mighty guns. He was adapting to the revolution he had witnessed aboard the *Litchfield* in 1929. One of his confidants was one of the navy's carrier zealots, Bill Halsey, his academy classmate, who, incidentally, had not taken any battleships along with him on the mission to Wake Island; they couldn't keep up with the *Enterprise*.

All year, Kimmel had peppered Stark with complaints and demands related to carriers. He objected, for example, to how Main Navy's Bureau of Aeronautics was handling Halsey's requests for additional late-model carrier planes. "Obstacles are offered to most of Halsey's recommendations," he wrote in February. "I cannot subscribe to these views. We must have the most modern planes in our carriers." He argued in May that the fleet was "woefully deficient" in carriers. In another memo, he emphasized that, far more than battleships, he needed "submarines, destroyers, carriers and cruisers," the stuff of quick, stealthy movement. "This is a vast ocean," he added then, and he wanted speedy ships and carrier planes—those "darting bolts of wrath"—to cover it, not more sluggish leviathans. On October 22, he wrote yet again: give me carriers. "The type of operations we have planned in the early stages of the war puts a premium on aircraft operations from carriers," he told Stark.

An admiral with such a thorough grasp of the power and nimbleness of carriers understood the significance of not knowing where the enemy's were. Missing from Layton's list on Tuesday, December 2, were the *Akagi*, *Kaga*, *Hiryu*, and *Soryu*, and when Kimmel asked Layton the obvious, "I said that I had no recent good indications of their locations." They had been engaged in exercises near Formosa earlier in the fall; that much the intelligence officer knew. But then their names and their units had fallen out of the transmissions overheard by the roofers. Not only were the carriers not speaking, they were not being spoken to. Layton could not be certain where they were, at least not enough to type their names onto his list.

"Then Admiral Kimmel looked at me, as sometimes he would, with somewhat stern countenance," Layton said. He considered Kimmel a "starchy" man, as so many did, but he liked his willingness to hear out subordinates.

"Do you mean to say," the admiral said, "that they could be rounding Diamond Head and you wouldn't know it?"

Beginning in January, about the time Kimmel had taken command, the word "surprise" had become common on American lips, as in: the Japanese could try to surprise us at Pearl Harbor. As in: they might try to surprise us at Pearl Harbor not only during a war—an obvious thing to attempt, given the importance of the naval base—but also *before* the legal formality of a declaration, as the very means by which they announce the war. They had done it to the Russians at Port Arthur. They might do it again.

"It is believed easily possible that hostilities would be initiated by a surprise attack upon the Fleet or the Naval Base at Pearl Harbor," Frank Knox wrote Henry Stimson, the secretary of war, on January 24. That could be a "major disaster." The attack might come in one of six ways, Knox felt, and he ranked them from most to least likely: air attack with bombs, air attack with torpedoes, sabotage, submarine attack in the waters outside the harbor, the mining of those waters, and naval bombardment of the harbor by surface ships. The last four possibilities were not as threatening or likely as the first two, Knox wrote. What worried him was "a striking force of carriers and their supporting vessels."

Surprise was equally on the mind of the army's General Marshall. "Out in Hawaii, the fleet is anchored but they have to be prepared against any surprise attack," the chief of staff told an army conference in Washington on February 19. "I don't say any probable attack, but they have to be prepared against a surprise attack from a trick ship or torpedo planes. Our whole Navy power in general is concentrated there."

And the possibility of surprise at Pearl—an "out of the blue" strike, as he called it—had also occurred to General Sherman Miles of Army Intelligence, "in view of the character of the Japanese." And to Bill Halsey, because of "their action against the Russians in 1904." Most important, it had occurred to Admiral Husband Kimmel. "The Japanese were known to make surprise attacks whenever they could," he said. "The only difference betwixt the Japanese and any other nation in that respect was that they were liable to do it without a declaration of war." In a "confidential letter" he wrote on October 14, Kimmel had reminded his entire command that Japan might attempt a predeclaration air assault on Pearl, or a "surprise submarine attack," or a combination of those two, an air raid and a submarine strike.

Two officers on Oahu, one army, one navy, had recently sketched a scenario of how the Japanese could—not that they would—execute a surprise attack on Pearl as the opening act of a war. The document, dated March 31, 1941, is so insightful it seems as if the duo journeyed to the future and back before typing it. Major General Frederick Martin, the commanding officer of the army's Hawaiian Air Force, and Rear Admiral Patrick Bellinger, who commanded the navy's patrol planes, had imagined a time, not far off, when diplomatic relations with Japan "are strained, uncertain and varying." They noted that Japan "has never preceded hostile actions by a declaration of war," and that Japan had eight aircraft carriers, seven of them fast. (They were writing before the *Zuikaku* and the *Shokaku* were finished.)

"It appears that the most likely and dangerous form of attack on Oahu would be an air attack," Martin and Bellinger wrote. "It is believed that at present such an attack would most likely be launched from one or more carriers which would probably approach inside of three hundred miles." Attacking at dawn would enable the Japanese to use the dark of night to approach, they said, although the Americans would then have many hours of daylight afterward to find and retaliate against the force. Attacking at dusk would preclude that kind of retaliatory strike, because darkness would soon envelop the escaping Japanese, but it would raise the chance of preraid discovery, because they would be approaching Oahu through many hours of daylight.

Overall, the two concluded, using the standard in-house word for Japan, "it appears possible that Orange submarines and/or an Orange fast raiding force might arrive in Hawaiian waters with no prior warning from our intelligence service." A successful attack from underwater or the air or both "might prevent effective offensive action by our forces in the Western Pacific for a long period." Or, in Frank Knox's words of January, it might be a major disaster.

Then just about everybody, navy and army, military and civilian, had relegated surprise to their mental back pages. The concept was an obligatory box that had now been ticked, an intellectual exercise that had now been completed but not taken too seriously. For all the official contemplation during 1941, the idea of a Japanese carrier surprise never rose higher than a long shot in most minds, whether those at Pearl or in Washington. Knox had called it "easily possible," but that was not the same as "likely." Martin and Bellinger had speculated that Japanese carriers "might" come, which was not the same as "would" or even "probably." The military affairs writer of the *New York Times*, Hanson Baldwin, himself a graduate of the Naval Academy, declared in *Harper's* in April, "The Japanese fleet is not built for trans-Pacific operations, but for work close to the Japanese Islands. (Ours is really the only 'blue water navy,' except for England's.)"

In the planning meeting in Kimmel's office on November 27, the army's Colonel James Mollison wondered aloud about the wisdom of reducing the number of Oahu's fighter planes to reinforce Wake and Midway. But Kimmel, mere weeks after having written to all of his officers about the theoretical possibility of a "surprise attack on ships in Pearl Harbor," had been so skeptical of Mollison's fear that he asked for Captain Soc McMorris's opinion. The war plans officer had provided comforting, 100 percent certitude: an air attack on Oahu would not happen. After all, could the Pacific Fleet do something like that? Sail all the way to Japan, executing all those refueling operations while on the high seas, and then launch an air strike on the Combined Fleet? It could not, not without sustaining losses greater than it inflicted. And if our boys can't do it, their boys can't do it.

"For us to make an attack on Japan would have required steaming long distance with [the] probability of detection," Soc Mc-

Morris would say later, "and then attack in the face of shore-based aircraft, where damage to [our] ships would be likely." Those ships that were not sunk might be too crippled to stagger home. Such a raid could well end in debacle. "We felt that the Japanese would find the same considerations would deter them from making such an effort against us."

Kimmel's chief of staff, Poco Smith, was convinced the Imperial Navy would realize that any force sailing to Pearl would be very easy to spot coming, "in which case they would [be] at a great disadvantage." The commandant of the Fourteenth Naval District, Admiral Claude Bloch, considered three thousand miles far too many to escape detection. Edwin Layton felt "Japan could not afford to gamble too much wherein she might lose the war in the first battle," the same sentiment the dubious Admiral Fukodome had expressed.

Kimmel regarded a surprise attack as only a "very remote" possibility, all but shoving it into the universe of the impossible. Only if evidence landed on his desk that an attack was likely—if the chance was, say, fifty-fifty or better—would he start taking precautions. But given what he knew about the difficulties of a cross-ocean expedition, Kimmel said he "arrived at the conclusion that an air attack on Pearl Harbor was not probable."

The Japanese, of course, had sifted the same military negatives. The astounding distance. The complexities of refueling while under way. The risk of calamitous discovery. They had calculated the odds they could pull off such a raid as just about that, fifty-fifty, perhaps a little better. Isoroku Yamamoto liked those numbers.

That Tuesday morning, Layton interpreted Kimmel's question about the four missing carriers coming around Diamond Head as sarcasm. To the degree the navy had theorized about a surprise raid, it had spoken only in terms of "a carrier" or "a two-carrier attack," or, vaguely, "carriers," although an army estimate had once mentioned "six," a number that had not imprinted itself in many minds. The navy had thought a great deal about how to use and group its own carriers, and massing them into a single offensive powerhouse—into something like a First Air Fleet—was not in its playbook yet. The US Navy had not traveled that far down the innovation highway.

Kimmel was merely ribbing him, Layton thought, for being unable to pinpoint all of Japan's warships. Given that radio messages were not even being sent *to* the four carriers—no commands, no intelligence updates, no weather reports—Layton's guess was they were not moving at all. They were sitting out the massive Japanese southern operation that was now about to begin and that already had five carriers, apparently. The missing quartet seemed "unconcerned with this entire matter," Layton felt, and—most likely, best guess— was bobbing benignly in the Inland Sea, and therefore inaudible.

In port, a warship does not have to broadcast strong radio signals to shore bases, the kind that distant eavesdroppers like those at Heeia might pick up. "They are on low-frequency, low-power circuits that cannot be heard," Layton said, "or on the ship-shore circuit, which is very low power, and sometimes they have a direct wire to the beach." Ships, in other words, drop off the grid in home waters. In the past six months, the Americans had lost track of Japanese battleships seven times, for spells of eight to fourteen days, and had lost carriers on twelve occasions, from nine to twenty-two days. Never had those missing ships suddenly turned up somewhere far away. Kimmel was as used to the pattern as Layton. "Units would disappear for four or five or six days and then they would come back again," the fleet commander said. "That was to be something to be expected."

Layton felt, too, that the southern operation was so mammoth the Japanese did not have enough destroyers and cruisers left over to properly protect the four carriers if they did go to sea. Rochefort thought so as well. Both men were guessing, if guessing reasonably. Actually, Layton was speculating even about the locations of the ships that *were* on his five-page list. "I underscored the word *thought* because I had no direct evidence." That was the nature of traffic analysis, "its faults and its promises, its inexactities." His list was, in fact, deeply flawed. Two of the five carriers he had placed with the southern invasion forces, the two biggest, were actually with the four he could not find. But he did not suggest to Kimmel that the four missing carriers, or any Japanese forces, were advancing anywhere at that moment under radio silence. "I wish I had." Nor did Rochefort suggest to Layton they were using radio silence. "Never," Layton said. "Never. Never." In other words, two of the Americans most familiar with Japan's culture and mind-set—one of whom had even met Yamamoto and considered him brilliant—did not see him coming.

Kimmel, of course, knew all about the benefits of radio silence. His ships engaged in it; Bill Halsey's forces on the way to Wake Island were observing it. "I believe that everyone who has worked with enemy radio intelligence," Layton said, "has always been aware that any force given sealed orders can get under way, go to sea, and as long as they don't use their radio, as long as they are not sighted, can move almost anywhere in the world." But at this moment, on this Tuesday, Layton was telling Kimmel the four carriers were in port, and the admiral had faith in his intelligence officer. But Kimmel's question about coming around Diamond Head, however jocular, does suggest that perhaps deep down, the invisibility of the Japanese four was bothering him.

———

Stanley Washburn of Lakewood, New Jersey, a newspaperman, a soldier, a propagandist, and a former Republican candidate for Congress, had just written to fellow Republican Frank Knox to offer a voice of Far East experience. Apparently during his newspapering days, Washburn had covered the Russo-Japanese War, and he told Knox in a letter on November 29 not to underestimate the Japanese. He had seen them in action, and they were smart, committed, creative, and willing to die. "In my experience, the Japanese never do what they're expected to do," Washburn warned.

Knox thought enough of Washburn's wisdom and credentials to pass the letter to Harold Stark. On Tuesday, December 2, Stark put a copy in the mail for Kimmel. By the time it arrived, its prediction was reality.

ELEVEN

THE SMOKE OF SECRETS

Wednesday, December 3

THE NEWEST MAGIC so startled Colonel Rufus Bratton of Army Intelligence that he asked one of his officers to march to the Japanese embassy and verify it by sight. Arriving from the Munitions Building, Bratton's scout could tell that on the grounds of their compound on Massachusetts Avenue, the Japanese had started a fire, not of wood but of paper, its remnants billowing into the warm and partly cloudy skies of Wednesday. So it was true, what Bratton had read: "Stop at once using one code machine unit and destroy it completely." The Japanese had two such machines at their embassy; Nomura would still need to have one, apparently. "When you have finished this wire me back the one word *haruna.*" It was the name of a battleship, among other things. "At the time and in the manner you deem most proper," the Foreign Office had continued, "dispose of all files of messages coming and going and all other secret documents."

Inside the compound, beyond the sight of any army watcher, Nomura was composing multiple replies, evidently shaken by both the instruction to begin cryptologic destruction and a second radiogram, quashing his suggestion of Monday for a parlay of Japanese and American leaders. He began bombarding the Foreign Office with observations that had an undercurrent of "please, don't do it." The Americans will shut our consulates if we pour more troops into Indochina, one radiogram said. They might go to war with us if we invade Thailand, the next said. Show them we have peaceful intent, a third said.

At Main Navy, the code-destruction intercept ripped a hole in the comforting blankie that the empire would never be so self-destructive as to war on a superpower. It clearly was taking steps to avoid the seizure of confidential documents, should the Americans burst into the Washington embassy in retaliation for attacks on American territory.

Harold Stark thought it was "one of the most telling and confirmative things that had happened, supporting our previous dispatches. It made a very deep impression on me," especially when coupled with another intercepted text, in which Tokyo gave identical orders for destruction to outposts in London and the Far East. The command to the Washington embassy "pointed right toward war," Stark said. Previously, in the war warning, he had been able to give the forces afloat only his best guess about which countries and possessions Japan might attack. But this decryption was "a beacon light."

Royal Ingersoll, the assistant chief of naval operations, ruled out the possibility that the dismantle-and-burn order indicated Japan was merely going to cut diplomatic ties. If that were all it had in mind, there would be no need to destroy anything. "The diplomats go home and they can pack up their codes with their dolls and take them home," he said. "Also, when you rupture diplomatic negotiations you do not rupture consular relations. The consuls stay on."

But the Japanese were ridding themselves of documents and machines not only at embassies but also at multiple consulates—Manila, Hong Kong, Singapore, and Batavia—"and that did not mean a rupture of diplomatic negotiations, it meant war," Ingersoll said—war with all the countries named in the radiograms, including the United States. "The inclusion of Washington in this dispatch is conclusive evidence."

To Admiral Richmond Turner, the head of war planning, it was "a definite and sure indication of war with the nations in whose capitals or other places those codes are destroyed." Bratton, the chief of Army Intelligence's Far Eastern Section, assumed the same thing, that "time was running out" and the next step was "probably a war." Admiral John R. Beardall, who was Roosevelt's naval aide, was "very much" affected by Japan's instructions to its outposts, concluding, "We were getting through with these diplomatic negotiations, and there was going to be war." He mentioned the instructions to Roosevelt a day or two later.

"Well, when do you think it will happen?" the president said. The war, that is.

"Most any time," Beardall replied.

Within a few hours, a dispatch composed by Arthur McCollum shot from Main Navy to the fleets in the Pacific. Unlike the war warning of November 27, the new text offered evidence that came straight from the Japanese themselves.

Highly reliable information has been received that categoric and urgent instructions were sent yesterday to Japanese diplomatic and consular posts at Hong-Kong X Singapore X Batavia X Washington and London to destroy most of their secret codes and ciphers at once and to burn all other important and confidential and secret documents.

McCollum's message had a mistake in chronology. Four of the cited cities had actually received their instructions on Monday, not "yesterday," Tuesday, a minor error. A second Main Navy message had a far greater flaw when it left five minutes after the first, sent by Naval Communications, an unnecessary duplication of McCollum's effort.

> Circular twenty four forty four from Tokyo one December ordered London X Hongkong X Singapore and Manila to destroy Purple machine XX Batavia machine already sent to Tokyo XX December second Washington also directed destroy Purple X All but one copy of other systems X And all secret documents XX British Admiralty London today reports embassy London has complied.

Unlike the first, this second dispatch mentioned the Purple machine, twice. It mentioned a Japanese text by number, 2444. Overwhelmed by a sense of urgency, Naval Communications had ignored the wisdom about not spreading the secret of Magic, even to Americans.

Neither of the two Main Navy dispatches said anything about Hawaii. In that, they were exactly like the November 27 war warning. Nor did either offer the commanders afloat, Kimmel and Hart, any wisdom about the significance of Japan's decision to start purging codes and machines. It was simply too self-evident. As usual, the two admirals were not told to report that they understood the import. As usual, Washington assumed they had.

Under partly sunny skies and with temperatures in the seventies, as they mostly were at that time of year, a great ship did indeed come around Diamond Head on Wednesday. It was the *Lurline* out of Los Angeles, as impressive as always, a Matson Line *M* on each of her twin funnels, bringing tourists to vacations and residents back to their homes on what would turn out to be her last carefree port call for many a month. While Kimmel's niece may have feared Japanese torpedoes when she and her children made the crossing in November, the islands remained as popular with mainlanders as ever, perhaps more so now that London lived under Nazi bombs and Paris, Amsterdam, and so many other European destinations lived under Nazi rule.

No doubt to the traditional welcome of band music and draped leis, the *Lurline* surrendered 793 passengers to the Honolulu pier on Wednesday morning: 741 who had not come to play football, 52 who had. The teams from San Jose State College in California and Willamette University in Oregon would each play the University of Hawaii, as well as each other, in a round-robin in paradise. The first game, between Willamette and Hawaii, was set for Saturday at Honolulu Stadium in verdant Manoa Valley, where mists sometimes floated down from the mountains "like great white parachutes." Most of the players would serve their country in the next four years. San Jose State's Kenneth C. Bailey would be killed in action; Willamette's Ted Ogdahl would be nearly bayoneted to death on a beach at Okinawa in 1945.

On their way to the Moana Hotel in Waikiki Beach, the teams traveled through a Honolulu in which General Walter Short's troops still stood their antisaboteur posts, but also a Honolulu that was beginning to look a lot like Christmas, or as much like it as a town that never knew snow could look. Four thousand lights illuminated the evenings along Fort Street downtown. Gift ideas crammed both newspapers. "Christmas has a year round meaning when you give electrical gifts," the advertisement of the Hawaiian Electric Company said. Sears suggested a Hawaiian-made "lounge coat" for $4.98, or a "slack suit" for $3.98. One essential component of the season was being imported, of necessity. "Here's the Good News, Folks," a *Star-Bulletin* headline proclaimed. "Yule Trees Are Coming." Precisely 12,995 bales from the Pacific Northwest—about 78,000 trees—were due in port on December 14. When not shopping, residents could sample the films playing at local houses, perhaps *A Slight Case of Murder* starring Edward G. Robinson, described as a "hilarious comedy-drama," or *Road to Zanzibar* with Bing Crosby, also described as a "hilarious comedy-drama."

Sometime on Wednesday, a Pan Am Clipper from San Francisco skidded onto the waters of Pearl Harbor, mail in its belly, one of the missives earmarked for Husband Kimmel. "Dear Mustapha," Betty Stark began, his preferred greeting in personal letters to the fleet commander. This one was dated eight days earlier, before the war warning, before the dispatches about Japanese code destruction. In it, Stark ricocheted from topic to topic: the dire need for more warships in the Atlantic; the plunge in navy recruiting that followed the sinking of the destroyer *Reuben James*; the president's grudging concession that his beloved naval service was not attracting enough volunteers to crew all the ships coming into commission and would have to use draftees, just like the army. Stark signed off with his usual admonition to "keep cheerful."

Then he appended a postscript. He had just come from a meeting with Cordell Hull and Roosevelt. "Neither would be surprised over a Japanese surprise attack," Stark said. Ambassador Joe Grew's letters warning of precisely that sort of thing had reached Hull by now. "From many angles," Stark continued, "an attack on the Philippines would be the most embarrassing thing that could happen to us. There are some here who think it likely to occur. I do not give it the weight others do." Japan would leave the United States and its lands alone during its next move, Stark predicted, and confine itself to "an advance into Thailand, Indochina, Burma Road area." What Roosevelt and America would do in that case, "I will be damned if I know. I wish I did."

Japan's consulate in Honolulu sat then, as it sits now, at Nuuanu Avenue and Kuakini Street, beside a shaded shallow creek in a residential neighborhood a half mile or so north of downtown. On Wednesday, agents of the Federal Bureau of Investigation did not actually observe the rising smoke of vanishing secrets there, but about noon, a source inside the consulate revealed that the Japanese were, indeed, immolating confidential material.

Special Agent in Charge Robert L. Shivers—"short, dark-haired, rather retiring" in one description; "smart and genteel" in another—had been in quasiretirement because of suspect health, but in 1939 had been recalled to duty by the director himself, J. Edgar Hoover, who had wanted his man to resuscitate the FBI's defunct Hawaiian office in light of looming war and all the residents of Japanese descent. Since then, Shivers had traveled the islands to get a feel for what the local Japanese might do if there was a conflict, but he never found evidence of what white residents kept telling him, which was that Hawaii's Japanese posed a threat. "They could only give you surmises, they could only tell you what they thought would happen," Shivers said, in part because Hawaii's Japanese community was "so closely woven together," hard for outsiders to penetrate.

On November 28, Hoover told Shivers of the parlous state of talks with Japan and that he must "be on the alert at all times, as anything could happen." Shivers, unlike others who got such war warnings during these days, had taken his to heart, scattering ten agents across Oahu "for the purpose of making additional contacts" with Japanese residents so the FBI would know "the state of mind of the civilian population" and know "of any untoward activity."

More than the civilians, Shivers worried about the diplomats, enough to wish that a patriotic American company or two would break federal law to help him find out what the consulate was doing in the way of espionage. He had tried to persuade the Oahu offices of the Radio Corporation of America, as well as Mackay Radio and Telegraph, to hand over the coded radiograms the consulate was sending through their offices, but "they refused to cooperate in this way, stating that they were prohibited by law and subject to prosecution." They indeed were: section 605 of the Federal Communications Act of 1934 made it a crime to disclose the contents of such messages. Shivers tried another tack. "Deeming that war with Japan and the Axis powers was imminent," he explained later, he asked Washington for permission to tap telephones, and got it on October 22.

On that Wednesday morning, the intelligence officer of the Fourteenth Naval District (both the district and the fleet had their own intelligence officer), Captain Irving H. Mayfield, called Shivers, wondering whether any documents were being burned at the consulate. Mayfield had just read Main Navy's messages about the instructions to Japanese outposts in Washington and elsewhere. Shivers told him he knew of nothing like that in Honolulu. A short while later, however, he called Mayfield back. Documents *were* being set afire on Nuuanu Avenue. The FBI had a tap on the phone of the consulate's cook, and Shivers's unwitting inside source had told "a Japanese person in Honolulu" that the consul general "was burning and destroying all his important papers."

That day, December 3, when he read that Japan was destroying its secrets in Washington and Manila, and when he learned later that the Honolulu consulate was, too, none of the deep worry that had washed over Main Navy washed over Husband Kimmel. Like so many of his countrymen, both civilian and military, the fleet commander did not think Japan was crazy enough to attack America first.

Not that he had a great deal of knowledge about the empire or how its people thought, unlike Isoroku Yamamoto, who knew a great deal about the United States. Kimmel's most memorable encounter with the Japanese had been his first, more than thirty years earlier, when he had sailed into Yokohama with Bill Halsey and Harold Stark and the Great White Fleet. The visit lasted only a few days. While doing postgraduate work at the Naval War College in 1926, Kimmel had written a paper about Far East issues, dispensing sympathetic bromides about the Japanese. "The United States has more contacts with Japan than any other power in the world save perhaps the British Empire," his thesis said, "and it behooves us to understand the aims and aspirations of this nation." If Kimmel had acquired any behooved understanding, it had come mostly long distance, while living and working among Americans too often given to dismissing the capabilities of the Japanese. He had had almost no contact with their contemporary leaders.

"I had never lived in Japan," he said. "I visited Japan on occasions, two or three times, but I had no opportunity to obtain any profound knowledge of the Japanese people by contacts with them." That did not make him derelict. It made him typical. Thomas Hart, the commander of the Asiatic Fleet, would remember that the navy paid "no particular attention" to inculcating officers in the psychology of the Japanese.

Kimmel thought Japan might bluff, it might rail, but it would never actually take on the United States by attacking Hawaii, the Philippines, or anywhere else. Quite apart from whether its navy could pull off the militarily breathtaking feat of sailing all the way to Hawaii without being detected, a comparison of national economies had long suggested to the admiral that Japan would behave as any nation would if its power were so conspicuously inferior. It would not self-annihilate by assaulting an atoll or island chain over which the Stars and Stripes waved, opening a war. No one had ever apprised him of any "Japanese 'mad dog' attitude,'" he said, some reckless and illogical mind-set "where they were going to strike out regardless of how much they got hurt."

Learning on Wednesday that their diplomats were ridding themselves of secrets in American cities, Kimmel—and Layton, too—reasoned that this was a predictable step Japan might take, not because it was going to attack the United States but because it feared the United States might attack *it*. If the Japanese invaded Thailand, for example, "the British or the Americans, or both of them, might jump on them and seize their codes and ciphers" in Japanese embassies and consulates in the Allied countries.

In other words, as he had with the war warning, as he had with Layton's report about the missing aircraft carriers, Kimmel infused the new piece of information with the meaning least likely to force him to disrupt Pearl's training routines and war plans. His was a casual, startling inattentiveness to the far more dangerous implication of code destruction: that it was a prelude to attack.

"The Department sent me a message that these codes were being burned," he said later, "and I feel, while that was good information, that they might very well have enlarged somewhat on what they believed it meant. I didn't draw the proper answer. I admit that. I admit that I was wrong."

If code burning did not fascinate Kimmel on Wednesday, something else in Washington's latest messages did: a single word, repeated twice, in the second dispatch. He promptly asked Layton if he knew what a "Purple" was. He did not. Layton tracked down the fleet security officer, who had earlier returned from the capital, and asked if he knew what a "Purple" was. He did: the American version of a machine the Japanese used to encipher and decipher dispatches.

Kimmel may not have been familiar with the color purple, or the existence of the machine, or the resulting Magic intercepts, but having held down jobs in the Washington bureaucracy on four occasions— in Ordnance, Budget, and twice in the office of the chief of naval operations—he knew about the navy's endless and expensive quests to penetrate Japan's encryption systems, and knew of earlier successes, too. From almost the moment of his ascension, he and Layton had been crusading for "information of a secret nature," as the admiral put it to Stark, the cracked-code intelligence that Pearl felt just had to exist back there on Constitution Avenue.

Surrounded by nothing but the sea, he often felt the isolation acutely. More than once, Kimmel had said to Layton, "I wish they would let us know more [about] what is going on back there." Back in Washington, he meant. Pearl was five and a half time zones and thousands of miles from national decision making. He rarely got much guidance about what the country—and thus the fleet—would do if Japan invaded Russia, or if it attacked British targets or Dutch targets but not American.

"The Commander-in-Chief Pacific Fleet is in a very difficult position," he had written Stark in May. "He is far removed from the seat of government, in a complex and rapidly changing situation. He is, as a rule, not informed as to the policy, or change of policy, reflected in current events and naval movements." He had all but ordered Stark—nominally, his superior—to make it "a cardinal principle" to send "all important [intelligence] developments as they occur and by the quickest secure means available." Layton had even written to his old friend from Japan days, Arthur McCollum, to ask for "dip" (diplomatic intercepts), so he could write more informed intelligence reports for the fleet. In return, Stark promised that naval intelligence would keep the Pacific Fleet "adequately informed concerning foreign nations, [and the] activities of these nations."

Sure enough, in July, Main Navy passed to Pearl the virtually verbatim contents of seven messages between Tokyo and several outposts. The flow then stopped. But now, on Wednesday, December 3, here was more "dip," summarized in the two dispatches about code burning, one of which spoke of Purple machines and referred to a Japanese dispatch by its number, 2444.

"I had asked for all vital information," Kimmel said. "I had been assured that I would have it. I appeared to be receiving it." He may not have known explicitly of America's greatest intelligence success—Purple and Magic—but the commander of the Pacific Fleet had the reinforced impression that Washington's cryptologic prowess was so good it knew all there was to know about whatever Japan was up to and was passing it along. It had his back.

Of course, even if Washington had indeed been sending him every intercept, the dip never at any time included the movements and timetables and intentions of the Imperial Navy.

Anyone with a car or a willingness to walk could easily see almost the entirety of Pearl Harbor without setting foot inside its gates. A journey from water's edge into the pineapple fields of Aiea Heights yielded a panoramic snapshot, literally. One day in 1936, before the fleet had taken up permanent residence at Pearl, it arrived at the base from the West Coast, and soon a civilian acquaintance of the fleet commander came aboard to present souvenir photos of the visit. There was the Pacific Fleet, impressively frozen on Kodak film, resting in a harbor that the visitors had thought was secure. "Well, he [the civilian] just stood up on the hill [in] back of it and took these pictures," said Arthur McCollum, who was aboard one of the visiting ships. By 1941, every American naval officer knew that observing the fleet at Pearl Harbor, counting it, taking note of its comings and goings, was one of the simpler tasks in the world of espionage. Kimmel knew it. He was once asked how close to the harbor he thought a civilian could get. "Oh, it is my recollection maybe one hundred yards, two hundred yards, something of that kind."

On September 24, Tokyo reached out to its Honolulu consulate to outline the proper manner in which to report the disposition of ships inside Pearl. "The waters are to be divided roughly into five sub-areas," it said. Area C, for example, would be East Loch, where the battleships tied up. The consulate should locate ships according to this grid, or plot, and briefly identify each by type. Cruiser, destroyer, and so on. "If possible," the Foreign Office added, "we would like to have you make mention of the fact when there are two or more vessels alongside the same wharf." Why, it did not say. It offered no rationale for the grid.

A few weeks later, Tokyo returned to the topic. "As relations between Japan and the United States are most critical, make your 'ships in harbor' report irregular, but at a rate of twice a week. Although you already are no doubt aware, please take extra caution to maintain secrecy." And just four days before, on November 29: "We have been receiving reports from you on ship movements, but in future will you also report even when there are no movements."

American listening stations were picking up so much Japanese radio traffic in various encrypted systems—some that had been solved by Washington, some not—it sometimes took days, even weeks, to decode and translate dispatches. Many were never fully read even when they could have been, or at least not when it would have mattered.

So it wasn't until October 9 that an English translation of Tokyo's grid system began circulating in Washington to the elite few eligible to receive such intelligence. The navy's Lieutenant Commander Kramer found the message strange, but not certifiably alarming. Those compulsive Japanese, they were always sucking up information. Admiral Wilkinson of Naval Intelligence said later, "The Japanese for many years had the reputation—and the facts bore out that reputation—of being meticulous seekers for every scrap of information, whether by photography or by written reports or otherwise." They were especially eager to know the travels of American warships, just as American intelligence labored to know theirs. On a wall at Main Navy, a large map of the Pacific had been divided into sectors, each named, and stickpins tracked the locations of the Imperial Fleet as best they could be discerned through radio analysis. Index cards recorded the history of each ship's movements.

Well before being told to use the grid, for example, the Honolulu consulate had reported to Tokyo on February 21 that "the capital ships and others departed from Pearl Harbor on the 13th and returned on the 19th." In June, the consulate noted, "two English converted cruisers entered Pearl Harbor." In August, the consulate in Panama detected "two United States freighters and 1 British freighter" passing through the Canal Zone. Tokyo asked the consulate in Seattle on October 16 to report each time more than "ten vessels of any type arrive or depart from port at one time." American listeners had snared all these diplomatic messages and many others like them, and forwarded them to Washington for decryption.

To Kramer, overlaying a grid on Pearl might have been a way of whittling verbiage in dispatches. "The Japanese were repeatedly and continually directing their diplomatic service to cut down traffic," he said. "They were repeatedly preparing and sending out abbreviations to be used with codes already in existence." McCollum wondered afterward if the goal was to give Tokyo a sense of how swiftly the fleet could funnel out of Pearl. It could go only single file, after all, given the constricted channel, and a mass sortie took time, upward of three hours. Whatever the motivation, the grid message "did not make much impression on my mind," McCollum said, "nor did it make much impression on the minds of any of the considerable number of what were supposed to be quite capable officers who saw this dispatch at that time." Nor had the follow-up instructions from Tokyo raised concerns, the one about twice-weekly reports, which was decrypted on December 3, or the one about reporting even when ships had not moved, which was read on December 5.

Bratton, of the Far Eastern Section of Army Intelligence, had been more curious about the grid message than most. After all, Oahu was the home of the fleet, whereas Seattle, for example, was not. "I felt that the Japanese were showing unusual interest in the port of Honolulu," he said, meaning Pearl, "and discussed this matter with my opposite numbers in the Navy on several occasions." They had told him not to worry. The grid represented the harmless gathering of minutiae. They also told him, he recalled, that when war did break out, "the fleet is not going to be there." It would have taken to sea. "So this is a waste of time and effort on the part of the Japanese consul."

It may have been. No evidence would surface that Yamamoto relied on the grid. In any event, what would become known as "the bomb plot" message, because it seemed to set up a map-plotting system to improve aerial attack runs, was never relayed to Kimmel, even though the topic was his warships, not negotiations. Nor were the follow-up messages that tweaked what Tokyo wanted. Kimmel may have interpreted their contents differently than Washington had. They were about his port, and seemed so obviously to have only military implications. "You tell a man he's got a snake under his desk," Layton said, "and he's going to jump."

Then again, the admiral might just as easily have imbued the bomb-plot messages with his usual equanimity. After all, he already knew he was being spied on. When it came to sleuthing, he considered the Japanese "most industrious."

In late November and early December, Vice Admiral Matome Ugaki, the Combined Fleet's chief of staff, had devoted some thought to what Yamamoto ought to say in an inspirational radio message to the strike fleet on the attack's eve. He settled on some version of what Lord Horatio Nelson had told the British fleet by signal flag as it began to engage the French and Spanish fleets off Trafalgar on October 21, 1805: "England expects that every man will do his duty."

Writing in his diary on Tuesday, December 2, Ugaki exulted at the good weather that hung over the northern Pacific. It was Providence. A high-pressure system was pushing east right behind the strike fleet, which must be keeping the seas relatively calm for them. "They'll be able to refuel, I'm sure," he wrote, although radio silence left him not really knowing. The magnitude of Japan's risk flooded his thoughts. "Under any circumstances," he wrote, "war decides the fate of a country. And in my view, the present war stakes the rise and fall of our empire."

By Wednesday, details had reached Japan of a news conference in Washington. Franklin Roosevelt had expressed his exasperation to reporters. Peace talks had started in April, he said, and then Japan moved its forces into all of Indochina. Peace talks had resumed, but now "the other day we got word from various sources that already, in Indochina, there are large additional bodies of Japanese forces—

various kinds of forces, naval, air, and land—and that other forces were on the way," the president said. So that morning, the State Department had, "at my request, very politely," asked the Japanese "as to what the purpose of this was, what the intention of the Japanese government in doing this was." Roosevelt hoped it would answer. "We are at peace with Japan," he had said. "We are asking a perfectly polite question."

In his diary entry for Wednesday, Ugaki mocked Roosevelt's naïveté and ignorance, the very idea of wondering about a few additional troops in Indochina when Japan had so much more in mind.

"Don't you know that a big dagger will be thrust into your throat in four days?"

Admiral Husband E. Kimmel, here savoring his elevation to commander of the Pacific Fleet in January 1941, had little contact with the Japanese during four decades of service, and had never heard of a " 'mad dog' attitude."

Deeply fond of the navy, Franklin Roosevelt relocated the fleet from the West Coast to Oahu in 1940, believing its power would intimidate belligerent Japan. Here he stands aboard the cruiser *Indianapolis* in 1936.

"You have told me that the operation is a speculation," Admiral Isoroku Yamamoto said to a critic of his plan to attack distant Oahu with aircraft carriers, "so I shall carry it out."

Lieutenant Commander Minoru Genda, arriving in New York in September 1940 on his way from London to Tokyo, held such unorthodox views about naval airpower that colleagues dubbed him "insane."

Even a close aide considered Harold R. Stark a poor choice to lead the navy, but almost everyone liked "Betty"— including Roosevelt, who here awards the admiral a commendation in 1942.

Putting to sea the day after the "war warning" in late November 1941, Admiral William F. Halsey told his ships he expected "to be in a fight" before seeing Pearl Harbor again.

Above all, the army's Lieutenant General Walter Short was worried not about an air attack on Oahu but about sabotage by some of its thousands of residents of Japanese descent.

Few Americans understood the potential adversary as well as Ambassador Joseph C. Grew, shown here golfing in Japan circa 1941. The empire, he believed, might go to war "with dangerous and dramatic suddenness."

"I should be kept out of heaven," Roosevelt said, in August 1941, for having chosen the National Mall as the site of the Navy and War Departments, seen here from the Washington Monument in 1938.

It was its most closely held secret: the Roosevelt administration was reading Japanese diplomatic messages, having broken their encryption system with machines similar to these, seen in 1944.

In their secret underground quarters at Pearl Harbor, Commander Joseph J. Rochefort and his eavesdroppers concluded from the patterns of Japanese radio traffic that "there was something afoot."

Unaware of the Pearl Harbor plan, Ambassador Kichisaburo Nomura, left, knew nonetheless that little time remained to "be the fire extinguisher." Here he stands with Secretary of State Cordell Hull and Special Envoy Saburo Kurusu on November 17, 1941.

Born in Japan and a student of the country, Captain Arthur H. McCollum sought twice in the last days before the attack to make sure Washington had told naval forces in the Pacific how grave the situation was.

His best guess, fleet intelligence officer Edwin T. Layton told Kimmel, was that the four Japanese aircraft carriers that had vanished from the radio waves were bobbing harmlessly in home waters.

Nearly half the production run of the navy's premier search aircraft, the PBY-5, was being diverted to allied nations that were already at war, leaving Oahu with too few.

In the last sentence of his last message from Oahu, the spy Takeo Yoshikawa, seen here in 1954, told Tokyo, "It appears that no air reconnaissance is being conducted by the Fleet air arm."

"Joined the ship Friday, got under way Saturday morning, and started the war on Sunday," said the new captain of the destroyer *Ward*, Lieutenant William W. Outerbridge, seen here in his 1942 identification photo.

"We have attacked . . . a submarine operating in defensive sea area," Outerbridge radioed Pearl, after the crew of the *Ward*'s number 3 gun had fired on a suspicious vessel off the entrance to the harbor an hour before the air raid began.

The inbound planes on his radar screen on the north shore of Oahu were "the largest group I had ever seen," said Private Joseph L. Lockard, who, along with George E. Elliott Jr., tried to warn army headquarters.

With torpedo tracks clearly visible in water once thought to be too shallow, three punctured battleships bleed semicircles of oil in the attack's opening seconds. A few minutes later, a bomb obliterated the *Arizona*, second from left, moored alongside a service ship.

The aftermath. In Dry Dock Number One, the battleship *Pennsylvania* looms over the badly damaged destroyers *Cassin* and *Downes*. On the far side of the harbor, smoke billows from the remains of the *Arizona*.

A letter writer told him suicide was a proper response to the disaster, but for the rest of his life, Kimmel, seen here testifying to Congress about the attack in 1946, believed the fault lay in Washington.

TWELVE

A TIME TO LOOK

Thursday, December 4

ODDLY, PERHAPS, for an army guy, Rufus Bratton kept wondering about the fleet, whether it was on the qui vive, a phrase more popular then than today. "I still felt uneasy about this thing," he said. The colonel was as familiar with the Japanese as his navy counterpart and friend, McCollum. He had learned the language in Tokyo; studied at the Japanese General Staff College; served as the assistant military attaché in Japan, and as the attaché, too. In toto, Bratton had lived about seven of his forty-nine years among the Japanese. Toward week's end, he made the long odyssey from Army Intelligence to McCollum's office to ask about Pearl. "I said to him, 'Are you sure these people are properly alerted? Are they on the job? Have they been properly warned?' He said, 'Oh, yes, the fleet is gone,' or 'is going to sea.'"

Or so McCollum had been led to conclude. Even now, three days after he had met with Stark, Ingersoll, and Turner, the precise intelligence and commands contained in their November 27 war warning

209

remained a mystery to him. He still had not seen a copy. "Possibly, it was none of my business," he said. But the man with the "nervousness of a terrier" even on noncrisis days had anxieties similar to Bratton's, even though the three top admirals in the navy had assured him the fleet was now wary and preparing.

Dispatches kept coming from watchers in the Far East—ashore, in submarines, in airplanes—about the southerly procession of Japanese warships. Main Navy had told its attachés in Tokyo, Bangkok, and other Asian cities to start getting rid of *their* codebooks and, as they finished the steps, to transmit the words "boomerang" or "jabberwock" to Washington in the clear, without encryption, so there would be no doubt they had done it.

McCollum had a strong sense of imminence, and for him, Stark's one warning was not enough, regardless of what it had said. He was not a seer. He had no foreboding about Pearl, the base. The Japanese did not care about the base. But he knew they cared about Kimmel's ships, and "would make a very definite attempt to strike the Fleet at or near the commencement time," wherever the ships were, in port or at sea. Even though he, too, believed the big Japanese carriers were probably in home waters, he now prepared a warning to supplement Stark's. To actually send it, though, McCollum had to first obtain the imprimatur not of Stark but of Richmond Turner, the head of war planning, who might have been the most memorable—and not in a good way—officer in the hierarchy of the navy.

"Richmond Kelly Turner was a son-of-a-bitch from a long line of bachelors," Joe Rochefort said, although he made that observation only after Turner had long been dead. "He was also a regular bull in a china shop. He was rigid, narrow, intolerant and had no use for intelligence in 1941." On one occasion, Turner had referred to sifting radio traffic for clues as "goddamn foolishness by these people." Edwin Layton called him "the Navy's Patton," with all the good qualities and terrible ones the comparison suggests.

An officer who had served under Turner aboard the destroyer *Mervine*, Joseph U. Lademan, described him as "intellectually brilliant," but dismissive of anyone who did not see the glory of his mind. "There was only one way to do a thing," Lademan said. "The Turner way." Vincenzo Lopresti, the quartermaster of the cruiser *Astoria* during the twenty-five months Turner was its captain, had witnessed sincere and consistent concern for enlisted men—and disdain for officers. Turner never sought their advice, and dressed them down publicly. "He was sure he knew it all," Lopresti said. For years afterward, Lopresti would remember how, whenever an officer gave an answer Turner thought wrong or illogical, he would "stamp his right foot lightly and utter the word 'balls.'"

Now fifty-six and possessed of "heavy, black, Mephistophelian eyebrows" and a "hot temper," Turner had decided that based on what he would later describe as his own "considerable study of the Japanese character and life and history," he was wise in the ways of the empire. The core of Turner's research, apparently, consisted of the roughly ten days he had spent in Japan in 1939 after the *Astoria* had conveyed home the ashes of the late Japanese ambassador, who had died in Washington. "He felt he knew a great deal about the Japanese," said one of Naval Intelligence's many recent directors, Alan Kirk. "We were clashing right along. It wasn't a very happy time there for me."

Turner had a pinched view of Intelligence's role. He saw it as a mere "collection agency," as Kirk recalled his phrase, a bunch of squirrels in uniform that were to gather acorns about foreign navies and pass them along, not ruminate about their meaning. It was fine if the squirrels gave the forces afloat neutral facts—ship X is at place Y, or the Japanese are dismantling their encryption systems—but not fine if they offered an opinion about what a piece of intelligence signified, or gave an estimate of what the Japanese might do next, at least not without first showing any proposed message to War Plans, home of the true global thinkers. "We had in our Division officers who were experienced in matters of that character," Turner said, "and more experienced than the officers of the Office of Naval Intelligence, who generally were more junior, and were trained rather for the collection and dissemination of information, rather than its application to a strategic situation."

Unfortunately for the admiral, navy regulations expressly stipulated that Naval Intelligence should not only collect, but also "evaluate," and said nothing about its estimates being vetted by anyone else. When the dispute had reached the chief of naval operations, he had cast his vote for Turner, regulations notwithstanding. Harold Stark genuinely liked him—there was no questioning the man's smarts—but no two personalities could have been more antithetical than those of the keep-cheerful CNO and the steamrolling director of War Plans. Betty had stepped out of Turner's way. It was another measure of the second-rate status of Naval Intelligence in 1941.

So it was that on Thursday, December 4, McCollum was compelled to visit room 2722 to secure Turner's consent for his new dispatch. Its precise wording has disappeared, because it was never sent. "When the dispatch does not go," McCollum said, "you wind it up and throw it in the wastebasket," and no copies are filed. His recollection would be that the message, first of all, had given a condensed version of the note he had read to Stark a few days earlier about Japanese ship movements, the return home of Japanese residents abroad, shifts in their espionage operations, and other intelligence. Then his new message told the Pacific forces what all this meant: "The Japanese were definitely bent on war, and that we could expect the opening of hostilities almost at any time." He was feeling more certain about that than he had been just three days before. "Japan would strike," he thought.

When the message was presented for his approval, Turner penciled out the estimate about the imminence of war, leaving only the data points. He then handed over the document McCollum had never seen—the war warning—and asked, "Did not [McCollum] think that was enough?" The opening sentence jarred him, as it had everyone who read it. "It does not come in the life of most naval officers to receive or see a message containing such words," he said later. To Turner, he then said, "Well, good gosh, you put in the words *war warning*. I do not know what could be plainer than that."

McCollum, however, was not satisfied and not finished. It surely annoyed him to have to be there at all, begging an admiral who possessed an amateur understanding of Japan. The Far Eastern Section was immersed in all things Japanese every day. Turner was not. McCollum had lived among them. Turner had not. McCollum had predicated in February the Japanese would occupy all of French Indochina, even as Turner was insisting, no, they would invade Siberia. In July, of course, the Japanese did what the junior officer had said they would do. Who was the strategic naïf?

Now, on Thursday, he refused to abandon the idea of a second warning just because Turner had showed him the first. The fleets needed a supplement. "I would like to see mine go" as written, he told Turner, who replied that he could send only the edited version, without the prediction of war. If he wished to send his original, Turner said, he would have to enlist Admiral Wilkinson—the director of Naval Intelligence at the moment—"and we will argue about it." If such an argument ever ensued, Turner won it; Stark had ensured he would. Later, Turner downplayed the exchange, saying that upon reading Stark's war warning, McCollum had concluded it was sufficient, and had promptly ripped his proposed dispatch in two, which seems most unlikely.

There will never be a way to know the impact a follow-up warning would have had if sent on Thursday. If McCollum's memory was accurate, his dispatch was much less ambiguous than the one of November 27. Stark's had noted only the possibility that Japan might strike American territory, the Philippines. McCollum's flat-out said Japan was going to war with the United States. Its writer had expertise when it came to the Japanese, and Layton at Pearl would have known that as he read the dispatch. They had been friends since Tokyo in '29. A second warning might have caused the fleet to snap to in ways it had not so far.

But it could just as easily have been dismissed as redundant, as Turner clearly thought it was. If McCollum's memory was correct, his dispatch said nothing about where the Japanese would commence the conflict he was predicting.

The Imperial Navy's second change of radio call signs was doing what it was intended to do, obfuscating its whereabouts and sowing confusion among the Americans. In the Dungeon on Thursday, the intelligence analysts were using Heeia intercepts to build their list of identified units back from nothing. They could work only so fast. "Almost a complete blank of information on the carriers today," Joe Rochefort's report for Tuesday had told Layton. Of two hundred new call signs at least "partially" identified by then, no carriers had turned up. Japanese radio operators must still be ignoring the four missing ones, which must still not be talking, which meant they could still be in home waters, or they could still not be. "It is evident that carrier traffic is at a low ebb," Rochefort had written. On the next day, he declared "no information" about carriers. On the next, he did not even bother to say he had none; by then, it was a given. "The carriers just completely dropped from sight," he said later. "Never heard another word from them."

With a copy to Kimmel on Thursday, an American naval attaché in the Far East reported that the British had told all friendly ships that were north of Hong Kong to "beat it south thereof," toward the Royal Navy's base at Singapore. They were to "bring such [ship]yard equipment as possible," to keep it out of the hands of the Japanese. Also on Thursday, also with a copy to Kimmel, Washington ordered the naval outpost on the island of Guam, nearly four thousand miles to the west of Pearl, to "destroy all secret and confidential publications and other classified matter, except that essential for current purposes," that is, for staying in touch. Guam should be ready to rid itself "instantly" of even this minimal encryption ability, Main Navy said, "in event of emergency." That would be an invasion.

Kimmel may have dismissed Japan's encryption destruction in Washington and Manila as merely a sign of its fear of an American declaration of war, but even he must have been having second thoughts if Main Navy thought Japan could try to seize Guam. "I was torn," he would say of this period. His contemplations of what to do, what defensive steps to take, if any, dueled constantly with his martial eagerness to take the fight to the Japanese as soon as he had permission. Only two days earlier, on Tuesday, he had made that perpetual desire for offensive action clear once again in a nine-page letter airmailed to Stark.

Anticipating war with Japan one day, the United States had been constructing naval and air stations not only at Midway and Wake, but also at a plethora of tiny isles dipping far down into the South Seas, nine by Kimmel's count, with more likely. The fleet would have to defend these obscure places—and in his mind, what a waste of his great ships that would be. The fleet must be footloose, not tied down as the guardian of outposts, inertly awaiting the Imperial Navy's appearance. "A fleet in being behind a series of defensive positions in the Central and South Pacific cannot contribute very much toward victory over a power some thousands of miles to the westward," Kimmel had written. Presumptuously, he had told Stark on Tuesday to build no more bases without an undisputed need.

It was a reprise of the theme—offense—that had permeated so many of his messages in 1941. In September, for example, after Roosevelt had given the Atlantic Fleet permission to shoot at German ships, Kimmel asked if his fleet could begin "direct offensive measures against German and Italian raiders" that ventured into his ocean. (No, Main Navy had replied. Let's not spread the war.) Going on the attack suited Kimmel's meticulous, take-charge personality. Train, make a plan, train, execute. Stark's war warning had been his get ready, get set to swoop down on the Marshalls and, if he got lucky, seduce the Japanese into a decisive trap. Even now, Kimmel's staff was working on an updated version of his November 30 memo, "Steps To Take" as soon as war broke out. "I considered my primary responsibilities out there offensive action, which we expected and hoped to undertake," Kimmel said, "and no man can get a proper view" of the decisions he made without understanding that.

To take the fight to the Japanese, the fleet needed long-range patrol planes winging far out in front of its advancing ships to scout enemy positions in the Marshalls and to look for imperial ships. But Kimmel also needed long-range patrol planes to defend Oahu. He didn't have enough to do both. The whole plane situation, in fact, drove the admiral crazy, and it was all Franklin Roosevelt's fault.

By December 1941, the nearly five thousand workers of Consolidated Aircraft in San Diego were rolling out the most coveted search plane in the English-speaking world at the rate of almost one a day. The PBY-5 was no show horse. It was slow. Its nose looked as if it had lost a bar fight. The wing was almost a free-floating, independent being, anchored to a pedestal that was mounted atop the fuselage. The fuselage itself sported large clear-plastic pimples for gazing out and down. What it lacked in charisma, the plane offered in functionality. A PBY-5 could keep its crew of seven to nine men aloft hour upon hour, searching as far as 1,400 miles before having to turn for home.

On his way back to Pearl in June after personally imploring Roosevelt not to steal any more of his warships for the Atlantic, Kimmel paid a visit to the Consolidated plant to exhort its workers to build more and faster. "You have to but recall that it was a single plane of the type you are building here that made possible the sinking of the German battleship Bismarck," the admiral had said, a nod to the grand British victory of the month before. "Had that plane missed contact, had she failed to maintain contact until other aircraft and surface ships arrived on the scene, the Bismarck would be afloat today."

He and General Walter Short had been battering the Navy and War Departments with pleas for more airplanes capable of searching far out to sea, not just PBYs but also army B-17s. Getting more patrol planes "was the thing I had stressed over and over again," Kimmel said. His need stemmed, in great part, from Oahu's most salient characteristic, its island-ness. A Japanese force bent on a raid could come from any direction, even looping around and sneaking in from the mainland side, to the east. A continuous, daily inspection of all the approach lanes—north, south, east, and west—would require dozens and dozens of aircraft devoted only to that purpose in a grinding cycle of flight, rest, repair, flight, rest, repair.

Pearl had thought a great deal about this numbing and intricate world of vectors and fuel capacities and engine wear and tear. Its best defense would not be to try to wipe out enemy planes as they appeared in the sky above the harbor but to catch and pulverize the carrier or carriers well out to sea, well before planes left the flight deck. Or as the Naval Institute's *Proceedings* had put it too flippantly, "Tackle the ball carrier before he crosses the line of scrimmage." Otherwise, once aloft, some enemy planes would inevitably make it all the way to Oahu, juke through antiaircraft fire, evade American fighter craft, and pounce on the ships in the pickle barrel of Pearl.

General Martin and Admiral Bellinger, in their prescient speculation of March, had chosen three hundred miles out as a possible launch point for the Japanese because it was far enough away to offer maximum protection to Japanese ships, but close enough that the attack planes would have fuel enough to make it back to their fleet. A launch at dawn made more sense than dusk. That way, the attack force could cover the last few hundred miles before takeoff wrapped in darkness. Given that there would be a poor chance of discovering the force precisely as it emerged into the sunshine of a new day, it had to be hunted for and found on the day prior, before it vanished overnight into the black. Doing the math—speed of ships, hours of darkness, three hundred miles away at launch—tacticians had concluded that Hawaii's patrol planes needed to sweep seven hundred miles from the islands in all directions, maybe eight hundred to be safe.

The PBY-5 did not come with radar; spotting was all by the eyes of the crew. The same crews could hardly search every day, not at sixteen hours per mission. Pilots, copilots, navigators would lose their edge, if not collapse. Bellinger figured, "A crew could conduct one patrol every third day of the type listed in the estimate." Aircraft would break down, too. Even those that did not would need maintenance, and every so often major overhauls. Taking everything into account, to keep aloft a daily, 360-degree defensive search for one month would require between 225 and 250 crews, and 150 to 170 planes, depending on how far out they traveled and how much visibility they enjoyed. Even then, even if Bellinger had every plane and airman he desired, the searchers would have only a 50 percent chance of peering in the right direction at the right moment, through clouds and haze, and seeing a node of enemy ships cutting through the immensity down below.

At his disposal in early December for protecting the nation's most vital base, Bellinger did not have 170 PBYs, or even 150. If all of his planes were in working order—and that was not the case at the moment—he had 81, roughly half the ideal. And he did not really have that many, either, because a number of his PBYs were based at Midway and could not be used for searching from Oahu. One day, an officer found Kimmel and Bellinger bent over a chart, drawing lines, hoping to devise a way to search with an inadequate stable of planes. The sight of them "trying to cut their cloth when there really was no cloth to cut was too much," the officer said.

The local naval district, the Fourteenth, was eager to take over the problem of defensive search from the fleet and had asked Washington "time and time again" for dozens and dozens of its own PBYs. By early December, it had scored none. General Short had asked for 184 B-17s so *he* could do the search, fulfilling the army's duty of protecting the fleet base. But at that moment, in the entire world, the Army Air Corps possessed only 148 B-17s, of which Short had a dozen, of which six were ready for long-range search.

Oahu lacked planes for the same reason Kimmel had been forced to hand over so many of his ships. There was a war in the Atlantic Ocean. Roosevelt was steering a huge percentage of the country's aircraft output to beleaguered friends. Helping others beat the Nazis over there today seemed preferable to having to fight the Nazis back here tomorrow. The pressure to give American planes to the Allies was "very insistent," army chief of staff Marshall said. Kimmel's predecessor, Richardson, had found that during the months he was in charge, the fleet was "well down on the Navy Department's priority list for receipt of additional patrol squadrons."

Since September 1940, when the first PBY-5 had emerged from Consolidated Aircraft's assembly line, the company had built 336 of them, but almost half had gone elsewhere: 97 to the Royal Air Force; 21 to the Royal Canadian Air Force; 18 to the Dutch; and 16 to the Royal Australian Air Force. The US Navy had gotten the rest, but it had deployed many of them to the Atlantic, where the shooting was. Army bombers were being shipped to the Allies, too. All told, between February 1, 1941, and December 1, the United States had turned over to British-aligned forces the astonishing sum of 3,814 aircraft—light bombers, heavy bombers, fighters, patrol planes. Roosevelt had memorably explained to the nation that if a neighbor's house is afire but he has no hose, and "if he can take my garden hose and connect it up with his hydrant, I may help to put out his fire." And so, a greater number of Consolidated Aircraft's PBY-5s had gone to the Royal Air Force than to the Pacific Fleet.

"There exists and will continue to exist for some time a shortage of patrol planes," Stark told all commanders in June. That hadn't changed by December. "The Department has no additional airplanes available for assignment," he wrote to Oahu on November 25.

By late 1941, Secretary of War Stimson was beginning to fear that Roosevelt was being too generous to the Allies, diminishing the security of his own country. "He is entirely in the hands of people who see only their side of the other nations, and who are wedded to the idea that with our weapons, they can win the war," Stimson wrote in his diary on October 15. "I am perfectly certain that they cannot, and perfectly certain that eventually we will have to fight and that this method of nibbling away at our store of weapons is reducing our weapons down to what I fear is a dangerous thing." Likewise, Republican congressman Robert F. Rich of Pennsylvania complained, "We are shipping out of this country the things that were manufactured for our own defense, and we could not defend our own shores if we were attacked."

Admiral Chester Nimitz, in charge of Main Navy's personnel office, was nagged by such concerns, too. He had written to Kimmel, an old friend, in March: "As you well know, this country is confronted with a most difficult problem—that of determining just how much of our total output shall go to Britain and her allies, and how much to keep for ourselves. A wrong guess may well make our own problem insoluble."

With the paucity of PBYs, a continuous, full-circle reconnaissance for any Japanese fleet that might be on its way to Oahu was impossible. "Very little discussion was required," Kimmel said. "We had gone up and down this scale dozens of times. We knew what we could do." For a 360-degree inspection, Oahu would have to send aloft the bulk of Bellinger's eighty-one PBYs on day one—and have few left over to send up on day two and day three. Unable to rotate crews and machines, Pearl would have to keep flying the same ones. Burnout would commence rapidly. Gaps would appear in the search circle. More and more sea would be left unexamined. And the attrition would eat up the airborne eyes the fleet needed for its opening offensive, when many of the PBYs would be flown to outer islands, closer to the enemy, to begin their scouting on behalf of the fleet.

"I had to decide what was the best use of the patrol planes as a matter of policy for the foreseeable future," Kimmel said, "and with their war task in front of me." It seemed to him far more likely that his ships and PBYs would soon be in hot pursuit of the Japanese down toward the Marshalls than that the Japanese would be coming to Oahu. To search for an approaching enemy fleet that was almost certainly not out there—it was "highly improbable," he maintained—would be a waste of resources, pointlessly cutting into his ability to carry out his plans. Martin and Bellinger had advised that, in light of the limited number of patrol planes, a 360-degree search should be undertaken only when "intelligence indicates that a surface raid is probable within rather narrow time limits." Kimmel took refuge in that standard. As yet, he did not have that kind of "probable" cause. So he would not search. In the recollection of his war plans officer, Soc McMorris, "This, in effect, accepted a calculated risk."

"Utilization of patrol planes for searching the Hawaiian area for a possible but improbable enemy," Kimmel said, "was of much less value than being prepared to immediately advance those planes to our distant island bases."

While a perfect search could not be done, a perfectly good one could be. Not all points of the compass posed an equal threat to Oahu. The seas to the south and west were dotted with those American island bases. The Japanese knew that. The fleet concentrated its training in those waters, too. The Japanese knew that. For them to try to thread through to attack Pearl from those directions would invite fatal exposure. Further, if the Japanese chose one of the two remaining alternatives—an attack from the east—they would have to pull off the longest journey of all from Japan, and after they attacked, Oahu and its planes would block the path between them and home.

At Pearl, it seemed that one compass sector—from west to north, and especially northwest to north—would beckon to the Japanese more obviously than the others, if they were bent on a surprise. "The air raid force on this place would have a better chance, a much better chance, to get in from the northward," Kimmel said. There were no bases to the north; no islands. Merchant ships were few. In the words of Richmond Turner, "Why, it is very easy to get in [from] there undetected." General Sherman Miles of Army Intelligence called the sector "the vacant sea, in which there are practically no ships and in which large movements of [war]ships could occur without anybody seeing them."

That area offered another inducement to the Imperial Navy, a technical one. Trade winds bathe the Hawaiian Islands, blowing from the northeast or east on many more days than not, rustling the palms constantly and taking the edge off the sun's heat, as any tourist knows. An aircraft carrier, even today, turns into the wind to launch and recover planes, in order to provide them with maximum lift as they race into the air or slowly descend. With the winds so reliably from the northeast and east, a carrier attacking Oahu from the south or southwest would have to keep sailing *toward* the island to recover its planes, rather than making its escape. But if attacking from the north, it could turn *away* from danger to recover them.

On Thursday, the man formally designated as Naval Air Pilot Number Four was at home on Oahu, in bed, suffering through a third day of a sore throat and laryngitis. Admiral Patrick Nieson Lynch Bellinger of Cheraw, South Carolina, the commander of the fleet's patrol planes, was fifty-six and a one-man record book. He had been the first American to pilot a warplane struck by a bullet in combat (Mexico, 1914), had set the American altitude record for a seaplane (ten thousand feet, 1915), had become the first navy pilot to act as a spotter for gunnery at sea (1916), and the first to test-fire machine guns in flight (1917).

Bellinger had been trying, while sick, to do paperwork. But he was also passing the time with the Honolulu newspapers, which "were all alarming," he thought, with their stories about the state of things with the Japanese. Of course, there existed better, and even more worrisome, intelligence than what was in the papers. Naval Air Pilot Number Four did not have it, though. Bellinger had not been shown the war warning, an uncharacteristic exclusion by the collegial Husband Kimmel, no doubt reflecting his opinion that no search was needed yet. "God only knows what I would have done," Bellinger said, "but I can say this: that I was very much surprised when I heard that there had been a [warning] message."

Nor had he been shown the dispatches about Japanese code burning, nor would he be shown the code-destruction order Main Navy sent to Guam on Thursday. Worst of all, Bellinger, coauthor of the report about how Japan might try to ambush Oahu with carrier planes, had not been told that four large Japanese carriers had evaporated from radio circuits. In fact, he had not spoken with Kimmel since the previous week.

If the fleet commander had given him all that intelligence, and if Kimmel had asked him what to do, Bellinger might have told him what he said later: He had sufficient PBYs to set aside some—enough, in fact—to support a fleet offensive at the start of the war and employ the rest to search the most dangerous wedge of the sky, straight north around to straight west. That way, Kimmel would still have had a fresh, intact group of planes and pilots even if all the others were used up in a fruitless search. How long could he have kept up that partial search? "For about two weeks, and maybe longer." It was a guess. He was short spare parts for the PBY-5s, which were the majority of his planes, and which were new and suffering shakedown glitches. He would not really know how long he could keep up an imperfect but focused search until he tried one.

As it happened, Admiral Nimitz had made a speech on Tuesday that, without mentioning airplanes, reflected the squeeze the navy faced. On the shores of Narragansett Bay in Newport, he had given the commencement address to the fifty-one officers of the Naval War College's latest class. They had spent only five months on the campus, the length of the postgraduate program having been cleaved in half because warships could no longer afford to have experienced officers absent for so long during what Nimitz told the graduates was "the world crisis." Likewise, the Naval Academy had cut its program to three years from four, to meet the demand for officers on new ships.

In the auditorium of Pringle Hall on Tuesday, Nimitz's concluding wisdom focused on what the graduates would encounter when they returned to their posts: shortages. They would have to live with them. "You must remember," he said, "that you in the field must make the best of what you have! Perfection, though desirable, is not attainable."

Had Bellinger been ordered, on the day of the war warning, to make the best of what he had and to begin searching to the north around to the west, the two-week period he believed possible would have ended on December 11.

THIRTEEN

OUT OF THEIR DEPTH

Friday, December 5

E VEN TO MANY of those on the mainland with no knowledge of code burnings and missing aircraft carriers, Friday felt as if a dreaded claxon was about to sound. News and editorial pages across the country "now present American involvement in a Pacific war as an imminent probability," according to a summary prepared for Treasury Secretary Morgenthau. Quietly, the administration had told leaders of Congress to keep both houses in session, instead of adjourning for the holidays. The Far East "looks pretty serious," one legislator told the *New York Times* after a ninety-minute briefing at the White House on Thursday. Asked if the cabinet session on Friday would be routine, Secretary of War Stimson replied, "No cabinet meetings are routine now."

"They don't mean business, Mr. President," Cordell Hull told the gathering at two o'clock that afternoon. The secretary of state had just come from a conversation with Nomura and Kurusu, who had presented their government's answer to Roosevelt's question from

earlier in the week. The empire's military enhancements in Indochina, they had said, merely reflected its fear that China was about
to attack the Imperial Army there. In that case, Hull had replied—no
doubt sarcastically—wouldn't it be simpler to just leave Indochina
altogether? "With every hour that passes, I become more convinced
that they are not playing in the open," Hull told the cabinet.

"He was very disgusted with the Japanese and used the strongest language I ever heard him use," Labor Secretary Frances Perkins wrote. Hull, who was now seventy and an object of veneration,
looked as dignified as any human could ever look, but he could star-
tle listeners with how profane he could be.

The cabinet began discussing where the empire would strike. Not,
the civilians kept hoping, American territory. Most likely Singapore.
Perkins would recall Roosevelt asking what should be done if only
the British or Dutch were attacked, and, as was the case when he had
asked a similar question in early November, the consensus was: go
to war. As for the Pacific Fleet, "Nobody asked where it was or how
it was dispersed," Perkins said. "It would have been extraordinarily
bad form to have asked. We would have been promptly told that the
admirals had charge of that."

On the floor of the House of Representatives on Friday, Republican Edwin A. Hall of New York argued for giving servicemen thirty
dollars each of federal money for bus and train fare, so they could see
their loved ones at Christmas. "As a mother wrote me not long ago,"
Hall said, "this may be the last chance that a great many boys have
to come home." The day before, John Taber, another New York Republican, had risen to speak in favor of adding $8 billion to defense
spending to show American resolve to Tokyo, although he would not
"be surprised if Japan takes a course that will force us to defend our
western coast, the Hawaiian Islands and the Philippines."

The most influential voice in American columnizing, or certainly one of them, believed the nation was "now really on the verge of actual, all-out war." Except not with the Nazis, as Republicans and isolationists had claimed for months would happen if the United States gave military aid to the British. Walter Lippmann's scorn for Roosevelt's opponents had oozed from every phrase of his Thursday piece in the *Washington Post*. He had mocked them for never having understood that the "direct and immediate threat to the United States was in the Pacific," and that helping Britain stay in the fight in Europe was the best way to free up the bulk of the navy to stand watch against Hitler's rampaging Asian ally. The national tussles over neutrality and armed escorts for convoys had been pointless. America was about to go to war on the overlooked side of the world.

In a letter that Friday, Franklin Roosevelt agreed that "the situation is definitely serious." He was writing to Wendell Willkie, the Indiana businessman whom he had defeated soundly only a year earlier. Although Willkie alleged during the 1940 campaign that Roosevelt would take the nation into war if given a third term, he was in reality a Republican of the Frank Knox stripe, the kind with an acute understanding of the threat posed by Germany and Japan. After the election, Willkie denounced the Axis powers as "madmen who are loose in the world," and confessed with a grin that he had been engaging only in "a bit of campaign oratory" when he painted Roosevelt as a warmonger. "He is *my* President now," Willkie said.

Roosevelt had dispatched him to London in February to confer with Winston Churchill, and now wanted him to do the same with the Australians and the New Zealanders, in light of "the Japanese matter." "There might be an armed clash at any moment if the Japanese continued [*sic*] their forward progress against the Philippines, Dutch Indies or Malays or Burma," he wrote to Willkie that Friday morning, December 5. "Perhaps the next four or five days will decide the matter."

The real name of the young man counting ships on Friday was Takeo Yoshikawa. But to his colleagues at the Japanese consulate, he was Tadashi Morimura. After the war, he would portray himself as the star of numerous risky espionage escapades during these months, such as taking a job at Pearl as a dishwasher to eavesdrop at the officers' mess; donning farmer's clothes to amble into forbidden military zones; diving into the harbor channel to see if underwater gates or nets had been emplaced to block submarines. A spy he was, yes. But his preferred methods leaned more toward boldly hailing a taxi so he could gaze on the fleet from any number of public places, as any non-Bond could. He did not even use binoculars; it was that easy.

Yoshikawa/Morimura, who was twenty-seven, had arrived from Yokohama in March with six $100 bills for expenses, presumably cab fares. By December, he had managed to alienate the bulk of his coworkers at the consulate, who noticed he was "frequently drunk, often had women in his quarters overnight, came to work late or not at all, as he pleased, insulted the Consul General on occasions, and generally conducted himself as if he were beyond penalty." He pretty much was. One consulate receptionist would remember that many times someone had to wake him up in the morning at his cottage, one of several small residences on the grounds.

His cover job, the only one most consulate employees believed he had, was to assist local Japanese with problems as outsiders in Hawaii. Often, they would come in and formally renounce their citizenship, and this perplexed the spy. He had assumed that with so many Japanese newspapers, schools, clubs, temples, and shrines, there would be plenty of tipsters to recruit for the cause. But he found Japanese religious and civic leaders "unanimously uncooperative," and the general population "essentially loyal to the United States."

He learned, in other words, what the FBI's Robert Shivers had: there was no teeming underground.

Yoshikawa had been living at home on the island of Shikoku in 1936, aimless, his career as a naval aviator cut short by persistent stomach pains, when an Imperial Navy officer came to his door on behalf of its intelligence service. Yoshikawa was invited to Tokyo to start absorbing all that he could about the ports and ships of the British and American navies, which he and most every naval officer assumed would be the enemies one day. He plunged into monthly issues of the US Naval Institute's *Proceedings*; combed *Jane's Fighting Ships*; stopped by embassies to pick up free copies of brochures about Western navies; and read naval attaché dispatches from Japan's embassies. He pored over photographs of American and British warships snapped by Japanese agents in the harbors of Singapore and Manila. He studied English, although to little evident effect.

By 1940, Yoshikawa was, at least in his opinion, the Imperial Navy's greatest living source of data about American naval prowess and habits. "I knew by then every U.S. man-of-war and aircraft-type by name, hull number, configuration and technical characteristics, and I knew, too, a great deal of general information about the U.S. naval bases at Manila, Guam and Pearl Harbor."

When he sailed for Honolulu aboard a Japanese merchant ship early in 1941, Yoshikawa traveled as Morimura, but without knowing of any plan to surprise the Americans. None had been fully formed and authorized, and even if one had been, its details would not have been passed along to a spy who stood a good chance of being stopped by the FBI and queried about his evident fascination with military airfields, potential landing beaches, and, of course, Pearl.

He inspected all the larger Hawaiian islands—Kauai, Maui, the Big Island. On Oahu, if he did not call a taxi, he would often summon Richard Kotoshirodo, a clerk at the consulate who had a 1937 Ford and was fond of Hawaiian shirts. Kotoshirodo was one of the few consulate workers with an excellent idea of what Yoshikawa had really come to do. He and the spy had been instructed never to ask Hawaiians about a specific place of interest, never to leave the highway to look at one, never to use a camera to photograph one, and to bring basic tourist maps, not the topographical kind. Yoshikawa never carried a notebook; all of his dispatches were written from memory. If asked, the men in the Ford were just sightseers. In Kotoshirodo's poor English, the rule was "no get caught." They never were.

Often Yoshikawa did his surveillance from a small peninsula that jutted into Pearl Harbor and featured a Japanese-owned soda shop he liked. Or he went into nearby Aiea Heights, near a sugar refinery, to soak up the view for thirty minutes or so. Anyone who knew the location of the Submarine Building down below could, and still can, see it from there, even the window of Husband Kimmel's corner office. There must have been days when Yoshikawa was looking down at the fleet as Kimmel was peering out at it.

The deeper into the fall of 1941, the more frequently Tokyo wanted Yoshikawa to report the comings, goings, and locations of ships in the harbor. Especially since receiving the instruction to use a grid system—it had arrived September 24—he sensed that the Imperial Navy was coiling for a great strike, for which he was providing critical intelligence.

On Tuesday, December 2, Tokyo made a very specific request. The Americans would not decrypt it until the end of the month, and by then it would not matter. "In view of the present situation," Foreign Minister Shigenori Togo wrote, "the presence in port of warships [he meant battleships], airplane carriers and cruisers is of utmost importance. Hereafter, to the utmost of your ability, let me know day by day. Wire me in each case whether or not there are any observation balloons above Pearl Harbor, or if there are any indications that they will be set up. Also advise me whether or not the warships are provided with anti-mine nets." Togo was referring to antitorpedo nets.

They were akin to underwater chain-link fences, suspended from buoys or booms across a harbor mouth, or at a short remove from the exposed sides of ships. Too few had been in place in the Gulf of Taranto on November 11, 1940. Toward midnight, under a robust, illuminating moon, a cluster of British carrier planes, so outdated they were biplanes, descended to the wave tops of the Mediterranean Sea and began closing on the oblivious Italian fleet, anchored in its home port in the heel of Italy. Of the eleven torpedoes that the Fairey Swordfish bombers loosed against their Axis enemy that night at Taranto, three plowed into the battleship *Littorio*, and one each found the battleships *Caio Duilio* and *Conte di Cavour*.

In Rome, the American naval attaché, Thomas C. Kinkaid, had recorded in his diary what the US consul in Naples had passed along to him: the raid, launched from the carrier *Illustrious*, had shattered Italian morale with its audacity. "The loss of ships in port without a chance to fight is a severe blow and a great humiliation—*brutta figura*," Kinkaid had written. "After the raid, there were street riots in Taranto, people complaining loudly of the poor ground defense, and the hardships they were enduring, and demanding peace."

Eleven days after the daring British torpedo strike, Harold Stark wrote James Richardson, who was still his commander in Hawaii. "Since the Taranto incident, my concern for the safety of the fleet in Pearl Harbor, already great, has become even greater," Stark wrote. While there might be acts of sabotage by the local Japanese if war broke out, "by far the most profitable object of sudden attack in

Hawaiian waters would be the Fleet units based in that area." Stark had then wondered, "Is it desirable to place torpedo nets within the harbor itself?"

The Bureau of Ordnance had concluded that a net placed ninety feet from a docked or anchored vessel—the most vulnerable kind—could stop 40 percent of the onrushing torpedoes; adding a second net farther out raised that figure to 90 percent. But in a harbor as congested as Pearl, protecting ships by putting them inside large corrals of cordoned water would shrink the width of channels and bedevil maneuvering. Nets would get in the way of PBY takeoffs and landings, too. They took a long time to emplace and, worse, a long time to remove, which could delay the fleet if it had to sail in a hurry. Richardson did not want the headaches, and besides, he thought it unlikely that Japanese carriers could get close enough in wartime to launch torpedo planes toward Pearl.

In February, Stark again raised the issue of air-launched torpedoes, this time with his new Pacific commander and this time offering comforting data, not trepidation. Providing his own italics, the chief of naval operations told Kimmel that at Taranto, "The *depths of water* in which the torpedoes were launched were *between 14 and 15 fathoms.*" That is, eighty-four to ninety feet. Thus, it was safe to assume, Stark believed, that an airplane dropping a torpedo needed "a minimum depth of water of seventy-five feet," otherwise the weapon would hit the bottom before it could level off, arm its warhead, and drive to the target. "One hundred and fifty feet of water is desired," Stark thought.

Pearl, at its deepest, was about forty-five.

But by June 13, Stark's office had reconsidered. It had new, cautionary thoughts. In recent tests, American and British torpedoes had been dropped into depths of "considerably less than 75 feet," Royal Ingersoll had written to Kimmel, and yet they had worked.

They had made "excellent runs." While it remained "much more likely" an attacker would still seek a depth of "at least 10 fathoms" (sixty-six feet) for an airborne torpedo attack, "it may be stated that it cannot be assumed that any capital ship or other valuable vessel is safe when at anchor from this type of attack."

"When the letter of June 13 was received at my headquarters," Kimmel said, "we went over this letter thoroughly, and my staff considered that, in view of the statements in this letter, that there was still no danger from torpedoes in Pearl Harbor." After all, he said, nowhere in Ingersoll's letter did it say "you can launch a torpedo at less than [sixty-six feet]."

It did not say you cannot, either.

In fact, Main Navy's whole point in the new message had been that with technology evolving so quickly, Kimmel should not assume that a harbor—his harbor—was too shallow. Ingersoll had written precisely to negate Stark's earlier assurances about depths. But Kimmel and his staff had not focused on what was new in the June 13 letter; they focused on its reassuring part, the likely sixty-six-feet part. That enabled them to continue to believe they had torpedo immunity, and to continue to dispense with the nets that made peacetime operations so messy. Their conclusion fit neatly with what they knew about their own navy's capability. According to Admiral William Pye, Kimmel's battleship commander, "most of our own torpedoes, dropped from planes at that time, were diving in the neighborhood of seventy-five feet before they ran." Once they finished analyzing Stark's June 13 letter, Kimmel and his staff never again revisited the question of whether the fleet was vulnerable to torpedo attack from the air while in port.

The Japanese, of course, knew the depth of Pearl Harbor. The Americans knew they knew. But they never seemed to have wondered whether their potential adversary, so often portrayed as me-

chanically challenged little Asians, might try to solve the problem
rather than live with it.

It is not clear which one of his vantage points Takeo Yoshikawa chose
on that Friday, but his spying eyes revealed a metamorphosed harbor.
The aircraft carrier *Lexington* was gone, as were several cruisers. Early
that morning, they had all sailed on a mission much like that of the *Enterprise* and her consorts, in this case shuttling marine dive-bombers
to Midway Island, not Wake. With their sortie, and with the third
Pacific Fleet carrier visiting the West Coast, no carriers remained at
Pearl. The *Lexington*, like the *Enterprise*, would live to seek revenge.

Even as she and the other ships made for the horizon, however, a
file of warships was coming down the channel from the open sea—
six destroyers, a cruiser, and three battleships, returning after a week
of exercises. Once inside the harbor, the battleships—the *Arizona*,
the *Nevada*, and the *Oklahoma*—were turned around to face out
for quick departure and then nudged into line with the four other
battleships already resting along the east side of Ford Island. At the
head of the queue by day's end was the *California*, by herself. Next,
side by side, were the *Oklahoma* and the *Maryland*. Following them,
also twinned, were the *West Virginia* and the *Tennessee*. Then came
the *Arizona*, which would never leave that spot, and behind her the
Nevada. Counting the *Pennsylvania*, which was in dry dock, all eight
of the battleships under Kimmel's immediate command were home
for the weekend.

Milo F. Draemel was aboard one of the smaller returning ships,
the light cruiser *Detroit*. A rear admiral, he commanded a group of
destroyers, and soon made his way to Kimmel's office to dissect the
just-completed sea exercises. As Draemel came out of their meeting,
the admiral's chief of staff handed him a two-day-old message, the

one about Japanese outposts being ordered to burn codes and documents. Quite alarmed, unlike almost everyone else at Pearl who had seen the note, Draemel returned to the *Detroit* thinking fleet headquarters would soon issue an alert "to meet an air attack." It seemed an obvious precautionary step.

"The Japanese policy had been to strike without a formal declaration of war," Draemel said. "Pearl Harbor offered a tempting target." Receiving no alert order, he was about to tell his destroyers on his own authority to man antiaircraft guns as long as the ships remained in harbor, but then decided that would usurp the power, and question the wisdom, of the fleet commander. Draemel noticed, too, that "liberty parties from all the other forces continued to go ashore as though the situation were normal." He must be overestimating the danger. Kimmel must know something he did not.

The number of Imperial Navy radio messages was soaring on Friday. Joe Rochefort had already delivered his daily report to Layton and Kimmel, but believed he could not wait the standard twenty-four hours to hand them the next one, due Saturday morning. What was happening was too unusual, even compared with earlier spikes. "Traffic volume heavy," Rochefort wrote to them that afternoon. "All circuits overloaded, with Tokyo broadcast going over full 24 hours." Many of the messages were "of high precedence, which appears to be caused by the jammed condition of all circuits." What the Japanese were saying was a coded mystery, as always. But they were saying a lot of it. Rochefort told his superiors he could find "no traffic" involving "the Commander Carriers." That had been true for well over a week.

Takeo Yoshikawa filed an intelligence report that afternoon, too: "The *Lexington* and five heavy cruisers left port on the same day.

The following ships were in port on the afternoon of the 5th: 8 battleships, 3 light cruisers, 16 destroyers." Whether he forgot to look
or forgot to include the answer, the message did not respond to Tokyo's question about torpedo nets. Yoshikawa would take care of
that tomorrow.

That Friday at noon, the *Lurline* bid farewell.

Once she cleared Honolulu harbor and curved around toward
distant California, Captain Charles Berndtson "ordered the customary three blasts on the whistle" in salute to the Royal Hawaiian
Hotel, passing to port along Waikiki Beach. Outrigger canoes and
small boats had come out to watch the great ship go, as they often
did, the paddlers waving good-bye and offering last alohas. Someone
had once written, "How many times have you watched from the pier
the expressions of departing visitors as they line the side of the ship's
deck, filling their eyes with a long, last look of Honolulu?" This exit
was happier. It was, the *Advertiser* said, the "big Mainland Christmas
rush." The *Lurline* overflowed with homebound military families,
defense workers, and tourists, so many passengers that 70 of the 765
did not have cabins to sleep in. In the evening, cots were to be set
up in the lounges, "men and women on opposite sides, separated by
a cloth partition." In its hold, the ship carried a record number of
bags of parcels; it was the season of gift giving. The ship's bars were
open, the weather beautiful.

The *Lurline* soon disappeared over the horizon, "bucking the
usual northeast trades." Halfway to San Francisco, on Sunday morning, her radio room would overhear a frantic flash from Pearl Harbor; Captain Berndtson would call for every knot the boilers could
muster; the crew would begin feverishly blacking out every porthole;
and the liner would be racing for her life.

FOURTEEN

YOUR MAJESTY

Saturday, December 6
Washington, DC

ESCORTED BY AN USHER, Lester Robert Schulz climbed the stairs to the second floor of the White House on a starry Saturday night, bearing a locked pouch and its key. He had not read the fifteen pages inside—they were far above his pay grade, which was lieutenant, navy—but he knew it was "some Magic material," because he had been instructed to await its delivery to the mansion instead of going home. Schulz, who was twenty-eight years old and wearing civilian clothes, was in his second week as Roosevelt's assistant naval aide, and in his second day actually working at the White House, out of an office in a corner of the mailroom. The pouch had been delivered to him five minutes earlier, at about half past nine. Elsewhere in the residence, the Canadian violinist Arthur LeBlanc was performing for the First Lady and thirty-four dinner guests.

The usher announced him, and Lieutenant Schulz walked into Roosevelt's study. It was a large, high-ceilinged oval of a room with too much to absorb at a glance. Nautical artwork, models of ships, piles of papers, snaking telephone cords, photos, books, the entire skin of a large animal overlaid on the carpeting. And an executive's carved and ponderous desk, at which sat the president of the United States, kept company by an adviser the lieutenant had met only the day before, Harry Hopkins. Schulz had the impression he was expected. Unlocking the pouch, he drew out the Magic pages and handed them to his commander in chief, who began reading. Hopkins began to pace.

Roosevelt had spent much of an exhausting day crafting a letter he had long thought of sending, and at last decided could do no harm. Four times during the year, brief notes of courtesy had traveled between the White House and the Imperial Palace: Hirohito offering "cordial congratulations" in January on Roosevelt's "third tenure"; the president thanking him; the American sending birthday wishes in April; the emperor giving condolences after Roosevelt's mother died in September. In the exchanges, they never broached politics. Roosevelt had never bypassed Japan's civilian and military leadership to speak with the divine figurehead. But by Saturday, in Cordell Hull's words, the president had come to believe "that he should not neglect even the slim chance" that peace might be salvaged by a letter.

"Only in situations of extraordinary importance to our two countries need I address to Your Majesty messages on matters of state," the president wrote Hirohito, who, at forty years old, was a generation younger. "I feel I should now so address you because of the deep and far-reaching emergency which appears to be in formation."

He noted that Japan and the United States had forged a peace almost a century earlier, when another president had extended "an offer of friendship"—Millard Fillmore, who had dispatched Commodore Matthew Perry in 1852 bearing gifts and a proposal for "commercial intercourse." That peace had never been broken, to this day. But now, Roosevelt went on, developments in the Pacific "contain tragic possibilities."

Before writing, the president had made certain of those developments, asking Hull for up-to-date numbers about Japan's rapid buildup of forces in its launchpad of Indochina, and the figures had been delivered to him earlier Saturday. The American consul in Hanoi estimated that transport ships had disgorged 3,400 trucks and tractors, 600 automobiles, 500 motorcycles, 200 tanks, 300 cannon, 2,000 machine guns, 1,300 submachine guns, and 2,100 pack-horses.

"During the past few weeks it has become clear to the world that Japanese military, naval and air forces have been sent to Southern Indochina in such large numbers as to create a reasonable doubt on the part of other nations that this continuing concentration in Indochina is not defensive in its character," Roosevelt's letter continued.

In light of that, "it is only reasonable that the people of the Philippines, of the hundreds of islands of the East Indies, of Malaya and of Thailand itself are asking themselves whether these forces of Japan are preparing or intending to make attack in one or more of these many directions." None of those places can live "indefinitely or permanently on a keg of dynamite." His fervent hope was "that Your Majesty may, as I am doing, give thought in this definite emergency to ways of dispelling the dark clouds" in order to "prevent further death and destruction in the world."

Their tone one of dignified sorrow, the five pages belie the notion of a president scheming to find a way into world war. Roosevelt had not threatened the emperor, or warned him. After finishing, he gave the letter to Hull with a cover note in his own handwriting. "Shoot this to Grew. I think [it] can go in gray code. Saves time." The gray code was a simple encryption system. "I don't mind if it gets picked up"—intercepted by the Japanese, that is. After all, it was intended for them, to be hand delivered by Ambassador Joe Grew. Riding the atmospheric waves, the letter departed Washington at nine that evening, not long before Lieutenant Schulz's arrival.

Throughout Saturday morning, a navy listening post on Bainbridge Island in Puget Sound, opposite Seattle, had scribbled down a flurry of encrypted Japanese messages, and sent them to Washington via teletype. After being decrypted and translated, the opening sentence of the first of the intercepts told army cryptographers that what would follow was a response to the Ten Points that Hull had presented ten days earlier as the foundation of any peace.

It was for this moment Nomura had been told to save one of his two decryption machines.

"The Government has deliberated deeply on the American proposal of the 26th of November," Foreign Minister Shigenori Togo explained to his ambassador, "and as a result we have drawn up a memorandum for the United States contained in my separate message #902, in English.

"This separate message is a very long one. I will send it in fourteen parts, and I imagine you will receive it tomorrow. However, I am not sure. The situation is extremely delicate, and when you receive it I want you to please keep it secret for the time being.

"Concerning the time of presenting this memorandum to the United States, I will wire you in a separate message. However, I want you in the meantime to put it in nicely drafted form and make every preparation to present it to the Americans just as soon as you receive instructions."

Actually, the fourteen parts of message #902 would not be coming the following day. They had been coming all that day, Saturday. And each part had, indeed, emerged from the decryption machines in English. Either Tokyo did not trust its embassy to accurately translate them, or it believed the complete text was too long to ask it to do so. By late afternoon Saturday, the Americans had thirteen parts, and had arranged them in order. Thirteen of fourteen were more than enough to see that the reply was a belligerent screed, a "go to hell," from a government convinced of its innocence. The United States and Great Britain had "brought about a situation which endangers the very existence of the empire." The two countries had done all they could to help China defeat Japan, to "maintain and strengthen" their power in Asia, to ruin Japan's economy with embargoes, to build military pressure. "The Japanese government cannot tolerate the perpetuation of such a situation."

Hull's Ten Points were "selfish," because they were too favorable to America. The Americans had "failed to display in the slightest degree a spirit of conciliation" after Japan proposed a meeting of national leaders. Roosevelt's demands for unfettered commerce and the evacuation of Japanese troops from China were "calculated to destroy Japan's position as the stabilizing factor of East Asia."

And Japan would not abandon its alliance with Germany and Italy.

"Therefore," part thirteen read, "viewed in its entirety, the Japanese government regrets it cannot accept the proposal as a basis of negotiation."

The punishment did not fit the language. For all of its vehemence, the document—or at least the document thus far—had not culminated in a declaration of war, or an ultimatum, or even the severance of formal ties. It had ended only with a rejection of the Ten Points, which the Americans had known was coming, because days earlier Magic had revealed Tokyo's complaints about Hull's "humiliating" proposal, and its promise to Nomura that negotiations would soon stop. The thirteen parts did not even go that far. They did not even say talks were finished. While earlier in the week, Main Navy had interpreted the destruction of encryption materials as proof of imminent war, these thirteen parts did not add up to that at all.

At Army Intelligence's Far Eastern Section on Saturday afternoon, Colonel Rufus Bratton plowed through the parts and concluded, "They contributed no additional information to the matters that we already had from Magic," a strangely nonplussed reaction from a man so deeply worried earlier in the week about what Japan might do. General George Marshall was at home in Arlington with his wife on Saturday evening, and no one at the Munitions Building thought it necessary to disturb the army chief of staff with a telephone call about the thirteen parts, let alone bring them to him.

That evening, General Sherman Miles, the head of Army Intelligence, was dining at the Virginia home of Admiral Theodore Wilkinson, the head of Naval Intelligence. After the thirteen parts had been delivered to them together, neither detected anything of military import, just more diplomatic pas de deux. "It was a justification of the Japanese position," Wilkinson said.

"We had already discounted through many days the fact that in all probability the Japanese reply to our note of November 26 would be unfavorable, and that was all that the first thirteen parts told us," Miles said. The answer was so expected that he and others had simply read right past the aggrieved and enraged tone and failed to connect it to all the other things, like code destruction, that had been happening. Japan was saying its "very existence" was at stake. Hull was seeking "to destroy Japan's position" in Asia.

At Main Navy, Kramer of Naval Intelligence read part eight first, because translated intercepts had come to him out of sequence. His initial impression was that it contained typical diplomatic bloviating. By the time he had all thirteen parts, he realized "this note was far, and appreciably, stronger language than earlier notes had been." He prepared copies and began making deliveries to higher authorities, chauffeured by his wife in their car. Kramer's first stop was 1600 Pennsylvania Avenue.

Roosevelt's naval aide, Admiral John Beardall, had not been there to receive Kramer, for he, too, was dining at the Wilkinson household in Virginia. But Beardall had known by late afternoon that the intercepts were being translated, and told his new, young assistant, Lester Schulz, to wait for them, giving him the key to the coming pouch. Kramer had handed the pouch to Schulz with "rather emphatic instructions to get to the President as quickly as possible."

Franklin Roosevelt took perhaps ten minutes to read the thirteen parts, which he then handed to Harry Hopkins, who read and gave them back. Lieutenant Schulz was still there, a witness. "The President then turned toward Mr. Hopkins and said in substance—I am not sure of the exact words, but in substance—'This means war.' Mr. Hopkins agreed."

To Schulz, it was clear from the conversation that followed that "this means war" did not equate to "tonight" or "tomorrow," or even to an attack on the United States. Roosevelt had already expressed similar general forecasts of Japanese intent to Wendell Willkie and to his own cabinet, although Schulz could not have known that, of course. In the study, Hopkins mused that whenever the Japanese had their forces arrayed "for their advantage," they would begin. "Indochina in particular was mentioned," Schulz said, "because the Japanese forces had already landed there and there were implications of where they should move next."

Everything Roosevelt had done to avoid this—moving the fleet to Pearl to give the Japanese pause, imposing embargoes to give them incentives to reverse course, sending the emperor a letter that very evening—was going to prove futile. The United States would have to go to war with Japan, which would lead to war with Germany. Schulz recalled Hopkins expressing the wish that the army and navy could preemptively strike at the empire's forces, before they could commence whatever was in the offing in the southwest Pacific. "The President nodded," Schulz said, "and then said in effect, 'No, we can't do that. We are a democracy and a peaceful people.'" At which point, Roosevelt "raised his voice and—this much I remember definitely—he said, 'But we have a good record.'"

Ordering a higher military alert never came up. The only place either Hopkins or the president mentioned by name was Indochina. Roosevelt, though, thought he ought to telephone Stark or, as Schulz recalled him saying, "Betty." Upon calling the admiral's residence, the Naval Observatory, the White House operator learned from a servant that Stark and his wife were at the National Theatre, enjoying a performance of *The Student Prince*. The president let him be.

When Betty and his wife returned home, the servant let them know Roosevelt had called, and the admiral promptly went upstairs to use the direct line to the White House. In years to come, Stark could not remember making this call, let alone what he and the president talked about. They talked so often, and so often late at night. He could not recall making the call even when presented with evidence that he had. His poor memory predictably fed thoughts that he and the president had plotted on the phone to let disaster happen, and that Stark was covering up. Whatever his flaws, Harold Stark was too honest, too decent, to have conspired.

The Starks had guests that evening. Navy captain Harold D.

Krick and his wife had dined with them at the observatory, gone to the theater with them, and returned with them to the house to pick up their car. Krick recalled later that as they entered the house, Stark was told that the president had called, and he went upstairs. A handful of minutes later, Stark returned, pessimistic about how things stood with Japan, but not panicked or nervous. When Krick mentioned the sequence to the admiral for the first time five years later, Stark assumed Roosevelt must have informed him of the thirteen parts during the call.

But the president "did not, certainly did not, impress [upon] me that it was anything that required action," Stark said. "I took none. I am certain that he gave me no directive or I would have carried it out." Even if Roosevelt had said something like "this means war," as he had said to Harry Hopkins, there would have been no further message to the Pacific, Stark said. He believed they were primed out there. Not that Main Navy was skittish about Pearl Harbor—it wasn't—but Kimmel had been warned, just to be safe. The army had warned Walter Short. While Main Navy was well aware that Oahu had far too few search planes, it believed Kimmel was making the best of what he had, and planes were out, trolling. Military intelligence in both services thought the fleet had left Pearl Harbor.

Washington, still, had not verified whether any of that was true.

It was already Sunday, December 7, in Tokyo; already evening, in fact. Joseph Grew was listening to the news on station KGO in San Francisco, a taste of America that could be picked up throughout Japan. To Grew's considerable surprise, the announcer suddenly said Roosevelt had sent a letter to the emperor. Any letter would come to the embassy first, and none had. The State Department had provided him with no guidance that one would be coming. Professional diplomat that he was, Grew began to prepare to deliver one, nonetheless. A member of his staff telephoned the Foreign Office to request an appointment for later that night, by which hour Grew hoped the letter would have arrived.

It had actually been in Japan for hours. Even the State Department's dispatches traveled as coded commercial radiograms, and at their end, the Japanese had taken to delaying those bound for the American embassy, which Grew did not know. "Finally, at 10:30 p.m., it came," he said, marked "triple priority." Even if it had been delivered instantly and Grew had placed it in the emperor's hands instantly, the Japanese had already selected their course.

At 12:15 a.m. Monday, December 8, having been driven through the dark streets of the capital, Grew showed the president's personal plea to Foreign Minister Togo. In Washington, it was 10:15 a.m. Sunday; in Honolulu, 4:45 a.m. Sunday. As was his diplomatic privilege, Grew asked for an audience with the emperor to deliver the letter. "I did not want any doubt as to getting it in his hands." Togo fussed about arranging that audience. He wanted time to study the letter first. The ambassador insisted on his rights, until Togo agreed.

That past November, Grew had reminded Washington of Japan's proclivity for suicidal acts of "dangerous and dramatic suddenness." He had cautioned it that "Japanese sanity cannot be measured by American standards of logic." He had underscored to it "the probability of the Japanese exploiting every possible tactical advantage, such as surprise and initiative." He had lived among the Japanese for ten years.

Yet as he returned to the embassy in the small hours to await the requested audience with Hirohito, not even Joseph Grew had detected any reason to believe the next twenty-four hours would differ by orders of magnitude from the previous twenty-four. They rarely do.

FIFTEEN

DINNER AT THE HALEKULANI

Saturday, December 6
Pearl Harbor

WITH THE DAWN of the 8,426th consecutive day of peace in America, the venerable *Ward* took in her lines and began slipping through the sedate waters of the harbor, bound for the channel and, unknowingly, history. She had been given unglamorous duty, a destroyer's. She was to carve lazy laps offshore, east to west and back, not even out of sight of the island, a sentinel primed to challenge any unknown vessel on or below the surface that inched toward the den of the fleet.

However prosaic the mission, the *Ward*'s leader could hardly have been happier. Stuck as a number two a week before, serving a captain he loathed, Lieutenant William Outerbridge had taken command of his new assignment less than a day earlier. "These boys on here," he had written to his wife, Grace, last night, "don't know how strange it is to me to be called 'captain,' but it is music to my ears."

Sooner than expected, his successor as executive officer of the *Cummings* had not only been named but also reported for his new assignment. Outerbridge was free at last, in time to take the *Ward* on a scheduled patrol. Things were moving with such velocity he had yet to unpack after his sudden transfer. "December is my lucky month," his letter to Grace had gone on. "I got a good ship, and the best wife in the world."

The *Ward* was a good one indeed, well trained and potent, armed with depth charges, torpedoes, and four four-inch deck guns. "I was particularly impressed with the spirit of the crew," he had written home. "They are almost all reserves, but are very much alive and full of pep. They seem to be much above average." It was a tribute to the skills of the *Ward*'s former captain. As for the captain of the *Cummings*, George Dudley Cooper, they had had a "heart to heart." It was unexpectedly pleasant. Of course, it hadn't cost Billy or Dud anything to be nice then, at the end of their professional marriage. "I'm glad I have finished with the *Cummings*," his letter said.

"Hope I can have a happy, hard working, and efficient ship. I can't tell you much about how it feels to be captain, but so far it is very fine."

As the *Ward* was plying through the second hour of Outerbridge's first day, a civilian scampered to the second deck of the Submarine Building, leaving his wife waiting in a rental car below. He probably noticed the array of seven states in their Battleship Row; observing was what he did in life. Joseph C. Harsch was a reporter for the *Christian Science Monitor* with a Gump-like knack for popping up where big events were about to happen. His memoirs would be called *At the Hinge of History*. For a good portion of the last two years, Harsch's turf had been western Europe, writing of Nazi conquest and fascist rallies. Now his newspaper wanted him in Moscow to record the Soviet side of the Eastern Front, and he was taking the long way, west across the United States, then to Oahu, then to Tokyo, then on.

Harsch, who was thirty-six, had arrived Wednesday aboard the *Lurline* with his wife, Anne. Their goal was a few days of Hawaiian interlude, but after just two, the journalist in Harsch had stirred. There had to be a good interview at that naval base down the coast from his hotel at Waikiki Beach, and when he called Kimmel's head-quarters, he was told to stop by the very next morning.

Entering the commander in chief's office, Harsch found him and much of his staff arrayed in a circle, seemingly quite relaxed— Kimmel had plopped his white buckskins on a coffee table—and ready to interview *him*. Here was a knowledgeable visitor from the front line of war come to remote Hawaii, and therefore he must tell them all about Europe's struggles, which Harsch began to do. "After about half an hour of being the subject of the questioning, I turned to the admiral and asked if it was my turn to ask a question." After all, Mrs. Harsch was still waiting downstairs, with swimsuits and a packed picnic lunch for a day of sightseeing. The reporter's one question to Kimmel was the most pressing one: Would there be war in the Pacific?

"Without a pause, immediately, almost casually, he replied no. His explanation—which I think I remember almost word for word—was the following," and Kimmel began speaking, not of Japan but of Russia. "Since you have been travelling," he said to Harsch, "you probably don't know that as of six days ago, the German high com-mand announced that German armies in Russia had gone into winter quarters." Endangered Moscow would not fall for now. The Soviets would remain in the war at least until spring. And as long as they did, Japan would not strike their allies, Great Britain and the United

States, lest Russia retaliate by attacking the empire. In sum, Kimmel said, "The Japanese are too intelligent to run the risk of a two-front war unnecessarily."

"I was fascinated," Harsch said. He did not know if Kimmel was merely brushing away a reportorial gadfly with a lame answer or if he believed what he had said. The journalist examined the faces of the other officers. "They showed no sign of being under strain or pressure. No one on the staff disagreed with what the admiral said about the prospects of war in the Pacific."

Harsch returned to his wife, and together they spent the day motoring all over Oahu—beaches on one side of the road, pineapple fields on the other—swimming, and eating their picnic lunch. They had no worries "because, after all, the admiral had assured me only that morning that there would be no war in the Pacific. It was a good day."

Actually, anxiety seemed to have suffused Kimmel at last. Why he picked Saturday to invite a reporter in for a chat is a conundrum. He could hardly have uttered the truth—that there *was* going to be war in the Pacific—without triggering a second question from Harsch, and a third, and a fourth, about when and where hostilities would start, about the fleet's strength, its tactics, and so on.

To a marine officer that day, Kimmel complained that "his stomach was acting up, because he felt like he did not know the whole story and frankly was worried." The officer tried to cheer him up, but "Admiral Kimmel was not impressed." During the entire ten months of his command, he had tailored even the smallest things to his liking, as he had throughout his entire career, whether it was reprimanding a ship that belched too much smoke or hoisting pennants to instruct a formation to "negative scatter." If two inventories of ammunition stocks disagreed, he could count them himself. If Oahu's roads were too crowded, rents too high, phones unreliable, he could dress down the Chamber of Commerce. If he did not know Roosevelt's strategy for containing the empire, he could—as he had in May—insist that Stark eliminate the "uncertainty, a condition which directly contravenes that singleness of purpose and confidence in one's own course of action so necessary to the conduct of military operations."

But here was uncertainty that could not be eliminated easily. On Saturday, he could not simply fire off a letter to the Japanese, insisting they disclose what they had in mind. "I sensed the deep feeling of concern and responsibility felt by the admiral," the marine officer said.

All week, clues of something massive under way, perhaps something crazy, had spilled into the Submarine Building. The Japanese had broken with past practice and changed radio call signs months too soon, hoping to befuddle the Pacific Fleet. Their circuits were now overflowing with traffic. Dozens upon dozens of their ships were moving. Four of their carriers had not been heard from in more than a week, and while Edwin Layton and Joe Rochefort presumed the ships were at home, there were never guarantees when it came to conclusions born of radio traffic.

Further, not only had Main Navy alerted Kimmel to a possible Japanese assault on the American territory of Guam, but he had also just learned that Washington's invasion fears were spreading to Wake, Midway, and other bases closer to Pearl. "In view of the international situation and the exposed position of our outlying Pacific islands," the department radioed him on Saturday, "you may authorize the destruction by them of secret and confidential documents now or under later conditions of greater emergency."

After Joseph Harsch and his spouse drove off into tropical leisure, Kimmel gathered with three senior officers to consider whether defensive steps were called for, whether this was, finally, the long-awaited moment when the fleet ought to shift out of training and into serious self-protection. "We didn't want to overlook anything, you see," Kimmel said. The Pacific "was growing increasingly critical."

Tellingly, Walter Short was not among the conferees. While the general and the admiral had conversed since the war warning, the topics involved mostly the outer islands. Kimmel did not know the precise alert level Short had chosen, nor did Short know the navy's. The navy believed that army radar was scanning, but it had not checked to see if it was, and did not know its hours of operation or that Short was using it only to hone the skills of his radar crews. Asked later if he had queried the general in these hours about whether the army had girded for the worst, Kimmel said, "In the specific terms that you have stated, perhaps not." He felt Short knew his business. Short felt Kimmel knew his.

It so happened that the previous week, the Naval War College had finished work on the latest edition of *Sound Military Decision*, an almost-unreadable staple that offered, among other things, advice on coming to the right responses to murky battlefield moments like this one. A commander must evaluate the situation "with intelligent suspicion," and take into account not only "what the enemy will probably do" but also "everything that the enemy can do." To assume he will, or will not, take a particular step "may be fraught with the most serious consequences for a commander."

That was especially true for an outpost. Army or navy bases on the mainland, or civilian leaders in their Washington, DC, offices, did not have to be as vigilant as a commander on the frontier. In his forward watchtower, the sentry could not indulge in the luxury of inattention or the assumption that others were taking care of matters. He was there to protect those to the rear, and that started, in Kimmel's case, with protecting himself, his men, and his ships. If there were no fleet, there would be nothing between the Japanese and the mainland. If there were no fleet, there would be no grand offensive, either. "In the Army," one general said, "we are taught that in case you have no information, you ought to be prepared for the worst, and in an outpost like Hawaii, they are always supposed to be awake and prepared for anything. That is why it is an outpost, so that people on the Mainland can go to sleep."

Earlier Saturday, a navy whaleboat had eased away from the officer's landing in Southeast Loch and made for the battleship *California*. It carried a piece of paper and Edwin Layton. The early morning was soothing, with scattered clouds; the warship ahead was beautiful, powerful, looming larger as the launch closed the gap. The *California* flew the flag of Admiral Pye, the second-highest-ranking officer in the fleet and somewhat of a consigliere to Kimmel, who wanted Pye's opinion about the paper Layton carried.

It was a message from Manila, from Admiral Hart, who was eighteen and a half hours deeper into Saturday than was Oahu. Some three dozen Japanese transports, escorted by twenty-eight warships, had been sighted surging around the tip of Indochina and into the Gulf of Siam, Hart reported. Lying directly ahead of them, only hours of sailing away, were the coasts of Thailand and British Malaya. To Layton, this was it. The war was on. The only remaining, and oft-debated, question was whether "they would leave us on their flank as a menace," Layton said, or attack the American airfields and naval installations in the Philippines to snuff the threat of retaliation for their invasions elsewhere.

Tommy Hart, as noted, thought they would attack him. Layton was inclined that way, too: "The Japanese have rarely left a strong enemy in an immediate flank." But aboard the *California*, Pye demurred. The Japanese would skirt the Philippines, the sage thought, for the same pragmatic reason endorsed by so many in the navy: America was just too muscular. Why would they pick a losing fight?

When Layton returned and relayed the gist, Kimmel "looked at me in the way he could look—right straight through you—and he snorted." He did that, "snorted like a horse," when he heard something of dubious validity, Layton knew. Once upon a time, the admiral believed what Pye did about America's being too intimidating to fight, but the snort suggested he now felt as Layton did, that the Japanese would indeed hit the Philippines to defuse a danger to their southern operation.

Of course, the Pacific Fleet was on the Japanese flank, too—much farther away, yes, but also much more powerful than anything in the waters of the Philippines. The Americans had advanced their great armada to Pearl to serve as a holstered threat, a curb on distant imperial aggression, never having wondered whether the Japanese might instead regard it as a bull's-eye they had to hit, an impediment to be overcome, just as the depth of the harbor was.

Kimmel and his men still possessed no incontrovertible evidence of onrushing Japanese raiders. *Sound Military Decision* urged commanders to credit the enemy "with the possession of good judgment," not rash instincts, and an attack on Oahu still seemed an astonishingly dangerous, if not logistically impossible, thing to try. The admiral's threshold still had not been met. An attack did not seem "probable," only remotely possible. The war was still going to open elsewhere.

At the meeting at the Submarine Building on Saturday, the leading officers of the Pacific Fleet opted to stand pat, to keep training in anticipation of their offensive missions. Kimmel encouraged and expected dissent, and "I had no advice from any one of them—I think I am fair in stating that—to take any measures other than the ones that we had laid down," he said. He was a man who liked things to stay as he had planned them. And so, the long-distance patrols that civilians on the mainland had been told for months were flying from Oahu did not now begin, not even in a limited way, thereby leaving the admiral blind by his own choice. The battleships and cruisers remained inside Pearl rather than sailing to safety. The level of readiness aboard anchored ships was not elevated.

It was a gamble, as much as Roosevelt's gift of American planes to other countries was a gamble, as much as Yamamoto's thrust to Oahu was. The memory banks of those at Pearl—and those in Washington—contained no solid images or estimates of the harm that could be inflicted on the fleet's men and their ships if the Japanese caught them inside the harbor. Martin and Bellinger had spoken of the damage possibly being great enough to threaten planned operations in the Western Pacific, and Frank Knox had suggested it could be a "major disaster." But nothing systematic had been compiled, no tables of projected losses if this many or that many battleships or carriers were surprised at their moorings. To estimate such damage, the size and potency of an attacking force must be estimated first, and while one report during the summer had mentioned six carriers, no American could really imagine the destructive punch of hundreds of warplanes delivered from the sea, because there was no precedent for such a thing. Navy minds weren't there yet. Taranto, after all, had been raided by only a single British carrier. And while torpedoes were dangerous weapons, they needed water deeper than Pearl's. Or so the fleet believed. All in all, there was a sense that nothing truly bad could happen under the sun of Oahu, even if the Japanese did show up. "I never believed that an air attack on Hawaii, on Pearl Harbor, would result in the destruction of the Fleet," Kimmel said.

Besides, he felt he held an ace. Washington, through its code breaking and other means, would know if probable danger was out there. "I felt that before hostilities came that there would be additional information, that we would get something more definite," he said. But to assume Washington would always know of the enemy's approach was to assume the empire could keep no secrets and could pull off no surprises. By definition, a surprise is what its recipient never sees coming.

Pencil in hand on Saturday, Takeo Yoshikawa sat in the Honolulu consulate, composing a careless and cocky sentence. Careless, because he used a word that happened to reflect the very essence of Japan's plan, though Yoshikawa did not actually know the plan; cocky, because he presumed to give Tokyo military advice. "I imagine," Yoshikawa wrote, "that in all probability there is considerable opportunity left to take advantage for a surprise attack against these places." No balloons that might entangle attacking aircraft were floating over Pearl Harbor, Ford Island, or nearby airfields, he wrote, and "in my opinion, the battleships do not have torpedo nets." The Americans were ripe.

He soon dispatched a second message, having visited the naval base once more, for what would be the last time. "The following ships were observed at anchor on the 6th: 9 battleships, 3 light cruisers, 3 submarine tenders, 17 destroyers, and in addition there were 4 light cruisers, 2 destroyers lying at docks. The heavy cruisers and airplane carriers have all left."

Yoshikawa may have voted himself Japan's greatest expert on the US Navy, but this missive bubbled with minor errors. The number of battleships was still eight, not nine; the number of cruisers was not seven, but eight, and two were the more intimidating heavy cruisers; the number of destroyers was thirty, not nineteen. He did get one thing absolutely correct.

"It appears that no air reconnaissance is being conducted by the fleet air arm."

Leaving his office at midafternoon, Kimmel returned to a brand-new dwelling. On the side of a nearby and long-dead volcanic bump called Makalapa, which offered an enviable panorama of the harbor, the navy was building ninety-seven residences for senior officers. The biggest dwelling, the one at 37 Makalapa Drive, boasted two stories, four bedrooms, four baths, and two lanais, its 5,052 square feet meant to serve as the official residence of the fleet commander and his family, if he had brought one along, which Kimmel had not. He must have done little with the place in the short time he had lived there. Upon seeing the interior of another officer's quarters one day, the admiral would remark that it was a home; he had a house.

Early that evening, after Kimmel had changed into civilian clothes, a 1937 Buick pulled up, driven by an enlisted man, Edgar C. Nebel, his regular driver. Together, they made the journey into Honolulu, then on to Waikiki Beach and the Halekulani Hotel. It being a Saturday night, the military was devoted to enjoying itself. Walter Short was the guest of honor at a charity dinner at Schofield Barracks, smack in the middle of Oahu. Edwin Layton and his wife were dining and dancing with other couples. Elsewhere, a "defense revue" was under way, with a cast of 135 soldiers, sailors, marines, and civilians, and music courtesy of a navy band, plus a production of something called *A Night at Dugan's Tavern*.

On this night of all nights, the presses broke at the *Honolulu Advertiser*. The seventy-page Sunday edition was going to remind residents on the front page that, as usual, Santa would be in the newspaper's lobby that day from nine a.m. to noon. The newspaper was also going to tell them the University of Hawaii had whipped Willamette 20–6 on Saturday. It was going to tell them in a giant headline: "FDR Will Send Message to Emperor on War Crisis." Its editorial page was going to mock the Japanese for saying they were only trying to rescue the Far East from horrible Westerners. "Nippon is saving China if she has to kill twice the several millions that the Nippon-created China Incident has already brought to death." And its Sunday magazine was going to have a photo spread on aircraft carriers, declaring, "Carrier-based aviation, which has undergone wide development in tactical scope and strategic conception, is destined to play a major role when the signal comes."

At the Halekulani Hotel, Kimmel sat down in a private room with about twenty of his officers and their wives. The hotel, which had opened in 1907 and is a much grander place today, hugged the water at Waikiki so closely that its cottages and palm trees were almost in the surf. Joseph Harsch and his wife were staying there; several officers lived there. The main dining room on that Saturday night, Harsch said, "was full of naval officers in their white uniforms and their wives in summer frocks, all behaving calmly and unworriedly as the admiral and his staff were that morning."

Kimmel had been reluctant to attend the gathering, but the wife of one of his admirals had pestered him for weeks about allowing her to organize an evening in his honor. "I had a pleasant enough time," he conceded, but as soon as propriety allowed, he had Nebel drive him back to 37 Makalapa Drive. In the morning, he was to play golf with Walter Short.

Every inch of their hulls now out of the water, three ships rested in the vast and illuminated canyon of Dry Dock Number One, where the welding and hammering went on deep into Saturday night, sparks cascading, smoke growing so thick the workers sometimes had to stop to let it clear. Two of the patients were destroyers, the

Cassin and the *Downes*, side by side at the head of the dry dock; the third, at the back end, dwarfed them. The *Pennsylvania*, Kimmel's ship, "was like a mother at rest in that concrete chamber," Ed Sheehan would recall, "with her destroyer-children safely tucked in for the night."

Sheehan was born in Massachusetts in 1918 and came to the islands in 1940 for the work, as so many had, starting as a helper in the navy yard and rising to shipfitter. "A carpenter working in steel and iron," he called himself. As time would tell, he had a poet's deftness with the language.

He was learning to surf, learning the ukulele, and learning there were no seasons in this exotic place. "There are only the times that are less gentle than others," he said. He repaired hulls. He manhandled decking into place for the welders. Or gun mounts, or ammunition bins. "I wanted to work with the big steel. It seemed somehow more important, permanent." The navy yard "reeked of boiling tar and burning metal," and there was "always the noise, the tooth-rattling tattoos of riveters and chippers, the sledgehammer blows ringing against resistant steel." All the months of summer and into the fall, the dockworkers had been cognizant that the Pacific was a tense ocean. "But, we thought and argued, these threats certainly could not be serious. Surely, the Men in Charge had everything under control."

That night, the work was on the *Downes*. She had a huge rectangular hole in her bow where thicker plating would be affixed, and they would soon perform the same surgery on the *Cassin*. They broke for lunch, and in the sudden quietude of the night, they could hear music floating through the yard—a radio, obviously. "Glenn Miller's reedy, 'Moonlight Serenade,'" Sheehan would remember. "Artie Shaw's clarinet in 'Moonglow.'"

A chief bosun's mate wrote Christmas cards. Someone griped about working on Saturday night. "The chief told him—quite cordially, I recall—to go fuck himself." Sheehan could see lights all over Pearl, on all kinds of warships. "The chief said the whole Fleet was in, except he hadn't seen any carriers lately. It was a lovely night, with stars pricking the infinite vault above, and air turning cool as time moved toward midnight."

SIXTEEN

FROM THE VACANT SEA

Sunday, December 7

TWO HUNDRED THIRTY MILES north of Pearl Harbor, in the last moments of the last night of its voyage from Hitokappu Bay, the strike fleet curved sharply to port, into the trade winds. Aboard the destroyer *Akigumo*, Executive Officer Sadao Chigusa could hear, but not see, aircraft engines leaping to life on the deck of the nearest carrier, the *Shokaku*. "We are in the very day to which we have been looking forward so eagerly," he told his diary.

After all the prognostications back home about inevitable discovery and naval doom, the Japanese had sailed the North Pacific for three thousand miles and twelve days, and encountered only the water. The skies had been free of enemy patrols. The seas had mostly been tranquil, despite the late season. Though challenging, the oil tankers had refueled the warships over and over without mayhem, the last time yesterday. Then, too plodding to keep up, they peeled away, to wait at a point of rendezvous, and the rest of the fleet—the destroyers, the cruisers, the battleships, and the six carriers—had revved off at twenty-four knots, straight south. With each passing mile of the vacant sea, the odds had risen they would win Isoroku Yamamoto's bet.

"I really couldn't find any other, better expression of our good fortune than the words, 'The grace of Heaven and the help of God,'" Chigusa wrote later. He put away his heavy coat; it had gotten warmer the farther east and south they had gone. He shaved his beard and cut his hair, to be groomed for battle. He told the *Akigumo*'s crew it could have any edible treat on its last evening of peace, and, as he had known the men would, they chose *ohagi*, a rice cake covered with bean jam. Because of rationing at home, "every Japanese hungered for sweets, and sailors were no exception," he said.

The closer the strike fleet sailed to Oahu, the stronger the signals of the island's commercial radio stations became, until the Japanese could hear Hawaiian music "as clearly as if we were there," said the First Air Fleet's chief of staff, Ryunosuke Kusaka. Judging by the unexcited broadcasts, the islanders frolicked in ignorance. Even with everything going so well, the fleet commander, Admiral Chuichi Nagumo, told Kusaka several times how deeply he regretted having agreed to lead such a hopeless expedition. He had fretted that the enemy would spot the blinker lights used to communicate ship to ship in lieu of radio; fretted about refueling; fretted that Tokyo would send a message to turn back but radio rooms would not pick it up, and the attack would go forward and he would be responsible for starting a war.

In fact, the strike fleet had picked up every vital message, none of which the Americans had snatched out of the Pacific skies. From the headquarters of the Combined Fleet, Admiral Matome Ugaki sent Yamamoto's final words of inspiration: "The fate of our Empire depends on this expedition. Each of you will do your duty, wearing yourself to the bone." In his diary, Ugaki had noted on Friday that turning back was no longer an option, "since the principle has been to accept a risk, whether we win the horse or lose the saddle." And to the Americans, he wrote in the diary, "Don't you know that the whole world will be panic-stricken within the next several hours to see such a world-shaking scene enacted?"

Aboard the flagship *Akagi*, Commander Minoru Genda was enjoying a great peace after bearing the weight of the stakes during the days and nights of the crossing. Genda had been to the United States, been to Hawaii. Americans probably had a better quality of life than the Japanese, he thought. Big houses. So many cars. Excellent food. But he was confident Japan had the better navy. The renegade who believed completely in air power was on the cusp of proving his point on a historic scale.

Genda was disappointed in one sense. Tokyo had relayed the last observations of the spy Takeo Yoshikawa, and the *Enterprise* and the *Lexington* were not in port. Initially, Yamamoto had made the Pacific Fleet's battleships the focal point of the attack, not because they were the most valuable ships but because the American public thought they were. Their destruction would weaken morale, "for the sinking of a battleship at that time was considered a most appalling thing, akin to the shock and astonishment that follows in the wake of such natural disasters as tornadoes, earthquakes and typhoons." But Genda had persuaded him to make the American carriers primary victims, too, and now they could not be.

Still, Yoshikawa had reported targets aplenty. One unknown— whether the Pacific Fleet would even be in Pearl Harbor—was now a known. As the operations officer, Genda would stay behind and wait. Watching the blue-white flames jetting from exhausts of the planes jamming the flight deck of the *Akagi*, "suddenly, I found a strange feeling in my heart. I felt very refreshed, as if all the uncertain things were cleared away."

The Japanese had gone back and forth on the amount of time to allow between when Ambassador Nomura gave some sort of vague war notice to the Americans and the arrival of the first planes over the harbor. Too much, and the fleet at Pearl might be waiting for them. Too little or none, and Japan might seem uncivilized and lawless. Admiral Osami Nagano, the chief of the Navy General Staff, told postwar American interrogators he had insisted to the emperor that "care should be taken to prosecute the war in a fair and honorable manner, to prevent criticism from any quarter." Personally, he had thought an hour's warning would be sufficient, but unbeknownst to him—or so he told his questioners—others had shrunk the window to thirty minutes. Whether thirty, sixty, or ninety minutes, the attack would have seemed equally enraging and immoral to its victims.

On the *Akigumo*, swells crashed over the bow. The trades were vigorous, and spray even reached the decks of the carriers. If this were a peacetime exercise, they would have stood down. But at six o'clock Hawaii time, "a set of flags located in the middle of the [*Akagi's*] mast suddenly went up and down quickly, the sign for take-off," Genda said. The first planes of the assault began lumbering forward on the six flight decks, full of ordnance and fuel, building speed, timing their liftoffs to each carrier's rise from the trough of the last wave.

"Within fifteen minutes, they had all been launched and were forming up in the still-dark sky, guided only by the signal lights of the lead planes," said the attack's airborne leader, Commander Mitsuo Fuchida. There were 183 of them. "After one great circling over the fleet formation, the planes set course due south for Oahu Island and Pearl Harbor. It was 6:15." He thought the sight "glorious, inspiring." There had never been anything remotely like it in the history of naval warfare. One hundred seventy more planes would follow right behind, as soon as they were elevated from hangar decks to the now-clear flight decks.

The forty torpedo planes of the first wave toted weapons cleverly altered. The Japanese had affixed additional small stabilizing fins to each eighteen-foot weapon to prevent it from spinning left or right as it plummeted from the plane to the sea. That would help reduce how deeply into the water each one plunged. That, in turn, would keep each one off the harbor bottom.

It would be the torpedoes that gutted the Pacific Fleet most of all.

The warm weather had fled Washington. The morning was season worthy, chilly and blustery but sunny, perfect for the Eagles and the Redskins at Griffith Stadium, ideal for George Marshall's postbreakfast horseback ride from Quarters One, his official residence at Fort Myer across the Potomac River. Normally on his Sunday excursions, "I rode at a pretty lively gait," the general said, "at a trot and a canter and at a full run down on the experimental farm where the Pentagon now is."

In its Sunday edition, the *New York Times* took note of the diplomatic gloom that had enveloped Washington the previous week, and the many high-level and secret meetings. One headline announced: "Big Forces Are Massed for Showdown in Pacific." Beneath another— "Navy Is Superior to Any, Says Knox"—the paper wrote that while issuing his annual report on Saturday on the condition of the fleets, the secretary said Americans "may feel fully confident in their Navy."

During the night, the listeners at Bainbridge Island on the West Coast overheard the fourteenth and final segment of Japan's reply to Cordell Hull. Its hostility mirrored that of the others. The United States and Britain were conspiring to thwart the empire, and all hope of peace "has finally been lost." In conclusion, "The Japanese Government regrets to have to notify hereby the American Government that in view of the attitude of the American Government it cannot but consider that it is impossible to reach an agreement through formal negotiations."

So Japan, it seemed, was going to do a bit more than reject the Hull proposal, as the thirteenth part had indicated last night. It was going to stop talking. That was unfortunate, and worrisome. But the Japanese would not be cutting relations, let alone declaring war, although there remained a curious dissonance between their listed, bitter grievances and what they intended to do about them. There was, as yet, no hint of when Ambassador Nomura was to present the document.

At the White House, the naval aide himself this time, Rear Admiral Beardall, shepherded the newest pouch of Magic to the second floor, where he found Franklin Roosevelt relaxing in bed at about ten a.m. The admiral waited as his president read the fourteenth part. The two did not usually discuss intercepts. That morning, "I do recollect him saying, though, which marks this in my mind, that it looked as though the Japs are going to sever negotiations, break off negotiations." The president showed "no alarm," Beardall said, nothing that "would indicate that he was expecting an attack." Unlike the previous evening, there was no "this means war."

Given the tense days, many officers of the War and Navy Departments were in their offices that Sunday. Colonel Rufus Bratton was at his desk at the Munitions Building—between eight and nine o'clock that morning, he recalled—when three additional messages from Tokyo to Nomura suddenly materialized, generated by the Purple machines and the translators.

Said the first:

Will the Ambassador please submit to the United States Government (if possible to the Secretary of State) our reply to the United States at 1 p.m. on the 7th, your time.

What had seemed an event that would take place in the dim future—the delivery—was roughly four hours away. Astoundingly, Tokyo wanted Nomura to roust Hull for an official meeting on a Sunday in Christmas season.

Bratton read the second dispatch, which had been sent right after the first. The Foreign Office, so often irritated by its inexperienced ambassador, was praising Nomura and special envoy Saburo Kurusu. They were no longer needed. "All concerned regret very much that due to failure in adjusting Japanese-American relations, matters have come to what they are now, despite all the efforts you two ambassadors have been making. I wish to take this opportunity to offer my deepest thanks to you both for your endeavors and hard work." Then Bratton read the third message, which had come right after the second. *Now* the embassy was to destroy the last encryption machine, it said, as well as remaining codebooks and any remaining secrets.

The specific time of delivery—one o'clock, Sunday—"immediately stunned me into frenzied activity because of its implications," Bratton said. At that hour or close to it, the Japanese might commence amphibious landings or air attacks somewhere. He telephoned Quarters One, only to learn that Marshall was still trotting and cantering his way along the Potomac River and back. Bratton urged the orderly who answered the phone to track down the general as swiftly as possible, "as I had an important message to deliver to him." He then called General Sherman Miles, the head of Army Intelligence, who said he would leave home at once.

Marshall did not return Bratton's call until after 10:00 a.m., and did not reach his office until 11:25. Waiting, "I kept looking at the clock on the wall, and at my watch," Bratton said. Marshall had never read any of the fourteen parts before now, and as he sat down at his desk and began to do so, both Bratton and Miles kept trying to get him to stop and shift his eyes to the one o'clock instruction. The general, engrossed in the longer document, ignored his subordinates and read on, until he finally came to the message with the time of delivery. He reacted like a fireman to the station house bell.

"General Marshall drew a piece of scratch paper toward him," Bratton said, "and picked up a pencil and wrote out in longhand a message to be sent to our overseas commanders," in Panama, the Philippines, and Hawaii. He read it aloud to a number of officers who had gathered. All agreed "the Japanese intended to attack us somewhere in the Pacific at or shortly after 1 p.m." In particular, Marshall felt, the Philippines "were going to get it." He telephoned his opposite number in Main Navy.

The chief of naval operations already knew the time of delivery. In fact, Harold Stark had known it for about an hour. Arthur Mc-Collum had handed him the intercept about 10:30 a.m. after Alwin Kramer brought it to McCollum from Naval Communications.

Kramer had done some calculations. One o'clock Sunday in Washington would be 2:00 a.m. Monday in Manila. If the Japanese were planning amphibious landings in the southwest Pacific, delivery at 2:00 a.m. in that part of the world would give them a diplomatic cushion of several hours before invading at first light, at 5:00 or 6:00. In passing, he had noted the delivery hour would be 7:30 a.m. Sunday in Hawaii, ninety minutes after "civil twilight," the time when there is enough light in a new day to see. But Kramer's concern was not Oahu. The deadline meshed with "the scheme that had been developing for the past week or so in the southwest Pacific." McCollum thought so, too. Not a man—not one in the Navy Department, not one in the War Department—wondered about Pearl.

On the phone now, Marshall told Stark about the message he intended to send to army commands. In the hour since he had learned of the delivery time, Stark had done nothing about it. "He didn't seem to be very much perturbed," McCollum said. Its possible military significance had not leaped out at him as it had at almost everyone else. To Marshall, he expressed no interest in having the army's bulletin also sent to navy commands in the Pacific. "We had sent them so much recently that it might be unnecessary," Stark said later, even though the hour of delivery was alarming, time-critical information.

Then, after he and Marshall hung up, Stark changed his mind and called back. Have your commanders in Hawaii and the Philippines pass the message to admirals Kimmel and Hart. Marshall amended it to read:

Japanese are presenting at 1 p.m. Eastern Standard time today what amounts to an ultimatum also they are under orders to destroy their code machine immediately stop Just what significance the hour set may have we do not know but be on alert accordingly stop Inform naval authorities of this communication.

As Bratton left Marshall's office with the new warning and headed to the army's dispatch center, a general told him that if there was any question about which destination—Panama, Hawaii, or the Philippines—should have priority, it was the Philippines. Dropping off the message, Bratton checked his watch. It was 11:58. Only later, too late, did he learn that the War Department's radio link to Honolulu, and on to Manila, had been disrupted all morning by atmospheric interference. Marshall's message had to go via Western Union. Neither commander in Hawaii would get it during peacetime.

It was roughly 5:00 a.m. in Hawaii when Stark first learned of the time of delivery. If he had been as immediately concerned as nearly everyone else, the navy might have gotten a message through to the Pacific outposts. Its radios were more powerful than the army's. For the rest of his life, Stark would regret not having sent his own message, or simply having picked up the telephone.

Twenty-four hours into his first patrol, Billy Outerbridge was asleep on a cot in the chart room near the bridge of the *Ward*. The night had been fitful. Shortly before 4:00 a.m., a navy minesweeper reported a periscope off the harbor entrance, and the *Ward* went to inspect, but found nothing and resumed her back-and-forth ritual. Then, at 6:37, a cry repeated twice—"Captain, come on the bridge!"—penetrated Outerbridge's unconscious, a summons he knew heralded something out of the ordinary.

The sun was ten minutes up. December 7 was going to be mild and partly cloudy.

Slipping on his glasses and robe—a kimono—Outerbridge reached the bridge to find the helmsman and several other men staring at a black object barely poking out of the water, perhaps seven hundred yards ahead. Off to port was a navy cargo ship, the *Antares*, towing a barge on a long line and headed into the harbor. The object, which was moving, seemed to be trying to sneak between the *Antares* and its tow, as if hoping to draft in the wake of the hauler.

A conning tower.

Without the shape of an American one.

Outerbridge may have been new to his job, but he knew his job. "One look he gave," the helmsman, H. E. Raenbig, said later, "and called General Quarters." Gun crews galloped toward their mounts, the ship sealed doors and hatches, a demand for ahead-full descended to the engine room, and the *Ward* shot forward, climbing from five knots to twenty-five, on a course to put herself between the *Antares* and the intruder, almost a ramming course.

The submarine, which bore no markings, seemed oblivious to the destroyer's rapid closure. She was a mere eighty feet long, Outerbridge estimated, a miniature version of the norm, a rusted oval, mossy, plagued by barnacles, both her bow and her stern awash as she plowed ahead. She appeared to have no deck guns. The crew of the *Ward* could not have known it, of course, but they were bearing down on one of a handful of tiny submarines the Imperial Navy hoped could sneak into the harbor.

A less-confident captain would have doubted this really could be the Japanese in the water off Oahu, and the end of peace. Billy Outerbridge told his boys to fire away. At a hundred yards, as the *Ward* cut across the prey's path, the forward four-inch gun spat, the shell roaring over the little vessel and into the sea beyond. At fifty yards, with the midget directly to starboard, the number three four-inch gun amidships fired, punching a hole in the conning tower at the water line. The mini recoiled. As the *Ward*'s momentum took her past, "the submarine appeared to slow and sink," Outerbridge said, submerging through the destroyer's wake. Four depth charges rolled off the *Ward*'s stern, set to explode at a hundred feet, and they did. "My opinion," said the enlisted man who did the dropping, W. C. Maskzawilz, "is that the submarine waded directly into our first charge."

The destroyer came about and retraced her path. An oil slick bloomed on the sea. Sound-detection equipment heard nothing from below.

Only a few minutes had slipped by. The *Ward* had fired the first shots of the war in the Pacific. Quickly, Outerbridge wrote, encoded, and radioed a message to Pearl: "We have dropped depth charges upon subs operating in defensive sea area." Then he reconsidered. The phrasing might suggest they had responded only to vague, underwater sound contacts, when they had seen an actual submarine on the surface. They had shelled it, and hit it. It was there. There was oil on the water. Two minutes later, Outerbridge sent a second version, more precise and more alarming. "We have attacked, fired upon and dropped depth charges on a submarine operating in defensive sea area."

Fired upon.

Outerbridge wanted to be absolutely certain he had been heard and understood.

"Did you get that last message?" he radioed.

It had left his ship at 6:54. Lieutenant Outerbridge had been sent out to be on guard, and he had been. The new captain and the old *Ward* had provided Pearl with a chance.

On the opposite side of Oahu, the two young privates of the army's mobile radar unit at Opana decided that someone higher in authority needed to know about the massive blob of unknown, inbound airplanes that erupted on their oscilloscope at 7:02 a.m. More accurately, after five or six minutes of pro and con, George E. Elliott Jr. convinced Joseph L. Lockard they ought to tell that higher authority, even if their training shift had ended at 7:00 and no one had given them any reason to think these were threatening days. "Private Lockard laughed at me, and told me I was crazy for wanting to do it." Even Elliott thought the planes were navy, but he wanted to report them anyway. There had never been a blob this big, and it was still coming.

Using a direct line, Elliott rang the command post specifically built for these moments. Radar contacts from units around the island were to be reported to Fort Shafter's information center, where they would be plotted on a map. Army and navy personnel would then figure out which ones were foes and which friendly, and coordinate any response of antiaircraft batteries and fighter planes. "I spoke in a very nervous voice," Elliott said. He had never called the center before.

Everyone had left it, except the switchboard operator and one other man.

Lieutenant General Walter Short had put his forces on alert for sabotage, not assault by air armada. He had put his radar units on a dawn shift for practice, not the real thing. Elliott told the center's operator that a "large" flight of planes was inbound, and he must "get somebody that would know what to do," and rang off. A few minutes later, in response, Lieutenant Kermit A. Tyler called Opana.

Tyler was an army fighter pilot. For the second time in his life, he had been ordered to spend an early-morning shift at the information center to learn to be a "pursuit officer," directing interceptors toward enemy contacts. It was a pointless assignment. There was no one there to teach him; the army had no fighter planes standing by to be directed; he had not been taught how radar worked; not a soul expected actual enemy contacts; and the navy provided no liaison officer to help the center with identifications. During the shift, Tyler watched plotters take early-morning reports of friendly planes, but then they left at seven a.m., leaving him by himself. An investigator later asked Tyler why he thought he was there. "Sir, I really don't know."

When he telephoned Opana and Lockard told him of the incoming aircraft, "I thought about it for a moment and said, 'Well, don't worry about it.'" He had a reason or two. "You see," Tyler said, "I had a friend who was a bomber pilot, and he told me any time that they play this Hawaiian music all night long, it is a very good indication that our B-17s were coming over from the mainland, because they use it for homing." He had heard such music on his radio as he drove to the center in the wee hours. A flight of B-17s had, in fact, been droning all night from California, and would arrive in the midst of World War II.

Told to forget it, George Elliott and Joseph Lockard watched the oscilloscope as the unidentified planes closed the distance. At about fifteen or twenty miles out, with the radar now getting return echoes from Oahu itself, the cluster vanished in the clutter.

Husband Kimmel, slated to golf that morning with Short, had not shaved or eaten breakfast before the telephone rang at 37 Makalapa Drive overlooking the harbor. Commander Vincent R. Murphy, the fleet's duty officer, told him a destroyer had attacked a submarine offshore. Give or take a few minutes, the time was 7:30, more than half an hour after Outerbridge had radioed that the *Ward* had opened fire.

In between, his message crawled up the chains of two navy commands, the Fourteenth Naval District and the fleet. On the district side, to which the *Ward* actually belonged, there had been skepticism. The chief of staff, Captain John B. Earle, had the impression "it was just another one of these false reports which had been coming in, off and on." He called Admiral Bloch, the district commandant, who wondered, "Is it a correct report, or is it another false report? Because we had got them before. I said, 'Find out about it.'" Just in case, Earle did order the on-call destroyer, the *Monaghan*, to head out and join the *Ward*.

Fleet duty officer Murphy learned secondhand of the *Ward*'s report sometime before 7:30, as he was getting dressed at home. He wanted details, such as whether there had been some sort of chase before the destroyer fired, but when he called the officer who had taken Outerbridge's message, his line was busy. Murphy then went to the Submarine Building, where his regular job was assistant war plans officer, and only then did he get through to the man who had Outerbridge's initial report. Murphy then called Kimmel.

In their analysis in March of how a surprise attack might unfold,

General Martin and Admiral Bellinger had speculated that "any single submarine attack [near Pearl] might indicate the presence of a considerable undiscovered surface force, probably composed of fast ships accompanied by a carrier." And now, on a Sunday morning in December, here was the anticipated harbinger: a destroyer had reported not merely that it might have heard a submarine, but that it had shot at one within sight of the harbor.

No one, in either command chain, reacted with alacrity to what the *Ward* had seen and done. Everyone remained in the vise grip of peace. What would have unfolded if the response in these last minutes had been faster is, of course, unknowable. There would not have been time for the fleet to flee its cramped home; but there might have been enough to sound general quarters on all ships and be waiting with all antiaircraft guns loaded and all eyes skyward.

On the phone, Kimmel told Murphy he was coming to the office, but he issued no orders. "I was not at all certain that this was a real attack," Kimmel said of Outerbridge's report. In a few minutes, the duty officer called the admiral back to say the *Ward* had filed a second message, about having detained a sampan. Then a yeoman burst into Murphy's office: "There's a message from the signal tower saying the Japanese are attacking Pearl Harbor and this is no drill."

Murphy relayed this to Kimmel on the phone. It was just before 8:00.

His uniform not yet buttoned, the commander in chief of the Pacific Fleet stepped out of his new home and into his yard. Aircraft were descending, climbing, darting, red balls visible on every wing. All residents of Oahu were habituated to military planes overhead, but only their own, the army's and the navy's, and for the rest of their lives they would speak of the shock of those alien red spheres, the improbability of it, the Japanese flying over the United States of America. Drawn by the crescendoing cacophony, Captain John Earle's wife emerged from her home next door to Kimmel's and joined him in the yard, two helpless witnesses to what the admiral understood instinctively was budding catastrophe. To Grace Earle, he seemed transfixed, incredulous, his face "as white as the uniform he wore."

Torpedo bombers skimmed directly past fleet headquarters to drop their 1,847-pound weapons into Southeast and East Lochs. The torpedoes did not impale in the mud, but rose, leveled off, armed themselves, and raced beneath the surface of a harbor that was not too shallow until they smashed into the hulls of Battleship Row, where there were no torpedo nets. Three pierced the *California*, Pye's ship, opening gaping holes. A half dozen riddled the *West Virginia*, which began to tip sharply to port; three, four, then more punctured the *Oklahoma*, which overturned in mere minutes, exposing its bottom to the heavens, trapping hundreds of men in an upside-down world; one hit the *Nevada*. A witness to the torpedoes' collisions with the big ships, Peter A. La Fata, a radioman third class aboard a nearby auxiliary ship, would recall "one hell of a mess, which made me feel like bawling, and I guess I did."

Even at some distance, Kimmel could see that one of his battleships had already begun to tip. His Buick pulled up. The driver, Edgar Nebel, had come unbidden. Kimmel dived in as someone else—perhaps another officer; he would not remember—leaped aboard, and they roared off to headquarters, a few minutes away. Perhaps before they left, perhaps as they raced, but a few minutes past 8:00, a terrifying, end-of-days detonation reverberated across the harbor and beyond. A bomb had plunged into the forward magazine of the *Arizona*, and she exploded and disappeared in a mountain of boiling, bluish-purple smoke that reached a thousand feet. Pieces of her rained down on nearby ships and Ford Island.

At 8:12, Kimmel's office radioed the first true communiqué of the fledgling Pacific war, addressed to the fleet—the *Enterprise* and the *Lexington*, still at sea, would need to know—and to Main Navy. "Hostilities with Japan commenced with air raid on Pearl Harbor," which oddly conveyed the idea the attack had concluded. It was in its infancy.

The cruiser *Helena* took a torpedo on her starboard side and began to settle amid fires, flooding, and darkness in her interior. The cruiser *Raleigh* was sliced open by a torpedo and began to list. The cruiser *Honolulu* lost electrical power to her two forward turrets when a near miss blew a hole in her hull, and flooding began. The destroyer *Shaw* erupted in a spectacular mushroom of flame and smoke. Two bombs struck the already torpedoed *West Virginia*. The minelayer *Oglala* rolled over. The old target ship *Utah* was holed by a torpedo and sank where she was moored. The battleship *Tennessee*, though spared torpedoes because she was tethered to the inside of the *West Virginia*, rocked from bombs that hit two of her turrets, the shrapnel killing her captain. In Dry Dock Number One, a bomb dropped onto the *Downes*, where shipfitter Ed Sheehan had been working only hours before, and touched off explosions and fires. One of the destroyer's deck-mounted torpedo tubes, weighing a thousand pounds, was sent tumbling up into the sky and came crashing down onto the dry-docked *Pennsylvania*, which had already suffered a bomb hit. The destroyer *Cassin* toppled off her dry-dock blocks, leaning into the *Downes* like a drunk passed out on a friend.

Oil plumes spread across the water from stricken ships and caught fire. Smoke grew so thick the tropical light dimmed. The noise was thunderous and continuous. Small boats, ignoring the strafing and falling bombs, sallied into East Loch to fish out men who had either escaped sinking ships or been blasted off them. "We [were] picking up sailors out of the water, all covered with oil, some of them missing parts of their bodies," enlisted man Richard Cunningham would remember, "and we'd haul them into this pristine officers' club boat, and soon it was just covered with oil. . . . We made boat load after boat load from the *Arizona* and from the *West Virginia* and from the *Oklahoma*."

Kimmel, watching from the Submarine Building's second deck, began to fear he would have nothing left. He was witnessing the death of the United States Pacific Fleet. For the first time in his career, he had failed, and spectacularly so. All of his assumptions were wrong, although he had copious company. The Imperial Navy could, indeed, sail thousands of miles and refuel repeatedly on the high seas. It would, indeed, take such a risk, however mindless. Japanese pilots were better than conventional wisdom suggested. Torpedoes could work in forty-five feet of water. Nets were necessary. The attack violated Kimmel's every notion of what was militarily and strategically sensible. Yet the Japanese were here. One had to admire them. The entire attack was "beautifully planned" and "beautifully executed," he would say, as if the enemy had engineered a feat beyond human conception. And, in a sense, it had.

Arriving from his apartment, Commander Arthur Davis, one of Kimmel's officers, found him "utterly shocked and crushed. . . . The attack just seemed to knock all the props away from him." When Edwin Layton got there, the admiral seemed "calm and collected," but clearly "shocked by the enormity of the thing that was happening to his command." Ensign Thomas J. Larson, who had landed in Hawaii only two days earlier and was now shuttling radio reports to Kimmel from ships in the harbor, said the admiral "was cursing, ranting and raving whenever he read all these dreadful messages I brought to him." Kimmel was surely all of those things: stunned, angry, devastated, and, above all, wrapped in anguish over the men who were dying, in his harbor, on his watch. "The world had exploded in his face," Layton said.

Paralysis did not come over him or headquarters. He was mad and going to find who did this to his fleet and his country. At 8:17, he radioed Patrick Bellinger and the patrol planes: "Locate enemy force." At 8:30, he radioed his two carriers at sea, so he could help them hunt, too: "Report position." But the Japanese were pouncing on Bellinger's PBYs wherever they sat on the tarmacs or waters of Oahu, until nearly half of his eighty-one planes had been obliterated. They had never been deployed to find the enemy coming, and would never be deployed for a grand offensive to the Marshalls. Many of Walter Short's fighter planes, which had been clumped together at army airfields for easier guarding against the saboteurs who never came, were being shot to pieces.

Yet out there in the harbor, something deeply heroic had begun. All the training Kimmel had insisted on through ten months of command, his endless emphasis on gunnery, on knowing the proper thing to do and the proper place to be, was now manifesting itself. Though as surprised as he, his men were shooting back, from the battleships, from the destroyers and cruisers, from rooftops and parking lots, from the decks of the submarines right below his windows. Within five minutes aboard most battleships, four on the cruisers, a curtain of bullets and antiaircraft shells began rising in quest of the buzzing attackers, the first of 284,469 rounds of every caliber the fleet would unleash. The sky erupted with hundreds of black dots, the bursts of antiaircraft shells. Shrapnel began falling on shore and water. An enraged enlisted man threw oranges at the Japanese. Offshore, the crew of the *Ward* broke out small arms and began firing at the enemy planes as they swept into or out of Pearl, although they had little hope of bringing one down. Even Outerbridge blazed away, after an experienced hunter aboard had calmly explained the concept of leading the prey.

On the battleship *Maryland*, Charles Mandell noticed that although "our antiaircraft crews were all youngsters, less than six months in the Navy," they stayed at their exposed mounts "in the face of strafing attacks by the Jap planes, working their guns to the maximum." Aboard the *Nevada*, the transition from peace to manic assault was so quick, "the result was a numbness," Ensign John Landreth said, yet the crew had been trained so well an "automatic functioning" began. On the severely damaged *Helena*, "all were cool, determined, resourceful, vigorous and, individually and collectively, conducted themselves with no hint of confusion or hysteria and with no thought of danger to themselves," her commanding officer wrote. "To point out distinguished conduct would require naming every person I observed." The Medal of Honor would be awarded to fifteen of Kimmel's men, the Navy Cross to sixty.

At 8:40, despite her wounds and without help from tugs, the *Nevada* began to try to save herself, pulling away from her mooring and inching down East Loch, the only big ship able to get under way. The Stars and Stripes fluttered at her stern, and her antiaircraft crews were still at their posts, firing through the smoke of fires on her decks. Those who saw her pass never forgot the sight. "The ship seemed surrounded by a horde of angry Jap planes," an ensign on another vessel said, "and waterspouts from the bombs they were now concentrating on this escaping target obscured much of the hull. It was a beautiful, yet horrible sight." Radioman Theodore C. Mason aboard the foundering *California* yelled encouragement as the *Nevada* went by, and "some of us were crying unashamed tears." "I had never seen anything so gallant," Mason said. Hit again and again, and with flames enveloping her bridge, the battleship gave up her flight and beached herself rather than sink and block the channel.

Layton's yeoman kept bringing him reports from "ships hit so far, those that were sinking, and others that were asking for assistance," and, Layton said, "it made me physically ill just to read it." The view from the Submarine Building "was pretty horrible to see. You knew that men were dying. There was the *Oklahoma*, upside down, oil burning on the water, and the sky a pall of black smoke. Things that you will never forget as long as you live." Headquarters rippled with "electric wonder about what was going to happen next," Layton said. At one point, he noticed a "short, slightly heavy-set officer" arrive, the rank of vice admiral on the shoulders of his white uniform, which was "spotted with fuel oil." He was still wearing a life jacket. His face was "blackened by smoke or soot. His eyes were almost shut. He looked dazed as he stared off into space, not saying a word." It was Admiral Pye, who had assured Layton the previous morning aboard the *California* that Japan would never attack the United States. Chaos reigned on his flooding ship, whose superstructure would soon be the only part of her poking above the surface of the harbor.

At some point amid the fury, marine colonel Omar Pfeiffer was standing with Kimmel and other officers in the war plans office, gazing through louvered windows at the disaster. "There was a ping as glass was broken," Pfeiffer said, "and when we turned, we saw a dark mark on Admiral Kimmel's uniform, above his heart." A bullet from an unknown gun, its velocity spent, had struck him, bruised him, and tumbled to the floor. He could not recall what Kimmel said next. Another man did: "It would have been merciful had it killed me."

Frank Knox, Harold Stark, and Richmond Turner were talking in the secretary's outer office when a courier from Naval Communications hustled through the door, bearing the first message, "Air Raid, Pearl Harbor, This Is No Drill." He handed it to Knox.

"My God, this can't be true! This must mean the Philippines!"

Knox, a civilian, was unused to navy acronyms and message forms. Stark looked at the dispatch and its sender.

CINCPAC.

Commander in Chief, Pacific.

"No, sir," Stark said. "This is Pearl."

At 2:20, Nomura and Kurusu entered Cordell Hull's office and handed him the fourteen-part note, whose delivery "had been delayed owing to the need of more time to decode the message," Nomura explained to the secretary of state. By now, Hull knew what Nomura did not, that an attack on Hawaii was under way. Hull knew the contents of the Japanese note, too, and knew this visit was a charade, and his anger was greater than at any other time in his fifty years of public service. Never, he told the diplomats sitting before him, had he seen an official document "more crowded with infamous falsehoods and distortions—infamous falsehoods and distortions on a scale so huge that I never imagined until today that any government on this planet was capable of uttering them." It was a declaration of war that did not even declare it. He all but told Nomura and Kurusu to get out.

As slightly more than fifty-five thousand watched at the Polo Grounds in New York City, the kickoff by the Brooklyn Dodgers— the Dodgers of the National Football League, not baseball—sailed down to the New York Giants' three-yard line, where Ward Cuff caught it, cut to his left, and, getting a terrific block from Tuffy Leemans, crossed the ten in stride. "Cuff's still going," the radio play-by-play man cried. "He's up to the twenty-five, and now he's hit, and hit hard about the twenty-seven yard line. Bruiser Kinard made the tack—" The network broke in midword. "We interrupt this broadcast to bring you this important bulletin from the United Press. Flash. Washington. The White House announces Japanese attack on Pearl Harbor."

As the news ricocheted around the country, several high-profile journalists and officials were enjoying a midafternoon Sunday dinner at a private home outside New York City. The phone rang. Japan had struck Oahu. "To that, there was instant reaction," the columnist Mark Sullivan, one of the guests, wrote. "It came from one of the half-dozen Americans most constantly in touch with the pulsing currents of world news. He said, 'It's a hoax.' And that was the judgment of all at the table."

In Long Beach, California, a woman named Clara May Morse sat down in the first seconds after the radio interruption to write a letter to one of her sons, Francis. "I heard all," she told him, "and am almost beside myself." Both Francis and his brother, Norman, were aboard the *Arizona*. None of the news flashes were mentioning the *Arizona*, or any ship, or any casualties, because nobody on the mainland knew anything. But Mrs. Morse had faith. "I am sure our USS fleet can handle it," she wrote Francis. "God bless our men and officers of the fleet. Help them to keep up and going." She was frantic, but tried not to let that seep into the letter. "Francis, I am alright and worried about my dear boys." Both of them, along with twenty-five other pairs of brothers on the *Arizona*, had perished by the time she wrote.

Grace Outerbridge picked up the phone on Jackdaw Street in San Diego to hear a friend say that Pearl—Billy's Pearl—was being bombed. "It is now 10 p.m.," she wrote her husband in longhand, "and I have been glued to the radio since 11:30 a.m. Incidentally, I am practically drunk." Her doctor had brought scotch and a sedative, and after getting the three boys to bed, she opened the bottle and took the pill. "Have been hoping and praying for your safety of," and the penmanship stopped. Grace had fallen asleep. She would not learn whether Billy was alive for six days, the worst of her life.

"This is the Emperor's reply to the President."

Foreign Minister Shigenori Togo laid—"slapped," in Joseph Grew's characterization—the fourteen-part document on a table. Awakened at the American embassy at seven a.m. Monday after only a sliver of sleep, and summoned to the Foreign Minister's official residence, the American ambassador had had no time to shave or eat, just as Kimmel had not. By then, the attack on the Pacific Fleet had ended. Grew did not know one had begun.

Togo, it seemed, had seen the emperor at three a.m., and Grew would not be given an audience to hand over Roosevelt's letter, as the ambassador had requested a few hours earlier. But the emperor would like the president to understand, if Grew would please convey the sentiment, that "the establishment of peace in the Pacific and consequently the world has been the cherished desire of His Majesty." Togo thanked Grew for his efforts, and escorted him out.

"I never understood why he did not tell me," Grew said, "whether he did not have the courage to do it, or whether he thought it was not diplomatic protocol. I have no idea." A few hours later, when the American embassy had finally heard the news, a low-level Foreign Office official arrived with a formal note. Grew declined to meet him. The worst possible outcome for a diplomat had happened. The Japanese official, a Mr. Ohno, read the note instead to First Secretary Edward S. Crocker.

"Excellency," the note from Togo to Grew said, "I have the honor to inform Your Excellency that there has arisen a state of war between Your Excellency's country and Japan, beginning today."

What a phrase, *the honor*.

"This is a very tragic moment," Crocker said.

"It is," Mr. Ohno said. "And my duty is most distasteful."

The Japanese confiscated the shortwave radios in the compound, and locked its outer gate. The Americans began tossing files into flames. "Throughout the day, fires were going in every fireplace," Grew said, adding, "The air was full of floating black pieces of soot, and the courtyard, towards dusk, looked like a veritable inferno."

Twenty-four hours earlier, almost exactly, Franklin Roosevelt had sat at his desk in the oval study, reading the first thirteen segments of Japan's message, having just sent a personal plea to the emperor for comity. Now, at 8:30 p.m. in Washington, seven hours into what would be the most enormous war in American history, chairs for the cabinet had been arced in a semicircle around the desk. A cigarette was clamped in the president's mouth. He looked gray, Frances Perkins, the labor secretary, thought. Earlier, on his way to the Oval Office in his wheelchair, the president had passed a Secret Service agent, who would remember that "his chin stuck out about two feet in front of his knees and he was the maddest Dutchman I, or anybody, ever saw." Roosevelt had already begun work on remarks he wished to give to Congress the following day, a speech of only five hundred or so words but one he understood would be "just about the equal in importance to the First Inaugural Address." Initially, the draft's first sentence said that December 7 was "a date which will live in world history." The president tinkered with that phrase, for the better.

"He opened by telling us that this was the most serious meeting of the cabinet that had taken place since 1861," Henry Stimson wrote in his diary, "and then he proceeded to enumerate the blows which had fallen upon us at Hawaii." To Perkins, Roosevelt seemed to struggle to describe what had befallen the fleet. "His pride in the Navy was so terrific." He told the cabinet that several battleships, destroyers, and smaller vessels had been sunk, but he could not be precise. Communication with Pearl and the other Pacific outposts was difficult. He did not know how many Americans had been killed or wounded. Guam and Wake Island had been attacked, he said, but confusion reigned about the Philippines. The Japanese had invaded the Malay Peninsula; the Dutch had declared war on the empire; the British Parliament would gather in special session the following morning. Attorney General Francis Biddle thought Roosevelt "was deeply shaken, graver than I [had] ever seen him."

At some point, the leaders of Congress entered the room. Someone asked how badly the attackers had been hurt. Roosevelt tamped out any hope that the navy and army had exacted a price. It had not been a two-way fight, the determination of the boys aboard the ships notwithstanding. "By far the greater loss has been sustained by us," he said. Any estimates of losses he provided must not leave the White House. "That information is of value to an enemy."

"Of course, it is a terrible disappointment to be President in a time of war," Roosevelt told them. But the brutal fact was "the principal defense of the whole West Coast of this country, and the whole west coast of the Americas, has been very seriously damaged today." The fleet, he meant. The members of Congress, Stimson wrote, "sat in dead silence." At the gates of the White House, crowds had gathered, and would soon begin singing "God Bless America."

Returning to his office just past eleven p.m., Treasury Secretary Henry Morgenthau told his waiting staff that Oahu was "much, much worse" than he had expected to hear. He did not understand how this could have happened. It made no sense. "It is going to be the most terrific shock this country has ever had." He said it again: He could not understand it. "They have the whole Fleet in one place. The whole Fleet was in this little Pearl Harbor base. The whole Fleet was there."

Not long past midnight, Harold Stark got through by phone to Oahu, where it was Sunday evening; where rumors of beach landings and parachutists and poisoned reservoirs were running wild; where scared antiaircraft crews were firing into the dark at what were only incoming American planes; where Robert Shivers and the FBI were rounding up 345 Japanese residents; and where shaken marine sentries were shooting at what turned out to be dogs.

The chief of naval operations had first spoken with Pearl five hours earlier, when the commandant of the Fourteenth Naval District called not long after the Japanese had finally left. "It's a pretty bad mess here," Claude Bloch said then, although he had far from a full picture of how bad. "The last report I had, there were thirty people dead and about four hundred patients." There were, in fact, more than two thousand dead. Bloch passed along a request: "I know Kimmel will welcome the addition of PBYs right away."

Since that first call, Kimmel had drawn up and sent an initial summary of the worst day in the history of the navy. "In spite of security measures," he wrote, "surprise attack by Japanese damaged all battleships except *Maryland*." Four of his big ships had been hurt badly, and a fifth, the *Arizona*, was a "total wreck." The cruisers *Honolulu*, *Helena*, and *Raleigh* were "unfit for sea." The destroyers *Shaw*, *Cassin*, and *Downes* were a "complete loss." Many, many airplanes, both army and navy, had been shot up. "Now have 2 carriers, 7 heavy cruisers, 3 squadrons destroyers and all available planes searching for enemy. Personnel behaving magnificently [in] face of furious surprise attack."

Twice Kimmel referred to surprise, as if it could not have been avoided or imagined, as if he needed Main Navy to understand this was treachery, not failure. And he had said "in spite of security measures," although there had been no search. It is not clear if Stark had read this dispatch by the time he made his midnight call. Most likely, he had.

Again, it was Bloch on the other end.

"I asked Kimmel," the commandant said to Stark, "and he said they had not located the Japs, the carriers. They have not located the two carriers." Even now, Pearl could not conceive of the Imperial Navy having employed three times as many.

"Did our patrol planes get them before they hit us?" Stark asked.

He had always assumed they were out, looking. He had never asked if they were. He was realizing they had not been.

"No," Bloch said, and began to ramble about the midget submarines that had been part of the attack. But the once-cheerful Betty would not relinquish the topic of search.

"Can you tell me how many and how far out the PBYs were scouting?"

"No, I cannot."

"Do you know how many were out?"

"No, I don't."

"What sectors were they in?"

"No, I don't. Kimmel knows that."

"Well, tell Kimmel that I will be asking him these questions, that I want to know how far out they were and in what sectors."

Actually, Bloch had a pretty good idea about the patrol planes.

"The answers will be sad," he finally confessed. "Very unsatisfactory. They caught us flat-footed."

EPILOGUE

O N THE EVENING of December 8, having hunted fruitlessly for the Japanese and needing replenishment, the *Enterprise* came home. As the carrier glided down the channel and into Pearl, Admiral Bill Halsey absorbed the vista in steeled silence until he was heard to mutter a vow. "Before we're through with them, the Japanese language will be spoken only in hell." From ashore, an army antiaircraft gunner yelled some hard-earned wisdom at Halsey, the *Enterprise*, and her escorts. "You'd better get the hell out of here, or the Japs will nail you, too."

The battered and scorched *Nevada* lay aground to one side. Ahead, the *Arizona* still burned wildly. All day, workmen had swarmed the exposed keel of the turned-turtle *Oklahoma*, trying to cut holes. Hundreds of sailors, living and dead, remained encased in her, the living tapping for help, running out of air. The harbor reeked of smoke and fuel, and defeat. "Oil was everywhere," Theodore Mason of the *California* said, "spreading out from the sunken ships in pernicious rings, mottling the water, blackening the shore. Drifting on the slow currents were life rafts, life jackets, pieces of boats and other flotsam." When enough of the sea had been pumped out of Mason's half-drowned ship to leave the water only thigh-deep belowdecks, men went wading to slip body bags over floating shipmates, cinching them together and lifting them out. "We didn't remove any of the dog tags," Jerod Haynes, an enlisted man, said. "We let whoever handled the bodies do that. All we did was get them out of the ship. We did that for about three weeks."

The unidentified dead were being fingerprinted, if they could be. Bodies were wrapped in canvas, placed in wood caskets, "and buried in two lots procured for this purpose and having in mind a national cemetery at a later date," a fleet surgeon, Elphege A. M. Gendreau, wrote to Washington. Such a cemetery did indeed come to pass, in the Punchbowl crater overlooking Honolulu and the blue Pacific. "A great number of men are missing," the doctor went on, "and will be unquestionably classified as dead." That came true as well.

The windows of fleet headquarters were painted over so operations could continue around the clock without emanations of light that might aid Japanese night raiders. But in their haste, the workmen had applied the masking black on the inside. "We had to endure the stifling [paint] fumes that intensified the cloying odor of burnt oil that hung over the harbor," Edwin Layton said. They were, of course, directing the war from those toxic rooms, although hardly the war Husband Kimmel had planned.

"With the losses we have sustained, it is necessary to revise completely our strategy of a Pacific war," a fleet memo said on Wednesday. Gone from its list of tasks were offensive forays. Holding on to Oahu, holding on to Pearl: "this mission is the immediate mission." America simply had to retain a forward port from which to begin to take back the far Pacific, where Japanese forces were marauding at will.

All of Hawaii was darkened at night, with heavy fines for violators. Schools and bars were shut; civilians were being relocated if they lived too close to possible targets, and limits were placed on the purchase of food, in order to curb hoarding. Waves of reinforcements—warships, warplanes, salvage engineers—were moving toward the islands from the West Coast. Having reached the Golden Gate without being torpedoed, the *Lurline* docked at 3:27 a.m. on Wednesday, and "even before the passengers were ready to leave the vessel," workmen hustled up gangways and began stripping away the peacetime elegance and creating "a drab, over-crowded military transport."

Frank Knox landed at Pearl that same Wednesday, having de-cided to make the long trip on Monday while listening to Roosevelt ask Congress to declare war on the empire. As good journalists do, the owner of the *Chicago Daily News* had to see the disaster first-hand, to ask what had happened, to understand what Kimmel—his man, his choice—had been thinking, or not. "The air was filled with rumors," the secretary of the navy said in a letter explaining his journey to a friend. "There was a prospect ahead of a nasty congressional investigation, and I made up my mind in a flash to go out there and get the actual facts." Nothing as catastrophically unexpected, as self-image shattering, had happened to the nation in its 165 years.

"America is speechless," Democratic congressman L. Men-del Rivers of South Carolina told the House on Monday. Another Democrat, Jerry Voorhis of California, said, "Millions of Americans had not believed such a thing could happen. They had believed the choice of war or peace was still theirs." Listening to their radios on Sunday, he said, "they began to realize that their world of that morn-ing was gone." Roy O. Woodruff, a Republican from Michigan, said the nation "is stunned by Hawaii. It is amazed by Pearl Harbor. It is utterly without explanation for what, on its face, appears to be an utterly inexplicable event."

It was brutally clear the military had not been patrolling the sea and sky as advertised, or at least not well. Clear, too, that Oahu was not an unassailable fortress; that the Japanese were not second-rate warriors; that little airplanes could kill muscular warships; that the navy was less capable than Knox had been saying.

"Where was the continuous reconnaissance?" the *Christian Science Monitor* asked.

"With astounding success, the little man has clipped the big fellow," *Time* said.

"The airplane is the master of the battleship," the *New York Times* said.

"Although this is contrary to expectations," the *Chicago Tribune* said, "there can be no doubt now about the morale of Japanese pilots, about their general abilities as flyers, or their understanding of aviation tactics." Overnight, the Japanese had morphed into gladiators.

Having served in the navy his entire adult life, Kimmel knew what befalls a losing admiral, and he suspected he did not have many hours left as commander in chief, but with an enemy out there and capable of anything, he would execute his responsibilities as long as he had them. On Thursday, he issued a public statement, acknowledging "hard blows" but promising to "deliver even harder ones." At this moment in time, he told his countrymen, "it is truly great to be an American. Victory for us is assured." The latter statement was certainly true; the former, hardly.

As soon as the *Enterprise* had docked, Halsey scurried to see his friend and classmate. He found Kimmel and his staff "haggard and unshaven," most of them not having slept much, "but their chins were up." To another officer, though, Kimmel seemed "just numb" during these days. "He kept sitting around, staring glazed-eyed into space, and thinking that the attack had not taken place."

Within twenty-four hours of the surprise, Democratic congressman John D. Dingell Sr. of Michigan demanded his court-martial, as well as Walter Short's. In the spirit of let's-give-'em-a-fair-trial-and-then-hang-'em, Dingell added that "hundreds of our boys have paid with their lives for the seeming deficiency of their superiors."

To Grace Earle, Kimmel's neighbor, the admiral seemed "awfully alone," which he was. He had no wife or other family on Oahu. "Every great man has to have his share of criticism," his brother Singleton wrote from Kentucky on Friday. "Sit steady in the boat, and everything will come out all right," adding he was sure his brother had done his best "with what you had to do with, and are not to blame." The admiral's oldest son, Manning, a naval officer serving on the East Coast, wrote simply, "My complete confidence and belief in you has not been shaken one bit, and I think you are the greatest Dad in the world." Manning would die at sea in 1944, when the Japanese sank his submarine.

About a week after the attack, on the day that a handsome drawing of Kimmel in resplendent white uniform appeared on the cover of *Time*, he wrote to Harold Stark. "If I am to be relieved I think my relief should be nominated, and that he should take over as soon as practicable," an honorable and professional offer. "I will, of course, stand ready to help him in every way I can. You must decide on the basis of what is best for the country. What happens to me is [of] no importance."

Two days later, on December 17, an officer happened to visit Kimmel about a personnel problem, not quite believing the admiral was personally delving into such trivia at a time like this, although that was Kimmel. "You're right," the admiral replied. "I do have other things to consider. Admiral Pye is going to relieve me in a few minutes."

Roosevelt, having received an unsparing report from Knox that neither Kimmel nor Short had taken the threat of an attack seriously, had removed them. William Pye was to take command at Pearl until the arrival from Washington of Admiral Chester Nimitz who, during the next four years, would lead the fleet across the Pacific and, eventually, to Japan.

"I am sorry this had to happen," Pye told Kimmel after each had read aloud his new orders, as protocol required, in a ceremony witnessed only by the officer who had come about the personnel matter. The temporary and the former commanders shook hands, and then Kimmel, the admiral who had never failed, left the Submarine Building, 319 days after taking command on the sunny afterdeck of the *Pennsylvania*.

The shock of Pearl Harbor was so great that no report by Knox or swift dismissal of Kimmel and Short could sate the nation. But an exhaustive inquiry, especially a public one, would entail risk. Roosevelt's senior commanders and cabinet officers—Stark, Marshall, Stimson, Knox, Hull, and others—would surely have to testify, and Washington had made multiple mistakes whose revelation could be demoralizing: Writing muddled warnings. Not passing to Pearl the intercepts revealing a Japanese mapping system for the harbor. Assuming—never verifying—that the fleet was on guard. Not grasping that Short had taken steps only against sabotage. Not insisting on a single commander on Oahu. Never taking seriously Knox's own early theories about a possible Japanese surprise. Not reacting to the one o'clock deadline on December 7 by picking up a phone to alert the Pacific commands, instead of sending a dispatch that arrived too late.

But America and its leadership had to get on with the winning of the new war, whose scope massively—if predictably—expanded on December 11 when Germany and Italy echoed Japan's decision to open hostilities. Not only that, any investigation might disclose the secret of Magic. So Roosevelt named a five-member Pearl Harbor commission, led by the chief justice of the Supreme Court, and circumscribed its mandate. It would confine itself to what had gone wrong on Oahu.

After days of closed hearings on the island, the commission's findings were delivered to the public on January 24, 1942. Kimmel and Short had not heeded the orders and implications of the November warnings, the commission said, otherwise army radar would have been in full operation and navy search planes would have been aloft. They had "failed to consult and cooperate," which was "a dereliction of duty." It was true, the report went on, that Oahu had lacked planes and other equipment, and true that Washington had misread Short's reply to the warning, and true that every American leader had expected an attack only in the southwest Pacific. But none of those truths relieved the two commanders of their obligation to ensure "the security of the Pacific Fleet and our most important outpost." "Each failed properly to evaluate the seriousness of the situation," the report said. "These errors of judgment were the effective causes for the effectiveness of the attack."

Kimmel and Short were now the Men Responsible.

On February 11, an attorney and former judge in Saint Louis wrote to Kimmel that given the findings, "you should try to show that you are a real man by using a pistol and ending your existence, as you are certainly of no use to yourself nor the American people."

By then, Kimmel had left Hawaii, and evidence suggests he never returned, even though he lived another quarter century. He and his wife took up temporary residence at a high-end hotel on the West Coast as he naively awaited another command, and a return to the war. "As you know, he is here brooding, of course, trying to see bits of clear sky through the clouds," an admiral wrote to Stark from San Francisco on February 13. The admiral, who was an old friend of Kimmel's, wondered whether Roosevelt could say publicly that the attack was really no one person's fault, that everyone in government bore a "share of responsibility." And couldn't he say something like "the frank and high-spirited attitude" of Kimmel and Short during the attack "is worthy of recognition"? No such exculpatory presidential statement was forthcoming.

Among his peers, Kimmel enjoyed immense sympathy, many telling him that in the same situation, they would have made the same choices. "The Navy, make no mistake, is behind you, and your friends and adherents and admirers are legion," one officer wrote to him. He heard from his predecessor, Richardson, who passed along another officer's quotation: "Poor Kimmel! No one ever worked harder than he did." He heard often from Harold Stark: "I know if I say 'keep cheerful' it may sound like a long call, but there is no difference in my feeling with regard to those two little words now than there has been before."

Kimmel retired, because that's what he concluded Washington wanted him to do. Walter Short retired, too, unwillingly.

The military damage of the attack—as opposed to the psychological— was far less than first imagined in Washington and in the country at large. Most ships of the fleet—and all of its aircraft carriers—were unscathed, and their crews remained well trained. The Japanese, strangely, had left untouched Pearl's tank farms of fuel oil, without which the surviving ships could not have sailed for long. Nor had they destroyed Pearl's dry docks, essential for making repairs. And feverish repairs on the battleships indeed commenced, in Hawaii and then on the West Coast. On June 6, 1944, many of the shells arcing over American troops as they assailed the beaches of German-held Normandy came from the *Nevada*'s guns. On September 2, 1945, having fought through horrific battles in the Pacific War, the *West Virginia* stood, fittingly, among the naval witnesses to the surrender of the Japanese in Tokyo Bay.

In the days immediately after the attack, perhaps the happiest man on Oahu—perhaps the only one—was Lieutenant William Outerbridge. "Joined the ship Friday, got under way Saturday morning, and started the war on Sunday," he said to his wife, Grace, in a letter that would not reach her in San Diego for days. "The *Ward* has a fine reputation now." The destroyer was being called "The Watchdog of Pearl Harbor," he said, even if her vigilance had turned out to be only another "what if" in the painful saga. "Have had the time of my life," Outerbridge wrote, somewhat insensitively, considering what had happened. "This life has its compensations."

Billy seemed not to realize that Grace might have no idea whether he was alive. In the naval community of San Diego, many wives did not know their spouses' fate. "Really, the atmosphere around here is ghastly," she wrote to Billy, hoping he was still out there to read a letter. The next day, she wrote, "Don't know how much longer I can stand it." The next day, the casualty lists came out. "I haven't been notified," Grace told her husband, "so I'm sure you must be alright." But even that hard data did not douse her anxiety. "Would give anything to know where you are, and what you're doing." Nearly a week after the attack, a telegram arrived at last, and Grace hesitated for several moments before opening it to find only five words.

Well and happy, William Outerbridge.

"I was so relieved, I sat down and bawled," Grace wrote back, "and then I fixed myself a drink, and drank it while I sat at the phone and called up all the folks who have been inquiring about you." She had gone through "just plain hell," but now, she said, "I feel like a new woman."

Billy Outerbridge and the *Ward* parted company in 1942, only to be reunited later in the war in surreal fashion. Escorting a convoy near the Philippine Islands, the *Ward* was set upon by Japanese bombers, one of them crashing into her starboard side at the waterline and exploding. With fires raging, and having no water pressure with which to fight them, the crew abandoned ship. Rather than leave a hulk adrift, the nearby destroyer *O'Brien* was ordered to sink the *Ward* with gunfire. She went down on the morning of December 7, 1944, three years to the day after she had tried to warn Pearl Harbor.

The captain of the *O'Brien* was Billy Outerbridge.

On June 18, 1942, the *Gripsholm*, a passenger liner of neutral Sweden, cast off in New York bearing 1,097 passengers, among them Ambassador Kichisaburo Nomura and Special Envoy Saburo Kurusu. Having spent six months in comfortable captivity at a resort in Virginia, the two diplomats and hundreds of other interned Japanese were bound for a port in what is now Mozambique, on the Indian Ocean coast of Africa. Not long after their arrival there, another passenger ship docked, the *Asama Maru*, with hundreds of Americans who had been detained by the Japanese, including Ambassador Joseph Grew, his wife, and the rest of the embassy family, who had endured spartan conditions inside its compound in Tokyo.

For several days, the two ships shared the port of what is present-day Maputo as the swap of nationals was arranged and provisions were delivered, and all that time Grew dreaded encountering Nomura. They were good friends, but Grew, as steeped as he was in protocol, did not wish to be photographed chatting with an enemy diplomat. Sure enough, one day, they did bump into each other on Maputo's main street. "Nomura smiled broadly at Grew," recalled Robert Fearey, Grew's young secretary, "and started over with his hand outstretched, trailed by Kurusu. Grew never slackened his pace. Bowing, coldly, he ignored the outstretched hand, and passed on. The incident long rankled with him, but he never doubted that he had done the right thing."

Minoru Genda, the devotee of carrier power who had turned Yamamoto's plan for surprise into reality, survived the war, becoming instrumental in rebuilding the air force of his nation, whose greatest ally became the United States. "Wars are fought and then they end," Genda said, "and when they end, we don't look back. Only forward." Likewise, Sadao Chigusa of the destroyer *Akigumo* not only lived through the hostilities but also rose to the rank of admiral in the postwar Japanese navy. One day, more than three decades after December 7, Chigusa was at home, preparing his wartime diary for publication, when his wife went to a chest of drawers and retrieved an envelope he never knew she had kept. Inside was the lock of hair he had snipped and sent her in the cold days before departure at Hitokappu Bay. "My eyes were moist with tears of thanks," Chigusa said.

Joe Rochefort blamed himself for Pearl Harbor, for not having imagined what the Imperial Navy was capable of doing, for not having recognized what the silence of the carriers had meant as he and his men sifted through radio traffic in the depths of the Dungeon. "I have often said that an intelligence officer has one task, one job, one mission," Rochefort said. "This is to tell his commander, his superior, today what the Japanese are going to do tomorrow." It was a noble sentiment, but the disaster of Pearl Harbor rested on far more shoulders than his alone.

Rochefort and his boys did exact near-perfect revenge, however. Cracking the enemy's main fleet code in 1942, they learned Japan planned to capture Midway Island and finally finish off the Pacific Fleet as it rushed forth to save the outpost. Their cryptologic breakthrough meant the planned ambush became American, one of history's greatest, game-changing military encounters. Off Midway on June 4, 1942, American carrier pilots—those of the *Enterprise* among them—sank four of the Japanese carriers that had surprised Pearl six months before. The Imperial Navy was never the same. As much as anyone's, that was Joe Rochefort's victory.

Edwin Layton got a measure of retribution for Pearl Harbor, too, although in a much more intimate way. Still serving as fleet intelligence officer, Layton learned from decrypted radio traffic the exact itinerary and timetable that Admiral Isoroku Yamamoto would follow during a flying inspection of his forces in the South Pacific. The thought of killing someone he knew and liked, with whom he had had such good times in Tokyo in 1939, bothered Layton. "He had been my 'official friend' four years ago," he said, but in the end, "I could not dismiss the fact that he was now my sworn enemy." On April 18, 1943, American fighter planes surprised and shot down the man who had planned Pearl Harbor.

———

In the spring of 1943, the battleship *Iowa*, newly commissioned, arrived in New York under the command of John McCrea, one of Harold Stark's former assistants. Remembering that Kimmel now worked in the city for an engineering company, McCrea sent an aide ashore to ask if the admiral wished to inspect the ship, which was far larger and more powerful than any he had served aboard or commanded. Anxious that the *Iowa*'s sailors not embarrass Kimmel with questions about Pearl Harbor, McCrea promised that no one but he and two other officers would know of his coming.

And so one day, a launch bearing a stately gentleman in civilian clothes pulled alongside the warship. After lunch, Kimmel toured every nook and cranny, as he had always done with ships. Briefly, he was back in the navy. At the gangway, preparing to return to shore, Kimmel reached out to shake hands with McCrea. "John, this is the nicest thing that has happened to me in a long, long while," he said, "and I'm grateful to you for doing it."

Far more than Walter Short, Kimmel obsessed in the months and years to come, especially about the allegation he had been derelict in the execution of his duties. He became convinced that the genesis of Pearl Harbor was Washington's failure to tell him of Japan's curiosity about ship locations in the port, and to make him privy to the fine points of negotiations and the raw output of the Purple machines. "I have an American's right to my day in court," he wrote in 1944.

In a closed, trial-like proceeding not long after that, a panel of three navy officers exonerated Kimmel, relying on the bizarre argument that he had not been told enemy carriers were coming and therefore had no reason to look. On the other hand, the panel said, Washington had had specific information Pearl Harbor was immediately endangered, but did not pass it along—which was not true.

Eventually, higher authorities in the Navy Department rejected the finding that Kimmel bore no responsibility, although they did agree that Harold Stark had not kept Oahu sufficiently informed about negotiations and had bungled his response on the morning of December 7. In the end, Kimmel's worst mistake "was his failure to conduct long-range reconnaissance in the more dangerous sectors from Oahu during the week preceding the attack," wrote the new navy secretary, James V. Forrestal. But Kimmel did not merit a court-martial.

Stark's career suffered, too, although not as much and not as publicly. Roosevelt, his friend and sponsor, squeezed him out as chief of naval operations in March 1942 by putting another admiral in charge of both wartime theaters, leaving Stark with only administrative and planning duties. It was a tacit recognition that his was not a military mind. He was sent to London to work with the British during the rest of the war, a job he performed well.

On December 12, 1944, after the findings of the three-officer court of inquiry were released, Stark wrote to Kimmel. "While I know nothing can ever undo much that has been done to you," he told him, "I want you to know that no one could have had greater satisfaction than I when I read the decision, recently published in the papers, that there was no grounds for courts martial for Pearl Harbor." He urged Kimmel to stay cheerful, and signed himself "Betty."

"Dear Stark," Kimmel wrote back. There would be no more "Dear Betty." As much as Kimmel blamed anyone, he blamed Stark for what had happened to him, and believed the former chief of naval operations had been dishonest in his testimony. "As I read your note of 12 December 1944 I am forced to conclude that your mind is affected or that you think mine is. I am convinced that you have betrayed me and the Navy, first by failing to supply me with essential information.... Furthermore, I have no desire to number among my friends any man who lies under oath as you did before [the] Court of Inquiry. May God forgive you for what you have done to me, for I never will."

It was not Stark, of course, who had decided that the Japanese would not be able to use torpedoes in the harbor, or who had valued his plans for an offensive over the need to ensure the security of the fleet, or who had interpreted every message in late 1941 in the most benign way, or who had not gathered with Walter Short to discuss what they faced.

Kimmel never mailed his brutal reply to Stark, concluding that cold silence was better. The two apparently never spoke again. The former fleet commander died on May 14, 1968, at the age of eighty-six. The former chief of naval operations died on August 20, 1972, at the age of ninety-one.

Late in 1945, with the war over and won, a joint committee of Congress began the first public investigation of Pearl Harbor, and it was lengthy, thorough, and politicized. The miracle of Magic was revealed. The roles played in Washington came out. The majority Democrats sought to shield the legacy of the now-dead Franklin Roosevelt, while the minority Republicans aimed to puncture it by proving that Washington had contributed to the success of the attack, which it had.

But even the Republicans concluded that Kimmel and Short had been given enough warning and information to do more than they did. "Admiral Kimmel should have been aware of the meaning of code destruction and of the Japanese reputation for surprise action," the Republicans wrote in their report. "He should have been vigilant."

While many decisions and actions led to December 7, its causes went beyond any individual on Oahu or in Washington. One was simply bad timing or luck: As with every innovation, someone gets there first. In this case, one nation was ahead of another in appreciating the lethal possibilities of massed aircraft carriers. But Japan's fortuitous realization could never have produced such success if not for American complacency, anchored in a belief that its Asian adversary lacked the military deftness and technological proficiency to pull off something so daring and so complicated, and a belief that Japan knew and accepted how futile it would be to go to war with a nation as powerful as the United States of America.

Assumption fathered defeat.

ACKNOWLEDGMENTS

S TART with those at Pearl Harbor itself.

    Surely no person is more in touch with the place and the event than Daniel Martinez, the longtime historian of the National Park Service's World War II Valor in the Pacific National Monument. Much in demand, Daniel nonetheless carved out hours to offer great wisdom. James Neuman, as historian of the naval base itself, squired me around what is still a huge, active, and understandably restricted military facility, answering endless questions and arranging a waterborne tour as well as visits to the Submarine Building (still in use), Husband Kimmel's residence on Makalapa Drive (still the official home of the Pacific Fleet commander), Ford Island, and the Dungeon. I am grateful to both Daniel and Jim, as well as to Scott Pawlowski of the National Park Service in Hawaii. Instrumental in making possible a trip to the base was Matthew Stroup of the Navy Office of Information East in New York City.

    On the army side, multiple kind hearts either arranged or led tours of Fort Shafter, Schofield Barracks, and the Tropic Lightning Museum. I am grateful to Kayla R. Overton, Dennis C. Drake, Adam K. Elia, Stefanie A. Gardin, James B. Guzior, and Kathleen H. Ramsden, all in Hawaii, and to Dean Welch of the army's Office of Public Affairs–Northeast in New York City.

    A great side benefit of compiling a work of history is encountering so many professionals who are dedicated to preserving it and who seem to have been born with the qualities of patience and curiosity. I have no doubt I will forget to list some of them here, but among those I have not are the archivists of the Naval Historical Collection at the Naval War College in Newport, Rhode Island: Evelyn Cherpak, Dara M. Baker, and especially Scott Reilly. They made it much easier to plow through the papers of Edwin T. Layton, B. Mitchell Simpson (Harold Stark's biographer), and the archives related to the history of the college itself.

At the Naval History and Heritage Command at the Navy Yard in Washington, DC, David J. Colamaria, Dale J. Gordon, Heidi Lenzini, and Paul Taylor—among others—made it possible to review the papers and photographs of so many essential participants in the events of December 7. The National Archives and Records Administration in College Park, Maryland, is huge (and beautiful), and many hands helped retrieve navy files and photographs, but my thanks go in particular to Holly Reed and Nathaniel Patch. No less vital were the staffs of several departments of the Library of Congress: the Manuscript Division, the Prints and Photographs Room; and the Newspaper and Current Periodical Reading Room, where I'd like to single out Amber Paranick for her help.

At Harvard University, Emily Walhout of the Houghton Library opened the door to the papers of Ambassador Joseph C. Grew. At the University of Pennsylvania, the Van Pelt Library's Nancy Shawcross oversaw the conversion of old tape recordings into compact discs, making it possible to hear Professor Donald G. Brownlow's decades-old interviews with many of those at the center of the events of 1941. Mark Sanolis at the library of the College of the Holy Cross in Worcester, Massachusetts, fished out the papers of Edward B. Hanify, who served as Husband Kimmel's attorney.

The American Heritage Center at the University of Wyoming in Laramie is the home of the papers of Husband Kimmel, as well as the papers of several other individuals with connections to the attack, and Amanda Stow was my principal contact there. The staffs of the Hawaii State Library in Honolulu and the Hamilton Library at the University of Hawaii at Manoa helped me find period maps, back issues of local publications, and personal reminiscences of December 7. Also on Oahu, Ann Yoklavich and Polly Tice of Mason Architects Inc. sent along essential information about the history of navy residences at Pearl Harbor.

For decades, the oral history program of the United States Naval Institute in Annapolis, Maryland, has made sure that the country has a record of the firsthand experiences of its leading naval officers. I am grateful to USNI's Janis Jorgensen for swiftly providing the transcripts of interviews with Edwin T. Layton, Arthur H. McCollum, Joseph J. Rochefort, and many others. In similar fashion, the Columbia Center for Oral History at Columbia University in New York City has captured the recollections of many navy and marine officers, and I thank the fine people there who made it possible to read the transcripts.

At the National Cryptologic Museum (which has an actual Purple machine) in Fort Meade, Maryland, the curator Patrick Weadon and librarian Rene S. Stein not only graciously fielded many questions, but also put me in touch with the retired historian Robert Hanyok of the National Security Agency, who made the Byzantine world of cryptology much more comprehensible. So did Dr. David A. Hatch, the NSA's chief historian.

It was always a treat to go to the Franklin D. Roosevelt Presidential Library and Museum in Hyde Park, New York, simply because the grounds include the president's home, and the history is enveloping. Every one of the staff members who helped me find the right Roosevelt papers, as well as numerous other records, could write a book about him, so deep is their knowledge. They are great. At the Dwight D. Eisenhower Presidential Library, Museum and Boyhood Home in Abilene, Kansas, Valoise Armstrong made sure that I got photocopies of the papers of William W. Outerbridge. At the Nimitz Library of the United States Naval Academy in Annapolis, Maryland, Jennifer A. Bryan and David A. D'Onofrio helped me with a microfilm copy of Admiral Kimmel's papers.

It's not possible to write about Pearl Harbor without visiting the Hornbake Library at the University of Maryland in College Park, the keeper of the papers of the historian Gordon Prange, who made the study of the Pearl Harbor attack his life's mission. Over the years, numerous efficient and congenial staff members helped me delve into Prange's notes, files, and, most important, his interviews with participants in the events, especially those on the Japanese side.

Scott Stephens of the National Climatic Data Center provided weather data for Honolulu and Washington in late 1941. Tosh Minohara, Hayoto Yukawa, and my cousin, Meg Sweeney, found answers in Japan to several questions. Yale University's library swiftly passed along to my local library a microfilm copy of the Henry L. Stimson diaries. And a special thanks to Mark Aldrich and Debbie Seracini, who plumbed the archives of the San Diego Air and Space Museum to come up with incredible statistics on the PBY-5.

I have the great good fortune to live within a dozen miles of the main branch of the New York Public Library. No matter how obscure or old, the right book was almost always somewhere in its closed stacks. During my many visits, the cast of people retrieving the tomes was ever changing, but they are collectively a gift, as is the library's beautiful Rose Reading Room.

Quite a few academics, friends, and authors offered guidance about either the attack itself or the art of writing a book. None of them is responsible for any conclusions or errors or clumsy writing here, but I would like to thank them: Stephen Budiansky, Paul Burtness, Larry Eichel, Douglas M. Goldstein, Trent Hone, Thomas Kimmel Jr., Kenneth D. Kitts, Warren U. Ober, Lynne Olson, Ray Panko, Jon Parshall, Norman Polmar, Barney Rubel, and David Von Drehle. Permit me to dedicate a separate sentence to a friend of many years, David Everett, whose advice proved why he was the academic director of the Writing Program at Johns Hopkins University in Washington.

Books have editors (usually), and the editor of this one was Simon & Schuster's Priscilla Painton, who has the perfect sense of what is too much, what is out of place, and what could be clearer. It's a cliché, but still: I feel fortunate and privileged to work with someone so calm and so good. And thanks to the equally able Sophia Jimenez, Megan Hogan, and Benjamin Holmes at S&S, as well as to mapmaker Robert Cronan.

Until this project, I never had a laptop and did not know I needed a magnifying glass. So they were the Christmas gifts that made it possible to take notes in archives and reading rooms, and to read the fine print of ancient newspapers, and they came from my spouse, Kathleen Carroll, and my son, Nick, who thought some technical assistance was in order if there was to be any book at all. Kathleen also relentlessly tracked down every single photo, and both wife and son assumed the burdens of the house, while offering endless understanding. There is no better pair, and they will forever have my love.

NOTES

PREFACE THE BOYS AT OPANA

xii *"here life is lived"*: Advertisement by the Hawaii Tourism Board, *Paradise of the Pacific*, December 1941, 2.

xii *"I mean, it was more practice"*: Congress of the United States, *Pearl Harbor Attack: Hearings Before the Joint Committee on the Investigation of the Pearl Harbor Attack* (Washington, DC: United States Government Printing Office, 1946), testimony of George Elliott, part 10, 5036. This forty-volume publication includes the testimony, findings, and exhibits of all previous investigations of the attack. Hereafter, the citation is *PHA*.

xii *"There was a sergeant"*: Elliott, *PHA*, part 32, 494.

xiii *"He was looking over my shoulder"*: Ibid., 488.

xiii *"It was the largest group"*: Testimony of Joseph L. Lockard, *PHA*, part 27, 532.

xiv *"very big and it was very noticeable"*: Elliott, *PHA*, part 10, 5041.

ONE AN END, A BEGINNING

1 *"convulsive lurch"*: Theodore C. Mason, *Battleship Sailor* (Annapolis, MD: Naval Institute Press, 1982), 174.

2 *"mighty thunderclaps"*: Ibid.

2 *"frightening"*: Transcript of the oral history of Hanson W. Baldwin, United States Naval Institute, February 24 and December 8, 1975, 325.

2 *"have a sixteen-inch gun go off"*: Ibid.

2 *"The ceremony is about to"*: CBS transcript of the change-of-command ceremony, February 1, 1941. The transcript can be found on reel 1 of a microfilm copy of the papers of Husband E. Kimmel, Nimitz Library of the United States Naval Academy, Annapolis, MD.

2 *"The greatest, most powerful"*: *Honolulu Advertiser*, September 14, 1940.

3 *"We hear the hum"*: CBS transcript.

4 *During annexation hearings*: These details and many others can be found in Tom Coffman's excellent history of the annexation, *Nation Within* (Kihei, HI: Koa Books, 1998).

4 *"With the dignity of their rank"*: CBS transcript.

4 *"My God, they can't do that"*: George C. Dyer, "My God, They Can't Do That to Me," *Air Raid: Pearl Harbor!* ed. Paul Stillwell (Annapolis, MD: Naval Institute Press, 1981), 44.

5 *"Unfortunately," he said later*: Testimony of James O. Richardson, *PHA*, part 1, 325.

5 *"confused by the multiplicity"*: James O. Richardson, thesis (record group 13, Student Theses, May 1934, Naval War College Archive, Newport, RI).

5 *"stamp collecting"*: James O. Richardson, *On the Treadmill to Pearl Harbor* (Washington, DC: Department of the Navy, Naval History Division, 1973), 382.

6 *"He already has a model"*: Letter of Grace Tully, December 4, 1941, papers of Franklin D. Roosevelt, President's Personal File 223, President's Naval History Collection, box 4, Franklin D. Roosevelt Presidential Library and Museum, Hyde Park, NY.

6 *"hate"*: Roosevelt to D. J. Callaghan, February 10, 1941, Roosevelt papers, President's Secretary's File, box 59, Navy File, January through June 1941.

6 *"Let me see"*: Ibid.

6 *catapults to launch*: Roosevelt to Royal E. Ingersoll, March 10, 1941, Roosevelt papers, President's Secretary's File, box 59, Navy File, January through June 1941.

6 *"the use of 70- and 77-foot"*: Roosevelt to James V. Forrestal, March 12, 1941, Roosevelt papers, President's Secretary's File, box 59, Navy File, January through June 1941.

6 *"Please speak to me"*: Roosevelt to Frank Knox, April 23, 1941, Roosevelt papers, President's Secretary's File, box 59, Navy File, January through June 1941.

6 *"If you do not tell"*: Richardson to Stark, January 26, 1940, *PHA*, part 14, 926.

7 *"I feel that any move"*: Richardson to Stark, May 13, 1940, *PHA*, part 14, 936.

7 *"aggressive"*: Richardson to Knox, September 12, 1940, *PHA*, part 14, 958.

7 *"Americans are perfectly willing"*: Richardson, *PHA*, part 1, 262–63.

8 *"Mr. President," he had said*: Richardson, *On the Treadmill to Pearl Harbor*, 435.

8 *"I thought that the President"*: Ibid., 436.

8 *"I can state with complete"*: Ibid.

8 *"I have never known"*: Ibid., 424.

9 *"had the air"*: *The Lucky Bag* (Annapolis, MD: First Class United States Naval Academy, 1904), 52.

10 *"Lieutenant Kimmel," his commanding officer*: Letter of Victor Blue, September 11, 1914, records of Husband Kimmel, file 6, 2, National Personnel Records Center, Archival Programs Division, Saint Louis, MO.

10 *"I recommend it highly"*: Joe Kyle to Kimmel, January 9, 1941, papers of Husband E. Kimmel, series II, box 2, folder 3, American Heritage Center, University of Wyoming, Laramie, WY.

10 *"I have heard for years"*: Husband Kimmel to Sibbella Kimmel, July 21, 1908, Kimmel papers, series II, box 2, folder 1.

10 *"met some of the native girls"*: Ibid.

11 *"As you know"*: Husband Kimmel to Sibbella Kimmel, March 22, 1908, Kimmel papers, series II, box 2, folder 1.

11 *"This boat for Sale"*: I am indebted to Thomas Kimmel Jr., the admiral's grandson, who allowed me to examine the papers of Manning Marius Kimmel, the admiral's brother. Among those papers is a 1939 clipping from an unnamed newspaper that recounts this episode.

11 *"intensely earnest"*: The Lucky Bag, 52.

11 *"He's the most honest, conscientious"*: Professor Donald G. Brownlow of the Haverford School on Philadelphia's Main Line taped interviews with many of those involved in the attack for his 1968 book, *The Accused: The Ordeal of Rear Admiral Husband Edward Kimmel* (New York: Vantage Press). Brownlow gave the recordings to the University of Pennsylvania. The donation has yet to be formally cataloged, but Penn's Van Pelt Library provided compact discs of selected tapes, from which this quote and others in this book are taken. This quote is from tape 34. Hereafter, the citation is Brownlow tapes.

11 *"invisible badges of success"*: Big Spring Herald, February 14, 1941.

12 *"a humdinger"*: Evaluation of Admiral W. V. Pratt, May 27, 1933, records of Husband Kimmel, file 8, 125, National Personnel Records Center.

12 *"absolutely top flight"*: Husband E. Kimmel, interview by Gordon Prange, November 29, 1963, papers of Donald M. Goldstein, series IX, box 23, folder 65, University of Pittsburgh.

12 *"I hadn't any intimation"*: Kimmel to Stark, January 12, 1941, papers of Harold Stark, series XIII, boxes 78 and 79, Naval History and Heritage Command, Washington, DC.

12 *"an engaging kind of chap"*: Brownlow tapes, tape 10.

12 *"Short, stocky, straightforward"*: Francis Biddle, *In Brief Authority* (Garden City, NY: Doubleday, 1962), 175.

13 *"irresponsible, erratic individual"*: Chicago Tribune, July 2, 1941.

13 *"Indifference to the outcome"*: Christian Science Monitor, January 18, 1941.

13 *"Always we must have"*: Roosevelt papers, President's Secretary's Files, box 62, Departmental Correspondence, Frank Knox, 1939–41.

14 *"He became very enthusiastic"*: Brownlow tapes, tape 34.

14 *"where they belong"*: Ibid.

14 *"Frank Knox and I"*: Melvin Maas to Kimmel, September 30, 1941, record group 313, Naval Operating Forces, Secret and Top Secret General Administrative Files, 1941–44, box 1, CINCUS files 1941–42 (Secret), Admiral Kimmel's Personal File, 1 January 1941–31 December 1941, National Archives and Records Administration II, College Park, MD.

14 *"My satisfaction is mixed"*: Husband Kimmel to Chester Nimitz, January 6, 1941, papers of Edward Hanify, box 17, folder 14, College of the Holy Cross, Worcester, MA.

15 *"Of course," he admitted*: Brownlow tapes, tape 34.

15 *"I didn't know it would be"*: J. W. Bunkley to Kimmel, January 9, 1941, Kimmel papers, series II, box 2, folder 3.

15 *"I confess it came sooner"*: Stark to Kimmel, January 13, 1941, PHA, part 16, 2144.

15 *"I am thankful"*: Ibid.
16 *"You are particularly fortunate"*: J. A. Furer to Kimmel, January 14, 1941, Kimmel papers, series II, box 2, folder 4.
16 *"I shall rest easier now"*: Edward C. Kalbfus to Kimmel, January 9, 1941, Kimmel papers, series II, box 2, folder 3.
16 *"electrified and delighted"*: Singleton Kimmel to Husband Kimmel, January 10, 1941, Kimmel papers, series II, box 2, folder 3.
16 *"Everybody we know"*: Ibid.
16 *"Hubbie has knocked"*: Ibid.
17 *"The greatest honor"*: Ibid.
17 *"All of you can take pride"*: *New York Times*, February 2, 1941.
17 *"is tempered by the fact"*: *Honolulu Advertiser*, February 2, 1941.
17 *"I can only say this"*: Ibid.
18 *"The crisp, blue-eyed"*: Ibid.
18 *"I hope you still think so"*: Joe Kyle to Kimmel, January 9, 1941, Kimmel papers, series II, box 2, folder 3.

TWO HITOPAKKU'S SECRET

19 *"Expressing my last gratitude"*: Translated excerpts of Sadao Chigusa's diary, as well as postwar commentary by him, can be found in Donald M. Goldstein and Katherine V. Dillon, eds., *The Pearl Harbor Papers* (Dulles, VA: Brassey's, 1993). This quotation appears on p. 182. Hereafter, the citation is Chigusa, *Pearl Harbor Papers*.
20 *"It was very cold"*: Ibid., 180.
20 *"a world of isolation"*: Ibid., 182.
20 *"No anchorage in these islands"*: "The Japanese Islands and Spheres of Control," 1940–41 edition, record group 4, box 95, folder 10, Naval War College Archives, Newport, RI.
21 *"something most serious"*: Chigusa, *Pearl Harbor Papers*, 175.
21 *"Our wardroom had been turned"*: Ibid., 173.
21 *"It is really encouraging"*: Ibid., 179.
21 *Thirty would be making*: The number of ships that made the crossing to Hawaii is difficult to pin down, with the discrepancies among sources apparently rooted in how many submarines and oil tankers made the entire voyage. Based on several sources in Japan, the total was thirty.
22 *The morning after his arrival*: Chigusa, *Pearl Harbor Papers*, 180.
22 *With the fleet gone*: Hiroyuki Agawa, *The Reluctant Admiral* (Tokyo: Kodansha International, 1979), 242. This biography was the source of many details about Yamamoto.
23 *"Boy, he was a good bridge player"*: Edwin T. Layton interview by John Costello and Roger Pineau, December 5, 1983, papers of Edwin T. Layton, box 30, folder 1, Naval War College, Newport, RI.
23 *"Few men could have been as fond"*: Agawa, *Reluctant Admiral*, 8.
23 *"possessed more brains"*: Testimony of Edwin T. Layton, *PHA*, part 26, 235.
23 *"Weird stuff"*: Layton interview with Costello and Pineau.

24   *"Many Japanese are hard to get to"*: Transcript of the oral history of Edwin T. Layton, United States Naval Institute (USNI), May 30, 1970, 58.

24   *"to be embraced in your arms"*: Translated excerpts of several of Yamamoto's personal and professional letters can be found in *Pearl Harbor Papers*. These quotations appear on p. 128.

24   *"rather unapproachable and taciturn"*: Agawa, *Reluctant Admiral*, 63.

24   *"He was famous for his geisha"*: Haruko Taya Cook and Theodore F. Cook, *Japan At War: An Oral History* (New York: New Press, 1992), 83.

25   *"a lot of steel"*: Layton, USNI oral history, 59.

25   *"There have not been many generals"*: *Japanese Times and Advertiser*, November 28, 1941, papers of Gordon Prange, series V, box 52, folder 19, Japanese Press Translated, November 1941, Hornbake Library, University of Maryland.

25   *"smart and dangerous"*: Prange papers, series V, box 74, folder 23. This is Poco Smith's recollection of Admiral Thomas C. Hart's notebook.

25   *"exceptionally able, forceful"*: Office of Naval Intelligence report, November 8, 1941, Far Eastern Section, Japanese Empire Desk (OP23F14), serials 1941–47, record group 38, NARA II.

25   *"may be expected"*: Ibid.

26   *"inevitable"*: Yamamoto, *Pearl Harbor Papers*, 115.

26   *"on its first day"*: Ibid., 117.

26   *"goes down to such an extent"*: Ibid., 116.

26   *"favored by God's blessing"*: Ibid., 117.

26   *"like going into the enemy's chest"*: The quotation comes from Gordon Prange's translation of Minoru Genda's 1972 book *Memoirs of the Pearl Harbor Naval Operation*, Prange papers, series V, box 20, folder 3.

26   *"For one week"*: Ibid., folder 2.

27   *"exercises in masturbation"*: Minoru Genda interview by Gordon Prange, March 21, 1947, Prange papers, series V, box 19, folder 6.

27   *"I even felt something very cold"*: Minoru Genda, "How the Japanese Task Force Idea Materialized," Prange papers, series V, box 20, folder 2.

28   *"Possible, right?"*: Ibid.

29   *"We knew that you were"*: Shigeru Fukodome interview by US Army interrogators, May 4, 1949, Prange papers, series V, box 18, folder 4.

29   *"Day and night"*: Walter Davenport, "Impregnable Pearl Harbor," *Collier's,* June 14, 1941, 75.

29   *"Destroyers, cruisers and aircraft carriers"*: *Chicago Tribune,* August 17, 1941.

30   *"would be detected long before"*: "Warning to the Enemy," *Paradise of the Pacific,* May 1941, 9.

30   *"Japan could lose the war"*: Shigeru Fukodome interview by Gordon Prange, May 2, 1950, Prange papers, series V, box 18, folder 5.

30   *"I like speculative games"*: Ryunosuke Kasaka interview by Gordon Prange, June 29, 1947, Prange papers, series V, box 58, folder 16.

32   *seventy-four times that of Japan*: Eri Hotta, *Japan 1941* (New York: Alfred A. Knopf, 2013), 224.

32   *"Japan's resources will be depleted"*: Ibid., 192.

32   *"My present situation is very strange"*: Yamamoto, *Pearl Harbor Papers*, 124.

33 *"little hope of success"*: Ibid., 118.

33 *"Military operations, in a war"*: Fukodome interview by US Army.

33 *"would not be altogether"*: Ibid.

33 *"occasionally, one must conjure up"*: Hotta, *Japan 1941*, 201.

34 *"But in this operation, we will meet"*: Gordon Prange, *At Dawn We Slept: The Untold Story of Pearl Harbor* (New York: McGraw-Hill, 1981), 344.

34 *"What came from his heart"*: Matome Ugaki, *Fading Victory: The Diary of Admiral Matome Ugaki* (Pittsburgh, PA: University of Pittsburgh Press, 1991), 25.

34 *"What a big drama"*: Ibid., 38.

34 *"An air attack on Hawaii!"*: Captured Japanese document written by Iki Kuramoti, *PHA*, part 13, 516.

34 *"Shiga stated that the consensus"*: Postwar interrogation of Yoshio Shiga, *PHA*, part 13, 645.

35 *"if you die in this operation"*: Gunichi Mikawa interview by Gordon Prange, January 12, 1949, Prange papers, box 62, folder 15.

35 *"off Hawaii in the greatest"*: Prange papers, series V, box 9, folder 18. The quotation is from an undated article that Sadao Chigusa wrote for the magazine of the American Chamber of Commerce in Japan.

35 *"I wrote my own farewell"*: Chigusa, *Pearl Harbor Papers*, 183.

35 *"All the crew were pleased"*: Ibid., 182.

35 *"And at 2230, I took my last"*: Ibid.

36 *"The sally of our great fleet"*: Ibid., 184.

36 *"it still remains very vivid"*: Yoshio Shiga interview by John Toland, papers of John Toland, Roosevelt Presidential Library, box 15, folder "The Rising Sun."

36 *"My elder brother"*: Chigusa, *Pearl Harbor Papers*, 186.

36 *"to do my best in war"*: Ibid.

37 *"Tears came to my eyes"*: Genda, "How the Japanese Task Force Idea Materialized."

38 *"For the first time in history"*: Jonathan Parshall and J. Michael Wenger, "Pearl Harbor's Overlooked Answer," *Naval History Magazine*, December 2011.

38 *"I pictured to myself the situation"*: Prange papers, series V, box 19, folder 8.

THREE THE ADMIRAL CHIEF OF THE PACIFIC FLEET

39 *"The day I arrived in Hawaii"*: Thurston Clarke, *Pearl Harbor Ghosts* (New York: Ballantine Books, 1991), 245.

39 *"I immediately got into a taxi"*: Otto Tolischus, *Tokyo Record* (New York: Reynal and Hitchcock, 1943), 3.

40 *"I marvel at the place"*: Helen Dauth to Singleton and Lambert Kimmel, November 1941, Kimmel papers, series II, box 2, folder 7.

40 *"bids fair to leap"*: Unsigned article, *Paradise of the Pacific*, September 1941, 3.

40 *"we didn't get bombed"*: Dauth letter, Kimmel papers.

40 *"He looks perfectly marvelous"*: Ibid.

41 *"for killing the fleet"*: Layton interviews with Costello and Pineau, September 27 and 28, 1983, Layton papers, box 30, folder 1.

41 *"We put on extra steam"*: Testimony of Husband Kimmel, *PHA*, part 6, 2748.

41 *"I believe that in my whole career"*: Transcript of the oral history of Omar T. Pfeiffer, Columbia Oral History Project, Columbia University, 1968, 168.

41 *"vehement castigation"*: Ibid.

41 *"Every command I ever had"*: Kimmel, *PHA*, part 6, 2748.

41 *"I set out"*: Ibid., 2499.

42 *"He couldn't do it any other way"*: Brownlow, *The Accused*, 27.

42 *"He was a dandy"*: Brownlow tapes, tape 34.

42 *"Within a matter of almost hours"*: William R. Smedberg III to Gordon Prange, letter, undated, Prange papers, series V, box 74, folder 14.

42 *"put us through the damnedest"*: Transcript of the oral history of William R. Smedberg III, USNI, May 1975 and December 1978, 182.

42 *"We were not being allowed to get home"*: Smedberg letter, Prange papers.

42 *"would come aboard ships"*: Transcript of the oral history of H. Kent Hewitt, Columbia Oral History Project, Columbia University, 1961, 13–4 to 13–5.

43 *"were falling all over"*: Ibid.

43 *"I don't give a dang"*: Ibid.

43 *"I note certain material"*: Kimmel to commander destroyers, August 7, 1941, NARA, record group 313, CINCUS files, box 1, "Admiral Kimmel's Personal File."

43 *On September 25, Kimmel*: Kimmel to William S. Pye, September 25, 1941, NARA II, record group 313, CINCUS files.

44 *"personally auditing the records"*: Testimony of William W. (Poco) Smith, *PHA*, part 26, 74.

44 *"The two papers disagreed"*: Ibid.

44 *"this movement of batteries"*: Kimmel to Claude C. Bloch, November 19, 1941, NARA II, record group 313, CINCUS Files.

44 *"like a man on roller skates"*: William W. Smith interview by Gordon Prange, undated, Prange papers, series V, box 55, folder 16.

44 *"rang my bell perhaps"*: Smith, *PHA*, part 26, 69.

45 *"Kimmel's staff was his family"*: Walter S. De Lany interview by Gordon Prange, November 2, 1962, Prange papers, series V, box 12, folder 27.

45 *"for a few months"*: Kimmel to Mrs. Abram Claude, January 28, 1941, Kimmel papers, series II, box 2, folder 4.

45 *"Well, to tell you the truth"*: William W. Smith interview by Gordon Prange, November 14, 1962, Prange papers, series V, box 74, folder 23.

45 *"did everything he could"*: Transcript of the oral history of George C. Dyer, USNI, April 1969–May 1971, 214.

45 *"keeping high the spirit"*: *Honolulu Star-Bulletin*, September 18, 1941.

46 *"They have with them the brisk"*: Garland Greene, "Progress Marches," *Paradise of the Pacific*, January 1941, 3.

46 *"There were new grills"*: *Honolulu Star-Bulletin*, July 11, 1941.

47 *"shortage of housing"*: *Honolulu Star-Bulletin*, October 7, 1941.

48 *"a bunch of slackers"*: *Hawaii Hochi*, September 23, 1941.

48 *"Kimmel was a real"*: Walter J. East interview by Gordon Prange, August 7, 1964, Prange papers, series V, box 13, folder 20.

48 *"mean, nasty old man"*: Ibid.

48   *"a lot of people didn't like Kimmel"*: Brownlow tapes, tape 34.
48   *"As long as Richardson commanded"*: Transcript of the oral history of Thomas C. Hart, Columbia Oral History Project, Columbia University, December 15, 1961, 144.
49   *"Kimmelite"*: Pfeiffer, Columbia oral history, 169.
49   *"The staff learned to understand"*: East interview by Prange.
49   *"was opinionated"*: Transcript of the oral history of John L. McCrea, USNI, May to October 1982, 95.
50   *"At an alarming rate"*: Kimmel to Stark, May 26, 1941, *PHA*, part 16, 2233.
50   *"There were times when 70 percent"*: Kimmel, *PHA*, part 6, 2500.
50   *"We cannot produce a satisfactory"*: Kimmel to Stark, April 22, 1941, *PHA*, part 16, 2230.
50   *"the highest state of efficiency"*: Testimony of William S. Pye, *PHA*, part 26, 158.
50   *"in my opinion, sir"*: Testimony of Willard A. Kitts, *PHA*, part 32, 388.
50   *"I feel that gunnery"*: Kimmel to Stark, August 12, 1941, *PHA*, part 16, 2244.
51   *"We are ready to do our damnedest"*: Ibid., 2245.
51   *"TALKS WITH JAPAN END"*: *Honolulu Advertiser*, November 27, 1941.
52   *"open to very serious question"*: Kimmel, *PHA*, part 22, 397.
52   *"There was a considerable difference"*: Ibid., 455.
53   *"the fleet offensively"*: Testimony of Charles H. "Soc" McMorris, *PHA*, part 26, 256.
53   *"The United States at that time"*: Testimony of Royal E. Ingersoll, *PHA*, part 26, 460.
54   *"Dear Mustapha"*: Stark to Kimmel, April 26, 1941, *PHA*, part 16, 2165.
54   *"We were continually"*: Testimony of Walter S. DeLany, *PHA*, part 26, 88.
54   *"for offensive operations"*: Kimmel to Stark, May 26, 1941, *PHA*, part 16, 2236.
55   *"to support active"*: Ibid.
55   *"bold offensive"*: Kimmel to Stark, September 12, 1941, *PHA*, part 16, 2248.
55   *"I must insist"*: Kimmel to Stark, November 15, 1941, *PHA*, part 16, 2252.
55   *"even on occasions"*: Ibid., 2253.
55   *"must not be considered"*: Ibid.
56   *"Just stop for a minute"*: Stark to Kimmel, November 25, 1941, *PHA*, part 16, 2224.
56   *"You cannot take"*: Ibid., 2223.
56   *"Would serve as bait"*: Kimmel, *PHA*, part 22, 397.
57   *"Why are you so worried"*: James A. Mollison interview by Gordon Prange, April 13, 1961, Prange papers, series V, box 62, folder 31.

FOUR **BETTY**

59   *That same Thursday arrived cloudless*: Throughout the book, descriptions of the weather are based on data provided by the National Climatic Data Center in Asheville, North Carolina.
60   *"He is not spectacular"*: *Washington Post*, June 4, 1939.
60   *"Tonight, the American"*: B. Mitchell Simpson III, *Admiral Harold R. Stark, Architect of Victory, 1939–45* (Columbia: University of South Carolina Press, 1989), 3.
60   *described him as "cheerful"*: Fitness reports written by Captain T. J. Senn, May 29,

1919; Captain W. M. Crose, July 10, 1920; and Captain W. K. Riddle, October 22, 1925, Stark papers, series III, box 23.

61 *"to be a gentleman"*: David W. Richmond interview by John Toland, papers of B. Mitchell Simpson, box 14, folder 1, Naval War College, Newport, RI.

61 *"dressed in blue silk"*: W. Larned Blatchford to B. Mitchell Simpson, September 28, 1978, Simpson papers, box 9, folder 3.

61 *"a disparaging remark"*: Ibid.

61 *"There was respect"*: Ibid.

61 *"NEVER heard a single"*: Harry J. Hansen to B. Mitchell Simpson, July 7, 1978, Simpson papers, box 8, folder 17.

61 *"Within a few days"*: Magruder H. Tuttle to B. Mitchell Simpson, August 22, 1978, Simpson papers, box 9, folder 3.

62 *"was a wonderful man"*: Smedberg, USNI oral history, 115.

62 *"He was a very simple sort of man"*: Ibid., 144.

62 *"I'll gladly relieve you"*: Unpublished manuscript of authorized biography by John C. Dingwell, 14–18, Stark papers, box 8.

62 *"Take good care"*: Stark to Roosevelt, July 28, 1933, Simpson papers, box 8, folder 8.

63 *"he had quite a bit"*: Smedberg, USNI oral history, 123.

63 *"Betty, I want this"*: Ibid., 129.

63 *"lunger, somebody who had a bright idea"*: Charles W. Wellborn Jr. interview by B. Mitchell Simpson, December 15, 1975, Simpson papers, box 11, folder 16.

64 *"defer to your better judgment"*: Stark to Roosevelt, February 11, 1941, *PHA*, part 16, 2151.

64 *"I considered every day of delay"*: Stark to Charles J. Cooke, July 31, 1941, *PHA*, part 16, 2175.

64 *"In the Atlantic"*: Ingersoll, *PHA*, part 9, 4249.

64 *"I confess to having used"*: Stark to Kimmel, February 10, 1941, *PHA*, part 16, 2147.

65 *"to some of my very pointed"*: Stark to Cooke, *PHA*, part 16, 2177.

65 *"Give us credit"*: Stark to Kimmel, March 22, 1941, *PHA*, part 16, 2160.

65 *"First, I will put"*: Stark to Kimmel, April 19, 1941, *PHA*, part 16, 2163.

65 *"God knows I would surrender"*: Stark to Cooke, *PHA*, part 16, 2177.

66 *"Believe it or not"*: Ibid.

66 *"He was a dear old man"*: Smedberg, USNI oral history, 123.

66 *"lacked decisiveness and fire"*: George C. Dyer to B. Mitchell Simpson, May 6, 1978, Simpson papers, box 8, folder 17.

66 *"probably not tough or ruthless enough"*: James L. Holloway Jr. to B. Mitchell Simpson, August 22, 1978, Simpson papers, box 8, folder 17.

66 *"He was rather too optimistic"*: Brownlow tapes, tape 34.

66 *"that he did not think"*: William A. Reitzel to B. Mitchell Simpson, November 22, 1977, Simpson papers, box 11, folder 14.

67 *"Halfway up the hill"*: Smedberg letter, Prange papers.

67 *"You will be unable to make up"*: unpublished Dingwell manuscript, 13–28, Stark papers, box 8.

68 *The army and navy*: Statistics on military production are from the Roosevelt

papers, President's Secretary's Files, box 95, subject file: Bureau of the Budget, for November 29 and December 31, 1941.

68 *"I know how bad"*: *Time*, September 22, 1941.

68 *"there must be statesmen"*: Ibid.

69 *"unless I am completely"*: Stark to Kimmel, April 4, 1941, *PHA*, part 16, 2161.

69 *"honestly sincere"*: Cordell Hull, *The Memoirs of Cordell Hull* (New York: Macmillan, 1948), 987.

69 *"tall, moon-faced, suave"*: Edwin T. Layton, *And I Was There: Pearl Harbor and Midway—Breaking the Secrets* (New York: William Morrow, 1985), 82.

69 *"I am old man"*: *Time*, September 22, 1941.

70 *"certainly occurred"*: Washington to Tokyo, July 30, 1941, *PHA*, part 12, 8.

70 *"a little too much wishful"*: Washington to Tokyo, September 29, 1941, *PHA*, part 12, 41.

70 *"appeasement measures"*: Washington to Tokyo, July 30, 1941, *PHA*, part 12, 8.

70 *"Admiral Nomura came in"*: Stark to Kimmel, September 29, 1941, *PHA*, part 16, 2213.

71 *"I am afraid"*: Washington to Tokyo, October 18, 1941, *PHA*, part 12, 79.

71 *"I know that for some time"*: Washington to Tokyo, October 22, 1941, *PHA*, part 12, 81.

71 *"a serious difficulty"*: Hull, *The Memoirs of Cordell Hull*, 1030.

71 *"to caution you again"*: Tokyo to Washington, September 26, 1941, *PHA*, part 12, 32.

71 *"Follow my instructions"*: Tokyo to Washington, November 4, 1941, *PHA*, part 12, 94.

72 *"absolutely necessary"*: Tokyo to Washington, November 5, 1941, *PHA*, part 12, 100.

72 *"redouble"*: Tokyo to Washington, November 11, 1941, *PHA*, part 12, 116.

72 *"There are reasons beyond"*: Tokyo to Washington, November 22, 1941, *PHA*, part 12, 165.

72 *"All over Tokyo"*: *Time*, September 22, 1941.

73 *"Nomura was extremely worried"*: Smedberg, USNI oral history, 157.

73 *"had no conception"*: Smedberg letter, Prange papers.

73 *"deeply impressed"*: Smedberg, USNI oral history, 157.

74 *"He fairly blew up"*: Henry L. Stimson, *The Henry Lewis Stimson Diaries, 1909–1945* (New Haven, CT: Manuscript and Archives, Yale University Library, 1973), entry for November 26, 1941.

75 *"there is nothing further"*: Ibid., August 8, 1941.

75 *"abject surrender to her demands"*: Testimony of Cordell Hull, *PHA*, part 11, 5392.

75 *"pacific settlement of controversies"*: The complete text of the two documents Hull presented can be found in *Peace and War: United States Foreign Policy, 1931–1941* (Washington, DC: United States Government Printing Office, 1943), which is available online at www.ibiblio.org/pha/paw/257.html. The quotations are on p. 809.

76 *"magnificent"*: Stimson diary, November 27, 1941.

76 *"In view of our negotiations"*: Washington to Tokyo, November 27, 1941, *PHA*, part 12, 182.

76   *"He [Hull] told me now"*: Stimson diary, November 27, 1941.
77   *"upon their return to me"*: Testimony of John L. McCrea, *PHA*, part 26, 294.
77   *"your flag officers and captains"*: Testimony of Harold R. Stark, *PHA*, part 5, 2110.
77   *"may be a matter of weeks"*: Stark to Kimmel, January 13, 1941, *PHA*, part 16, 2144.
77   *"grave"*: Navy Department to forces afloat, October 16, 1941, *PHA*, part 14, 1402.
77   *"Personally,"* he had said: Stark to Kimmel, October 17, 1941, *PHA*, part 16, 2214.
77   *"worser and worser"*: Stark to Kimmel, November 7, 1941, *PHA* part 16, 2220.
78   *"The words 'war warning'"*: Testimony of Richmond Turner, *PHA*, part 26, 280.
78   *"because I remember"*: McCrea, *PHA*, part 26, 295.
78   *"We pondered almost an entire"*: Stark, *PHA*, part 32, 51.
79   *"I thought it was very plain"*: Stark, *PHA*, part 5, 2447.
79   *"all out"*: Ibid.
79   *"so outstanding"*: Ibid.

FIVE IT DOESN'T MEAN US

81   *"This dispatch is to be considered"*: The full text of the navy "war warning" can be found in *PHA*, part 14, 1406.
82   *"sitting at a desk"*: Stark, *PHA*, part 5, 2143.
82   *"I have been concerned"*: King to Stark, January 21, 1941, Simpson papers, box 8, folder 10.
83   *"the front"*: *Time*, November 24, 1941.
83   *"wiry little man"*: Ibid.
83   *"I sort of feel finished"*: James Leutze, *A Different Kind of Victory* (Annapolis, MD: United States Naval Institute, 1981), 205.
83   *"I could think of no one"*: Stark to Hart, November 1, 1941, *PHA*, part 16, 2454.
83   *"Of the three"*: Hart, Columbia oral history, 90.
83   *"was the smartest"*: Richmond interview with Toland.
83   *"This . . . is . . . a . . . war . . . warning"*: Brownlow tapes, tape 34.
84   *"When asked about it"*: Hart, Columbia oral history, 92.
84   *"both weaker and slower"*: Testimony of Thomas C. Hart, *PHA*, part 10, 4814.
84   *"Did they dare"*: Hart, *PHA*, part 10, 4812.
84   *"My own estimate was"*: Ibid.
85   *"sleeps like a criminal"*: Brownlow tapes, tape 34.
85   *"Really,"* he said: Adolph A. Hoehling, *The Week Before Pearl Harbor* (New York: Norton, 1963), 206.
85   *"to talk back to him"*: East interview by Prange.
85   *"why he gave so much hell"*: Brownlow, *The Accused*, 78.
86   *"I'll put a phonograph"*: Ibid.
86   *"wolf" dispatches*: Testimony of William F. Halsey, *PHA*, part 26, 320.
86   *"indicated a very serious"*: Pye, *PHA*, part 27, 544.
86   *"exasperating and unsettling"*: Layton, *And I Was There*, 120.
86   *"glad to have"*: Kimmel, *PHA*, part 6, 2617.
88   *"a shock to me"*: Layton, *PHA*, part 10, 4866.
88   *"I not only never saw"*: Kimmel, *PHA*, part 6, 2630.

88   *"very doubtful"*: Stark to Kimmel, November 24, 1941, *PHA*, part 14, 1405.

88   *"a surprise aggressive movement"*: Ibid.

88   *"indicated to us"*: Husband Kimmel, *Admiral Kimmel's Story* (Chicago: Henry Regnery, 1955), 7.

89   *"tended to, and did"*: Kimmel, *PHA*, part 32, 267.

89   *"Now, war was getting closer"*: Kimmel, *PHA*, part 6, 2659.

89   *"Without exception, everyone believed"*: Testimony of Claude Bloch, *PHA*, part 32, 313.

89   *"There was some doubt"*: Bloch, *PHA*, part 27, 787.

90   *"It seemed to us"*: McMorris, *PHA*, part 26, 259.

90   *"slipped my mind"*: Stark, *PHA*, part 32, 87.

90   *"Probably," he said*: Stark, *PHA*, part 5, 2200.

91   *"We had assumed when we sent"*: Ibid., 2203.

92   *"then there must have been"*: Kimmel, *PHA*, part 6, 2632.

92   *"A commander-in-chief is considered"*: Ingersoll, *PHA*, part 9, 4244.

93   *"I had every confidence in him"*: Stark, *PHA*, part 32, 56.

94   *"nasty, suspicious"*: William Outerbridge to Grace Outerbridge, December 1, 1941, papers of William W. Outerbridge, Eisenhower Presidential Library, Abilene, KS, box 2, Letters to His Wife, March–April and November–December 1941.

94   *"a small person"*: Ibid., November 7, 1941.

94   *"It would tickle me"*: Ibid., November 27, 1941.

94   *"Hope someone in the [personnel]"*: Ibid., November 18, 1941.

94   *"I wish I could be there"*: Ibid., November 7, 1941.

94   *"As a matter of fact"*: Ibid., November 18, 1941.

95   *"If I am killed"*: Ibid., April 7, 1941.

95   *"I wonder what the Japs"*: Ibid., November 27, 1941.

SIX **MACHINE GUN SHORT**

97   *After shedding the ropes*: Details of the *Enterprise*'s departure that morning can be found in E. B. Potter's *Bull Halsey* (Annapolis, MD: Naval Institute Press, 1985).

98   *"He grins more readily"*: William F. Halsey and J. Bryan III, *Admiral Halsey's Story* (Washington, DC: Zenger, 1980), xi.

98   *"one of the six most startling"*: Ibid., x.

98   *"to get [to] the other fellow"*: Halsey, *PHA*, part 23, 613.

98   *"When we get to Tokyo"*: John W. Dower, *War Without Mercy* (New York: Pantheon Books, 1986), 79. This is a superb book on the racial and cultural aspects of the war in the Pacific.

99   *"without doubt the most"*: Husband Kimmel to Sibbella Kimmel, October 23, 1908, Kimmel papers, series II, box 2, folder 1.

99   *"the government did itself proud"*: Husband Kimmel to Sibbella Kimmel, November 3, 1908, Kimmel papers, series II, box 2, folder 1.

99   *"I felt that the Japs"*: Halsey and Bryan, *Admiral Halsey's Story*, 12.

99   *"Use your common sense"*: Ibid., 74.

99   *"On leaving port"*: Halsey, *PHA*, part 23, 608.

100 *"Goddammit, Admiral"*: Halsey and Bryan, *Admiral Halsey's Story*, 76.

100 *"I felt that we were going"*: Halsey, *PHA*, part 26, 323.

100 *"It is part of the tradition"*: E. B. Potter, *Bull Halsey*, 6.

100 *"Wake, you know"*: Kimmel, *PHA*, part 28, 928.

101 *"vital places"*: *Honolulu Star-Bulletin*, November 28, 1941.

101 *"one sees trains"*: John Willis, "Panorama of Activity," *Paradise of the Pacific*, October 1941, 28.

101 *"Ever and anon, echoes"*: Ibid.

101 *"hostile action possible"*: The complete text of the army "war warning" can be found in *PHA*, part 14, 1328.

102 *"a bird of passage"*: Kimmel, *PHA*, part 28, 934.

102 *"If such be the case"*: Kimmel to Stark, October 17, 1941, *PHA*, part 17, 2467.

102 *"astounded"*: Kimmel, *PHA*, part 22, 324.

102 *"old Army and Navy feuds"*: George C. Marshall to Walter Short, February 7, 1941, *PHA*, part 15, 1602.

102 *"entirely inadequate"*: Kimmel, *PHA*, part 32, 283.

103 *"As with the British"*: Layton interviews with Costello and Pineau, September 27 and 28, 1983.

103 *"In the operations between our planes"*: Smith, *PHA*, part 26, 53.

104 *"had no imagination"*: Gordon W. Prange, *The Verdict of History* (New York: McGraw-Hill, 1986), 337.

104 *"penetrating intellect"*: Charles Anderson, *Day of Lightning, Years of Scorn* (Annapolis, MD: Naval Institute Press, 2005), 60.

104 *"charisma to move"*: Ibid.

104 *"headline-generating"*: Ibid., 48.

104 *"personal qualities, [his] good scholarship"*: Ibid., 12.

104 *"inspecting and reporting upon"*: Ibid., 46.

104 *"somewhat austere" and "disciplined"*: Ibid., 60–61.

104 *"I guess he was about"*: Robert J. Fleming Jr. interview by Paul B. Ryan, March 31, 1975, Prange papers, series V, box 14, folder 15.

105 *"a very superior officer"*: Testimony of George C. Marshall, *PHA*, part 32, 553.

105 *"is the, rather than a"*: Marshall to Short, February 7, 1941, *PHA*, part 15, 1601.

105 *"very direct, even brusque"*: Ibid.

105 *"had, in the past"*: Ibid.

105 *"I told him then"*: Kimmel, *PHA*, part 28, 932.

105 *"approachable and cooperative"*: Short to Marshall, February 19, 1941, *PHA*, part 15, 1602.

105 *"extremely friendly"*: Testimony of Walter C. Short, *PHA*, part 32, 170.

106 *"'Really,' Short said, 'I felt'"*: Ibid., part 27, 218.

107 *"When you have a responsible"*: Kimmel, *PHA*, part 22, 406.

107 *"would hesitate lots of times"*: Short, *PHA*, part 22, 84.

107 *"would have resented"*: Short, *PHA*, part 27, 194.

107 *"felt that he could be"*: Short, *PHA*, part 7, 3039.

107 *"The raiding force"*: "Report on the Establishment of an AWS in Hawaii," August 31, 1944, *PHA*, part 31, 3158.

108 *"We were never able to get"*: Testimony of C. A. Powell, *PHA*, part 29, 1993.

108 *"However much I should have"*: Kimmel, *PHA*, part 22, 409.

108 *"wipe out virtually overnight"*: *Honolulu Advertiser*, August 9, 1941.
108 *"While there is splendid"*: Melvin Maas to Halsey, October 20, 1941, papers of William F. Halsey, box 15, Special Correspondence, Melvin Maas, 1938–53, Library of Congress, Washington, DC.
109 *"It wouldn't work"*: Testimony of Patrick N. L. Bellinger, *PHA*, part 26, 129.
109 *"all military and naval"*: Mass to Halsey, October 20, 1941, Halsey papers.
109 *"The only foreseeable"*: Ibid.
109 *"In my opinion"*: Ibid.
109 *"No change therein"*: Kimmel to Stark, November 13, 1941, Kimmel papers, series II, box 2, 15.
110 *"to all practical purposes"*: Army "war warning," *PHA*, part 14, 1328.
110 *"to meet any action"*: Testimony of Leonard T. Gerow, *PHA*, part 29, 2184.
110 *"If that statement was made"*: Testimony of James A. Mollison, *PHA*, part 27, 414.
111 *"in some way"*: Testimony of Frederick L. Martin, *PHA*, part 28, 972.
111 *"All you had to do"*: Short, *PHA*, part 22, 104.
111 *"Whoever wrote it"*: Short, *PHA*, part 27, 201.
111 *"I did not pin him down"*: Ibid., 202.
112 *"of that many people"*: Testimony of Kendall J. Fiedler, *PHA*, part 28, 1540.
112 *US senator Guy M. Gillette*: *Honolulu Star-Bulletin*, November 27, 1941.
112 *"indispensable"*: *New York Times*, March 2, 1941.
113 *"For whatever their citizenship"*: Ibid.
113 *"There are great areas"*: Martin, *PHA*, part 28, 990.
113 *"all members of that group"*: *Honolulu Star-Bulletin*, July 19, 1941.
113 *"and it was a comparatively"*: Fiedler, *PHA*, part 28, 1539.
114 *"No, there was none"*: Martin, *PHA*, part 28, 970.
114 *"My feelings on that"*: Testimony of George Bicknell, *PHA*, part 10, 5103.
114 *"no instance of sabotage"*: Robert Shivers to J. Edgar Hoover, December 15, 1941, NARA II, record group 65, Files of the Federal Bureau of Investigation, box 87, War Situations-Pearl Harbor Folder.
114 *"Japanese populace as a whole"*: Ibid.
114 Desired that you initiate: War Department to Short, November 28, 1941, *PHA*, part 14, 1330.
115 Report department alerted: Short to War Department, November 28, 1941, *PHA*, part 14, 1330.
115 *"I had an immense number"*: Marshall, *PHA*, part 3, 1421.
116 *"I told them as plainly"*: Short, *PHA*, part 32, 188.
116 *"If they didn't know"*: Short, *PHA*, part 27, 163.
117 *"defense of these islands"*: Short to Marshall, March 3, 1941, *PHA*, part 15, 1606.
117 *"With the present international"*: Ibid.
117 *"to get the battle"*: Short, *PHA*, part 22, 102.

SEVEN AMBASSADOR JOE AND PRESIDENT FRANK

119 *"as high as $25"*: *New York Times*, November 29, 1941.
120 *"who knows that he is going to be defeated"*: Testimony of Joseph C. Grew, *PHA*, part 2, 566.

120 *"I haven't packed a thing"*: Joseph C. Grew, diary entry for November 29, 1941, papers of Joseph C. Grew, Houghton Library, Harvard University, Cambridge, MA.

120 *"I feel somewhat 'Wild West'"*: Ibid., October 19, 1941.

121 *"one of my principal duties"*: Robert A. Fearey, "My Year With Ambassador Joseph C. Grew," 4. The self-published memoir is available on the website of the Library of Congress at www.loc.gov/item/mfdipbib000360.

121 *"His putting style"*: Ibid., 5.

121 *"Dear Frank"*: Grew to Roosevelt, December 14, 1940, *PHA*, part 2, 630.

121 *"I find that diplomacy"*: Ibid., 631.

121 *"What a sad change"*: Grew to Mrs. S. V. R. Crosby, April 18, 1941, Grew papers, Grew letters 1941.

122 *"crafty, haughty, blood-sucker"*: *New York Times*, August 19, 1941.

122 *"the soul of a prostitute"*: *New York Times*, November 6, 1941.

122 *"not the Japan that"*: Grew to Roosevelt, December 14, 1940, *PHA*, part 2, 632.

122 *"more cocky and self-assured"*: Tolischus, *Tokyo Record*, 9.

122 *"an instinctive reaction"*: Ibid.

122 *"were full of war talk"*: Ibid., 7.

122 *"If I can help only a mite"*: Grew to Anita Grew English, July 28, 1941, Grew papers, Grew Letters 1941.

123 *On the evening of September 6*: Grew described the circumstances of his meeting with Konoye during testimony to Congress, *PHA*, part 2, beginning at p. 663.

123 *"At that time in Japan"*: Ibid., 716.

123 *"Few are completely satisfied"*: *New York Times*, August 3, 1941.

124 *"He knew a good deal more"*: Grew, *PHA*, part 2, 640.

124 *Forty commodities were being rationed*: The details of the economic impact of the sanctions are taken from the *New York Times*, September 22, 1941, and from a lecture by A. E. Hindmarsch, August 15, 1941. The lecture can be found in the Naval War College Archives, record group 15, box 9, folder 2, "Japanese Foreign Policy," 1941.

125 *"act of the highest statesmanship"*: Grew to Hull, August 19, 1941, United States Department of State, *Foreign Relations of the United States* (Washington, DC: United States Government Printing Office, 1966), Diplomatic Papers 1941, vol. IV, 382.

125 *"but his own life"*: Ibid.

125 *"one of the worst international desperadoes"*: Hull, *PHA*, part 2, 552.

125 *"on the rampage"*: Ibid.

125 *"We asked ourselves"*: Ibid., 425.

126 *"Konoye repeatedly stressed"*: Grew to Hull, September 6, 1941, *Peace and War*, 733.

126 *"electrify the Japanese people"*: Grew, *PHA*, part 2, 717.

126 *"Grew had been in Japan"*: Fearey, "My Year With Ambassador Joseph C. Grew," 9.

126 *"entirely unconfirmed reports"*: *New York Times*, September 3, 1941.

127 *"The only plan the President"*: *New York Times*, September 4, 1941.

127 *"It would be a very simple thing"*: Grew diary, October 19, 1941.

127 *"I don't like heroics"*: Ibid.

127 *"Appeasement. Is that what"*: Ibid., October 13, 1941.

128 *"The Administration is reported certain"*: *Chicago Tribune*, November 29, 1941.

128 *"grinning, bowing, breath-sipping little man"*: *Time*, December 22, 1941.

128 *"The Japanese mind works by intuition"*: New York Times, September 7, 1941.

128 *"devoid of what Westerners call logic"*: Dower, *War Without Mercy*, 96.

128 *"We just don't think the way they do"*: Fiedler, *PHA*, part 28, 1535.

129 *"I believe that it was the consensus"*: Testimony of Alwin D. Kramer, *PHA*, part 9, 3959.

129 *"conceive of Japan being crazy enough"*: New York Times, October 17, 1941.

129 *"The Japanese are not going to risk"*: *Congressional Record*, February 19, 1941, 1198.

129 *"The reason is Japan"*: Honolulu Star-Bulletin, December 2, 1941.

129 *"The answer to the question is simple"*: Lecture by Commander J. L. Hall, "Naval Operations of the Russo-Japanese War," Naval War College Archives, record group 14, box 9.

130 *"an uncertain and dangerous hypothesis"*: Grew to Hull, November 3, 1941, *Peace and War*, 773.

130 *"an all-out, do-or-die"*: Ibid.

130 *"I am not in touch"*: Ibid., 774.

130 *"my purpose is only to ensure"*: Ibid.

130 *"Japanese sanity cannot"*: Ibid.

130 *"the need to guard against"*: Grew to Hull, November 17, 1941, *Peace and War*, 787.

131 *"Therefore, you are advised"*: Ibid., 788.

131 *"We must purge"*: New York Times, November 30, 1941.

131 *"utterly stupid"*: Grew diary, November 29, 1941.

131 *"Once again I am impressed"*: Ibid.

132 *"He looked very tired"*: Washington to Tokyo, November 27, 1941, *PHA*, part 12, 194.

132 *"was very anxious"*: Grace Tully, *FDR, My Boss* (New York: C. Scribner's Sons, 1949), 249.

132 *"The President arrived here"*: New York Times, November 30, 1941.

132 *"closer than at any"*: New York Times, November 29, 1941.

133 *"a source of unquestioned"*: Washington Post, November 29, 1941.

133 *"I think I could tell you for background"*: Roosevelt press conference, November 28, 1941. Transcripts of all of Roosevelt's press conferences can be found here: www.fdrlibrary.marist.edu/archives/collections/franklin/?p=collections/finding aid&id=508.

133 *"I think a study of the map"*: Ibid.

133 *"I don't think any more can be said"*: Ibid.

134 *"inferior"*: Marshall-Stark memo to Roosevelt, November 5, 1941, *PHA*, part 14, 1061.

134 *"The most essential thing"*: Marshall-Stark memo to Roosevelt, November 17, 1941, *PHA*, part 14, 1083.

134 *"As you know," he had written*: Harold Ickes, *The Secret Diary of Harold L. Ickes* (New York: Simon & Schuster, 1953), 567.

134 *"Dear Joe"*: Roosevelt to Grew, January 21, 1941, *PHA*, part 2, 632.

135 *"It was the consensus"*: Stimson diary, November 28, 1941.

135 *"the press is prepared"*: The diaries of Henry Morgenthau, Roosevelt Presidential

Library, vol. 466, November 27–30, reel 130, entry for November 28. The quotation is from a memo by Alan Barth.

135 *"every sign that there will"*: Ibid.

135 *"take steps now to keep Japan"*: Roosevelt papers, President's Secretary's Files, box 157, Subject File, Public Opinion Polls, 1935–41. This report is dated December 5, 1941.

135 *"in case we struck Japan down there"*: Stimson diary, November 7, 1941.

136 *"the people are unanimous"*: Washington to Tokyo, August 16, 1941, *PHA*, part 12, 17.

136 *"This is really a discovery of a place"*: Elliott Roosevelt, ed., *F.D.R.: His Personal Letters* (New York: Duell, Sloan and Pearce, 1950), 566.

136 *"completely blotted out"*: Roosevelt's Thanksgiving remarks can be found at http://georgiainfo.galileo.usg.edu/topics/history/related_article/fdrs-visits-to -georgia/background-to-fdrs-ties-to-georgia/fdr-postponed-thanksgiving-dinner -remarks-nov.-29-1941.

137 *"Mr. Hull was deeply worried"*: Tully, *FDR, My Boss*, 250.

137 *"that the showdown had come"*: *New York Times*, December 1, 1941.

137 *"This may be the last time"*: Tully, *FDR, My Boss*, 251.

138 *"The Pacific is so wide!"*: Ugaki, *Fading Victory*, 29.

EIGHT THEIR MAIL, OPENED AND READ

139 *"It was a crime"*: Roosevelt press conference, August 19, 1941.

140 *"Well, you two ambassadors"*: Tokyo to Washington, November 28, 1941, *PHA*, part 12, 195.

141 *"long-suffering and conciliatory"*: Ibid.

141 *"would greatly injure"*: Tokyo to Washington, November 29, 1941, *PHA*, part 12, 199.

141 *"now you want them to stretch out"*: Transcript of Kurusu telephone call with Foreign Office, November 30, 1941, *PHA*, part 12, 207.

141 *"I looked on them as I would a witness"*: Hull, *PHA*, part 2, 447.

141 *"a priceless assett"*: Testimony of Sherman Miles, *PHA*, part 3, 1362.

142 *When the sender typed a second* m: David Kahn's chapter on Magic in *The Codebreakers* (New York: Scribner, 1967, 1996) was invaluable in explaining how a Purple machine operated, and also provided additional details about the American cryptologic effort against the Japanese.

142 *"take measures to secure"*: Tokyo to Washington, July 31, 1941, *PHA*, part 12, 9.

143 *"now reached a point"*: Ibid., October 21, 1941, 81.

143 *"Nay, when it comes"*: Ibid., November 4, 1941, 93.

143 *"the order and method of destroying"*: Tokyo to Washington, November 15, 1941, *PHA*, part 12, 137.

143 *"had to sign a paper never to"*: Stark, *PHA*, part 5, 2468.

143 *"collected all of these pouches"*: Testimony of Rufus S. Bratton, *PHA*, part 29, 2451.

144 *"with a folder"*: Smedberg, USNI oral history, 100.

144 *"the extreme importance"*: Testimony of Leigh Noyes, *PHA*, part 10, 4717.

144   *"reading Ambassador Nomura's"*: Berlin to Tokyo, May 3, 1941, *PHA*, part 4, 1861.

144   *"the most stringent"*: Washington to Tokyo, May 5, 1941, *PHA*, part 4, 1862.

145   *"Especially in view of"*: Memo from Alwin D. Kramer, May 17, 1941, papers of William F. Friedman, National Security Agency, Pearl Harbor Research Records, folder 203. The Friedman papers are available online at www.nsa.gov /public_info/declass/friedman_documents/index.shtml.

145   *The secret held*: Kahn, *The Codebreakers*, 30.

145   *"dealt with administrative"*: Bratton, *PHA*, part 29, 2450.

145   *"It was entirely too voluminous"*: Marshall, *PHA*, part 33, 824.

145   *"and read every day"*: Ibid.

146   *"only a single frame"*: William F. Friedman, "Certain Aspects of Magic in the Cryptological Background of the Various Official Investigations into the Attack on Pearl Harbor," SRH-125, 63. This illuminating article can be found at nsa .gov/public_info/_files/friedmanDocuments/PearlHarborResearchRecords /FOLDER_204/41762819080196.pdf.

146   *"I said, 'It's not magic'"*: Transcript of the oral history of Arthur H. McCollum, USNI, 1970–71, 282.

146   *"did not necessarily reflect the opinion"*: Ibid., 284.

147   *"what in the world"*: Testimony of Roscoe Schuirmann, *PHA*, part 33, 758.

147   *"Undoubtedly, it [was] intended"*: Kramer, *PHA*, part 36, 342.

147   *"In case of a [sic] Japan–U.S."*: Tokyo to Washington, November 19, 1941, *PHA*, part 12, 154.

148   *"created a sense of infallibility"*: Layton, *And I Was There*, 81.

148   *"pure blind"*: Stimson diary, August 9, 1941.

148   *"They have already"*: Ibid.

149   *roughly nineteen messages*: I am indebted to Robert Hanyok, retired historian of the National Security Agency, for the calculation of the number of daily Japanese naval messages.

150   *"brainwashed"*: Transcript of the oral history of Joseph J. Rochefort, USNI, August-December 1969, 53.

150   *"habit of caustic speech"*: W. J. Holmes, *Double-Edged Secrets* (Annapolis, MD: Naval Institute Press, 1979), 3.

150   *"was worn thin"*: Transcript of the oral history of Edwin T. Layton, National Security Agency, February 7–8, 1983, 9.

151   *"It makes you feel"*: Rochefort, USNI oral history, 16.

151   *"Being a little bit nuts"*: Ibid., 13.

151   *"I like to consider"*: Ibid., 14.

151   *"He was inspired"*: Transcript of the oral history of Thomas H. Dyer, USNI, August-September 1983, 86.

151   *"was intuitive, quick, sharp-thinking"*: Forrest R. Biard, "Breaking Japanese Naval Codes: Pre-Pearl Harbor to Midway," *Cryptologia* 30, no. 2 (2006): 153.

151   *"He can translate"*: Elliot Carlson, *Joe Rochefort's War* (Annapolis, MD: Naval Institute Press, 2011), 57.

151   *"to pick up the mores"*: Rochefort, USNI oral history, 65.

152   *"perhaps fairly well fitted"*: Ibid., 144.

153 *"there were very long"*: Ingersoll, *PHA*, part 9, 4241.

153 *"it certainly is an inexact"*: Layton, *PHA*, part 10, 4836.

153 *"With all modesty"*: Rochefort, USNI oral history, 105.

153 *"a very, very good estimate"*: Testimony of Joseph J. Rochefort, *PHA*, part 28, 866.

153 *"there was something afoot"*: Rochefort, *PHA*, part 23, 679.

154 *"secret communication methods"*: Fourteenth Naval District Communication Intelligence Summary, September 10, 1941, summaries for 16 July to 31 December 1941 5510/4, intelligence records of inactive naval stations, box 3, records of the Naval Security Group Central Depository, Crane, IN, record group 38, NARA II.

154 *"preparations are increasing"*: Ibid., September 28, 1941.

154 *"is unprecedented"*: Fourteenth Naval District Communications Intelligence Summary, November 3, 1941, *PHA*, part 17, 2603.

154 *"The literal reading of this"*: Ibid.

154 *"a strong force"*: Fourteenth Naval District to Navy Department, November 26, 1941, *PHA*, part 15, 1887.

155 *"rather extraordinary"*: Layton, *PHA*, part 10, 4893.

NINE THE TALENTS OF NIPPON

157 *"highly dramatic"*: Washington to Tokyo, December 1, 1941, *PHA*, part 12, 210.

157 *"EXPECT JAP ANSWER"*: *Chicago Tribune*, December 1, 1941.

157 *"deeply pained expression"*: Washington to Tokyo, December 1, 1941, *PHA*, part 12, 210.

158 *"be in a position"*: Ibid., 215.

158 *"a ten-minute broadcast"*: *Peace and War*, 817.

158 *"expand to obtain"*: Ibid., 819.

158 *"bluster and blood-curdling"*: Ibid.

158 *"One of these days"*: Ibid., 817.

158 *"seemingly happier"*: *New York Times*, December 2, 1941.

158 *"departed grimly"*: Ibid.

158 *"We feel, however"*: Washington to Tokyo, December 1, 1941, *PHA*, part 12, 214.

159 *"The four offices"*: Tokyo to Washington, December 1, 1941, *PHA*, part 12, 209.

159 *"the keenness, as well as"*: Hoehling, *The Week Before Pearl Harbor*, 65.

159 *"He has the manners"*: *The Lucky Bag*, 1921, 344.

160 *"All Orange service"*: Arthur H. McCollum intelligence report, December 1, 1941, Far Eastern Section, Japanese Empire Desk (OP23F14), serials 1941–47, record group 38, NARA II.

160 *"has marshaled its full naval"*: Ibid.

161 *"It was as plain as the nose"*: McCollum, USNI oral history, 301.

161 *"my recollection is we had none"*: Stark, *PHA*, part 5, 2252.

161 *"very great difficulty"*: Testimony of H. H. Smith-Hutton, *PHA*, part 32, 642.

161 *"on the railway trip from Tokyo"*: Grew, *PHA*, part 2, 578.

162 *"The Japanese were past"*: Ibid.

162 *"the Japanese, as a race"*: Dower, *War Without Mercy*, 103.

163 *"they're carried on the backs"*: McCollum, USNI oral history, 272.

163 *"I based that opinion"*: Testimony of Wilson Brown, *PHA*, part 26, 149.

163 *"in technical achievements"*: Donald W. Mitchell, "How to Beat Japan," *The Nation*, August 30, 1941, 178.

163 *"only fair"*: *Chicago Tribune*, November 29, 1941.

164 *"good"*: Bellinger, *PHA*, part 22, 587.

164 *"The Japanese are, by nature"*: *The Aeroplane*, March 7, 1941, as reprinted in the June 1941 issue of *Proceedings*.

164 *"The Japanese have known"*: Joseph C. Grew, "Report from Tokyo: A Message to the American People," 1942, Kimmel papers, box 1, folder 16.

165 *"There were a great many"*: McCollum, USNI oral history, 403.

165 *"For a long time, I have"*: Charles Healey Day, guest column, *Chicago Tribune*, December 26, 1941.

165 *"In all the modern achievements"*: *New York Times*, September 7, 1941.

165 *"would only half believe"*: McCollum, USNI oral history, 273.

165 *"just would not take seriously"*: Howard Young, "Racial Attitudes and the U.S. Navy's Unpreparedness for War With Japan," in *New Aspects of Naval History* (Baltimore: The Nautical and Aviation Publishing Company of America, 1985), 179.

165 *"the constant daily drumfire"*: McCollum, USNI oral history, 273.

166 *"We pushed this out"*: Ibid., 156.

166 *"Usually and unfortunately"*: Ibid., 153.

166 *"The Japanese were probably"*: Ibid., 155.

167 *"the kiss of death"*: Gordon Prange, *The Verdict of History*, 288.

167 *"There was no training"*: Layton interview with Costello and Pineau, December 5, 1983.

168 *"attendance at two"*: Testimony of Theodore S. Wilkinson, *PHA*, part 4, 1725.

168 *"He is by reputation"*: Testimony of Arthur H. McCollum, *PHA*, part 8, 3411.

168 *"He read this document"*: Ibid., 3384.

168 *"Many Japanese residents"*: "Memorandum for the Director," December 1, 1941, *PHA*, part 36, 660. All subsequent quotations in this and the next paragraph come from this memo.

169 *"Japan had taken every possible step"*: Arthur H. McCollum to Husband Kimmel, May 21, 1944, Toland papers, box 121, McCollum folder.

170 *"whether or not the fleets"*: McCollum, *PHA*, part 8, 3385.

170 *"categorical assurance"*: Ibid.

170 *"was not Navy custom"*: Stark, *PHA*, part 5, 2445.

171 *"the weakest of all"*: Stimson diary, December 1, 1941.

171 *"You may tell the boys"*: William Outerbridge to Grace Outerbridge, November 29, 1941, Outerbridge papers.

171 *"Being on one of"*: Ibid., December 5, 1941.

172 *"near the commissary"*: Ibid., November 30, 1941.

172 *"The mess of moving"*: Ibid., November 29, 1941.

172 *"If Japan just stays quiet"*: Ibid., November 30, 1941.

TEN **THE SHIPS THAT WERE NOT THERE**

174 *"His two great failings"*: *The Lucky Bag*, 1924, 190.

174 *"Merely glance at the above"*: Ibid.

174   *"one-channel man"*: Layton, *And I Was There,* 495. Although this is Layton's autobiography, the quotation about his character appears in a note by his coauthors, who attribute the statement to Admiral Arleigh Burke.

174   *"I found the Japanese"*: Layton, USNI oral history, 8.

175   *"an easy-to-meet"*: Layton, NSA oral history, 8.

175   *"the kind who would give"*: Layton, *And I Was There,* 39.

176   *"Me no here"*: Ibid., 50.

176   *"I went around"*: Ibid.

176   *"to celebrate the successful"*: Ibid.

177   *"So I had to go over"*: Layton, NSA oral history, 84.

177   *"And this infuriated me"*: Joseph J. Rochefort interview by Gordon Prange, August 26, 1964, Prange papers, series V, box 70, folder 23.

177   *"You undoubtedly have known"*: Transcript of the oral interview of Thomas H. Dyer, National Security Agency, January 29, 1982, 56.

177   *"The fact that service"*: Fourteenth Naval District Communication Intelligence Summary for December 1, 1941, *PHA,* part 17, 2636.

177   *"It appears that the Japanese"*: Ibid.

178   *"they were doing everything"*: Layton, *PHA,* part 36, 129.

178   *"crucial meeting today"*: *Honolulu Advertiser,* December 1, 1941.

178   *"In the newspapers"*: Kimmel, *PHA,* part 6, 2806.

178   *"a great deal of confusion"*: Smith, *PHA,* part 26, 68.

178   *"He might have asked me"*: Stark, *PHA,* part 32, 116.

179   *"Steps To Be Taken"*: Kimmel's "Steps to Be Taken" memos, one of November 30 and one of December 5, can be found in *PHA,* part 17, 2714.

179   *The result—five typewritten pages*: Layton's full memo of December 1, 1941, can be found in *PHA,* part 17, 2667.

180   *"aviation enthusiasts who claim"*: Admiral J. K. Taussig, "The Case for the Big Capital Ship," *Proceedings,* July 1940.

180   *"The gun for many years"*: Ibid.

181   *"A fleet which lacks aviation"*: "The Employment of Aviation in Naval Warfare," 1937, Naval War College Archives, record group 15, box 7, folder 25. This was a standard lecture apparently given by several instructors.

181   *"so fast one could barely"*: *New York Times,* February 14, 1929.

182   *"Obstacles are offered"*: Kimmel to Stark, February 18, 1941, *PHA,* part 16, 2229.

182   *"woefully deficient"*: Kimmel to Stark, May 26, 1941, *PHA,* part 16, 2236.

182   *"submarines, destroyers"*: Kimmel to Stark, August 12, 1941, *PHA,* part 16, 2243.

182   *"This is a vast ocean"*: Ibid.

183   *"The type of operations"*: Kimmel to Stark, October 22, 1941, *PHA,* part 16, 2250.

183   *"I said that I had"*: Layton, *PHA,* part 36, 127.

183   *"Then Admiral Kimmel looked"*: Layton, *PHA,* part 36, 128.

183   *"Do you mean to say"*: Ibid.

184   *"It is believed easily possible"*: Frank Knox to Henry Stimson, January 24, 1941, *PHA,* part 14, 1000.

184   *"a striking force of carriers"*: Ibid., 1001.

184   *"Out in Hawaii"*: Notes of army's General Council Meeting, February 19, 1941, *PHA,* part 15, 1627.

184   *"out of the blue"*: Miles, *PHA*, part 35, 102.

184   *"in view of the character"*: Ibid., part 2, 819.

184   *"their action against"*: Halsey, *PHA*, part 23, 620.

184   *"The Japanese were known"*: Kimmel, *PHA*, part 6, 2704.

184   *"confidential letter"*: The complete text of Pacific Fleet Confidential Letter No. 2CL-41 (Revised) can be found in *PHA*, part 26, 475.

185   *"are strained, uncertain"*: The document that came to be known as the Martin-Bellinger Report can be found in *PHA*, part 22, starting on p. 349.

185   *"It appears that the most likely"*: Ibid., 350.

185   *"it appears possible"*: Ibid., 349.

186   *"The Japanese fleet is not built"*: Hanson W. Baldwin, "The Naval Defense of America," *Harper's*, April 1941, 458.

186   *"For us to make an attack"*: McMorris, *PHA*, part 26, 249.

187   *"We felt that the Japanese"*: Ibid.

187   *"in which case"*: Smith, *PHA*, part 36, 220.

187   *"Japan could not afford to gamble"*: Layton, *PHA*, part 26, 235.

187   *"arrived at the conclusion"*: Kimmel, *PHA*, part 6, 2753.

188   *"unconcerned with this entire matter"*: Layton, *PHA*, part 10, 4903.

188   *"They are on low-frequency"*: Layton, *PHA*, part 23, 659.

188   *"Units would disappear"*: Kimmel, *PHA*, part 28, 928.

189   *"I underscored the word"*: Layton, *PHA*, part 36, 150.

189   *"its faults and its promises"*: Ibid., 129.

189   *"I wish I had"*: Layton, *PHA* part 10, 4840.

189   *"Never," Layton said*: Layton, NSA oral history, 133.

189   *"I believe that everyone"*: Layton, *PHA*, part 10, 4839.

190   *"In my experience"*: Stanley Washburn to Frank Knox, November 29, 1941, Hanify papers, box 17, folder 15.

ELEVEN **THE SMOKE OF SECRETS**

191   *"Stop at once"*: Tokyo to Washington, December 2, 1941, *PHA*, part 12, 215.

192   *"one of the most telling"*: Stark, *PHA*, part 32, 61.

192   *especially when coupled*: Tokyo to Washington, December 1, 1941, *PHA*, part 12, 209.

192   *"pointed right toward war"*: Stark, *PHA*, part 5, 2263.

192   *"a beacon light"*: Stark, *PHA*, part 32, 132.

192   *"The diplomats go home"*: Ingersoll, *PHA*, part 9, 4226.

193   *"and that did not mean"*: Ibid.

193   *"a definite and sure"*: Testimony of Richmond Kelly Turner, *PHA*, part 4, 2002.

193   *"time was running out"*: Bratton, *PHA*, part 9, 4577.

193   *"very much" affected*: Testimony of John R. Beardall, *PHA*, part 11, 5284.

193   *"Well, when do you"*: Ibid.

193   *"Highly reliable information"*: Navy Department to Pacific commands, December 3, 1941, *PHA*, part 14, 1407.

194   *"Circular twenty four"*: Ibid., 1408.

195   *It was the* Lurline: Details of the Hawaiian visit of the two football teams are

taken from an article in the *Santa Rosa (CA) Press-Democrat*, December 6, 2011.

195 *"like great white parachutes"*: Willard Brown, *Paradise of the Pacific*, November 1941, 18.

195 *San Jose State's*: Press Democrat, December 6, 2011.

195 *"Christmas has a"*: Honolulu Star-Bulletin, November 26, 1941.

196 *"Here's the Good News"*: Honolulu Star-Bulletin, December 5, 1941.

196 *"Neither would be surprised"*: Stark to Kimmel, November 25, 1941, *PHA*, part 16, 2224.

197 *"short, dark-haired, rather retiring"*: Hoehling, *The Week Before Pearl Harbor*, 85.

197 *"smart and genteel"*: FBI news release marking the sixty-eighth anniversary of the attack, available at www.fbi.gov/news/stories/2009/december/shivers_120709.

197 *"They could only give you"*: Testimony of Robert L. Shivers, *PHA*, part 23, 857.

197 *"be on the alert"*: Affidavit of Robert L. Shivers, April 10, 1945, *PHA*, part 35, 43.

197 *"for the purpose of"*: Federal Bureau of Investigation report, February 11, 1942, NARA II, record group 65, box 89, War Situations-Pearl Harbor Folder, 100-97-1-Sec. 2, 1/3.

198 *"they refused to cooperate"*: Ibid.

198 *"Deeming that war"*: Ibid.

198 *"a Japanese person"*: Shivers affidavit, *PHA*, part 35, 43.

199 *"The United States has more contacts"*: Commander H. E. Kimmel, thesis (Naval War College Archives, record group 13, Student Theses, December 23, 1925).

199 *"I had never lived"*: Kimmel, *PHA*, part 6, 2564.

199 *"no particular attention"*: Hart, Columbia oral history, 127.

200 *"Japanese 'mad dog'"*: Kimmel, *PHA*, part 6, 2637.

200 *"the British or the Americans"*: Ibid., 2596.

200 *"The Department sent me"*: Kimmel, *PHA*, part 22, 379.

201 *"information of a secret"*: Kimmel to Stark, February 18, 1941, *PHA*, part 16, 2229.

201 *"I wish they would"*: Layton, *PHA*, part 32, 583.

201 *"The Commander-in-Chief Pacific Fleet"*: Kimmel to Stark, May 26, 1941, *PHA*, part 16, 2238.

201 *"a cardinal principle"*: Ibid.

202 *"adequately informed concerning"*: Stark to Kimmel, March 22, 1941, *PHA*, part 16, 2160.

202 *"I had asked for all"*: Kimmel, *PHA*, part 6, 2540.

203 *"Well, he [the civilian]"*: McCollum, USNI oral history, 213.

203 *"Oh, it is my recollection"*: Kimmel, *PHA*, part 6, 2568.

203 *"The waters are"*: Tokyo to Honolulu, September 24, 1941, *PHA*, part 12, 261.

203 *"As relations between Japan"*: Tokyo to Honolulu, November 15, 1941, *PHA*, part 12, 262.

203 *"We have been receiving"*: Tokyo to Honolulu, November 29, 1941, *PHA*, part 12, 263.

204 *"The Japanese for many years"*: Wilkinson, *PHA*, part 4, 1747.

204 *"the capital ships and others"*: Honolulu to Tokyo, February 21, 1941, *PHA*, part 12, 258.

204 *"two English converted"*: Honolulu to Tokyo, June 14, 1941, *PHA*, part 12, 261.

204 *"two United States freighters"*: Panama to Tokyo, August 20, 1941, *PHA*, part 12, 271.

204 *"ten vessels of any type"*: Tokyo to Seattle, October 16, 1941, *PHA*, part 12, 309.

204 *"The Japanese were repeatedly"*: Kramer, *PHA*, part 9, 4177.

205 *"did not make much"*: McCollum, *PHA*, part 8, 3391.

205 *"I felt that the Japanese were showing"*: Bratton, *PHA*, part 9, 4534.

205 *"the Fleet is not going to be there"*: Ibid.

206 *"You tell a man"*: Layton, NSA oral history, 94.

206 *"most industrious"*: Kimmel, *PHA*, part 6, 2576.

206 *"They'll be able"*: Ugaki, *Fading Victory*, 33.

206 *"Under any circumstances"*: Ibid.

206 *"the other day we got"*: Roosevelt press conference, December 2, 1941.

207 *"Don't you know that a big dagger"*: Ugaki, *Fading Victory*, 35.

TWELVE A TIME TO LOOK

209 *"I still felt uneasy"*: Bratton, *PHA*, part 29, 2444.

209 *"I said to him, 'Are you sure'"*: Bratton, *PHA*, part 9, 4580.

210 *"Possibly, it was none"*: McCollum, *PHA*, part 8, 3388.

210 *"would make a very"*: Ibid., 3436.

210 *"Richmond Kelly Turner was"*: Rochefort interview by Prange.

210 *"goddamn foolishness"*: Rochefort, USNI oral history, 306.

211 *"the Navy's Patton"*: Layton, *And I Was There*, 96.

211 *"intellectually brilliant"*: George C. Dyer, *The Amphibians Came to Conquer: The Story of Richmond Kelly Turner* (Washington, DC: US Department of the Navy, 1972), 77.

211 *"There was only one way to do"*: Ibid.

211 *"He was sure he knew"*: Vincenzo Lopresti, "Notes on Admiral Turner," papers of Richmond Kelly Turner, Naval History and Heritage Command, Washington, box 34, series XVI.

211 *"stamp his right"*: Ibid.

211 *"heavy, black, Mephistophelian"*: Hoehling, *The Week Before Pearl Harbor*, 54.

211 *"considerable study of the Japanese"*: Turner, *PHA*, part 26, 272.

211 *"He felt he knew"*: Transcript of the oral history of Alan G. Kirk, Columbia Oral History Project, Columbia University, 1962, 180.

212 *"We had in our Division"*: Turner, *PHA*, part 4, 1914.

212 *"When the dispatch"*: McCollum, *PHA*, part 8, 3390.

212 *"The Japanese were definitely"*: Ibid., 3436.

213 *"Japan would strike"*: McCollum, *PHA*, part 8, 3438.

213 *"Did not [McCollum] think"*: Ibid., 3388.

213 *"It does not come"*: Ibid., 3412.

213 *"Well, good gosh"*: Ibid., 3388.

213 *"I would like to see"*: Ibid.

213 *"and we will argue"*: Ibid.

214 *"Almost a complete"*: Fourteenth Naval District Communications Intelligence Summary for December 2, 1941, *PHA*, part 17, 2638.

214   *"It is evident"*: Ibid.
215   *"The carriers just completely"*: Rochefort, *PHA*, part 23, 679.
215   *"beat it south"*: NARA II, record group 80, Pearl Harbor Liaison Group, box 31, Narrative Statement of Evidence at Navy Pearl Harbor Investigations, 1945, 560.
215   *"destroy all secret"*: Navy Department to Naval Station Guam, December 4, 1941, *PHA*, part 14, 1408.
215   *"I was torn"*: Kimmel, *PHA*, part 32, 659.
216   *"A fleet in being"*: Kimmel to Stark, December 2, 1941, Kimmel papers, box 35, folder 2.
216   *"direct offensive measures"*: Kimmel to Stark, September 12, 1941, *PHA*, part 16, 2248.
216   *"I considered my primary"*: Kimmel, *PHA*, part 6, 2838.
217   *"You have to but recall"*: *Chicago Tribune*, June 24, 1941.
217   *"was the thing"*: Kimmel, *PHA*, part 6, 2722.
218   *"Tackle the ball carrier"*: Logan C. Ramsey, "Aerial Attacks on Fleets at Anchor," *Proceedings*, August 1937.
218   *"A crew could conduct"*: Bellinger, *PHA*, part 26, 124.
219   *"trying to cut their cloth"*: William Furlong interview by Gordon Prange, November 11, 1962, Prange papers, series V, box 18, folder 11.
219   *"time and time"*: Bloch, *PHA*, part 27, 773.
220   *"very insistent"*: Marshall, *PHA*, part 3, 1390.
220   *"well down on the Navy Department's"*: Richardson, *On the Treadmill to Pearl Harbor*, 354.
220   *Since September 1940*: Archivists at the San Diego Air and Space Museum provided the statistics on the production and distribution of the PBY-5.
220   *"if he can take my garden"*: Doris Kearns Goodwin, *No Ordinary Time* (New York: Simon & Schuster, 1994), 194.
220   *"There exists and will continue"*: Stark to all commands, June 14, 1941, box 6, folder A16, War Operations 16 June 1941 to 10 September 1941, Secret and Top Secret General Administrative Files, 1941–44, group 313, NARA II.
220   *"The Department has no"*: Stark to Claude C. Bloch, November 25, 1941, *PHA*, part 17, 2472.
220   *"He is entirely in the hands"*: Stimson diary, October 15, 1941.
221   *"We are shipping out"*: *Congressional Record*, December 5, 1941, 3480.
221   *"As you well know"*: Nimitz to Kimmel, March 3, 1941, *PHA*, part 16, 2154.
221   *"Very little discussion"*: Kimmel, *PHA*, part 6, 2730.
221   *"I had to decide what was"*: Ibid., 2535.
222   *"highly improbable"*: Kimmel, *PHA*, part 22, 384.
222   *"intelligence indicates that a surface raid"*: Martin-Bellinger Report, *PHA*, part 22, 351.
222   *"This, in effect, accepted"*: McMorris, *PHA*, part 36, 182.
222   *"Utilization of patrol planes"*: Kimmel, *PHA*, part 22, 328.
222   *"The air raid"*: Ibid., 388.
223   *"Why, it is very easy"*: Turner, *PHA*, part 32, 619.
223   *"the vacant sea, in which"*: Miles, *PHA*, part 27, 58.
224   *"were all alarming"*: Bellinger, *PHA*, part 26, 127.

224   *"God only knows"*: Bellinger, *PHA*, part 8, 3486.
224   *"For about two weeks"*: Ibid., 3465.
225   *"You must remember"*: Commencement address of Admiral Chester W. Nimitz, December 2, 1941, Naval War College Archives, record group 16, Addresses, 1885–1983.

THIRTEEN OUT OF THEIR DEPTH

227   *"now present American involvement"*: Morgenthau diary, vol. 469, reel 130, December 5–6, 1941.
227   *"looks pretty serious"*: *New York Times*, December 5, 1941.
227   *"No cabinet meetings"*: *New York Times*, December 6, 1941.
227   *"They don't mean business"*: Frances Perkins, "The President Faces War," in Stillwell, *Air Raid: Pearl Harbor!*, 113.
228   *"With every hour that passes"*: Ibid.
228   *"He was very disgusted"*: Ibid., 114.
228   *"Nobody asked where it was"*: Ibid., 115.
228   *"As a mother wrote me"*: *Congressional Record*, December 5, 1941, 9460.
228   *"be surprised if Japan"*: Ibid., 9438.
229   *"now really on the verge"*: *Washington Post*, December 4, 1941.
229   *"direct and immediate threat"*: Ibid.
229   *"the situation is definitely serious"*: Roosevelt to Wendell Willkie, December 5, 1941, *PHA*, part 17, 2457.
229   *"madmen who are loose"*: Goodwin, *No Ordinary Time*, 213.
229   *"a bit of campaign"*: Ibid., 214.
229   *"He is my President"*: Ibid.
229   *"the Japanese matter"*: Roosevelt to Willkie, December 5, 1941, *PHA*, part 17, 2457.
230   *"frequently drunk"*: Navy report on Japanese espionage, February 15, 1943, *PHA*, part 35, 363.
230   *"unanimously uncooperative"*: Takeo Yoshikawa, "Top Secret Assignment," *Proceedings*, December 1960. The article provides details of Yoshikawa's life.
231   *"I knew by then"*: Ibid.
232   *"no get caught"*: Navy report on Japanese espionage, *PHA*, part 35, 366.
232   *"In view of the present"*: Tokyo to Honolulu, December 2, 1941, *PHA*, part 12, 266.
233   *Toward midnight, under a robust*: For a detailed analysis of the British raid, see Angelo N. Caravaggio's "The Attack at Taranto," in *Naval War College Review* (summer 2006).
233   *"The loss of ships in port"*: Papers of Thomas C. Kinkaid, Naval History and Heritage Command, Washington, box 1, series I, folder 1, Diary 1938–41, entry for November 17, 1941.
233   *"Since the Taranto"*: Stark to Richardson, November 22, 1940, *PHA*, part 14, 973.
234   *"The depths of water"*: Stark to Kimmel, February 15, 1941, *PHA*, part 17, 2701.
234   *"considerably less than"*: Navy Department to all commands, June 13, 1941, *PHA*, part 17, 2705.
235   *"When the letter of June 13"*: Kimmel, *PHA*, part 32, 226–27.
235   *"you can launch"*: Kimmel, *PHA*, part 6, 2592.

235 *"most of our own"*: Pye, *PHA*, part 26, 167.
237 *"to meet an air attack"*: Milo F. Draemel to "Frederick and Eleanor," January 17, 1963, Prange papers, series V, box 13, folder 4.
237 *"The Japanese policy had been"*: Ibid.
237 *"liberty parties from all the other"*: Ibid.
237 *"Traffic volume heavy"*: Fourteenth Naval District Communication Intelligence Summary, December 5, 1941, *PHA*, part 17, 2641.
237 *"The* Lexington *and five"*: Honolulu to Tokyo, December 5, 1941, *PHA*, part 12, 269.
238 *"ordered the customary"*: Toland papers, box 120, folder SS *Lurline* (No. 1). This file contains an account of the last peacetime voyage, written by the ship's chief officer.
238 *"How many times"*: ECG, "On Leaving Hawaii," *Paradise of the Pacific*, January 1941, 23.
238 *"men and women"*: Toland papers, chief officer's account.
238 *"bucking the usual"*: Ibid.

FOURTEEN YOUR MAJESTY

239 *"some Magic material"*: Testimony of Lester Robert Schulz, *PHA*, part 10, 4661.
240 *"cordial congratulations"*: Roosevelt papers, President's Office Files, box 197, Japan, folder 1941–42.
240 *"that he should not neglect"*: Written statement of Cordell Hull, *PHA*, part 11, 5372.
240 *"Only in situations of extraordinary"*: Roosevelt to Hirohito, December 6, 1941, *Peace and War*, 828.
240 *"an offer of friendship"*: Ibid.
241 *"contain tragic possibilities"*: Ibid.
241 *Before writing, the president*: Hull's report to Roosevelt on the Japanese buildup in Indochina can be found in *PHA*, part 20, 4120.
241 *"During the past few weeks"*: Roosevelt letter, 829.
241 *"it is only reasonable"*: Ibid.
241 *"indefinitely or permanently"*: Ibid., 830.
241 *"that Your Majesty"*: Ibid.
241 *"Shoot this to Grew"*: Photostat copy of Roosevelt's memo, *PHA*, part 14, 1238.
242 *"The Government has deliberated deeply"*: Tokyo to Washington, December 6, 1941, *PHA*, part 12, 238.
243 *"brought about a situation"*: Japanese message to Cordell Hull, December 7, 1941, *PHA*, part 12, 240. All subsequent quotations from the message can be found on pages 239–45.
244 *"They contributed no additional"*: Bratton, *PHA*, part 9, 4516.
244 *"It was a justification"*: Wilkinson, *PHA*, part 4, 1763.
244 *"We had already discounted"*: Miles, *PHA*, part 2, 942.
244 *"this note was far"*: Kramer, *PHA*, part 8, 3899.
245 *"rather emphatic instructions"*: Kramer, *PHA*, part 33, 857.
245 *"The President then turned"*: Schulz, *PHA*, part 10, 4662.
245 *"for their advantage"*: Ibid.
246 *"The President nodded"*: Ibid., 4663.

247 *"did not, certainly did not"*: Stark, *PHA*, part 11, 5545.
248 *"Finally, at 10:30 p.m."*: Grew, *PHA*, part 2, 570.
248 *"I did not want any doubt"*: Ibid.

FIFTEEN DINNER AT THE HALEKULANI

249 *"These boys on here"*: William Outerbridge to Grace Outerbridge, December 5, 1941, Outerbridge papers. Subsequent Outerbridge quotations in this section come from this letter.
251 *"After about half an hour"*: Joseph C. Harsch, *At the Hinge of History: A Reporter's Story* (Athens: University of Georgia Press, 1993), 72.
251 *"Without a pause"*: Ibid.
251 *"Since you have been travelling"*: Ibid.
252 *"The Japanese are too intelligent"*: Ibid.
252 *"I was fascinated"*: Ibid.
252 *"They showed no sign"*: Ibid., 73.
252 *"because, after all, the admiral"*: Ibid.
252 *"his stomach was acting up"*: Pfeiffer, Columbia oral history, 174.
252 *"Admiral Kimmel was not impressed"*: Ibid.
253 *"uncertainty, a condition which"*: Kimmel to Stark, May 26, 1941, *PHA*, part 16, 2238.
253 *"I sensed the deep feeling"*: Brownlow, *The Accused*, 127.
253 *"In view of the international situation"*: Navy Department to Kimmel, December 6, 1941, *PHA*, part 14, 1408.
254 *"We didn't want to overlook"*: Brownlow tapes, tape 34.
254 *"was growing increasingly critical"*: Kimmel, *PHA*, part 22, 328.
254 *"In the specific terms"*: Kimmel, *PHA*, part 32, 264.
254 *"with intelligent suspicion"*: United States Naval War College, *Sound Military Decision* (Annapolis, MD: Naval Institute Press, 1942), 199. This book is available online at www.gutenberg.org/files/28178/28178-h/28178-h.htm.
255 *"In the Army"*: This observation was made by General George Grunert during an army inquiry into the Pearl Harbor attack, *PHA*, part 27, 791.
255 *"whether or not they would"*: Layton, *PHA*, part 26, 237.
255 *"The Japanese have rarely left"*: Layton, *PHA*, part 36, 145.
256 *"looked at me"*: Layton, USNI oral history, 75.
256 *"snorted like a horse"*: Layton, NSA oral history, 89.
256 *"with the possession of good judgment"*: *Sound Military Decision*, 141.
256 *"I had no advice from any"*: Kimmel, *PHA*, part 22, 384.
257 *"I never believed that an air"*: Kimmel, *PHA*, part 6, 2591.
257 *"I felt that before hostilities"*: Kimmel, *PHA*, part 32, 659.
258 *"I imagine," Yoshikawa wrote*: Honolulu to Tokyo, December 6, 1941, *PHA*, part 12, 269.
258 *"The following ships were observed"*: Ibid., 270.
258 *"It appears that no air"*: Ibid.
259 *"FDR Will Send Message"*: *Honolulu Advertiser*, December 7, 1941.
260 *"Nippon is saving"*: Ibid.

260 *"Carrier-based aviation"*: Ibid.
260 *"was full of naval officers"*: Harsch, *At the Hinge of History*, 73.
260 *"I had a pleasant enough time"*: Brownlow tapes, tape 32.
261 *"was like a mother at rest"*: Ed Sheehan, *Days of '41* (Honolulu, HI: Pearl Harbor–Honolulu Branch 46 Fleet Reserve Association Enterprises, 1976), 122.
261 *"A carpenter working in steel and iron"*: Ibid., 39.
261 *"There are only the times"*: Ibid., 115.
261 *"I wanted to work"*: Ibid., 39.
261 *"reeked of boiling tar"*: Ibid., 104
261 *"But, we thought and argued"*: Ibid., 67.
262 *"The chief told him"*: Ibid., 123.
262 *"The chief said"*: Ibid.

SIXTEEN FROM THE VACANT SEA

263 *"We are in the very day"*: Chigusa, *Pearl Harbor Papers*, 192.
264 *"I really couldn't find"*: This quotation comes from Gordon Prange's copy of Chigusa's diary, Prange papers, series V, box 9, folder 18.
264 *"every Japanese hungered for sweets"*: Chigusa, *Pearl Harbor Papers*, 191.
264 *"as clearly as if"*: This quotation comes from a translation of Ruyonosuke Kusaka's 1952 book *Combined Fleet*, Prange papers, series V, box 58, folder 17.
264 *"The fate of our Empire"*: Ugaki, *Fading Victory*, 38.
265 *"since the principle has been"*: Ibid.
265 *"Don't you know that the whole world"*: Ibid., 40.
265 *"for the sinking of"*: Prange papers, series V, box 19, folder 11. The quotation is Prange's characterization in his notes of a conversation between Genda and Admiral Takijiro Onishi about the impact of attacking battleships.
265 *"suddenly, I found"*: Genda memoirs, Prange papers, series V, box 20, folder 3.
266 *"care should be taken"*: Prange papers, series V, box 63, folder 19. Military officials interrogated Nagano in prison after the war. The quotation comes from the notes of those interviews.
266 *"a set of flags"*: Genda, "How the Japanese Task Force Idea Materialized."
266 *"Within fifteen minutes"*: Mitsuo Fuchida, "I Led the Air Attack on Pearl Harbor," in Stillwell, *Air Raid: Pearl Harbor!*, 8.
266 *"glorious"*: Mitsuo Fuchida interview by Gordon Prange, December 10, 1963, Prange papers, series V, box 16, folder 1.
267 *"I rode at a pretty lively"*: Marshall, *PHA*, part 3, 1108.
267 *"Big Forces Are Massed"*: *New York Times*, December 7, 1941.
267 *"may feel fully"*: Ibid.
267 *"has finally been lost"*: Tokyo to Washington, December 7, 1941, *PHA*, part 12, 245.
268 *"I do recollect"*: Beardall, *PHA*, part 11, 5274.
268 *"Will the Ambassador"*: Tokyo to Washington, December 7, 1941, *PHA*, part 12, 248.
269 *"All concerned regret"*: Ibid.
269 *"immediately stunned me"*: Bratton, *PHA*, part 9, 4517.
269 *"as I had an important"*: Bratton, *PHA*, part 29, 2346.

269 *"I kept looking at the clock"*: Ibid., 2420.

270 *"General Marshall drew"*: Bratton, *PHA*, part 9, 4518.

270 *"the Japanese intended"*: Ibid.

270 *"were going to get it"*: Marshall, *PHA*, part 23, 1081.

270 *"the scheme that had been"*: Kramer, *PHA*, part 8, 3909.

270 *"He didn't seem to be"*: McCollum, USNI oral history, 417.

271 *"We had sent them"*: Stark, *PHA*, part 23, 1082.

271 *"Japanese are presenting"*: Marshall to army Pacific commands, December 7, 1941, *PHA*, part 15, 1640.

272 *"Captain, come on"*: William Outerbridge to Grace Outerbridge, December 14, 1941, Outerbridge papers.

272 *"One look he gave"*: Statement of H. E. Raenbig, Outerbridge papers, box 2, Statements Concerning the Attack, 7 December 1941 (I).

273 *"the submarine appeared"*: Outerbridge report to commanding officer, December 13, 1941, Outerbridge papers, box 2, Official Papers USS *Ward* December 1941.

273 *"My opinion," said the enlisted man*: Statement of W. C. Maskzawilz, Outerbridge papers, box 2, Statements Concerning the Attack, 7 December 1941 (I).

273 *"We have dropped"*: Radio Log, Section Base, Bishop's Point, December 7, 1941, *PHA*, part 37, 704.

273 *"We have attacked"*: Ibid.

274 *"Private Lockard laughed"*: Elliott, *PHA*, part 32, 489.

274 *"I spoke in a very"*: Elliott, *PHA*, part 10, 5041.

275 a *"large" flight of planes*: Ibid., 5068.

275 *"get somebody that"*: Elliott, *PHA*, part 27, 521.

275 *"Sir, I really don't"*: Testimony of Kermit A. Tyler, *PHA*, part 27, 570.

275 *"I thought about it"*: Tyler, *PHA*, part 22, 221.

275 *"You see," Tyler said*: Tyler, *PHA*, part 27, 569.

276 *"it was just another"*: Testimony of John B. Earle, *PHA*, part 23, 1052.

276 *"Is it a correct"*: Bloch, *PHA*, part 22, 499.

277 *"any single submarine"*: Martin-Bellinger Report, *PHA*, part 22, 350.

277 *"I was not at all"*: Kimmel, *PHA*, part 22, 319.

277 *"There's a message"*: Testimony of Vincent R. Murphy, *PHA*, part 26, 210.

278 *"as white as"*: Prange, *At Dawn We Slept*, 507.

278 *"one hell of a mess"*: Statement of Peter A. La Fata, papers of Walter Lord, Naval History and Heritage Command, box 3, Pearl Harbor Book Questionnaires, La Fata-La Bage folder.

279 *"Hostilities with Japan"*: Kimmel to all ships and stations, December 7, 1941, *PHA*, part 23, 935.

279 *"We [were] picking up sailors"*: Transcript of the oral history of Richard Cunningham, December 6, 2003, 5, National Museum of the Pacific War, Fredericksburg, TX.

280 *"beautifully planned"*: Kimmel, *PHA*, part 22, 388.

280 *"utterly shocked and crushed"*: Arthur C. Davis interview by Gordon Prange, January 30, 1963, Prange papers, series V, box 12, folder 24.

280 *"calm and collected"*: Edwin T. Layton interview by Gordon Prange, July 22, 1964, Prange papers, series V, box 58, folder 23.

280 *"was cursing, ranting and raving"*: Papers of Thomas J. Larson, the American Heritage Center, University of Wyoming, box 1, folder 12.

281 *"The world had exploded"*: Layton, *And I Was There*, 317.

281 *"Locate enemy force"*: Kimmel to Patrol Wing Two, December 7, 1941, *PHA*, part 23, 935.

282 *"our antiaircraft crews"*: Statement of Charles Mandell, Lord papers, box 3, Magee-Merdinger folder.

282 *"the result was a numbness"*: Statement of John Landreth, Lord papers, box 3, La Fata-La Bage folder.

282 *"all were cool"*: Action report of commander of the USS *Helena*, December 14, 1941, available at www.ibiblio.org/hyperwar/USN/ships/logs/CL/cl50-Pearl.html.

282 *"The ship seemed surrounded"*: Statement of C. J. Merdinger, Lord papers, box 3, Magee-Merdinger Folder.

282 *"some of us were crying"*: Mason, *Battleship Sailor*, 228.

283 *"ships hit so far"*: Layton, *And I Was There*, 316.

283 *"was pretty horrible"*: Layton, USNI oral history, 93.

283 *"electric wonder"*: Layton, *And I Was There*, 316.

283 *"short, slightly heavy-set"*: Layton, USNI oral history, 94.

283 *"There was a ping"*: Pfeiffer, Columbia oral history, 175.

283 *"It would have been merciful"*: Prange, *At Dawn We Slept*, 516.

284 *"My God, this can't be true"*: Testimony of John H. Dillon, *PHA*, part 8, 3829.

284 *"had been delayed"*: *Peace and War*, 830.

284 *"more crowded with"*: Ibid., 831.

284 *"Cuff's still going"*: The Internet Archive has collected broadcasts from this period at www.archive.org/details/WWII_News_1941. The clip from the Dodgers-Giants game is Number 74.

285 *"To that, there was instant"*: *Washington Post*, December 14, 1941.

285 *"I heard all"*: Gary A. Yarrington, *World War II: Personal Accounts Pearl Harbor to VJ Day* (Austin, TX: Lyndon Baines Johnson Foundation, 1992), 71.

285 *"It is now 10 p.m."*: Grace Outerbridge to William Outerbridge, December 7, 1941, Outerbridge papers, box 2.

286 *"This is the Emperor's"*: Grew, *PHA*, part 2, 570.

286 *"the establishment of peace"*: Grew diary, December 8, 1941.

286 *"I never understood"*: Grew, *PHA*, part 2, 570.

286 *"Excellency," the note*: Grew diary, December 9, 1941.

287 *"Throughout the day"*: Ibid., December 8, 1941.

287 *"his chin stuck out about two feet"*: Robert J. C. Butow, "How Roosevelt Attacked Japan at Pearl Harbor: Myth Masquerading as History," *Prologue*, fall 1996.

287 *"just about the equal"*: "FDR's 'Day of Infamy' Speech: Crafting a Call to Arms," *Prologue*, winter 2001. The article, published in the magazine of the National Archives and Records Administration, quotes a letter from FDR to one of his sons about the importance of the speech.

287 *"He opened by telling"*: Stimson diary, December 7, 1941.

287 *"His pride in the Navy"*: Perkins, "The President Faces War," in Stillwell, *Air Raid: Pearl Harbor!*, 118.

288 *"was deeply shaken"*: Biddle, *In Brief Authority*, 206.

288 *"By far the greater loss"*: Transcript of Roosevelt's remarks to the cabinet and members of Congress, December 7, 1941, *PHA*, part 19, 3504.

288 *"Of course, it is a terrible"*: Ibid., 3505.

288   *"The principal defense"*: Ibid.
288   *"sat in dead silence"*: Stimson diary, December 7, 1941.
288   *"much, much worse"*: Morgenthau diary, vol. 470, reel 131, December 7–9, 1941, entry for December 7.
288   *"It is going to be"*: Ibid.
289   *"It's a pretty bad mess here"*: Transcripts of these two phone conversations are in the Stark papers at the NHHC.
289   *"in spite of security measures"*: Kimmel, *PHA*, part 24, 1365.
290   *"I asked Kimmel"*: Stark transcript, NHHC.

EPILOGUE

291   *"Before we're through with them"*: Halsey and Bryan, *Admiral Halsey's Story*, 81.
291   *"You'd better get the hell"*: Potter, *Bull Halsey*, 13.
291   *"Oil was everywhere"*: Mason, *Battleship Sailor*, 249.
292   *"We didn't remove"*: Transcript of the oral history of Jerod Haynes, National Museum of the Pacific, September 29, 2000, 8.
292   *"and buried in two lots"*: Roosevelt papers, President's Secretary's File, box 59, Navy File, July to December 1941.
292   *"We had to endure"*: Layton, *And I Was There*, 325.
292   *"With the losses we have"*: *The Nimitz Gray Book*, Naval War College, Naval Historical Collection, vol. 1, 8.
292   *"this mission is the immediate"*: Ibid., 9.
293   *"even before the passengers"*: Toland papers, box 120, folder SS *Lurline* (No. 1), chief's account.
293   *"The air was filled with rumors"*: Frank Knox to Paul Mowrer, December 18, 1941, papers of Frank Knox, Library of Congress, box 4, General Correspondence.
293   *"America is speechless"*: *Congressional Record*, December 8, 1941, 9526.
293   *"Millions of Americans had not"*: Ibid., 9530.
293   *"is stunned by Hawaii"*: Ibid., 9522.
294   *"Where was the continuous"*: *Christian Science Monitor*, December 8, 1941.
294   *"With astounding success"*: *Time*, December 15, 1941.
294   *"The airplane is the master"*: *New York Times*, December 11, 1941.
294   *"Although this is contrary"*: *Chicago Tribune*, December 12, 1941.
294   *"hard blows"*: *Christian Science Monitor*, December 12, 1941.
294   *"haggard and unshaven"*: Halsey and Bryan, *Admiral Halsey's Story*, 81.
294   *"just numb"*: Davis interview by Prange.
295   *"hundreds of our boys"*: *New York Times*, December 9, 1941.
295   *"awfully alone"*: Grace Earle to Gordon Prange, October 16, 1964, Prange papers, series V, box 13, folder 15.
295   *"Every great man"*: Singleton Kimmel to Husband Kimmel, December 12, 1941, Kimmel papers, series II, box 2, folder 7.
295   *"My complete confidence"*: Manning Kimmel to Husband Kimmel, December 18, 1941, Kimmel papers, series II, box 2, folder 7.
295   *"If I am to be relieved"*: Kimmel to Stark, December 15, 1941, Stark papers, series XIII, boxes 78 and 79.
295   *"You're right," the admiral replied*: Draemel letter, Prange papers.

296 *"I am sorry this had to happen"*: Milo F. Draemel interview by Gordon Prange, January 17, 1963, Prange papers, series V, box 13, folder 5.

297 *"failed to consult"*: PHA, part 39, 20.

297 *"you should try to show"*: George E. Mix to Kimmel, February 11, 1941, Kimmel papers, series II, box 3, folder 1.

298 *"As you know, he is here"*: John W. Greenslade to Stark, February 13, 1942, Stark papers, series XIII, boxes 78 and 79.

298 *"The Navy, make no mistake"*: Willard A. Kitts III to Kimmel, March 18, 1942, Kimmel papers, series II, box 3, folder 2.

298 *"Poor Kimmel!"*: James O. Richardson to Kimmel, February 24, 1942, Kimmel papers, series II, box 3, folder 1.

298 *"I know if I say"*: Stark to Kimmel, February 16, 1942, Kimmel papers, series II, box 3, folder 1.

299 *"Joined the ship Friday"*: William Outerbridge to Grace Outerbridge, December 14, 1941, Outerbridge papers.

299 *"The Ward has a fine"*: Ibid.

299 *"Have had the time"*: Ibid.

299 *"Really, the atmosphere"*: Grace Outerbridge to William Outerbridge, December 9, 1941, Outerbridge papers.

299 *"Don't know how much"*: Grace Outerbridge to William Outerbridge, December 11, 1941, Outerbridge papers.

299 *"I haven't been notified"*: Grace Outerbridge to William Outerbridge, December 12, 1941, Outerbridge papers.

299 *"Well and happy"*: A copy of the telegram is in the Outerbridge papers.

300 *"I was so relieved"*: Grace Outerbridge to William Outerbridge, December 13, 1941, Outerbridge papers.

301 *"Nomura smiled broadly"*: Fearey, "My Year With Ambassador Joseph C. Grew," 31.

301 *"Wars are fought"*: New York Times, August 17, 1989.

301 *"My eyes were moist"*: Chigusa, Pearl Harbor Papers, 183.

302 *"I have often said"*: Rochefort, USNI oral history, 112.

302 *"He had been my"*: Layton, And I Was There, 475.

303 *"John, this is the nicest thing"*: McCrea, USNI oral history, 94.

303 *"I have an American's"*: Kimmel statement of May 17, 1944, Hanify papers, box 17, folder 17.

304 *"was his failure"*: James V. Forrestal, Secretary of the Navy, July 12, 1945, PHA, part 39, 368.

304 *"While I know nothing"*: Stark to Kimmel, December 12, 1944, Hanify papers, box 17, folder 18.

304 *"Dear Stark"*: Unsent letter from Kimmel to Stark, December 28, 1944, Hanify papers, box 17, folder 18.

304 *"As I read your note"*: Ibid.

305 *"Admiral Kimmel should have been"*: The minority report of Senators Homer Ferguson and Owen Brewster, Joint Committee on the Investigation of the Pearl Harbor Attack. The findings of the joint congressional committee constitute the only unnumbered volume of the forty-volume PHA series. If it were numbered, it would be the fortieth volume. This finding is on p. 554.

SELECTED BIBLIOGRAPHY

GOVERNMENT PUBLICATIONS

Congress of the United States. *Congressional Record.* Washington, DC: United States Government Printing Office, 1941.

Congress of the United States. *Pearl Harbor Attack: Hearings Before the Joint Committee on the Investigation of the Pearl Harbor Attack.* Washington, DC: United States Government Printing Office, 1946.

Department of State. *Foreign Relations of the United States.* Washington, DC: United States Government Printing Office, 1966.

Department of State. *Peace and War: United States Foreign Policy, 1931–1941.* Washington, DC: United States Government Printing Office, 1943.

United States Naval War College. *Sound Military Decision.* Annapolis, MD: Naval Institute Press, 1942.

ORAL HISTORIES

Columbia Center for Oral History, Columbia University, New York, New York

Hart, Thomas C.
Hewitt, H. Kent
Ingersoll, Royal E.
Kirk, Alan G.
Pfeiffer, Omar T.

Oral History Collection, National Museum of the Pacific War, Fredericksburg, Texas

Cunningham, Richard
Haynes, Jerod

Oral History Collection, National Security Agency, Fort Meade, Maryland

Capron Jr., James B.
Dyer, Thomas H.
Layton, Edwin T.

Oral History Program, United States Naval Institute, Annapolis, Maryland

Baldwin, Hanson W.
Dyer, George C.
Dyer, Thomas H.
Layton, Edwin T.
McCollum, Arthur H.
McCrea, John L.
Rochefort, Joseph J.
Smedberg, William R. III
Wellborn, Charles Jr.

COLLECTIONS OF RECORDS AND PERSONAL PAPERS

Arnold, Henry, Library of Congress, Washington, DC.
Bloch, Claude C., Library of Congress, Washington, DC.
Brownlow, Donald G., Van Pelt Library, University of Pennsylvania, Philadelphia, Pennsylvania.
Friedman, William F., National Security Agency, www.nsa.gov/public_info/declass /friedman_documents/index.shtml.
Goldstein, Donald M., University of Pittsburgh, Pittsburgh, Pennsylvania.
Grew, Joseph C., Harvard University, Cambridge, Massachusetts.
Halsey, William F., Naval History and Heritage Command, Washington, DC.
Hanify, Edward B., College of the Holy Cross, Worcester, Massachusetts.
Ickes, Harold L., Library of Congress, Washington, DC.
Kimmel, Husband E., American Heritage Center, University of Wyoming, Laramie, Wyoming.
Kinkaid, Thomas C., Naval History and Heritage Command, Washington, DC.
Knox, Frank, Library of Congress, Washington, DC.
Larson, Thomas J., American Heritage Center, University of Wyoming, Laramie, Wyoming.
Layton, Edwin T., Naval Historical Collection, Naval War College, Newport, Rhode Island.
Lord, Walter, Naval History and Heritage Command, Washington, DC.
Morgenthau, Henry, Franklin D. Roosevelt Presidential Library, Hyde Park, New York.
Naval War College Archives, Naval War College, Newport, Rhode Island.

Outerbridge, William W., Dwight D. Eisenhower Presidential Library, Abilene, Kansas.

Prange, Gordon W., University of Maryland, College Park, Maryland.

Roosevelt, Franklin D., Franklin D. Roosevelt Presidential Library, Hyde Park, New York.

Simpson, B. Mitchell, Naval Historical Collection, Naval War College, Newport, Rhode Island.

Stark, Harold R., Naval History and Heritage Command, Washington, DC.

Toland, John, Franklin D. Roosevelt Presidential Library, Hyde Park, New York.

Turner, Richmond Kelly, Naval History and Heritage Command, Washington, DC.

NEWSPAPERS, PERIODICALS

Atlantic
Big Spring Herald
Chicago Tribune
Christian Science Monitor
Collier's
Harper's
Hawaii Hochi
Honolulu Advertiser
Honolulu Star-Bulletin
The Nation
New York Times
Paradise of the Pacific
Press Democrat
Proceedings
Time
Washington Post

SELECTED ARTICLES

Baldwin, Hanson W. "The Naval Defense of America." *Harper's Magazine*, April 1941.

Barnhart, Michael A. "Planning the Pearl Harbor Attack: A Study in Military Politics." *Aerospace Historian*, December 1982.

Biard, Forrest R. "Breaking of Japanese Naval Codes: Pre-Pearl Harbor to Midway." *Cryptologia* 30, no. 2 (2006).

Burtness, Paul S., and Warren U. Ober. "Communication Lapses Leading to the Pearl Harbor Disaster." *The Historian*, winter 2013.

————. "President Roosevelt, Admiral Stark, and the Unsent Warning to Pearl Harbor: A Research Note." *Australian Journal of Politics and History* (December 2011).

————. "Secretary Stimson and the First Pearl Harbor Investigation." *Australian Journal of Politics and History* (April 1968).

Butow, Robert J. C. "How Roosevelt Attacked Japan at Pearl Harbor: Myth Masquerading as History." *Prologue*, fall 1996.

————. "The Hull-Nomura Conversations: A Fundamental Misconception." *The American Historical Review* (July 1960).

Campbell, Mark A. "The Influence of Air Power Upon the Evolution of Battle Doctrine in the US Navy, 1922–1941." Thesis, University of Massachusetts, 1992.

Caravaggio, Angelo N. "The Attack At Taranto." *Naval War College Review*, summer 2006.

————. " 'Winning' the Pacific War: The Masterful Strategy of Commander Minoru Genda." *Naval War College Review*, winter 2014.

Carlson, Elliot. "Did Joe Rochefort Unwittingly Mislead Admiral Kimmel About Pearl Harbor?" *Proceedings*, December 2011.

Conroy, Hilary. "The Strange Diplomacy of Admiral Nomura." *Proceedings of the American Philosophical Society*, 1970.

Evans, David C. "Planning Pearl Harbor." *Hoover Digest*, no. 2 (1998).

Friedman, William F. "Certain Aspects of Magic in the Cryptological Background of the Various Official Investigations into the Attack on Pearl Harbor." National Security Agency, 1957.

Ford, Harold P. "The Primary Purpose of National Estimating." *Studies in National Intelligence*, fall 1991.

Gannon, Michael. "Reopen the Kimmel Case." *Proceedings*, December 1994.

Genda, Minoru. "Tactical Planning in the Imperial Japanese Navy." *Naval War College Review*, October 1969.

Hanyok, Robert J. "Catching the Fox Unaware." *Naval War College Review*, autumn 2008.

————. "How The Japanese Did It." *Naval History Magazine*, December 2008.

Hone, Thomas C. "December 7, 1941: The Destruction of the Battle Line at Pearl Harbor." *Proceedings*, December 1977.

Hosoya, Chihiro. "Japan's Decision for War." *Hitotsubashi Journal of Law and Politics*, April 1967.

Kahn, David. "The Intelligence Failure of Pearl Harbor." *Foreign Affairs*, winter 1991.

————. "Pearl Harbor and the Inadequacy of Cryptanalysis." *Cryptologia*, October 1991.

Parshall, Jonathan, and Michael J. Wenger. "Pearl Harbor's Overlooked Answer." *Naval History Magazine*, December 2011.

Pfeiffer, David A. "Sage Prophet or Loose Cannon: Skilled Intelligence Officer in World War II Foresaw Japan's Plans, but Annoyed Navy Brass." *Prologue*, summer 2008.

Ramsey, Logan C. "Aerial Attacks on Fleets at Anchor." *Proceedings*, August 1937.

Taussig, Joseph K. "The Case for the Big Capital Ship." *Proceedings*, July 1940.

Yoshikawa, Takeo. "Top Secret Assignment." *Proceedings*, December 1960.

BOOKS

Agawa, Hiroyuki. *The Reluctant Admiral: Yamamoto and the Imperial Navy*. Tokyo, New York: Kodansha International, 1979.

Anderson, Charles Robert. *Day of Lightning, Years of Scorn*. Annapolis, MD: Naval Institute Press, 2005.

Beach, Edward L. *Scapegoats: A Defense of Kimmel and Short at Pearl Harbor*. Annapolis, MD: Naval Institute Press, 1995.

Belote, James H., and William M. Belote. *Titans of the Seas: The Development and Operations of Japanese and American Carrier Task Forces During World War II*. New York: Harper and Row, 1975.

Ben-Zvi, Abraham. *Prelude to Pearl Harbor: A Study of American Images toward Japan 1940–41*. New York: Vantage Press, 1979.

Biddle, Francis. *In Brief Authority*. Garden City, NY: Doubleday, 1962.

Boesewetter, Monica Low. *Gone with the Dawn: Pearl Harbor Memories of Youth*. Bloomington, IN: Xlibris, 2002.

Borch, Fred, and Daniel Martinez. *Kimmel, Short and Pearl Harbor: The Final Report Revealed*. Annapolis, MD: Naval Institute Press, 2005.

Borg, Dorothy, and Shumpei Okamoto, editors. *Pearl Harbor As History: Japanese-American Relations 1931–41*. New York: Columbia University Press, 1973.

Bowles, John. *The Day Our World Changed: Punahou '52 Remembers Pearl Harbor*. North Liberty, IA: Ice Cube Press, 2004.

Brinkley, David. *Washington Goes to War*. New York: Alfred A. Knopf, 1988.

Brown, David K. *Nelson to Vanguard: Warship Development 1923–1945*. London: Chatham Publishing, 2000.

Brownlow, Donald Grey. *The Accused: The Ordeal of Rear Admiral Husband Edward Kimmel*. New York: Vantage Press, 1968.

Budiansky, Stephen. *Battle of Wits: The Complete Story of Code-Breaking in World War II*. New York: Free Press, 2000.

Burtness, Paul S., and Warren U. Ober, editors. *The Puzzle of Pearl Harbor*. Evanston, IL: Row, Patterson, 1962.

Butow, Robert J. C. *Tojo and the Coming of the War*. Princeton, NJ: Princeton University Press, 1961.

Carlson, Elliot. *Joe Rochefort's War: The Odyssey of the Codebreaker Who Outwitted Yamamoto at Midway*. Annapolis, MD: Naval Institute Press, 2011.

Clarke, Thurston. *Pearl Harbor Ghosts: A Journey to Hawaii Then and Now*. New York: William Morrow, 1991.

Coffman, Tom. *Nation Within: The History of the American Occupation of Hawaii*. Kihei, HI: Koa Books, 1998.

Coletta, Paolo E. *Patrick N. L. Bellinger and U.S. Naval Aviation*. Lanham, MD: University Press of America, 1987.

Collier, Richard. *The Road to Pearl Harbor 1941*. New York: Atheneum, 1981.

Conroy, Hilary, and Harry Wray. *Pearl Harbor Reexamined: Prologue to the Pacific War*. Honolulu: University of Hawaii Press, 1990.

Cook, Haruko Taya, and Theodore F. Cook. *Japan at War: An Oral History*. New York: New Press, 1992.

Costello, John. *Days of Infamy: MacArthur, Roosevelt, Churchill: The Shocking Truth Revealed*. New York: Pocket Books, 1994.

Dingman, Roger. *Deciphering the Rising Sun: Navy and Marine Corps Codebreakers, Translators and Interpreters in the Pacific War*. Annapolis, MD: Naval Institute Press, 2009.

Dower, John W. *War Without Mercy: Race and Power in the Pacific War*. New York: Pantheon, 1986.

Dull, Paul S. *A Battle History of the Imperial Japanese Navy, 1941–1945*. Annapolis, MD: Naval Institute Press, 1978.

Dyer, George C. *The Amphibians Came to Conquer: The Story of Richmond Kelly Turner*. Washington, DC: US Department of the Navy, 1972.

Evans, David C., editor. *The Japanese Navy in World War II: In the Words of Former Japanese Naval Officers*. Annapolis, MD: Naval Institute Press, 1986.

Evans, David C., and Mark R. Peattie. *Kaigun: Strategy, Tactics and Technology in the Imperial Japanese Navy, 1887–1941*. Annapolis, MD: Naval Institute Press, 1997.

Farley, Jim. *Jim Farley's Story: The Roosevelt Years*. New York: Whittlesey House, 1948.

Feis, Herbert. *The Road to Pearl Harbor: The Coming of the War Between the United States and Japan*. Princeton, NJ: Princeton University Press, 1950.

Ford, Douglas. *The Elusive Enemy: U.S. Naval Intelligence and the Imperial Japanese Fleet*. Annapolis, MD: Naval Institute Press, 2011.

Gannon, Michael V. *Pearl Harbor Betrayed: The True Story of a Man and a Nation Under Attack*. New York: Henry Holt, 2001.

Gillon, Steven M. *Pearl Harbor: FDR Leads the Nation Into War*. New York: Basic Books, 2011.

Goldstein, Donald M., et al. *The Way It Was: Pearl Harbor, The Original Photographs*. Washington, DC: Brassey's, 1991.

Goldstein, Donald M., and Katherine Dillon. *The Pearl Harbor Papers: Inside the Japanese Plans*. Washington, DC: Brassey's, 1993.

Goodwin, Doris Kearns. *No Ordinary Time: Franklin and Eleanor Roosevelt: The Home Front in World War II*. New York: Simon & Schuster, 1994.

Grew, Joseph C. *Ten Years in Japan*. New York: Simon & Schuster, 1944.

Halsey, William F., and Jay Bryan III. *Admiral Halsey's Story*. New York: Whittlesey House, 1947.

Hamer, David. *Bombers Versus Battleships: The Struggle Between Ships and Aircraft for the Control of the Surface of the Sea*. Annapolis, MD: Naval Institute Press, 1998.

Hanyok, Robert J., and David P. Mowry. *West Wind Clear: Cryptology and the Winds Message Controversy*. Fort Meade, MD: Center for Cryptologic History, National Security Agency, 2008.

Harsch, Joseph C. *At the Hinge of History: A Reporter's Story*. Athens: University of Georgia Press, 1993.

Heinrichs, Waldo H. Jr. *American Ambassador Joseph C. Grew and the Development of the United States Diplomatic Tradition*. Boston: Little, Brown, 1966.

———. *Threshold of War: Franklin D. Roosevelt and American Entry into World War II*. New York: Oxford University Press, 1988.

Hoehling, Adolph A. *The Week Before Pearl Harbor*. New York: Norton, 1963.

Holmes, W. J. *Double-Edged Secrets*. Annapolis, MD: Naval Institute Press, 1979.

Hone, Thomas C., and Trent Hone. *Battle Line: The United States Navy 1919–1939*. Annapolis, MD: Naval Institute Press, 2006.

Hone, Thomas C., Norman Friedman, and Mark Mandeles. *American and British Aircraft Carrier Development 1919–1941*. Annapolis, MD: Naval Institute Press, 1999.

Hotta, Eri. *Japan 1941: Countdown to Infamy*. New York: Alfred A. Knopf, 2013.

Hoyt, Edwin P. *Yamamoto: The Man Who Planned Pearl Harbor*. Guilford, CT: Lyons Press, 1990.

Hull, Cordell. *The Memoirs of Cordell Hull*. New York: Macmillan, 1948.

Ickes, Harold L. *The Secret Diary of Harold L. Ickes*. New York: Simon & Schuster, 1953–54.

Janis, Irving L. *Groupthink: Psychological Studies of Policy Decisions and Fiascos*. Boston: Houghton Mifflin, 1983.

Kahn, David. *The Codebreakers: The Story of Secret Writing*. New York: Scribner, 1996.

Kam, Ephraim. *Surprise Attack: The Victim's Perspective*. Cambridge, MA: Harvard University Press, 1988.

Kimmel, Husband E. *Admiral Kimmel's Story*. Chicago: Henry Regnery Co., 1955.

Kinzey, Bert. *Attack on Pearl Harbor: Japan Awakens a Sleeping Giant*. Blacksburg, VA: Military Aviation Archives Inc., 2010.

Kirkpatrick, Lyman B. *Captains Without Eyes: Intelligence Failures in World War II*. New York: Macmillan, 1969.

LaForte, Robert S., and Ronald E. Marcello, editors. *Remembering Pearl Harbor: Eyewitness Accounts by U.S. Military Men and Women*. Wilmington, DE: Scholarly Resources, 1991.

Lambert, John W., and Norman Polmar. *Defenseless: Command Failure at Pearl Harbor*. St. Paul, MN: MBI Publishing, 2003.

Landauer, Lyndall Baker, and Donald A. Landauer. *Pearl: The History of the United States Navy in Pearl Harbor*. Stow, MA: Flying Cloud Press, 1999.

Lawrence, David. *Diary of a Washington Correspondent*. New York: H. C. Kinsey and Company, 1942.

Layton, Edwin T. *And I Was There: Pearl Harbor and Midway—Breaking the Secrets.* New York: William Morrow, 1985.

Leutze, James. *A Different Kind of Victory: A Biography of Admiral Thomas C. Hart.* Annapolis, MD: Naval Institute Press, 1981.

Levite, Ariel. *Intelligence and Strategic Surprises.* New York: Columbia University Press, 1987.

Lewin, Ronald. *The American Magic: Codes, Ciphers and the Defeat of Japan.* New York: Farrar, Straus and Giroux, 1982.

Lord, Walter. *Day of Infamy.* New York: Holt, 1957.

Lu, David John. *From the Marco Polo Bridge to Pearl Harbor: Japan's Entry into World War II.* Washington, DC: Public Affairs Press, 1961.

Marshall, Jonathan. *To Have and Have Not: Southeast Asian Raw Materials and the Origins of the Pacific War.* Berkeley, CA: University of California Press, 1995.

Mason, Theodore C. *Battleship Sailor.* Annapolis, MD: Naval Institute Press, 1982.

McIntire, Ross T. *White House Physician.* New York: G. P. Putnam's Sons, 1946.

Melosi, Martin V. *The Shadow of Pearl Harbor: Political Controversy Over the Surprise Attack 1941–1946.* College Station, TX: Texas A&M University Press, 1977.

Miller, Edward S. *War Plan Orange: The US Strategy to Defeat Japan, 1897–1945.* Annapolis, MD: Naval Institute Press, 1991.

Millis, Walter. *This is Pearl! The United States and Japan 1941.* New York: William Morrow, 1947.

Morison, Samuel Eliot. *History of United States Naval Operations in World War II,* vol. 3: *The Rising Sun in the Pacific, 1931–April 1942.* Annapolis, MD: Naval Institute Press, 1954.

Nofi, Albert M. *To Train the Fleet for War: The U.S. Navy Fleet Problems 1923–1940.* Newport, RI: Naval War College Press, 2010.

Olson, Lynne. *Those Angry Days: Roosevelt, Lindbergh, and America's Fight Over World War II, 1939–1941.* New York: Random House, 2013.

Parker, Frederick D. *Pearl Harbor Revisited: United States Navy Communications Intelligence 1924–1941.* Fort Meade, MD: Center for Cryptologic History, National Security Agency, 2013.

Peattie, Mark R. *Sunburst: The Rise of Japanese Naval Air Power, 1909–1941.* Annapolis, MD: Naval Institute Press, 2001.

Polmar, Norman. *Aircraft Carriers: A Graphic History of Carrier Aviation and Its Influence on World Events.* Garden City, NY: Doubleday, 1969.

Potter, Elmer B. *Bull Halsey.* Annapolis, MD: Naval Institute Press, 1985.

Prange, Gordon. *At Dawn We Slept: The Untold Story of Pearl Harbor.* New York: McGraw-Hill, 1981.

———. *December 7, 1941: The Day the Japanese Attacked Pearl Harbor.* New York: McGraw-Hill, 1988.

———. *The Verdict of History.* New York: McGraw-Hill, 1986.

Pratt, Fletcher. *The Navy's War*. New York: Harper and Brothers, 1944.

Richardson, James O. *On the Treadmill to Pearl Harbor: The Memoirs of Admiral James O. Richardson as Told to George C. Dyer*. Washington, DC: Naval History Division, Department of the Navy, 1973.

Richardson, K. D. *Reflections of Pearl Harbor: An Oral History of December 7, 1941*. Westport, CT: Praeger, 2005.

Roosevelt, Elliott, editor. *FDR: His Personal Papers*. New York: Duell, Sloan, and Pearce, 1947.

Rosenberg, Emily S. *A Date Which Will Live*. Durham, NC: Duke University Press, 2003.

Satterfield, Archie. *The Day the War Began*. Westport, CT: Praeger, 1992.

Sheehan, Ed. *Days of '41: Pearl Harbor Remembered*. Honolulu, HI: Pearl Harbor-Honolulu Branch 46 Fleet Reserve Association, 1976.

Shirley, Craig. *December 1941: 31 Days That Changed America and Saved the World*. Nashville, TN: Thomas Nelson, 2011.

Simpson, B. Mitchell. *Admiral Harold R. Stark: Architect of Victory 1939–1945*. Columbia: University of South Carolina Press, 1989.

Smith, Douglas V. *One Hundred Years of U.S. Navy Air Power*. Annapolis, MD: Naval Institute Press, 2010.

Spector, Ronald H., editor. *Listening to the Enemy: Key Documents on the Role of Communications Intelligence in the War with Japan*. Wilmington, DE: Scholarly Resources, 1988.

Stille, Mark. *Imperial Japanese Navy Aircraft Carriers, 1921–45*. New York: Osprey Publishing, 2005.

Stout, Rex, editor. *The Illustrious Dunderheads*. New York: Alfred A. Knopf, 1942.

Stillwell, Paul, editor. *Air Raid: Pearl Harbor! Recollections of a Day of Infamy*. Annapolis, MD: Naval Institute Press, 1981.

Stimson, Henry L. *The Henry Lewis Stimson Diaries, 1909–1945*. New Haven, CT: Manuscript and Archives, Yale University Library, 1973.

Thomas, Evan. *Sea of Thunder*. New York: Simon & Schuster, 2006.

Thompson, Robert Smith. *A Time for War: Franklin Delano Roosevelt and the Path to Pearl Harbor*. New York: Prentice Hall Press, 1991.

Toland, John. *Infamy: Pearl Harbor and Its Aftermath*. Garden City, NY: Doubleday, 1982.

Tolischus, Otto D. *Tokyo Record*. New York: Reynal and Hitchcock, 1943.

Travers, Paul J. *Eyewitness to Infamy: An Oral History of Pearl Harbor*. Lanham, MD: Madison Books, 1991.

Tully, Grace. *FDR, My Boss*. New York: Charles Scribner's Sons, 1949.

Ugaki, Matome. *Fading Victory: The Diary of Admiral Matome Ugaki 1941–1945*. Pittsburgh, PA: University of Pittsburg Press, 1991.

Utley, Jonathan G. *Going to War With Japan, 1937–41*. Knoxville: University of Tennessee Press, 1985.

Van der Vat, Dan. *Pearl Harbor: The Day of Infamy: An Illustrated History*. New York: Basic Books, 2001.

Vlahos, Michael. *The Blue Sword: The Naval War College and the American Mission, 1919–1941*. Newport, RI: Naval War College Press, 1980.

Vogel, Steve. *The Pentagon, a History: The Untold Story of the Wartime Race to Build the Pentagon—and Restore It Sixty Years Later*. New York: Random House, 2007.

Wallin, Homer N. *Pearl Harbor: Why, How, Fleet Salvage and Final Appraisal*. Washington, DC: Naval History Division, 1968.

Weintraub, Stanley. *Long Day's Journey into War: December 7, 1941*. New York: Dutton, 1991.

West, Rodney T. *Honolulu Prepares for Japan's Attack*. Self-published, 2002.

Wheeler, Gerald E. *Prelude to Pearl Harbor: The United States Navy and the Far East, 1921–1931*. Columbia: University of Missouri Press, 1963.

Wilhelm, Maria. *The Man Who Watched the Rising Sun: The Story of Admiral Ellis M. Zacharias*. New York: F. Watts, 1967.

Willmott, H. P. *Empires in the Balance: Japanese and Allied Pacific Strategies to April 1942*. Annapolis, MD: Naval Institute Press, 1982.

Wohlstetter, Roberta. *Pearl Harbor: Warning and Decision*. Stanford, CA: Stanford University Press, 1962.

Wukovits, John. *Admiral "Bull" Halsey: The Life and Wars of the Navy's Most Controversial Commander*. New York: Palgrave Macmillan, 2010.

Yarrington, Gary A. *World War II: Personal Accounts Pearl Harbor to VJ Day*. Austin, TX: Lyndon Baines Johnson Foundation, 1992.

Zacharias, Ellis M. *Secret Missions: The Story of an Intelligence Officer*. New York: G. P. Putnam, 1946.

Zimm, Alan D. *The Attack on Pearl Harbor*. Havertown, PA: Casemate, 2013.

IMAGE CREDITS

1. Copyright Bettmann/Corbis.
2. Courtesy of the Franklin D. Roosevelt Presidential Library.
3. Courtesy of the Naval History and Heritage Command.
4. Copyright Bettmann/Corbis.
5. Courtesy of the Naval History and Heritage Command.
6. Copyright Associated Press.
7. Copyright Bettmann/Corbis.
8. Courtesy of the Naval History and Heritage Command.
9. Courtesy of the Naval History and Heritage Command.
10. Copyright Associated Press.
11. Courtesy of the Naval History and Heritage Command.
12. Copyright Associated Press.
13. Courtesy of the Naval History and Heritage Command.
14. Courtesy of the Naval History and Heritage Command.
15. Courtesy of the National Archives and Records Administration.
16. Copyright Associated Press.
17. Courtesy of the Naval History and Heritage Command.
18. Courtesy of the Naval History and Heritage Command.
19. Copyright Bettmann/Corbis.
20. Courtesy of the Naval History and Heritage Command.
21. Courtesy of the National Archives and Records Administration.
22. Photo by George Skadding/The LIFE Picture Collection/Getty Images.

INDEX

ABOUT THE AUTHOR

STEVE TWOMEY began his career in journalism as a copyboy at the *Chicago Tribune* when he was in high school. After graduating from Northwestern University, he began a fourteen-year career at the *Philadelphia Inquirer*, during which he won the Pulitzer Prize for feature writing, and then worked at the *Washington Post* for thirteen years. More recently, he has written for *Smithsonian* and other magazines and has taught narrative writing at the graduate schools of New York University and the City University of New York. The ghostwriter of *What I Learned When I Almost Died* and the author of *Countdown to Pearl Harbor*, Twomey lives in Montclair, New Jersey, with his wife, Kathleen Carroll. They have an adult son, Nick.